SYLVIA PORTER'S 1982 INCOME TAX BOOK

Other Avon Books by Sylvia Porter:

SYLVIA PORTER'S NEW MONEY BOOK FOR THE 80's

SYLVIA PORTER'S 1982 INCOME TAX BOOK

THE COMPLETE LINE-BY-LINE GUIDE FOR
FILLING OUT 1981 INCOME TAX RETURNS
AND FOR 1982 TAX PLANNING

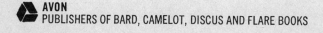
AVON
PUBLISHERS OF BARD, CAMELOT, DISCUS AND FLARE BOOKS

AVON BOOKS
A division of
The Hearst Corporation
959 Eighth Avenue
New York, New York 10019

Copyright © 1981 by Sylvia Porter
Published by arrangement with the author
International Standard Serialization Number (ISSN): 0491-8738
ISBN: 0-380-77925-x

Cover design by Lembit Rauk
Book design by Bobye List

First Avon Printing, December, 1981

The Library of Congress has cataloged this work as follows:

Porter, Sylvia Field, 1913—
    Sylvia Porter's income tax guide.
    1960, 1964, 1969, 1975, 1981, 1982
    Greenwich, Conn., Hall House, etc.

        4 v. 28 cm.

    Title varies slightly.
    Key title: Sylvia Porter's income tax guide, ISSN 0491—8738
    1. Income tax—United States—Popular works.   I. Title.
KF6369.6.P6   343'.73'052   64—118
                             MARC—S

Library of Congress   [r76]rev   OCAT

CONTENTS

List of Money-Saving Tax Tips and Keynotes 7

How to Use This Guide 9

Introduction 11

The Great New Tax Breaks   11
IRA and Keogh Plans   12
Estate and Gift Taxes   13
More Tax Breaks for Individuals in '82   14
    Dependent-Care Credit on Employment-Related Expenses ● Two-Earner Married-Couple Deduction ● Charitable-Contributions Deduction ● Tax-Deferred Stock Dividends from Domestic Public-Utility Companies
Stockholders and Depositors Get New Tax Break on '81 Returns   15

Simple Form 1040A 17

Is the "Short" Tax Form 1040A for You?   19
Who Must Use Form 1040   19

Line-by-Line Guide to Form 1040 23

Filing Status   25
Exemptions   26
Income   32
    Compensation ● Interest Income ● Schedule B ● Dividend Income ● Refunds of State and Local Income Taxes ● Capital Gains and Losses from Sale or Exchange of Property ● Schedule D ● Rents and Royalties, Partnerships, Estates or Trusts ● Schedule E ● Form 4562 ● Unemployment Compensation ● Other Income
Adjustments to Income   61
    Moving Expenses ● Employee Business Expenses ● Expense-Account Deductions ● Payments to an Individual Retirement Arrangement ● Payments to a Keogh Retirement Plan ● Alimony ● Disability Income Exclusion
Adjusted Gross Income   77
Tax Computation   77
    Itemized Deductions ● Schedule A ● Medical Expenses ● Taxes ● Interest Deductions ● Charitable Contributions ● Casualty or Theft Losses ● Miscellaneous Deductions ● Figuring Your Tax

6

Credits   102
   Credit for Political Contributions ● Credit for the Elderly ● Schedules
   R & RP ● Credit for Child and Dependent-Care
   Expenses ● Investment Credit ● Residential Energy Credits
Other Taxes   113
   Self-Employment Tax ● Minimum Tax ● Other Taxes
Payments   114
   Total Federal Income Tax Withheld ● Estimated Tax
   Payments ● Earned Income Credit ● Excess FICA and RRTA Tax
   Withheld
Refund or Balance Due   117
Signing   119

Schedule C   121

Income   123
   Gross Receipts Less Allowances, Rebates, and Returns ● Cost of
   Goods Sold and/or Operations ● Schedule C-1 ● Gross
   Profit ● Other Income
Deductions   127
   Amortization ● Bad Debts ● Schedule C-2 ● Depreciation and
   Obsolescence ● Insurance ● Interest on Business
   Indebtedness ● Retirement Plans ● Rent on Business
   Property ● Repairs ● Taxes on Business and Business
   Property ● Wages ● Other Business Expenses
Expense Account Information   134
   Schedule C-3

Schedule SE   135

1981 Tax Table   139

   1987 Tax Table ● 1981 Tax Rate
   Schedules and Tax Computation Worksheet

Other Federal Forms and Schedules   147

   1981 Earned Income Credit Table ●
   Schedule A ● Schedule G ● Form 3468 ●
   Form 4797 ● Form 3903 ● Form 2106 ●
   Form 2119 ● Form 4726

1982 Tax Planning Section   163

Index   167

LIST OF MONEY-SAVING TAX TIPS AND KEYNOTES

Key Changes in 1981 Form 1040A   19

Earned Income Credit   21

Which Capital Expenditures Count as Support of a Dependent?   27

Children of Divorced or Separated Parents   29

Claiming Friends and Cohabitors as Dependents   32

Investing Less than $10,000 to Get Higher Interest for Bank C.D.s Has Tricky
    Tax Consequences   36

Other Income   38

Special 20-percent Ceiling on Long-Term Capital Gains after June 9, 1981   40

What Are Capital Assets?   40

Do You Dabble in the Market?   47

Vacation-Home Expenses   56

Renting Out Your Home or Summer Home for Short Time Can Give Tax-Free
    Income   57

Which Unemployment Benefits Are Exempt and Which Are Not?   60

Barter Transactions   60

Medicare Benefits and Premiums for Elderly   61

Adjustments to Income   62

Mini-Guide: Your Guide to Expense-Account Deductions   65

The Employee's Office-at-Home Deduction   68

Expense-Account Records to Protect Your Deduction   69

How to Reduce Expense-Account Record-Keeping   69

Deduction for Driving to Work with Tools   73

8

How to Boost Deductions for Cars Used for Both Business and Pleasure 73

Did You Buy a Car for Business Use during 1981? 74

Self-Employed (Keogh) and Individual Retirement Plans (IRAs) Attractive 74

Important Medical-Expense Rules 80

Handle Support Payments for Your Parents to Get Maximum Tax Break 83

Which Taxes Are Deductible? 84

Mortgage Points on Buying House 86

How Do Your Deductions Compare? 89

Use of Car in Connection with Charitable Work 91

Back Up Your Checks to Charity 91

If You Were Hit by Hurricanes, Floods, Drought, or Other Disasters 93

If Your Property Damage Resulted from an Event Labeled as a Disaster by the President 94

Expenses of Visiting Your Broker 96

Cost of Hunting for a Job 97

Teachers' Travel Expenses 98

Deducting the Costs of Qualifying for a "Specialty" 99

Correcting Oversights on Your 1980 Return 99

Income Averaging 102

You Can Get a Child-Care Credit for Payments to Your Parent 109

Important Points to Note on Energy Credit 112

Asking for an Automatic Extension to File Your Return 116

Don't Overlook Your 1982 Declaration of Estimated Tax! 118

Common Errors 119

What Are the Chances of Your Return Being Audited? 119

Property Depreciation Rules 129

Can You Prove That You Filed Your Return on Time? 134

How to Use This Guide

This guide is arranged in the same order as the lines on Form 1040, a formula designed to make it as easy as possible to fill out the long form so you achieve the maximum tax savings.

Collect all your records, canceled checks, bills, etc., for 1981. Place blank copy of Form 1040 alongside this Guide. Then you are ready to read my line-by-line explanation of how to fill in the form.

Following a simple summary of what each line requires, you will find a series of questions and answers that will help you decide the correct way to fill in the line for your particular situation.

In addition to the questions and answers, you will find dozens of Tax Tips that point the way to vital tax-saving opportunities that may never before have even occurred to you.

Before you begin to fill out Form 1040, though, check out my summary of important tax developments of 1981, beginning on page 11, to find out whether *any* of them affect your 1981 Form 1040 or will affect your 1982 tax status.

After you have completed filling out your return for 1981, make a firm pledge to yourself to take full advantage of the record-keeping section beginning on page 163. You can use it during all of 1982 to keep the records in this Guide that you will need in order to prepare for filling out your 1982 return in 1983.

Who Must File a Return, Using Either Short Form 1040A or Form 1040

File a return, even if you owe no tax if you are:	And your gross income is at least:
Single (also legally separated, divorced, or married living apart from spouse for the entire year with dependent child) and are under 65	$3,300
Single (also legally separated, divorced, or married living apart from spouse for the entire year with dependent child) and are 65 or older	$4,300
A person who could be claimed as a dependent on your parent's return and you show taxable dividend income, interest income, or other types of unearned income of $1,000 or more.	$1,000
A qualifying widow or widower with dependent child and are under 65	$4,400
A qualifying widow or widower with dependent child and are 65 or older	$5,400
Married filing jointly, living together at end of 1981 (or at date of death of husband or wife), both are under 65	$5,400
Married filing jointly, living together at end of 1981 (or at date of death of husband or wife), one is 65 or older	$6,400
Married filing jointly, living together at end of 1981 (or at date of death of husband or wife), both are 65 or older	$7,400

File a return, even if you owe no tax if you are:	And your gross income is at least:
Married filing separate returns, or married but not living together at end of 1981	$1,000
A person who can exclude income from sources within U.S. possessions	$1,000
Self-employed and your net earnings from self-employment were at least	$ 400
You received any advance earned income credit payments from your employer during 1981.	

Even though you are not required to file a return, according to the list above, you should nevertheless file a return if either:

1. Income tax was withheld from you that you are entitled to get back as a refund, or:

2. You are eligible to take the earned income credit. (See page 21.)

Your return in either of these cases will be a refund claim for you.

Also, even if your income is less than indicated in the list above, you must file a return if you owe any taxes, such as Social Security taxes on tips you did not report to your employer, and so on.

These rules are for all U.S. citizens and resident aliens, also for nonresident aliens who are married to U.S. citizens or residents at the end of 1981 and file a joint return.

For those who can and want to use Form 1040A, see page 19. For those who must use or should use Form 1040, it may also be necessary to fill out the following separate schedules, as well as others.

If you received more than $400 of dividends (including capital-gain distributions) or more than $400 of interest, or any amount of interest from All-Savers Certificates, you must fill out Schedule B, Form 1040, giving the details.

If you itemized your deductions instead of taking the flat standard deduction, you will fill out the itemized deductions on Schedule A, Form 1040.

If you sold or exchanged property, such as stock or a house, you must fill out Schedule D, Form 1040.

If you had income from rents, royalties, partnerships, estates, or trusts, you must fill out Schedule E, Form 1040.

If you claim a credit for the elderly, you must file a Schedule R or RP, Form 1040.

If you are a business or professional person, or a farmer, your Form 1040 package will contain other schedules in addition to those listed above.

Business or professional persons must fill out Schedule C, Form 1040.

Farmers must fill out Schedule F. (This Guide does not cover Schedule F.)

Self-employed persons must compute their Social Security Self-Employment tax on Schedule SE unless they also had $29,700 or more of wages and tips subject to Social Security taxes.

Introduction

The Great New Tax Breaks

Most of the well-publicized changes in the 1981 tax law which apply to you, as an individual taxpayer, become effective in years after 1981. For instance, the widely hailed "indexing" of tax brackets to reflect the rate of inflation won't go into effect until 1985—some time away. But there are significant changes that are retroactive to 1981 or became effective in 1981. To summarize a few for you:

1. The first rate-reduction stage of the '81 tax law went into effect for 1981. When you file your 1981 tax return this spring, you will be given a credit of 1.25 percent of the tax calculated under the 1980 rates. If you must use the Tax Tables to determine your 1981 tax, you'll find that the IRS has prepared new Tax Tables to reflect the 1.25-percent credit ($1.25 for each $100 of tax). If you must use the tax-rate schedules to figure your tax, you will have to make the computation yourself.

Under the tax law, you get only a 1¼-percent reduction for 1981—but a further 8¾-percent reduction in 1982, another 9-percent reduction in 1983, and still another 4 percent after 1983.

Now, postponing income into later years in the 1980s and accelerating deductions into earlier years in this decade come into focus as top-notch tax strategies! Millions of you—in occupations ranging from sales to medicine and law—can easily shift portions of your income from one year to the next and by so doing can cut your federal income taxes substantially. Millions of you can speed up deductions from one year to another and by so doing also reduce your tax debts to the IRS. Start thinking about how to arrange these shifts to benefit yourself on your 1982 tax return—which you will file in the spring of 1983—*now,* when you can move your funds with ease.

2. As of calendar 1982, all income—whether earned or unearned—will *not* be taxed at more than a 50-percent rate. This means that long-term capital gains, no matter how great, are being taxed at no more than 20 percent (50 percent of the 40 percent of long-term capital gains subject to tax). In addition, long-term capital gains from sales made *after June 9, 1981,* are under the 20-percent-ceiling rate. The benefit of this, however, is restricted to individuals whose 1981 taxable income, including 40 percent of the capital gains, is more than $41,500 if single, or $60,000 if married.

3. No matter what your age, if you sell your house at a profit, you can defer tax on the profit if you buy another principal residence within an 18-month period before and after the sale, at a price at least equal to your selling price. This period has been extended from 18 months to two years for residences sold *after July 20, 1981.* But if you, an individual, sold a residence before July 21, 1981, and the old 18-month period expires on or after July 20, 1981, you are given an extra six months (meaning up to two years total).

4. If you are 55 years of age or older, you, as an individual, have been able to exclude $100,000 of any gain on your residence, whether you bought a new home or not. The exclusion limit has been raised to $125,000 for sales made after July 20, 1981.

5. As a qualified oil-royalty owner, you were allowed a credit of up to $1,000 against the windfall-profit tax during 1980. This was boosted to $2,500 for 1981.

6. Since October 1, 1981, and until December 31, 1982, you can buy a one-year tax-exempt savings certificate from a bank or other qualified institution at a rate of 70 percent of the yield on a one-year U.S. Treasury bill. But you can exclude a lifetime total of only $1,000 of exempt interest earned—or $2,000 for a joint return. Thus, if the current investment yield on a 52-week U.S. Treasury bill was about 15 percent, this would allow you to invest a maximum of $20,000, if married, at about a 10-percent tax-exempt yield for one year (70 percent of the current-Treasury-bill yield).

If you will look at this objectively, you will realize that if you are in an income-tax bracket of 30 percent or less, you get no tax break from these certificates. If you earn 14.5 percent on a taxable Treasury bill (or bank certificate of deposit, etc.), and pay a 30-percent income-tax rate, you will have roughly the same 10-percent after-tax result as from a one-year tax-exempt savings certificate. (So much for all the publicity about a savings certificate for lower-income individuals.)

7. Individuals who engage in straddles as a tax shelter have lost their anticipated tax benefits for property acquired and positions established after June 23, 1981. (This tax dodge has been an open scandal.)

8. Currently, if you owe the IRS taxes for underpayment of estimated tax, there is a penalty imposed at a rate of 12 percent a year—or if the IRS owes you a refund, it pays you interest at a 12-percent annual rate. But starting February 1, 1982, the IRS has raised the rate to 20 percent a year.

9. A new penalty tax has been added for individuals, or those managing a closely held corporation or a personal-service corporation, who inflate valuations on property acquired within five years in order to reduce their income tax. This applies to returns filed after 1981—*which includes 1981 returns.* If the overvaluation is between 150 percent and 200 percent of the correct valuation, the penalty tax is 10 percent of the income-tax underpayment. If the overvaluation is over 200 but not over 250 percent, the penalty tax is 20 percent, and if more than 250 percent, 30 percent.

No penalty applies if the underpayment of tax is less than $1,000. There even you had reasonable grounds for your valuation. (Don't hope too much.)

10. Until now, expenses involved in an adoption have not been deductible. Beginning with 1981, though, an exception to this general rule has been made for the expenses of adopting a "child with special needs," for whom adoption-assistance payments are made under Social Security. If you adopt a child of this nature, you may take an itemized deduction for the reasonable costs of the adoption procedure—such as adoption fees, court costs and attorney fees—up to $1,500. Adoption expenses for any other children are still not deductible.

IRA and Keogh Plans

Right now, start to plan how you can get the maximum benefits from the tax breaks in the new tax law liberalizing Individual Retirement Account (IRA) and Keogh plans as of calendar 1982—the best "tax shelters" ever created for us as individuals.

The rules on IRAs have been made much more favorable to you in two significant ways. You will be a fool if you ignore them.

The limit on the amount you will be able to contribute to a regular IRA and deduct each year has been raised, from the previous lesser of $1,500 or 15 percent of your compensation to the lesser of $2,000 or 100 percent of your compensation. In itself, the 33⅓-percent boost in the dollar ceiling that you can set aside for your retirement and deduct on your tax return from $1,500 to $2,000 is an important tax break. But far more valuable is the change in the alternative limit from the previous 15 percent of compensation to 100 percent of compensation, particularly to all of you who had (or will earn) less than $10,000 of compensation during the year.

The low 15-percent alternative limit has meant that if you earned, say, only $6,000 during 1981 from part-time or temporary jobs, you could contribute and deduct only $900 instead of $1,500 for the year. But beginning in '82, the new alternative limit of 100 percent of compensation won't bar you from contributing and deducting up to the $2,000 limit if your compensation in '82 is at least $2,000.

If you qualify to set up a spousal IRA because you have a nonearner spouse, the previous $1,750 limit on annual deductible contributions to a spousal IRA is raised to $2,250 a year beginning in 1982. And the rule requiring the spousal IRA contributions to be divided equally between the spouses is repealed, so you can divide them as you prefer.

In addition to boosting the deductible, tax-sheltered amounts you can contribute toward your retirement, the new law greatly broadens the number of you who will be able to use IRAs. Up to 1982, only if you were *not* an active participant in an employer-sponsored qualified employee benefit plan could you use IRAs. Thus, millions of employees covered by their employers' qualified pension, profit-sharing, etc., plans were barred from setting up IRAs—even if they desperately wanted to supplement their coverage on their own.

This limit is eliminated, beginning in 1982. As an employee covered by an employer's qualified benefit plan, you, too, will be able to create and deduct contributions to an IRA. This can be enormously helpful to you!

The new law also actually enables you, if you are an employer with a qualified benefit plan, to offer your employees the tax benefits of the new IRAs, so they don't have to set up separate IRAs for themselves. As an employer, you must amend your plan to provide for voluntary contributions by your employees. These voluntary employee contributions will be deductible by the employee and subject to the same limits and withdrawal rules as contributions to an IRA are.

The IRA rules also are expanded to cover a divorced spouse whose former spouse set up a spousal IRA at least five years before the divorce, if the former spouse contributed under the spousal IRA rules at least three of the five years before the divorce. If these requirements are met, then, beginning in '82, the divorced spouse can contribute each year to the spousal IRA and deduct up to the lesser of $1,125 or the sum of the divorced spouse's compensation and alimony included in gross income.

Warning: If your IRA (or an individually directed account in a qualified plan) invests in a "collectible" after December 31, 1981, this is to be treated as a distribution from the IRA to you, the IRA's owner. "Collectibles" are defined as any work of art, rug or antique, metal or gem, stamp or coin, alcoholic beverage, or any tangible property added to the list by the Treasury. This means you no longer will be able to invest your IRA funds in collectibles, because you will be taxed on the amount of the investment—as if the IRA had distributed that amount to you in cash.

Keogh plans (tax-sheltered retirement plans for use by self-employed individuals) also are liberalized. Before 1982, a deductible contribution to a Keogh plan of the profit-sharing type was limited to the lesser of 15 percent of self-employment earnings or $7,500. Starting with

1982, the limit is the lesser of 15 percent of self-employed earnings or $15,000. This will benefit you, however, only if you earn over $50,000.

It will be easier, too, to avoid penalty tax on contributions that are erroneously made in excess of the deductible limit. If the excess funds are distributed back to the contributor on or before the due date for filing the income-tax return for the year, there will be no penalty tax.

Estate and Gift Taxes

Recheck your will at once! Even if you are in a mid-income bracket and think you have no assets worth "estate planning," you're almost surely *wrong*. Your life insurance, home, benefits under pension or profit-sharing plans, union or fraternal assets, etc., easily can put your estate in the high six figures. Your spouse and children could be vitally involved in the new tax law's spectacular liberalization of federal estate and gift taxes.

Immediate action is imperative because the exemption from estate and gift taxes rises *gradually* from 1981's $175,000 to $600,000 in 1987. In sum, each year the exemption becomes more valuable.

Also, because of the drastic cutting of these taxes, you must reexamine any life-insurance coverage you may have taken out to provide funds to pay estate taxes that will no longer exist.

The whole setup on giving gifts to people you love has been so altered that ignorance can be shockingly costly. Here's a rundown:

1. If you are married, you can now avoid estate taxes *completely* on your death, simply by giving all of your estate to your spouse by will, or, before death, by lifetime gift (after '81). Even an estate running into the millions may be transferred on death or during life to a spouse, free of gift and estate taxes. (Until the end of '81, this exemption was limited to the higher of half your estate or $250,000, whichever was larger.)

On the surviving spouse's death, the estate will be entitled to the then applicable exemption ($600,000 if the survivor dies after '86), and only the total over the exemption will be subject to estate tax.

While the new law lets you transfer your entire estate to your spouse free of gift or estate tax, either by lifetime gift or by will at your death, you might want to leave certain property at death instead of transferring it to your spouse by lifetime gift. If you own appreciated property that you expect your spouse to sell after receipt from you, he or she will have a much smaller income tax, or no tax at all, on the appreciation if you leave it by will rather than by lifetime gift. You might be holding stock, say, for which you paid $10,000, but which is now worth $100,000. You escape the gift tax by giving the stock during your lifetime, but your spouse will have to pay tax on a $90,000 capital gain on sale ($100,000 price less your $10,000 cost). If you leave it by will, there will be no estate tax, but your spouse will have zero gain subject to tax on sale, because the cost basis will go up to the $100,000 estate-tax value ($100,000 price less $100,000 estate value).

2. If you wish to pass part (or all) of your estate to your children or others, gift-tax free, you can give each child or other donee up to $10,000 *per year* after '81 (limit has been $3,000 per donee per year). For instance, if you have three married children and three grandchildren, then, starting January 1, 1982, you can give each married child, each spouse of the married children, and each grandchild $10,000 each year, or a total of $90,000 each and every year, free of gift tax.

If your spouse joins with you in making the gifts, then you can give up to $20,000 to each donee each year free of tax. If you make gifts to a service-provider for medical care or tuition for a donee, these gifts have unlimited exclusion.

If you are a typical middle-income person, the right to give away these totals free of tax represents practically no limits at all.

3. If on death you still leave a taxable estate, after transfers to your spouse and tax-free gifts, the '81 estate-tax exemption of $175,625 has increased to $225,000 for those dying in '82, to $275,000 in '83, $325,000 in '84, $400,000 in '85, $500,000 in '86 and $600,000 thereafter.

4. If you own property with your spouse as tenants by the entirety or in joint tenancy with right of survivorship, you will each be treated for estate-tax purposes—starting in 1982—as owner of 50 percent of the property, regardless of how much, if any, of the purchase price was paid by each of you. For instance, if you are a married couple owning a home jointly with right of survivorship, but only one of you actually paid for it, each spouse will nevertheless be considered a half owner for estate-tax purposes.

5. The top 70-percent bracket on estate-tax rates will be reduced gradually, starting in '82 to 65 percent, to 60 percent in '83, to 55 percent in '84, to 50 percent in '85. This is strictly for the very, very rich (the 50-percent rate will help only the few with taxable estates above $2,500,000).

One tightening-up provision in the new law: Allowing a parent's estate to exclude payments of $5,000 a year to an orphaned child for each year the child is under 21 is repealed after 1981.

More Tax Breaks for Individuals in '82

Dependent-Care Credit on Employment-Related Expenses

If you must spend money to take care of children and dependents in order to work for pay, you will get significantly higher tax credits in 1982 than in 1981. Begin planning now how to get your maximums.

In 1982, you will be allowed a credit on up to $2,400 of employment-related expenses if you have one dependent (as against 1981's $2,000), or up to $4,800 if you have two or more dependents (instead of 1981's $4,000). Under the old law, you are entitled to a 20-percent credit, limiting your maximum for '81 to $400 or $800. Under the new law, the percentage credit allowed beginning in '82 will depend on your adjusted gross income (income before deducting your itemized deductions).

If your adjusted gross income is less than $10,000, your percentage allowed is 30 percent of expenses up to $2,400 or $4,800. For every $2,000 of added adjusted gross income you have, the 30 percent drops 1 percentage point (but not to less than 20 percent). Under this formula, if your adjusted gross income is over $28,000, you will be back to 20 percent—and your maximum credit for '82 will be limited to $480 or $960.

Under '81 law, expenses incurred for services outside the household don't qualify for the credit unless for the care of a dependent under the age of 15. In '82, expenditures for older children and for out-of-home, noninstitutional care of a disabled spouse or dependent also are eligible for the credit.

The law also gives employers a way to provide employees' child- and dependent-care expenses as tax-exempt income to their employees. To qualify, the employer's plan is hedged with the usual antidiscrimination rules.

Note: Under these new plans, you, an employee, could save much more in taxes than the $960 maximum credit otherwise allowed. For instance, if you're an employee for whom the firm pays $4,000 of child-care expenses and you are in the 40-percent bracket, you would in effect save $1,600 instead of being limited to the $960 maximum credit. Plan now with your employer how this can be worked out.

Two-Earner Married-Couple Deduction

The so-called marriage penalty, under which a married couple can pay more in taxes than would be due if they were not married and had filed single returns, is eased after '81 by allowing a flat deduction in arriving at adjusted gross income (before itemized deductions or standard deduction) based on the earnings of the lower-earning spouse. For '82, it will be 5 percent of the lower-earning spouse's earned income, up to $1,500 (on $30,000 of earned income) and after '82, 10 percent, up to $3,000.

Earned income for this purpose will be computed without regard to community-property laws, the 30-percent limitation on certain compensation from a trade or business in which capital and personal services are material income-producing factors, or any deferred compensation including pensions, etc. This deduction is allowed beginning in '82 for every two-earner married couple regardless of whether there would or would not have been a marriage penalty. There is to be no relief for spouses covering *unearned* income, though.

If you're a couple with only earned income, this new deduction could even result in a marriage *bonus*. Thus, in 1983, if your total income is earned, with one spouse earning $40,000 and the other $10,000, you'll have an estimated $200 marriage bonus from the new deduction, instead of a penalty.

Charitable-Contributions Deduction

If you have been using the zero-bracket amount (standard deduction) and not itemizing your deductions, you haven't obtained any benefit from charitable contributions. To encourage you to make some contributions, beginning in '82 the new law will allow you to deduct 25 percent of your charitable contributions up to $100 for '82 and '83 (a maximum deduction of $25), in addition to your zero-bracket amount. Higher amounts will be allowed in '84, and '85, and '86. The ceiling applies for both single and joint returns, but is halved for married persons filing separately.

Tax-Deferred Stock Dividends from Domestic Public-Utility Companies

The new law allows domestic public-utility companies to set up plans to permit investors in their shares to receive tax-deferred stock dividends that then can be sold as capital gain. Under the general rules, if a corporation gives its shareholders the choice of receiving a dividend either in cash or in additional stock, all shareholders are taxable on the amount of the dividend as ordinary dividend income, even those who choose to take the dividend in additional shares rather than cash. But under the new law, domestic public-utility companies (electricity, gas, water, phone, etc.) may adopt plans that will allow individual investors to elect to receive their dividends in additional stock rather than cash. If you, a shareholder, choose stock, the stock dividend will not be taxable to you, as it otherwise would be under the general rules because of the choice between cash and stock.

However, there is a limit on the amount of such stock dividends that may be treated as tax-deferred in a year.

If you are married persons filing a joint return, you can exclude up to $1,500 of such dividends from income each year, while other investors can exclude up to $750 a year.

If you, the investor, hold these stock-dividend shares for at least a year before you sell them, the entire proceeds of the sale will be taxed as a long-term capital gain. Thus, you, the investor, get a double benefit from electing to take your dividend in the form of stock rather than cash. First, you defer paying any tax on it until you sell it. When you sell after a year, you have in effect converted your dividend into capital gain.

But if you, the investor, sell your dividend stock *within* a year after it is distributed to you, the proceeds will be taxed to you as ordinary income just as if paid in cash—not as capital gain.

This new exclusion of stock dividends from domestic public-utility corporations will apply to distributions in 1982 through 1985. Corporations which adopt plans for such elective stock dividends will undoubtedly publicize them for potential investors. They will become major lures for buyers.

The new law also includes unfavorable changes beginning in 1982 that you must not overlook.

For 1981, the law allows you, an individual, to exclude from income up to $200 ($400 on a joint return) of any combination of dividends and interest from domestic sources. (See below.) For 1982, this exclusion is repealed and is replaced by an exclusion that applies only to dividends. The amount of exclusion for 1982 will be $100 of dividends on a separate return and $200 on a joint return. The $200 exclusion on the joint return can be based on any combination of dividends of the husband and wife; it is not limited to $100 per spouse as in past years.

Beginning in 1982, the civil penalty for claiming withholding allowances based on false information goes up from the previous $50 to $500. This puts a premium on care and accuracy if you file claims for withholding allowances.

The Tax Court is the taxpayer's chief area for litigating disputes with the IRS. Until 1982, the court was authorized to charge a fee of up to $10 for filing a petition with the court. Beginning with calendar year 1982, the court is authorized to charge up to $60. What the court will do under its higher authorization is, as of today, a big question.

Stockholders and Depositors Get New Tax Break on '81 Returns

For 1981 only, the previous special exclusion for dividends has been expanded to include interest as well as dividends, and has been increased in amount and further liberalized.

Under the rules that applied to your 1980 return, each person was allowed to exclude from income up to $100 of dividends received by him or her during the year. There was no such exclusion for interest you received from banks, savings and loans, corporation bonds, etc., (except that tax-exempt interest on state and local obligations is entirely exempt from federal income tax).

If you were a husband and wife filing a joint return, each of you was separately allowed an exclusion of up to $100 on your own dividends, and neither of you could take the other's unused exclusion.

For instance, say that in 1980 Mrs. Smith received $200 in dividends on stock she owned in her own name. Her husband received $25 in dividends on stock he owned in his own name. Applying each one's $100 dividend exclusion separately, Mr. Smith's entire $25 of dividends was excluded, but only $100 of Mrs. Smith's $200 of dividends was excluded. She couldn't apply Mr. Smith's $75 of unused exclusion to any part of her own dividends.

So the Smiths reported $100 of taxable dividends on their joint return for 1980.

But the results are drastically different on the 1981 return.

1. The dividend exclusion has been changed to a combined dividends-plus-interest exclusion. Dividends and interest are added together in applying the exclusion.

2. The amount of the exclusion for the combined dividends-plus-interest is up to $200 for a single individual and up to $400 on a joint return of a husband and wife. The $400 exclusion on the joint return applies regardless of whether the dividends and interest come from the husband's or wife's ownership.

Again, to illustrate, say that Mr. Smith received $25 of dividends on his own stock in 1981. Mrs. Smith received $200 on her own stock, and Mrs. Smith also earned $300 of interest in 1981 on a bank account in her own name. Between them, their combined dividends and interest in 1981 totaled $525. On their 1981 joint return they exclude $400 of the $525 so that they are taxed on only $125. It makes no difference that only $25 of the combined total came from Mr. Smith and $500 came from Mrs. Smith.

Simple Form 1040A

Is the "Short" Tax Form 1040A for You?

You can qualify to report your 1981 income tax on simple Form 1040A if (1) your 1981 income consisted of only wages, salaries, tips, interest, dividends and unemployment compensation; (2) your taxable income (which is your adjusted gross income less your exemptions) is less than $50,000; (3) you don't itemize your deductions; (4) you don't claim any adjustments to income, such as moving expenses; and (5) you don't claim any credits other than the political contributions credit or the earned income credit.

If in 1981 you received more than $400 in interest, or any amount of interest from All-Savers Certificates, you must list the payers and the amounts they paid in Part I on Page 2 of Form 1040A. Also, if you received more than $400 of ordinary dividends and nontaxable distributions in 1981, you must list the payers and the amounts they paid in Part II on Page 2 of Form 1040A. If you received $400 or less of interest (other than on All-Savers Certificates) or of dividends, you just enter the total amounts without filling in Parts I and II. Interest on All-Savers Certificates must be reported in Part I no matter how small the amount.

Once you have arrived at your taxable income by subtracting your exemptions from your adjusted gross income, you simply pick out your tax from the appropriate tax table. These tax tables automatically incorporate the standard deduction (zero bracket amount) to which you are entitled as well as the 1981 tax cut.

You Must Use Form 1040 and Can't Use Form 1040A If:

• Your taxable income is $50,000 or more.
• At any time during the year you had an interest in or signature or other authority over a bank account, securities account, or other financial account in a foreign country.
• You were a grantor of or a transferor to a foreign trust that existed during 1981.

• You had income other than wages, salaries, tips, interest, dividends, and unemployment compensation.
• Your spouse files a separate return and itemizes deductions, except that you can still use Form 1040A if you have a dependent child and can meet the tests on page 100 for Married Persons Who Live Apart (and Abandoned Spouses).

• You can be claimed as a dependent on your parents' return and had interest, dividends, or other unearned income of $1,000 or more.

• You are a qualifying widow(er) with a dependent child. (See page 101.)

• You were a nonresident alien during any part of 1981 and do not file a joint return.

• You were married to a nonresident or dual status alien at the end of 1981 who had U.S.-source income and you do not file a joint return, except that you can still use Form 1040A if you meet the tests on page 95 for Married Persons Who Live Apart (and Abandoned Spouses).

• You itemize deductions.

• You file any of these forms:

Form 1040-ES, Declaration of Estimated Tax for Individuals, for 1981 (or if you want to apply any part of your 1981 overpayment to estimated tax for 1982).

Schedule G (Form 1040), Income Averaging.

Form 2119, Sale or Exchange of Principal Residence.

Form 2210, Underpayment of Estimated Tax by Individuals.

Form 2555, Deduction from, or Exclusion of, Income Earned Abroad.

Form 4563, Exclusion of Income from Sources in United States Possessions.

Form 4868, Application for Extension of Time to File U.S. Individual Income Tax Return.

• You owe any of these taxes:

Uncollected employee Social Security (FICA) tax on tips shown on your Form W-2.

Social Security (FICA) tax on tips if you received more than $20 in any month and you did not report all of them to your employer (Form 4137).

Tax on individual retirement arrangement (IRA) (Form 5329).

Tax on self-employment income (Schedule SE).

• You claim income such as:

Moving expenses due to a change in jobs (Form 3903 or Form 3903F).

Employee business expenses such as travel (Form 2106).

Payments to an individual retirement arrangement (IRA) or to a Keogh plan.

Interest penalty on early withdrawal of savings.

Alimony paid.

Disability Income exclusion (Form 2440).

Repayment of Sub-pay under the Trade Act of 1974.

• You claim any of these tax credits:

Credit for the elderly if you are 65 or over, or under 65 with a pension from a federal, state, etc. retirement plan (Schedules R and RP).

Credit for child- and dependent-care expenses (Form 2441).

Investment credit (Form 3468).

Overpaid windfall profit tax (Form 6249 or 6249A).

Foreign-tax credit (Form 1116).

WIN credit (Form 4874).

Jobs credit (Form 5884).

Credit for federal tax on special fuels, nonhighway gasoline, and lubricating oils (Form 4136).

Credit or refund for federal tax on gasoline, diesel fuel, and special fuels used in qualified taxicabs (Form 4136-T).

Credit for taxes paid by a regulated investment company (Form 2439).

Credit for residential energy-saving items (Form 5695).

Credit for alcohol used as fuel (Form 6478).

Credit for increasing research activities.

Check your actual deductions before choosing between Form 1040A and Form 1040.

Even if you are eligible to use the shorter Form 1040A, you will generally pay *less tax* by using regular Form 1040 if:

1. You are married filing jointly and your itemized deductions total more than $3,400.

2. You are single or an unmarried head of household and your itemized deductions total more than $2,300.

3. You are married filing separately and your itemized deductions total more than $1,700.

In filling out Form 1040A, note these points:

1. If you want IRS to figure your tax, skip lines 13b through 18 and sign and date your return. (Attach Form(s) W-2 to Form 1040A.)

If you are filing a joint return and both you and your spouse have income, you should show the income of each separately in the space to the right of lines 8a through 8d so IRS can figure your tax the way that gives you the smaller tax.

You should file on or before April 15, 1982. IRS will then figure your tax and send you a refund check if you have overpaid or bill you if you did not pay enough.

2. If you made qualified political contributions during 1981, you may take a credit on line 13a of Form 1040A for a specified amount of these contributions. For an explanation of which political contributions qualify for credit and how much credit you can take, see the detailed discussion page 102.

3. If you worked for more than one employer during 1981 and together they paid you more than $29,700 in wages, too much Social Security tax may have been withheld from your wages. Add up all of your FICA and RRTA taxes collected by your various employers. If the total is more than $1,975.05 you should enter that excess over $1,975.05 at line 13b. On a joint return, such excess amounts must be figured separately for the husband and the wife. If you include any excess on line 13b, write "excess FICA" and the amount to the left of the line 13b entry space.

4. If you compute your own tax on Form 1040A, you must use the Tax Tables reproduced in the official form booklet and shown on pages 139-145.

TAX TIP: Earned Income Credit

The job of figuring out your 1981 earned income credit is easier because of an IRS table that is reproduced on page 147. If you show less than $10,000 on line 11 of Form 1040A or line 31 of Form 1040, and meet the other requirements for a refundable earned income credit as shown on page 22, you fill in the information required by the Worksheet, then get the amount of your credit from the table on page 147.

For example, suppose Mr. and Mrs. Smith live with their baby in their own home. Mr. Smith earned only $2,500 of wages in 1981 and received $500 of interest from their bank account. The Smiths drew on their savings for the rest of their needs.

Smith is eligible for the earned income credit because he meets all the tests listed on page 22. He files Form 1040A to claim the refundable credit, even though he is otherwise not required to file a return.

In order to claim his credit, Mr. Smith fills in Form 1040A through line 10. Then he uses the Worksheet on page 22 and table on page 147 to get the amount of his credit. The Worksheet shows that his credit will be based on the $2,500 he fills in at line 7 of Form 1040A. The table then shows that the credit on $2,500 is $248, which he enters on line 13c. Smith then completes lines 13a through 14 and 16 of Form 1040A, signs (with his wife) and dates the return, attaches Copy B of his Form W-2 and mails it to IRS. He will then receive his $248 refundable credit.

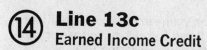

⑭ Line 13c
Earned Income Credit

What Does the Earned Income Credit Do?

The earned income credit helps many taxpayers who have a child and have incomes under $10,000. If you can take the earned income credit, you can subtract it from tax you owe or get a refund even if you had no tax withheld from your pay. The credit can be as much as $500.

What is Earned Income?

In most cases, you had earned income if you worked last year. Earned income includes:

• wages, salaries, tips, and

• anything else of value (money, goods, or services) you get from your employer for services you performed regardless of whether it is taxable.

Note 1: *In addition to the income listed above, the following are examples of amounts received from your employer that must be included in line 1 of the worksheet, but not on Form 1040A, line 7—*
a. *Housing allowance (or rental value of a parsonage) for members of the clergy.*
b. *Meals and lodging.*

Earned income does **not** include items such as interest, dividends, social security payments, welfare benefits, nondisability pensions, veterans' benefits, workmen's compensation, or unemployment compensation (insurance).

Who Can't Take the Earned Income Credit?

You can't take the earned income credit if:

1. You are **Single** (Filing Status Box 1); **OR**
2. You are **Married filing a separate return** (Filing Status Box 3); **OR**
3. Your income is **$10,000 or more.**

Note 2: *If you got advance earned income credit payments, you must file a tax return. Report these payments on line 15b of Form 1040A. If you expect to answer YES to all the questions below for 1982 and want to get advance payments of the credit, file Form W–5 with your employer.*

If you are not required to file a return but can claim the earned income credit, file Form 1040A to get a refund of your credit.

All you need to do is:

1. Fill in Form 1040A through line 10. Do not check the Presidential Election Campaign Fund box(es).
2. Use the Earned Income Credit Worksheet on this page to figure your credit.
3. Fill in Form 1040A, lines 13a through 14 and 16.
4. Sign and date the return.
5. Be sure to attach the first copy or Copy B of Form(s) W–2.

If you want IRS to figure your earned income credit for you, skip instructions **2** and **3** above, but please provide all the other information requested.

If you want IRS to figure your tax, including the Earned Income Credit, answer the questions below, but do not fill in the Earned Income Credit Worksheet.

To see if you can take the Earned Income Credit, fill in Form 1040A through line 10, and answer the following:

	Yes	No
1. Is the amount you listed on Form 1040A, line 10, less than $10,000?	☐	☐
2. Did you receive any wages, salaries, tips, or other earned income (see "What is Earned Income?" on page 13)?	☐	☐
3. Did you have a child **(see note 3 below)** who lived with you in the same principal residence in the United States during all of 1981?	☐	☐

4. If you checked Filing Status **Box 2** on Form 1040A, did you claim your child as a dependent on Form 1040A, line 5c? **OR**

   If you checked Filing Status **Box 4** on Form 1040A, **and your child was married for 1981,** did you claim that child as a dependent on Form 1040A, line 5c? **OR**

   If you checked Filing Status **Box 4** on Form 1040A, **and your child was unmarried for 1981,** did you enter that child's name on Form 1040A, line 4 (or 5c if you claimed that child as a dependent)?   ☐   ☐

Note 3: *For this purpose, the word* **child** *means:*
- Your son or daughter.
- Your stepchild, adopted child, or a child placed with you by an authorized placement agency for legal adoption (even if the child became your stepchild or adopted child, or was placed with you during the year).
- Any other child whom you cared for as your own child for the whole year, unless the child's natural or adoptive parents provided more than half of the support for that year.

If you answered NO to **any** question, you can't take the earned income credit. Do not fill in the worksheet. Instead, put "No" on line 13c.

If you answered YES to **all** the questions, you may be able to take the credit. Use the Earned Income Credit Worksheet below to figure the amount of any credit.

Earned Income Credit Worksheet
(Keep for your tax records)

1. Amount from Form 1040A, line 7. (See **Note 1** under "What is Earned Income?")	$
2. Amount from Form 1040A, line 10.	
3. If line 2 above is **not over $6,000,** use the amount on line 1 to find the credit in the table on page 23. Enter the credit here and on Form 1040A, line 13c.	
4. If line 2 is **over $6,000:**	
a. First, find the amount from line 1 above in the table on page 23, and enter the credit for that amount here. $_____	
b. Second, find the amount from line 2 in the table, and enter the credit for that amount here. $_____	
c. Enter the amount from 4a or 4b, whichever is smaller, here and on Form 1040A, line 13c.	$

For example, in our filled-in form, the Browns' earned income credit was figured as follows:

Earned Income Credit Worksheet

1. Amount from Form 1040A, line 7. (See **Note 1** under "What is Earned Income?")	$9,080.00
2. Amount from Form 1040A, line 10.	$9,180.00
3. If line 2 above is **not over $6,000,** use the amount on line 1 to find the credit in the table on page 23. Enter the credit here and on Form 1040A, line 13c.	SAMPLE
4. If line 2 is **over $6,000:**	
a. First, find the amount from line 1 above in the table on page 23, and enter the credit for that amount here. $116.00	
b. Second, find the amount from line 2 in the table, and enter the credit for that amount here. $103.00	
c. Enter the amount from 4a or 4b, whichever is smaller, here and on Form 1040A, line 13c.	$103.00

Form **1040** Department of the Treasury—Internal Revenue Service
U.S. Individual Income Tax Return **1981**

For the year January 1–December 31, 1981, or other tax year beginning , 1981, ending , 19 . | OMB No. 1545-0074

Use IRS label. Otherwise, please print or type.

Your first name and initial (if joint return, also give spouse's name and initial) | Last name | **Your social security number**

Present home address (Number and street, including apartment number, or rural route) | **Spouse's social security no.**

City, town or post office, State and ZIP code | Your occupation ▶ | Spouse's occupation ▶

Presidential Election Campaign
▶ Do you want $1 to go to this fund? . . . . |__| Yes |__| No
▶ If joint return, does your spouse want $1 to go to this fund? . . | Yes | No

Note: Checking "Yes" will not increase your tax or reduce your refund.

Filing Status

Check only one box.

1 |__| Single

For Privacy Act and Paperwork Reduction Act Notice, see Instructions.

2 |__| Married filing joint return (even if only one had income)
3 |__| Married filing separate return. Enter spouse's social security no. above and full name here ▶ ------------------
4 |__| Head of household (with qualifying person). (See page 6 of Instructions.) If he or she is your unmarried child, enter child's name ▶ ------------------
5 |__| Qualifying widow(er) with dependent child (Year spouse died ▶ 19). (See page 6 of Instructions.)

Exemptions

Always check the box labeled Yourself. Check other boxes if they apply.

6a |__| Yourself |__| 65 or over |__| Blind
b |__| Spouse |__| 65 or over |__| Blind

} Enter number of boxes checked on 6a and b ▶ |__|

c First names of your dependent children who lived with you ▶ ------------------
----

} Enter number of children listed on 6c ▶ |__|

d Other dependents:

(1) Name	(2) Relationship	(3) Number of months lived in your home	(4) Did dependent have income of $1,000 or more?	(5) Did you provide more than one-half of dependent's support?

Enter number of other dependents ▶ |__|

Add numbers entered in boxes above ▶ |__|

e Total number of exemptions claimed . . . .

Income

Please attach Copy B of your Forms W-2 here.

If you do not have a W-2, see page 5 of Instructions.

7 Wages, salaries, tips, etc. . . . . | **7** |
8a Interest income (attach Schedule B if over $400 or you have any All-Savers interest) . . | **8a** |
b Dividends (attach Schedule B if over $400) . . . . . . | **8b** |
c Total. Add lines 8a and 8b . . . . | **8c** |
d Exclusion (See page 9 of Instructions) . . . . | **8d** |
e Subtract line 8d from line 8c (but not less than zero) . . . . | **8e** |
9 Refunds of State and local income taxes (do not enter an amount unless you deducted those taxes in an earlier year—see page 9 of Instructions) . . . . | **9** |
10 Alimony received . . . . | **10** |
11 Business income or (loss) (attach Schedule C) . . . . ▶ | **11** |
12 Capital gain or (loss) (attach Schedule D) . . . . | **12** |
13 40% of capital gain distributions not reported on line 12 (See page 9 of Instructions) . | **13** |
14 Supplemental gains or (losses) (attach Form 4797) . . . . | **14** |
15 Fully taxable pensions and annuities not reported on line 16 . . . . | **15** |
16a Other pensions and annuities. Total received . . . . | **16a** |
b Taxable amount, if any, from worksheet on page 10 of Instructions . . . . . . | **16b** |
17 Rents, royalties, partnerships, estates, trusts, etc. (attach Schedule E) . . . . . | **17** |
18 Farm income or (loss) (attach Schedule F) . . . . ▶ | **18** |
19a Unemployment compensation (insurance). Total received | **19a** |
b Taxable amount, if any, from worksheet on page 10 of Instructions . . . . . . | **19b** |
20 Other income (state nature and source—see page 11 of Instructions) ▶ ------------------ | **20** |

Please attach check or money order here.

21 **Total income.** Add amounts in column for lines 7 through 20 . . . . ▶ | **21** |

Adjustments to Income

(See Instructions on page 11)

22 Moving expense (attach Form 3903 or 3903F) . . . . | **22** |
23 Employee business expenses (attach Form 2106) . . . | **23** |
24 Payments to an IRA (enter code from page 11 ....) . | **24** |
25 Payments to a Keogh (H.R. 10) retirement plan . . . . | **25** |
26 Interest penalty on early withdrawal of savings . . . . | **26** |
27 Alimony paid . . . . | **27** |
28 Disability income exclusion (attach Form 2440) . . . . | **28** |
29 Other adjustments—see page 12 ▶ | **29** |
30 **Total adjustments.** Add lines 22 through 29 . . . . ▶ | **30** |

Adjusted Gross Income

31 **Adjusted gross income.** Subtract line 30 from line 21. If this line is less than $10,000, see "Earned Income Credit" (line 57) on page 15 of Instructions. If you want IRS to figure your tax, see page 3 of Instructions . . . . ▶ | **31** |

☆ U.S. GOVERNMENT PRINTING OFFICE : 1981—O-343-057

343-057-1

Form 1040 (1981)   Page **2**

Tax Compu- tation (See Instruc- tions on page 12)	**32a** Amount from line 31 *(adjusted gross income)*	**32a**		
	32b If you do not itemize deductions, enter zero . . . . } If you itemize, complete Schedule A (Form 1040) and enter the amount from Schedule A, line 41 . . . }	**32b**		
	Caution: If you have unearned income and can be claimed as a dependent on your parent's return, check here ▶ ☐ and see page 12 of the Instructions. Also see page 12 of the Instructions if: ● You are married filing a separate return and your spouse itemizes deductions, OR ● You file Form 4563, OR ● You are a dual-status alien.			
	32c Subtract line 32b from line 32a	**32c**		
	33 Multiply $1,000 by the total number of exemptions claimed on Form 1040, line 6e . .	**33**		
	34 Taxable Income. Subtract line 33 from line 32c	**34**		
	35 Tax. Enter tax here and check if from ☐ Tax Table, ☐ Tax Rate Schedule X, Y, or Z, ☐ Schedule D, ☐ Schedule G, or ☐ Form 4726	**35**		
	36 Additional Taxes. (See page 13 of Instructions.) Enter here and check if from ☐ Form 4970, } ☐ Form 4972, ☐ Form 5544, or ☐ Section 72(m)(5) penalty tax . . . . }	**36**		
	37 **Total.** Add lines 35 and 36 . . . . ▶	**37**		
Credits (See Instruc- tions on page 13)	**38** Credit for contributions to candidates for public office . . . **38**			
	39 Credit for the elderly *(attach Schedules R&RP)* **39**			
	40 Credit for child and dependent care expenses (*attach Form 2441*) . . **40**			
	41 Investment credit *(attach Form 3468)* **41**			
	42 Foreign tax credit *(attach Form 1116)* **42**			
	43 Work incentive (WIN) credit *(attach Form 4874)* **43**			
	44 Jobs credit *(attach Form 5884)* **44**			
	45 Residential energy credit *(attach Form 5695)* **45**			
	46 **Total credits.** Add lines 38 through 45	**46**		
	47 **Balance.** Subtract line 46 from line 37 and enter difference (but not less than zero) . ▶	**47**		
Other Taxes (Including Advance EIC Payments)	**48** Self-employment tax *(attach Schedule SE)*	**48**		
	49a Minimum tax. Attach Form 4625 and check here ▶ ☐	**49a**		
	49b Alternative minimum tax. Attach Form 6251 and check here ▶ ☐	**49b**		
	50 Tax from recomputing prior-year investment credit *(attach Form 4255)*	**50**		
	51a Social security (FICA) tax on tip income not reported to employer *(attach Form 4137)* . .	**51a**		
	51b Uncollected employee FICA and RRTA tax on tips *(from Form W-2)*	**51b**		
	52 Tax on an IRA *(attach Form 5329)*	**52**		
	53 Advance earned income credit (EIC) payments received *(from Form W-2)*	**53**		
06	**54** **Total tax.** Add lines 47 through 53 . . . . ▶	**54**		
Payments Attach Forms W-2, W-2G, and W-2P to front.	**55** Total Federal income tax withheld **55**			
	56 1981 estimated tax payments and amount applied from 1980 return . **56**			
	57 Earned income credit. If line 32a is under $10,000, see page 15 of Instructions **57**			
	58 Amount paid with Form 4868 . . . . **58**			
	59 Excess FICA and RRTA tax withheld (two or more employers) **59**			
	60 Credit for Federal tax on special fuels and oils *(attach Form 4136 or 4136-T)* **60**			
	61 Regulated Investment Company credit *(attach Form 2439)* **61**			
	62 **Total.** Add lines 55 through 61 . . . . ▶	**62**		
Refund or Balance Due	**63** If line 62 is larger than line 54, enter amount **OVERPAID** . . . . ▶	**63**		
	64 Amount of line 63 to be **REFUNDED TO YOU** . . . . ▶	**64**		
	65 Amount of line 63 to be applied to your 1982 estimated tax . . . ▶ **65**			
	66 If line 54 is larger than line 62, enter **BALANCE DUE.** Attach check or money order for full amount payable to "Internal Revenue Service." Write your social security number and "1981 Form 1040" on it. ▶ (Check ▶ ☐ if Form 2210 (2210F) is attached. See page 16 of Instructions.) ▶ $	**66**		

Please Sign Here	Under penalties of perjury, I declare that I have examined this return, including accompanying schedules and statements, and to the best of my knowledge and belief, it is true, correct, and complete. Declaration of preparer (other than taxpayer) is based on all information of which preparer has any knowledge. ▶ _____ Your signature Date _____ ▶ _____ Spouse's signature (if filing jointly, BOTH must sign even if only one had income)
Paid Preparer's Use Only	Preparer's signature ▶ _____ Date _____ Check if self-employed ▶ ☐ Preparer's social security no. _____ Firm's name (or yours, if self-employed) and address ▶ _____ E.I. No. ▶ _____ ZIP code ▶ _____

343-057-2

Line-by-Line Guide to Form 1040

Form **1040**	Department of the Treasury—Internal Revenue Service **U.S. Individual Income Tax Return**	**1981**	

For the year January 1–December 31, 1981, or other tax year beginning , 1981, ending , 19 . | OMB No. 1545-0074

Use IRS label. Otherwise, please print or type.

Your first name and initial (if joint return, also give spouse's name and initial) | Last name | Your social security number

Present home address (Number and street, including apartment number, or rural route) | Spouse's social security no.

City, town or post office, State and ZIP code | Your occupation ▶ | Spouse's occupation ▶

Presidential Election Campaign ▶ Do you want $1 to go to this fund? . . . . Yes / No

If joint return, does your spouse want $1 to go to this fund? . . . Yes / No

Note: *Checking "Yes" will not increase your tax or reduce your refund.*

If you are married, filling out your name at the top of your return is important, because here is where you make a decision on whether you should fill in your spouse's and your name or just your own. Include your spouse's Social Security number on your return—if you file a joint return. Even if you don't work, make sure to get a Social Security identification number for your return.

If you received a form package with a preprinted label address on it, use the preaddressed return label. If the label is wrong, cross out the incorrect information and write in the correct information.

Write your and your spouse's occupations in the box under your social security numbers.

How to Give to the Presidential Campaign

You have the right to earmark $1 of your 1981 taxes ($2 on a joint return) for use by various parties in the next presidential election campaign. You do this by checking the "Yes" box under your name and address.

FILING STATUS

Filing Status Check only one box.

1 ___ Single
2 ___ Married filing joint return (even if only one had income)
3 ___ Married filing separate return. Enter spouse's social security no. above and full name here ▶
4 ___ Head of household (with qualifying person). (See page 6 of Instructions.) If he or she is your unmarried child, enter child's name ▶
5 ___ Qualifying widow(er) with dependent child (Year spouse died ▶ 19). (See page 6 of Instructions.)

For Privacy Act and Paperwork Reduction Act Notice, see Instructions.

Lines 1–5: Filing Status

In checking the box above which applies to you, you have indicated which column in the official Tax Table you must use to find your tax.

This is explained on pages 100-101, where you will be shown how to work out the amount of tax on your taxable income.

Q. Should I file a joint return with my wife, even if she has no earnings or income of her own?

A. Generally, yes. With some exceptions, you usually will pay less tax by filing a joing return with your wife, because this entitles you to the tax benefits of income splitting.

EXEMPTIONS

Exemptions	6a	☐ Yourself		☐ 65 or over		☐ Blind	} Enter number of boxes checked on 6a and b ▶	☐
Always check the box labeled Yourself. Check other boxes if they apply.	b	☐ Spouse		☐ 65 or over		☐ Blind		

c First names of your dependent children who lived with you ▶ - } Enter number of children listed on 6c ▶ ☐

d Other dependents: (1) Name	(2) Relationship	(3) Number of months lived in your home	(4) Did dependent have income of $1,000 or more?	(5) Did you provide more than one-half of dependent's support?	Enter number of other dependents ▶ ☐

e Total number of exemptions claimed . . . . Add numbers entered in boxes above ▶ ☐

Line 6: Exemptions

Every taxpayer is entitled to reduce his taxable income by a flat $1,000 amount for each exemption. There are two classes of exemptions: (1) personal, and (2) dependency.

Personal exemptions refer to the amounts that can be claimed because of yourself and your spouse.

Dependency exemptions refer to the amounts allowed because you support certain persons, such as your children, relatives, etc.

The information needed for arriving at the number of your exemptions is entered on lines 6a, 6b, 6c, 6d, and 6e. On line 6a, you claim the exemptions for yourself. At line 6b, you claim the exemptions for your spouse. At line 6c, you claim exemptions for your dependent children who lived with you. At line 6d, you claim any other dependents. At line 6e, you enter the totals of lines 6a, 6b, 6c, and 6d.

Personal Exemptions for Yourself and Spouse

You can claim one $1,000 exemption for yourself.

You can claim another $1,000 exemption if you are 65 years old or older.

You can claim still another $1,000 exemption if you are blind.

Also, if you file a joint return with your spouse, you can claim a $1,000 exemption for her or him, another $1,000 if your spouse is 65 or over, and still another $1,000 if your spouse is blind.

If you file a separate return you can claim the various $1,000 exemptions for your spouse only if he or she has no gross income of his or her own.

Check the appropriate boxes of 6a and 6b and put the total of boxes checked in the right hand column.

Q. I reached my 65th birthday on July 1. Am I entitled to only half the $1,000 exemption for being 65?

A. No, you are entitled to the full $1,000, as long as your 65th birthday isn't later than January 1, 1982.

Q. My spouse died during the year, at the age of 69. Can I claim any exemptions for her (or him)?

A. Yes, you can claim all the exemptions your spouse was entitled to on the date of death. Thus, you can claim his or her own personal exemption, plus another exemption since he or she was over 65 years of age.

These can be claimed on your separate return if your spouse had no gross income. If your spouse did have income, you can still get the exemptions by filing a joint return.

Q. I have been losing my eyesight gradually. What does the law consider as blindness to permit me to claim the added exemption?

A. The blindness test is based on your condition on the last day of the year. This key date applies to both you and your spouse except that in the event of death, the day of death is used. Thus, if a husband or wife dies and was blind on the day of death, the exemption is allowed in full.

Blindness is defined as a condition where the central visual acuity does not read 20/200 in the better eye with correcting lenses, or the widest diameter of the visual field subtends an angle no greater than 20 degrees.

If you are totally blind, meaning you cannot tell light from darkness, merely attach a statement to that effect to your return. If you are partially blind, attach a statement from a qualified physician or registered optometrist that you meet the above tests. If you have already attached such a statement with your return for a previous year, merely attach a statement referring to this earlier statement.

Q. I was divorced in December. Since I supported my wife, can I claim her exemption as either a personal or dependency exemption?

A. No. Since the key date is the end of the year, you are treated as unmarried and cannot claim an exemption for your former wife. And since a wife is never considered a dependent, you can't claim a dependency exemption for her.

Q. I was legally separated from my wife during the year. Does this eliminate any claim for exemptions?

A. Yes. The same rules apply to you as to a divorced person.

For Your Children and Other Dependents

The tax law permits an exemption to be claimed by you for each person who qualifies as your dependent.

To be able to claim an exemption for a dependent, the following tests must be met:

1. You must furnish over half the support (with an exception explained on page 28).

2. Your dependent *cannot* have gross income of $1,000 or more during the year unless he or she is a child under 19 or, if over that age, is a full-time student or is pursuing a full-time on-farm training course. The exception for children applies also to foster children who were members of the household for the entire taxable year.

3. If not related to you, your dependent must be a member of your household and live with you for the entire year. But if a close relative, it makes no difference where your dependent lives.

For this purpose your close relatives are:

a. Your child, or your grandchild, great grandchild, etc. (a legally adopted child is considered your child);

b. Your stepchild, but not the stepchild's descendant;

c. Your brother or sister, half brother or half sister, stepbrother or stepsister;

d. Your parent, grandparent, or other direct ancestor, but not foster parent;

e. Your stepfather or stepmother;

f. A brother or sister of your father or mother;

g. A son or daughter of your brother or sister;

h. Your father-in-law, mother-in-law, son-in-law, daughter-in-law, brother-in-law, or sister-in-law.

4. The individual supported must be a citizen or resident of this country, or a resident of Canada, Mexico, the Canal Zone or the Republic of Panama for the year you claim an exemption; or was an alien child adopted by and living with a U.S. citizen abroad.

5. Even if all the above tests are met, the exemptions are lost if the supported person files a joint return with his or her spouse.

The first names are listed, and the number of dependent children who lived with you is entered at line 6c on page 1. No explanation is required. If you have any other dependents, including children living away from home, parents, etc., fill out the information required on line 6d.

Add lines 6a through d to give you your total exemptions on line 6e.

TAX TIP: Which Capital Expenditures Count as Support of a Dependent?

In figuring support, include such capital items as a car or furniture only if those items are actually given to, or bought by, the dependent for his use or benefit.

IRS gives the following examples of capital expenditures that do or don't qualify as a support payment for a dependent.

"Situation 1. A power mower costing $200 was purchased by the custodial parent for a 13-year-old child to whom the parent had assigned the duty of keeping the lawn trimmed. The lawn mower was supplied to make the chore more palatable to the child."

This is not support for the child because the lawn mower is a family item which will benefit all members of the household.

"Situation 2. A television set costing $150 was purchased by the non-custodial parent as a Christmas gift for a 12-year-old child and was set up in the child's bedroom. The taxpayer bought the television set on credit and made no payment on the charge in the year of purchase but paid the entire amount of the charge in the following year."

The TV set is an item of support up to its fair market value, $150. It is included as support in the year of the gift even though the parent made no payment.

"Situation 3. An automobile costing $5,000 was purchased by the custodial parent of a 17-year-old youth. The automobile was titled and registered in the parent's name and was used by the parent and the youth equally."

Because the parent continued to own the car, the cost of the car is not support. But out-of-pocket expenses of operating the auto for the dependent's benefit are part of the dependent's support furnished by the parent.

"Situation 4. In a year when a parent furnished all of the ordinary support required by a youth who otherwise qualified as the parent's dependent, the youth purchased an autombile costing $4,500, using personal funds to make the purchase. The total support furnished by the parent in that year amounted to $4,000."

The car is part of the youth's support paid by him. The parent therefore can't claim him as a dependent because the parent furnished less than half the son's support.

Figuring Support

Q. What does support mean for purposes of figuring out whether I have given more than half the support to the persons I claim as dependents?

A. Support is not only the cash you give. It also includes board, clothing, maid service in the home, lodging, education, medical and dental care, recreation, transportation, and similar necessities. If you furnish any goods, the fair market value is taken into account.

However, support does not include any income taxes or Social Security taxes paid for the person, life-insurance payments, or purchases of capital items such as an auto. Nor does it include the value of your own services performed for the dependent.

Q. How do I figure whether I furnished over half of the support of the person?

A. Simply compare the amount of support provided by you with the amount of support which the individual received from all sources including his own funds and including his Social Security benefits, gifts, savings, welfare benefits, etc.

Q. My father has only $4,000 of income, but he used $5,500 of his capital for his support, while I spent about $5,700 for his support. Can I claim him as a dependent, since payments for his support came out of capital?

A. No. It makes no difference where the funds came from. Since your $5,700 was less than half the total support, you can't claim your father as a dependent.

In figuring whether you furnished more than half the support, all funds used for the support, whether from capital, Social Security benefits, life-insurance proceeds, welfare-society payments, etc., are considered.

Q. My mother lives with us. In computing whether I furnish half her support, do I figure the cost of her lodging as a portion of the cost of running the house, or do I figure lodging is worth what I could have received in rent?

A. You use the fair rental value of the lodging, not a fraction of your actual cost.

Q. My mother lived with and was supported by me in Florida for four months of last year. She spent the other eight months with my sister, who supported her in Rhode Island. Does my sister get the $1,000 exemption?

A. You can't tell from these facts. The length of her stay with you is unimportant. The key is who paid more money for her support during the year. For example, if you spent $3,200 on your mother's support during the four months she was with you while your sister spent only $3,100 on her during her eight months of support, you take the $1,000 exemption.

Q. My daughter received a $4,000 scholarship from her college last year. I contributed only $3,700 to her support during the year, which is less than half the total amount she used during the year. Do I lose the dependency exemption?

A. No. The value of scholarships doesn't count as support for a child who is a full-time student. Thus, you contributed the full support of $3,700 and get the exemption for your daughter.

Q. My son entered military service last year. Does that bar me from claiming him as a dependent?

A. Not necessarily. Compare how much you spent for his support during the part of the year before he entered service with the amount of his pay and value of his food, etc., after he entered service. If you spent more, then you contributed more than half to his support and can claim him as a dependent. But if he was 19 or over during the year and his military pay was $1,000 or more, you can't claim him.

If the individual is in the armed forces or one of the service academies for the full year, he or she can't be claimed as a dependent, whether an officer or enlisted person.

Q. My father received $4,600 in Social Security payments during the year. I also helped support him. Can I claim an exemption for him?

A. Although an adult whose gross income is $1,000 or more can't be claimed as a dependent, your father's receipt of $4,600 in Social Security does not disqualify him. Social Security is not considered as gross income at all; therefore your father had no gross income and qualified to be claimed as a dependent. But, although Social Security isn't gross income, it is counted as part of the money your father spent for his support. Thus, if he spent the entire $4,600 on his support and you contributed less than that to him during the year, you didn't furnish more than half his support during the year and you can't claim him as a dependent. You could claim him, though, if you had contributed $4,605.

Q. I am divorced and pay my former wife $5,200 a year for child support. Can I claim a $1,000 exemption?

A. That isn't an easy question to answer. You can if your $5,200 is more than half the cost of the child's support. Since you provide $1,200 or more of child support for each child, you are entitled to the exemptions unless your wife proves that she provided a greater amount. If she makes such a claim, each of you will have to furnish an itemized statement of your expenditures to the other.

The best procedure to follow is to claim the exemption if you cannot obtain the information on total support and you feel you have furnished more than half the cost.

TAX TIP: *Children of Divorced or Separated Parents*

Divorced or separated parents can avoid unpleasant arguments and unnecessary litigation over which one can claim the dependency exemption for their children.

The parent who has custody of the child for the greater part of the year (usually the mother) will generally get the dependency exemption, except that the other parent (usually the father) can have the exemption if *either* (1) he contributed at least $600 to the child's support during the year, and the divorce or separation decree or a written agreement provides that he gets the exemption, *or* (2) he contributed $1,200 or more for each child supported during the year and the parent having custody (wife) doesn't prove that she contributed more. If she claims she contributed more than he did, then each parent is entitled to an itemized statement of expenses claimed by the other.

These rules apply only where the parents together furnish more than half of a child's total support for the year (thus it wouldn't apply if grandparents contributed 75 percent of the child's total support) and the child is in the custody of one or both parents for more than half the year (thus it wouldn't apply if the child was in the custody of grandparents for seven months of the year).

If divorced or separated parents can work the dependency exemptions out sensibly between them, then they can agree in writing which one or ones of the children the father can take. If he contributes at least $600 for each one of them during the year, he can take the dependency exemptions without any trouble from the Treasury.

Where a husband and wife can't agree on who should get the dependency exemptions for their children, the husband is not up against the stone wall of being unable to prove he contributed more than half the support. If he contributed $1,200 or more during 1981 for *each* child, he is entitled to get the figures from his wife if she claims she contributed more than he did.

Before making any agreements about dependency exemptions, parents should bear in mind that medical-expense and child-care deductions will depend on who gets the dependency exemptions.

Q. I am divorced. My ex-husband gives me $2,500 a year toward our child and my father gives me $3,500, which I use to support the child. Can my father claim the child or do I?

A. The answer depends upon how the money received from your father was given. If he gave it to you with no strings attached to be used as you wished, you are using your money to support the child. However, if your father specified that his money was to be used to support the child, your father could claim the exemption.

Q. I am divorced. I live with my three minor children in a four-bedroom, two-and-a-half-bathroom house that has a fair rental value of $900 a month exclusive of utilities. For purposes of deciding whether my divorced husband or I contribute more than half of the support of the children, do I figure that the $900 rental value of my house is divided equally among me and my children?

A. The Treasury says yes, but a Tax Court decision said that a larger percentage of the $900 should be allocated to you as an adult. That, of course, lowers the amount of support you are considered to have contributed to your children.

Q. My brother and I each contributed $4,000 to the support of my mother, while my sister contributed $600. Our mother has no income. Who gets the dependency exemption for her?

A. No one can get it unless a multiple-support agreement is filed, because no one of you furnished more than half of the dependent's total support. However, any one of you who furnished more than 10 percent of the support can claim the exemption if all the others who furnished more than 10 percent agree to it. Because your sister didn't contribute more than 10 percent, she can't claim the exemption, and her agreement is not required to let either you or your brother get the exemption. Suppose he agrees that you get it. Then he gives you a statement that he is "waiving" the exemption. You attach his waiver to your own tax form and you claim the exemption.

Get special Form 2120 for this purpose from your local director and attach it to the return of the person who claims the exemption.

Q. My mother and father live in their own apartment. Dad's income from Social Security was $3,000, Mother's income was $1,500. I contributed $5,000 towards their support. Can I claim my mother as a dependent?

A. You can claim both your mother and father. Here is how this works: First you figure out how much the members of the household, your mother and father, spent for their support. Here it totals $4,500. Unless there is specific proof of how much was spent for each member of the household (which is highly unlikely), the total is divided equally between them. This means that $2,250 (half of $4,500) was spent to support each of your parents.

In the same way, your contributions for support, from outside the household, are also considered spent equally for the members of the household in the absence of either proof of specific spending for each or of a specific designation of your contribution for some particular member of the household. So here you spent $2,500 for each parent's support. Since this is more than the $2,250 spent by your mother and father, you can claim both parents as dependents. (Your father's Social Security payments don't count in figuring the $1,000 gross income test which can disqualify a dependent.)

Q. I am the sole support of my 66-year-old mother. During the year, my mother received Medicare hospital benefits that amounted to more than the amount that I contributed to her support during the year. Does that mean that I can't claim her as a dependent because I didn't contribute more than half her total support during the year?

A. You can claim her as a dependent. Both the Medicare hospital reimbursements (Part A) and the reimbursements for doctor care (Part B) are entirely excluded from support in determining dependency. This means that you contributed your mother's entire support for the year, and that entitles you to claim her as your dependent.

Q. Does the same rule apply to Medicaid payments received?

A. The Tax Court says that Medicaid payments are treated the same as Medicare. However, the IRS contends that Medicaid payments *are* part of support.

Q. My daughter is a student nurse at an accredited school of nursing. She receives free room and board. Do I have to consider the value of this free board and lodging in determining whether I supply half her support?

A. No. This is viewed as a scholarship, which is disregarded.

Q. I paid most of the costs of my child's wedding. For purposes of determining whether I get the dependency exemption for her, can I count those expenses as part of the support that I contributed for her during the year?

A. Yes. IRS has ruled that a parent could count as support for dependency purposes the amount that the parent spent for his child's wedding apparel and accessories, for a wedding reception, and for flowers for the wedding party, church, and reception.

Q. I am a widow and receive $200 a month Social Security benefits for my 15-year-old son. It cost me $3,000 to support him last year. Can I claim a dependency credit for him?

A. No. Since the Social Security payments are considered as belonging to your son, he contributed $2,400 toward the total support of $3,000, or more than half.

Q. My mother is a patient in a state hospital. I pay $3,500 toward the cost of keeping her in the hospital. Can I claim a dependency credit for my mother?

A. Probably no. When a parent is in a state institution, or in an old-age home supported by a religious, fraternal, or charitable organization, you must figure in the amounts spent by the state or organization. Thus if we assume that the average cost of a patient is $8,000, you don't meet more than half the cost.

Q. My father is in a mental hospital. During 1981, I paid $700 toward his support and promised to pay the hospital over the next two years the $7,500 which the hospital paid for my father's support during 1981. Can I claim my father as a dependent?

A. Yes. The Treasury says that if you take what it calls an affirmative step during the year to provide support, and incur an unconditional obligation to pay for this support, you are regarded as providing the dependent's support in the amount of the obligation you incur this year even though you don't pay till a later year.

Q. In computing whether half the support is furnished, the fair rental value of lodgings is included. Can I also figure the cost of heat, taxes, etc., which I paid on my house as contributed for the support?

A. No. The fair rental value already includes such costs for running your home as heat, electricity, water, taxes, repairs, interest, depreciation, paint, insurance, etc.

Of course, if you compute the fair rental value of your home or of an apartment *excluding* such items as heat and utilities, the cost of the heat and utilities would be added to the fair rental value.

Q. My father lives in his own house and I help support him by giving him $450 per month. The fair rental value of his house is $3,500 and my father spent $1,500 of his own money for support. Do these figures add up to my contributing more than half his support?

A. Yes. Your father's total support was the $5,400 you paid plus $3,500 for the fair rental value of the house plus $1,500 of his own money, or $10,400. Since you spent $5,400, or more than half, you can claim him as a dependent.

Q. I support my 67-year-old mother. Can I claim her as a dependent and take another dependency claim because she is over 65?

A. No. Although a taxpayer and his wife get an extra dependency exemption at 65 or over, there is no similar extra exemption for a dependent who is 65 or over.

Q. My 20-year-old daughter was married last Novem-

ber. I provided for more than half her support, and she has no income. Does the fact that she is married bar me from claiming her as a dependent?

A. No. You can claim her as a dependent so long as she does *not* file a joint return with her new husband. Check with your new son-in-law to see whether it is more advantageous to have him claim the extra exemption on a joint return or to have you take the exemption.

Q. I am divorced. I paid $900 to send my child to summer camp. Can I count that as support that I furnished?

A. A court has held that it is support despite the Treasury argument that it shouldn't be considered support because it wasn't a "necessity of life." The court also rejected the Treasury's argument that the amount paid was unreasonably high, therefore not necessary.

Q. I contributed the major support for my married daughter, who is filing a joint return with her husband. Can I claim her as a dependent?

A. No. You can't claim a married person as a dependent if he or she files a joint return with his or her spouse. But note the above answer, which emphasizes that if she doesn't file a joint return, you can claim the exemption. Check with your daughter and son-in-law to see who gets the greater benefit.

Q. Our baby was born last December 31. Do we get any kind of exemption for the baby?

A. You can claim a full exemption for the baby though it was alive for only one day during the year.

Q. My mother died January 5, 1981. I had become her sole support in December 1980. Can I get any part of an exemption for her for 1981?

A. You can get the entire exemption for her even though she lived only five days in 1981.

Gross-Income Test

Q. What is the point of the requirement that certain dependents must have less than $1,000 "gross" income? What's the difference between that and taxable income?

A. Gross income is the income you must include on a tax return before taking deductions from that income. For example, your father may rent a small piece of property to a tenant for $5,000 which nets him only $950 after he deducts all expenses. He cannot be claimed as a dependent because his gross income is over $1,000 although his net or taxable income is under $1,000.

Q. Our 16-year-old son had $1,000 of income during the year from his summer-vacation work and from

interest on his savings account. Does this disqualify him as my dependent even though we contributed much more than $1,000 to his support?

A. No, the requirement that a dependent must have under $1,000 of gross income during the year does not apply to a child under 19. Not only do you get a dependency exemption for the child, but he also can take a personal exemption on his own tax return.

Q. I contributed more than half the support of my uncle, but he has much more than $1,000 of income from Social Security. Can I claim an exemption for him?

A. Yes. The $1,000 gross-income test refers only to taxable income. It does not include tax-free income such as municipal-bond interest, Social Security, etc.

Q. My son is 23 years old and attends college. During the summer he worked and earned $1,500. However, we contributed considerably more than $1,500 in supporting him. Does the $1,500 earnings bar us from claiming him as a dependent?

A. No. Since your son was a full-time student, you can claim him as a dependent despite his over-$1,000 earnings.

A student is a person who, during each of 5 calendar months of the year, is (1) enrolled full time at an educational institution which maintains a regular faculty and curriculum and has a body of students in attendance, or (2) attending a full-time on-farm training course under the supervision of an agent of a state or a political subdivision of a state or of an educational institution which maintains a regular faculty and curriculum and has a body of students in attendance.

This rule also applies to foster children who were members of the taxpayer's household for the entire taxable year.

Q. My son works on a job in private industry under his vocational high school's prescribed course of classes-plus-job. Is he a full-time student?

A. Yes.

Q. Does taking correspondence courses qualify a child as a full-time student?

A. No.

Who Can Qualify as a Dependent

Q. We have a housekeeper who gets a flat monthly sum plus her board and lodging. She has no other income. Can I claim her as a dependent?

A. No. You haven't furnished her support. She has worked for it and supported herself.

TAX TIP: Claiming Friends and Cohabitors as Dependents

Q. I'm taking care of a friend who has been down and out for some time. He's living with us until he can get back on his feet. Can I claim him as a dependent?

A. Yes, you can, even though he is not a relative. You may claim a nonrelative as a dependent if: during the year his gross income was under $1,000; you furnished more than half his support; that person had your home as his principal place of abode; and he was a member of your household for the entire year. Temporary absences caused by vacations, illness, etc., don't disqualify him.

Q. I have been living, unmarried, with a person of the opposite sex, whom I have been supporting. Can I claim her (or him) as a dependent?

A. If the above tests for a dependent are met and the local law does not declare it illegal for an unmarried man and woman to live together, then you can.

Q. I support my wife's uncle in a separate house. Since my wife's uncle is no close relative of mine, am I barred from taking the exemption?

A. No. If you file a joint return, the dependent qualifies as a close relative if he is related to either of you.

Q. I took care of a foster child last year. Although we were paid for this, we spent much more on the child than we were paid. Can we claim an exemption?

A. Yes. If the child was with you and you furnished more than half of the support during the year, you can take the exemption.

Q. During the year a child was placed with me for legal adoption by an authorized placement agency. Can I take a dependency deduction for the child?

A. Yes, if you contributed more than half of its support, even though you didn't have the child in your household for the entire year.

You now have the top guides on claiming your maximum exemptions on lines 6a, 6b, 6c, and 6d of page 1. On line 6e, enter the total of exemptions you claim.

INCOME

Income

Please attach Copy B of your Forms W-2 here.

If you do not have a W-2, see page 5 of Instructions.

Please attach check or money order here.

7 Wages, salaries, tips, etc.	7	
8a Interest income (*attach Schedule B if over $400 or you have any All-Savers interest*)	8a	
b Dividends (*attach Schedule B if over $400*)	8b	
c Total. Add lines 8a and 8b	8c	
d Exclusion (*See page 9 of Instructions*)	8d	
e Subtract line 8d from line 8c (but not less than zero)	8e	
9 Refunds of State and local income taxes (*do not enter an amount unless you deducted those taxes in an earlier year—see page 9 of Instructions*)	9	
10 Alimony received	10	
11 Business income or (loss) (*attach Schedule C*)	11	
12 Capital gain or (loss) (*attach Schedule D*)	12	
13 40% of capital gain distributions not reported on line 12 (See page 9 of Instructions)	13	
14 Supplemental gains or (losses) (*attach Form 4797*)	14	
15 Fully taxable pensions and annuities not reported on line 16	15	
16a Other pensions and annuities. Total received	16a	
b Taxable amount, if any, from worksheet on page 10 of Instructions	16b	
17 Rents, royalties, partnerships, estates, trusts, etc. (*attach Schedule E*)	17	
18 Farm income or (loss) (*attach Schedule F*)	18	
19a Unemployment compensation (insurance). Total received	19a	
b Taxable amount, if any, from worksheet on page 10 of Instructions	19b	
20 Other income (state nature and source—see page 11 of Instructions)	20	
21 **Total income.** Add amounts in column for lines 7 through 20	21	

Line 7: Compensation

On line 7, you report all your salary, wages, bonuses, etc. and your spouse's, if your spouse is filing a joint return with you. This is normally your full compensation, copied from the Form W-2 which your employer has given you; it is not reduced by your payroll deductions. The totals for yourself and your spouse are entered here. Attach Copy B of Form W-2 to the front of Form 1040.

On line 7, enter the total amount of any wages, salaries, bonuses, commissions, tips, and other compensation you have received and which are shown on your 1981 Form W-2 from your employer or employers.

If you're filing a joint return as a husband and wife who are both working, you must include the same type of information for both of you.

Q. I am a beauty-parlor operator. Are the tips I get from customers nontaxable gifts, or compensation which I must report as income?

A. Tips given for services must be reported as income. Examples are tips to barbers, waiters, cab drivers, etc.

Q. Instead of receiving a salary, I am paid by commissions and bonuses. Are these income to me?

A. Yes.

Q. I received a real estate lot worth $5,000 from my employer for helping him sell ten lots. Is this income to me?

A. Yes. If your employer pays you for your services by giving you property (instead of, or in addition to cash) you report as income the value of the property at the time you received it.

Q. My employer had his painter do $700 worth of painting on my home as part payment for the work I did for my boss. Do I have to include this in income?

A. Yes. If you are given services as compensation for your work, you must report as income the value of the services you received.

Q. My employer withholds from my weekly pay a certain amount for income taxes, a certain amount for union dues, a certain amount for my savings-bond purchase plan, and a certain amount for a health-insurance plan. Do I have to report any of these amounts as income?

A. Yes. Even though the money withheld for these purposes by your boss never reaches you, it's income, which you must report in the year your employer withholds it from you.

Q. I contribute to a group life-insurance plan which my employer set up. My payments are withheld by my boss from my pay. Are they part of my income?

A. Yes, regardless of whether the coverage is group-term or group-permanent.

Q. After I became involved in a collection suit for furniture I bought, my employer paid part of my salary directly to my creditor and the creditor also officially attached my wages. Are the amounts that went to my creditor income to me?

A. Yes, and you include it in income in the year you would have otherwise received it.

Q. My employer pays premiums on my behalf under our group life-insurance plan. Are the premiums he pays for my coverage taxable income to me?

A. That depends. If the insurance is of the group-term type, which is the more common one, your employer's premium payments for your coverage are *not* income to you to the extent that your coverage does not exceed $50,000. To the extent your coverage exceeds $50,000, your employer's premium payments for that excess will result in taxable income to you. Also, if the insurance is of the group-permanent type (your employer will tell you which kind you have), his premium payments for your coverage *are* and must be reported as income by you, unless your right to the permanent insurance or equivalent benefits is forfeitable in case you leave or lose your job.

Q. My employer contributes a certain amount to our group hospitalization plan in addition to what we employees have withheld from our pay. Do I have to report his payment on my behalf as income?

A. No.

Q. I receive a vacation allowance from a vacation fund set up under a labor agreement and based on the number of weeks I worked. Is this taxable income to me, as it would be if it were ordinary vacation pay from my employer?

A. Yes.

Q. When my previous job was ended, my former employer gave me severance pay. Is this taxable income to me?

A. Yes.

Q. I was invited by a firm in another city to go there for a job interview. The firm paid all my expenses of traveling to and from the interview. Is this income to me?

A. No. It isn't income to you, whether or not you went to work for that firm.

Q. I had a two-year employment contract that my previous employer wanted to terminate last year. He paid me a certain sum to cancel the contract. Is that income to me?

A. Yes.

Q. I am one of the teachers who went on a strike that was considered illegal under our state law. When we returned to work, one week's pay was deducted from our salary as a penalty under the state law for an illegal strike. Do I have to report that penalty as my salary or do I just deduct that week's pay from the amount of salary I report as my income?

A. You can't deduct the week's pay that was taken away from you as a penalty. You must report it as part of your income even though you never received it.

Q. My employer gives his salesmen prizes, either in cash or various household appliances, for meeting certain quotas. Are these prizes and special rewards tax-free gifts or taxable income?

A. Taxable income. The property should be reported in income at its fair market value.

Q. For reaching the highest sales quota, my employer gave me and my family an expense-paid vacation trip. Must I report this as income?

A. Yes, you report the fair market value of the trip as income.

Q. My employer permits all the employees in his department store to buy various items at a special employee discount. Do I have to report the discounts that I received on my purchases as income?

A. No. Courtesy discounts on purchases from your employer aren't taxable income to you if they are of relatively small value, are offered to employees generally, and are intended merely to promote the health, good will, contentment, or efficiency of the employees.

But if your employer lets you buy property at a reduced price, intending this to be part of your compensation, you must include in your income the difference between what you paid and what the property is worth.

Q. My employer pays for a health-reconditioning program for me and other executives in the firm. Is this taxable income to me?

A. Generally, amounts paid by your employer for a reconditioning, health-restoring, or executive-rehabilitation program for you are taxable compensation to you. Examples of such programs are athletic-club memberships, ocean cruises, visits to resort areas, etc.

Q. I am a life-insurance agent. Are my commissions on policies I bought for my own children and grandchildren taxable income to me, or merely a reduction of the price of the policies?

A. They are taxable income to you.

Q. My employer furnishes me with supper money when I have to work overtime. Is the supper money taxable to me?

A. No, according to an old Treasury ruling.

Q. My boss furnishes me with meals as part of my job arrangement. Is the value of the meals taxable income to me?

A. Not if the meals are furnished on your employer's business premises for his convenience. For example, he may want you on call even during meal hours.

Q. I work at a hospital, which furnishes me with lodging. Is the value of the lodging taxable to me?

A. Not if the employer furnishes it on his business premises for his convenience and you are required to live there as a condition of your employment. If, instead of furnishing the lodging free, your employer deducted a charge for it from your pay, that amount would still be tax-free to you.

If you are given the choice of free lodging on the employer's premises or a rental allowance for living elsewhere and you choose to live on the premises, the value of the lodging furnished by your employer is taxable income to you.

Q. My employer makes contributions on my behalf to a Treasury-approved pension plan set up for his employees. Do I have to pay tax on these contributions?

A. No. You will pay a tax on them only when they are ultimately paid out to you.

Q. My employer makes contributions on my behalf to a Treasury-approved profit-sharing or thrift plan. Do I have to pay a tax on these contributions?

A. No. As in the case of the Treasury-approved retirement plan, you will pay the tax only when the money is ultimately paid out to you.

Line 8a: Interest Income

On line 8a, Form 1040, you enter the total amount of interest income which you received. If the total is over $400, or if you have any amount of interest on All-Savers Certificates, you also list on Part I of separate Schedule B the details as to the amount paid by each payer of interest.

Except for interest you receive from All-Savers Certificates and from bonds or other obligations of states, municipalities, and other political subdivisions, interest you get is fully taxable and should be included in income. Even interest on tax refunds is taxable.

This includes interest on bank accounts, bonds, building-and-loan accounts, credit-union accounts, loans, notes, refunds of tax, savings-and-loan accounts, and U.S. savings bonds.

Schedules A&B (Form 1040) 1981   **Schedule B—Interest and Dividend Income**   OMB No. 1545-0074   Page **2**

Name(s) as shown on Form 1040 (Do not enter name and social security number if shown on other side) | Your social security number

Part I — Interest Income

If you received more than $400 in interest or you received any interest from an All-Savers Certificate, you must complete Part I and list ALL interest received. Also complete Part III if you received more than $400 in interest. See page 8 of the Instructions to find out what interest to report. Then answer the questions in Part III, below. If you received interest as a nominee for another, or you received or paid accrued interest on securities transferred between interest payment dates, please see page 20 of the Instructions.

Name of payer	Amount
1a Interest income (other than qualifying interest from All-Savers Certificates).	
1b Total. Add above amounts	
1c Qualifying interest from All-Savers Certif-icates. (List payers and amounts even if $400 or less.) See page 20 of Instructions.	
1d Total.	
1e Exclusion (See page 20 of Instructions) .	
1f Subtract line 1e from line 1d.	

Caution: *No part of the amount on line 1f may be excluded on Form 1040, line 8d .*

2 Total interest income (add lines 1b and 1f). Enter here and on Form 1040, line 8a . . . .

Part II — Dividend Income

If you received more than $400 in gross dividends (including capital gain distributions) and other distributions on stock, complete Part II and Part III. Please see page 9 of the Instructions. Then answer the questions in Part III, below. If you received dividends as a nominee for another, please see page 21 of the Instructions.

Name of payer	Amount
3	
4 Total. Add above amounts	
5 Capital gain distribu-tions. Enter here and on line 13, Schedule D. See Note below . . .	
6 Nontaxable distribu-tions (See Instructions for adjustment to basis)	
7 Total (add lines 5 and 6)	
8 Total dividend income (subtract line 7 from line 4). Enter here and on Form 1040, line 8b	

B

Note: *If you received capital gain distributions for the year and you do not need Schedule D to report any other gains or losses or to compute the alternative tax, do not file that schedule. Instead, enter 40% of your capital gain distributions on Form 1040, line 13.*

Part III — Foreign Accounts and Foreign Trusts

If you received more than $400 of interest or dividends, OR if you had a foreign account or were a grantor of, or a transferor to, a foreign trust, you must answer both questions in Part III. Please see page 21 of the Instructions.

	Yes	No
9 At any time during the tax year, did you have an interest in or a signature or other authority over a bank account, securities account, or other financial account in a foreign country?		
10 Were you the grantor of, or transferor to, a foreign trust which existed during the current tax year, whether or not you have any beneficial interest in it?		

If "Yes," you may have to file Forms 3520, 3520-A, or 926.

For Paperwork Reduction Act Notice, see Form 1040 Instructions.   343-059-1

☆ U.S. GOVERNMENT PRINTING OFFICE : 1981—O—343-059

If you list interest or dividends on Schedule B, be sure to answer No to questions 9 and 10 in Part III unless you are one of the relatively few individuals who have foreign bank accounts or foreign trusts.

Q. I received $100 of All-Savers interest in December, 1981. Since this is tax-exempt interest, do I ignore reporting it?

A. No. Even though this is tax-exempt interest and even though you had less than $400 of taxable interest in 1981, you must report the $100 of All-Savers interest on line 1c of Part I of Schedule B and show the same $100 amount as an exclusion (subtraction) on line 1e. The net result is that you show the IRS that your $100 of All-Savers interest is tax-exempt because it does not exceed the $1,000 or $2,000 limit that applies to you (see number 6 of the Great New Tax Breaks, beginning at page 11).

Q. I have $5,000 on deposit in an out-of-town savings-and-loan account and don't send my passbook in to have the interest entered. Do I hold off reporting the interest until I do send in the passbook?

A. No. Interest is considered received when the bank credits it to your account and it can be withdrawn by you, even though it isn't entered in your passbook. You should include in your interest income the amount of interest which the bank has credited you for 1981.

Q. I have some coupon bonds with coupons due December 31, 1981. However, I didn't get to the vault to clip them and make a deposit until 1982. In which year, 1981 or 1982, do I include the coupon interest?

A. In 1981. The interest is taxable when the coupon is due and payable even though you have not collected it.

Q. I am a widow and my husband left me $25,000 of life insurance, which will be paid in ten $3,000 annual instalments. Is any part of this taxable as interest?

A. No. The tax law permits up to $1,000 a year of interest earned on life-insurance proceeds payable at death in instalments to be exempt. Thus, of the $3,000 received by you, one-tenth of $25,000, or $2,500, is a receipt of the proceeds which would have been paid at death. The added $500 is interest, but since it doesn't exceed $1,000 it is exempt.

Q. I cashed in $1,000 of Series E bonds in 1981 when they matured. How much do I include in income?

A. The balance over what you paid in for them is interest and is taxable as income.

TAX TIP: *Investing Less than $10,000 to Get Higher Interest for Bank C.D.s Has Tricky Tax Consequences*

Many banks have made the higher interest rates payable on their six-month $10,000 certificates of deposit available to individuals with less than $10,000. This is done by lending the depositor the amount needed to make up $10,000, at generally one percent interest charged by the bank over the interest earned by the depositor on the money borrowed.

Even though you as a depositor consider that you have received a net return on your money deposited (your total interest on $10,000 less the interest the bank charged you), IRS requires you and the banks to report that you have received the full interest paid you on the $10,000. You must include that full amount as interest income. You separately deduct the interest charged by the bank as an itemized deduction on your Schedule A. If you use the standard deduction (zero-bracket amount), you will have no interest deduction but you will still have to report the entire interest income on the $10,000.

Line 8b: Dividend Income

If your gross dividends, including capital-gain distributions from mutual funds and other distributions on stock, are $400 or less, just enter the amount of gross dividends *excluding* any capital-gain distributions and nontaxable distributions, at line 8b of Form 1040. For example, if you had $300 of regular dividends and $100 of capital-gain distributions from your mutual fund, enter $300 at line 8b. If more than $400, you must also fill out Part I of separate Schedule B, listing the details as to payers of dividends and amounts paid by each.

If you received capital-gain distributions such as from mutual funds, and you don't have to file a separate Schedule B because your gross dividends don't exceed $400, then you report the capital-gain distribution in one of two ways, depending on whether you have to fill out separate Capital Gains Schedule D for any reason. If you have to report gains or losses on Schedule D, then you enter your capital-gain distribution on Schedule D.

Thus, in the example above, where you received $300 of regular dividends and $100 of capital-gain distributions from your mutual fund, you would enter the $300 of regular dividends at line 8b, and 40 percent of your $100 capital gain at line 13 of Form 1040.

If you received capital-gain distributions and do have to use separate Schedule B because your gross dividends including capital-gain distributions exceed $400, you first show your capital-gain distributions separately at line 5 of Part II of Schedule B. Then, just as explained above, you report 40 percent of the capital-gain distributions directly on line 13 of Form 1040 if you don't otherwise have to use separate Capital Gains Schedule D. But if you do have to use Schedule D for reporting gains or losses, etc., then you enter the capital-gain distribution at line 13 of Schedule D.

If your total dividends, including capital-gain distributions, exceed $400, here is how you should fill out your required Schedule B. In Part II you list and total the gross amount of all the dividends and other distributions on stock received by you or your spouse in 1981 including capital-gain distributions and nontaxable distributions. Include here any dividends received by you through a partnership of which you are a member, or as the beneficiary of a trust, or through a nominee or other intermediary. If you received these amounts through a nominee or other intermediary, list his name. List each payer and the amount paid.

On stocks held by your broker in "street name," you got an information return from the broker giving you one total figure for all dividends received in your account during 1981 on such stock. You do not break this figure down into dividends received from each corporation. Instead, you enter on line 3 of Part II the name of your broker as the payer and the one total figure of dividends received from the broker.

The total of all dividends in line 3 is entered on line 4.

At line 5 of Part II, you give the amount of dividends included on line 3, which are considered to be capital-gain distributions. The distributing corporation will usually notify you to this effect when it sends you this kind of dividend.

Also enter this amount on separate Schedule D, Part II, line 13, with the following exception: If you wouldn't need the separate Schedule D to report any other gains or losses, you need not file a Schedule D just to report this capital-gain distribution. Instead, enter 40 percent of the capital-gain distribution on line 13 of Form 1040.

At line 6, you state the amount of any dividends included in line 3 which are considered to be nontaxable, as for example where the distribution is considered a return of your capital. Here too, the distributing corporation will generally let you know if this is so (when it sends you this kind of distribution).

At line 7 of Part II, you add up the figures on lines 5 and 6. At line 8 you subtract this total from line 4, and what is left is your total amount of dividends before exclusions. Enter this same figure on line 8b of Form 1040.

Q. I haven't sent in my savings account book in a Federal Savings and Loan Association for the end of the year. Do I have to include the dividend, which hasn't been credited in my book?

A. Yes, but report it under interest, not dividends. If your account with the association has been credited, the fact that you haven't sent in your book doesn't bar the income from being taxed. You have "constructively" received the interest.

Q. What about the dividends I have received from my mutual life-insurance company or on veterans' life insurance?

A. These dividends are not taxable at all.

Q. My securities are held by my broker on margin. All dividends are left in the account. Are these taxed?

A. Yes. The dividends are treated as received by you. Your broker reported this total to you on an information form which you should have received from him.

Q. I am a member of a partnership that owns stock. Do I show my share of the dividends here?

A. Yes. Obtain the information necessary to fill out this schedule from the partnership return Form 1065 filed by the partnership.

Q. I own stock in a corporation that has been liquidating. I received liquidating dividends last year. Are these included here?

A. No. Liquidating dividends are treated as part of the sales price for the stock. If the liquidating dividends haven't yet equaled your cost (basis) of the stock, you have no income. However, any receipts over your cost are taxed as long-term capital gains in '81, if you have held the stock for more than one year. Show the gain in separate Schedule D.

Q. I received certain stock rights on my shares last year. Are these dividends?

A. No. And they generally are not taxable. In your case, if you merely exercised the rights, you are not taxed until you sell the stock. If you sold the rights, the gain is a capital gain as discussed on page 43.

Q. I received a stock dividend of 5 shares for each 100 I owned. The stock dividend was worth $50. Is this included here?

A. No. Stock dividends are not taxable unless you had the option to receive cash or other property instead of the stock dividend. Generally, no such right attaches to stock. A notice that the corporation will sell a fractional share due you is not an option that makes the stock dividend taxable.

Q. I sold some shares in November, but received a

dividend on the stock in December 1981. Is this a dividend or part of the sale price?

A. It is a dividend. You sold your shares after the dividend date. Therefore, you are taxed on a dividend even though you sold the stock before actually receiving the dividend.

Q. I receive a dividend on my life-insurance policies each year. Is this taxable?

A. No. These dividends just cut your insurance costs and can be ignored.

Q. I own stock in a mutual fund. How do I report the dividends I received?

A. The regular dividend portion is shown on line 8b with your other dividends. If you received a capital-gain distribution either alone or in addition to your regular

dividend, this is shown on either Schedule D or line 13 of Form 1040, as explained above.

Q. I have a small interest in a corporation that elected not be be taxed as a corporation. How do I handle the dividends I received?

A. Check with the accountant or lawyer who prepared the corporation's return. These corporations pass-through their income somewhat in the fashion of a partnership, and you may well be taxed on more than you actually received. In addition, none of the amounts received qualifies as a real dividend, and these amounts are not to be shown here. Instead, show your share of both the distributed and undistributed current taxable income as ordinary income in Part II of separate Schedule E, except that any portion taxable as a long-term capital gain is shown in separate Schedule D.

Line 8c: The $200-$400 Exclusion

You add together the total amount of interest you report on line 8a plus the total amount of dividends you report on line 8b to determine the figure for line 8c.

Line 8d: Exclusion

From the combined total of interest and dividends at line 8c, you exclude (subtract) up to $200, or up to $400 on a joint return, regardless of which spouse received the interest and dividends. But you cannot reduce the amount on line 8c below zero.

Note that the amount of interest paid to you by an individual—for example, a loan you made to a friend or relative—does *not* qualify for the exclusion.

Nonqualifying Corporations

Dividends from certain corporations such as foreign corporations—so-called nonqualifying corporations—aren't eligible for the exclusion.

Q. I received dividends from a Canadian corporation. Do they qualify for the exclusion?

A. No, because they were received from a foreign corporation.

KEYNOTE: Other Income

All income from sources other than wages, dividends, and interest is entered on lines 9 through 20. This includes some from business, which must be shown on separate Schedule C; gains and losses from sales or exchanges of property, which must be shown on separate Schedule D; rents and royalties, income or losses from partnerships, estates or trusts, or small business corporations, all of which must be shown on separate Schedule E; and farm income or losses, shown on separate Schedule F.

After you get the total for each of these four separate

Schedules on which you may have to report income, you enter the total for each separate Schedule on the proper line. Thus total income from Schedule C goes on line 11, from Schedule D on line 12 and so on. If you have any miscellaneous income that doesn't fit into these lines, enter it on line 20, giving the nature and source of the miscellaneous income.

To make it easier for you to follow my explanation, I have put off the discussion of the Business Schedule C for line 11 to begin on page 123.

Line 9, Refunds of State and Local Income Taxes

State and local income-tax refunds are entered here. However, do not include any state or local income-tax refund you received in 1981 for a pre-1981 year in which you claimed the federal standard deduction. Do not include any federal income-tax refund.

Line 10, Alimony Received

If alimony received is deductible by your spouse on your spouse's return, you are taxed on it. Otherwise you are not. To see whether the alimony is deductible by your spouse look at the explanation of alimony deductions under line 27.

Line 11, Business Income

See my discussion of Business Schedule C, which begins on page 123.

Line 12, Capital Gains and Losses from Sale or Exchange of Property

If you sold or exchanged property in 1981, you must first fill out separate Schedule D.

The net gain or loss from sale or exchange of capital assets on Schedule D is entered at line 12.

If you didn't sell or exchange any property during 1981, skip the following discussion of separate Schedule D. If you did sell or exchange property in 1981, you must write the details on separate Schedule D and include it on line 12 of Form 1040. If you have to fill out Schedule D Supplement, Form 4797, you show the income from that schedule on line 14.

Any gains which you realize on the sale of any property, stock, bonds, cars, boats, etc., are subject to tax although the law imposes a much lower tax on these gains than on your salary, interest, dividends, etc. if the property was held for more than a year. Losses which you sustain on the sale of various types of property are subject to different tax treatment. Some losses—for instance, on personal items such as cars, boats, houses—are completely disregarded and can't be used for any tax purposes. Others— for instance, on bonds and other securities—can be used to offset similar gains, but if the losses exceed the gains, only a limited amount can be used to reduce your income from salary, dividends, etc.

Additional key points are:

While you may have made a sale at a profit, you may not have to pay any immediate tax on the entire profit if you have received only a portion of the sales price. (See page 48.)

If the sale involved your residence, any gain may be exempt if you buy another home, within 18 or 24 months, or if you are 55 or over, as explained on page 43.

If any of your stocks or securities with interest coupons or in registered form become worthless during the year, the loss is a capital loss and you treat it as though they were sold on the last day of the year.

Most persons make sales only in connection with their stock-market activities, their homes, or real property owned by them. The following discusses these areas.

The transactions are reported on Schedule D if they involve capital assets such as stock, bonds, your house, etc. If you sold or exchanged property other than capital assets, such as depreciable property used in your trade or business, you would report such transactions on a separate Form 4797.

Long-term capital gains are given a real tax break. Only 40 percent of your net long-term capital gains are included in your income. The remaining 60 percent is completely tax exempt.

TAX TIP: *Special 20-percent Ceiling on Long-Term Capital Gains after June 9, 1981*

The '81 Tax Act provided that the 1981 tax on net long-term capital gains on *sales* made after June 9, 1981 (or the net long-term capital gains for all of 1981, if that is lower) can't exceed 20 percent. That is a top tax rate of 50 percent on the 40 percent of long-term capital gains included in income. This affects only single persons with taxable income of over $41,500 or joint returns with taxable incomes over $60,000. (See page 11.)

KEYNOTE: *What Are Capital Assets?*

Everything that you own is considered a capital asset *except* the following:

1. Stock in trade;

2. Real or personal property includable in *inventory*;

3. Real or personal property held for *sale to customers*;

4. Accounts or notes *receivable* acquired in the ordinary course of a trade or business for services rendered, or from the sale of any of the properties above, or for services rendered as an employee;

5. Depreciable property used in your trade or business (even though fully depreciated);

6. Real property used in your trade or business;

7. A *copyright*, or a *literary*, musical, or *artistic* composition, letters or memorandums or similar property, if your personal efforts created such property, or if you acquired it from the creator under circumstances entitling you to the creator's basis (for example, by gift or transfer in trust); and

8. Certain *short-term obligations*, federal, state and municipal.

Special Rule on Sale of Business Machinery, Equipment, Land, Buildings, Etc.

While real and depreciable property used in your trade or business is *not* a capital asset, there is a special tax break allowed. If the items were held for more than a year, the gains can be taxed as long-term capital gains on your '81 return. This can give you a full deduction if you lose when you sell, a long-term capital gain if you have a profit from sale.

But where you sell depreciable property at a profit, you may find that some or all of the profit will be taxed to you as ordinary income rather than capital gain under the so-called "depreciation recapture" rules. These rules apply to depreciation taken on personal property (other than livestock) after 1961, on elevators and escalators after June 30, 1963, and on livestock, after 1969.

The recapture rules for real property are more complicated. They apply generally if speedy depreciation has been deducted.

Capital Losses of Earlier Years Can Be Used in 1981

Before you start to fill out Schedule D of your 1981 return, look at Schedule D of Form 1040 for 1980 to see whether you had any capital losses which you couldn't use up in 1980. These unused capital losses can be deducted from your '81 net capital gains. To the extent the capital losses exceed the net capital gains, you can deduct them against up to $3,000 of '81 ordinary income. Any capital losses that you can't deduct this way can be carried over to '82.

Any losses you realized in and carried over from 1965-1980 are treated in 1981 as short-term if they were short-term in those years, and long-term if long-term in those years.

Deducting Net Capital Losses from Ordinary Income

Net capital losses left after all capital gains are offset are deductible against up to $3,000 of ordinary income for '81. Under this rule, any unused long-term or short-term capital losses carried over from years before 1970 and any net short-term capital losses you took after '69 can be deducted $1 for $1 from your ordinary income up to $3,000 for '81. But any *long-term* capital losses *you took after 1969* are deductible under this rule only on a $2-for-$1 basis. For example, if the only entry on your 1981 Schedule D is a $3,000 *long-term* capital loss, you can only deduct $1,500 from your 1981 ordinary income. But if your $3,000 loss in 1981 was *short-term,* you can deduct $3,000 from your 1981 ordinary income.

SCHEDULE D
(FORM 1040)
Department of the Treasury
Internal Revenue Service

Capital Gains and Losses
(Examples of property to be reported on this Schedule are gains and losses on stocks, bonds, and similar investments, and gains (but not losses) on personal assets such as a home or jewelry.)
▶ Attach to Form 1040.   ▶ See Instructions for Schedule D (Form 1040).

OMB No. 1545–0074

1981

14

Name(s) as shown on Form 1040

Your social security number

Part I   Short-term Capital Gains and Losses—Assets Held One Year or Less

D

a. Kind of property and description (Example, 100 shares 7% preferred of ''Z'' Co.)	b. Date acquired (Mo., day, yr.)	c. Date sold (Mo., day, yr.)	d. Gross sales price less expense of sale	e. Cost or other basis, as adjusted (see instructions page 23)	f. LOSS If column (e) is more than (d) subtract (d) from (e)	g. GAIN If column (d) is more than (e) subtract (e) from (d)
1						

2a Gain from sale or exchange of a principal residence held one year or less, from Form 2119, lines 7 or 11 . . . .

  b Short-term capital gain from installment sales from Form 6252, line 19 or 27 . . .

3 Enter your share of net short-term gain or (loss) from partnerships and fiduciaries .

4 Add lines 1 through 3 in column f and column g . . . . ( )

5 Combine line 4, column f and line 4, column g and enter the net gain or (loss) . . . .

6 Short-term capital loss carryover from years beginning after 1969 . . . . ( )

7 Net short-term gain or (loss), combine lines 5 and 6 . . . .

Part II   Long-term Capital Gains and Losses—Assets Held More Than One Year

8						

9a Gain from sale or exchange of a principal residence held more than one year, from Form 2119, lines 7, 11, 16 or 18 . . . .

  b Long-term capital gain from installment sales from Form 6252, line 19 or 27 . . . .

10 Enter your share of net long-term gain or (loss) from partnerships and fiduciaries .

11 Add lines 8 through 10 in column f and column g . . . . ( )

12 Combine line 11, column f and line 11, column g and enter the net gain or (loss) . . . .

13 Capital gain distributions . . . .

14 Enter gain from Form 4797, line 5(a)(1) . . . .

15 Enter your share of net long-term gain from small business corporations (Subchapter S) . . . .

16 Combine lines 12 through 15 . . . .

17 Long-term capital loss carryover from years beginning after 1969 . . . . ( )

18 Net long-term gain or (loss), combine lines 16 and 17 . . . .

Note: *Complete this form on reverse. However, if you have capital loss carryovers from years beginning before 1970, do not complete Parts III or V. See Form 4798 instead.*

For Paperwork Reduction Act Notice, see Form 1040 instructions

343–061–1

Part III   Summary of Parts I and II

19 Combine lines 7 and 18, and enter the net gain or (loss) here . . . .
    NOTE: *If line 19 is a gain complete lines 20 through 22. If line 19 is a loss complete lines 23 and 24.*

20 If line 19 shows a gain, enter the smaller of line 18 or line 19. Enter zero if there
    is a loss or no entry on line 18 . . . .

21 Enter 60% of line 20 . . . .
    If line 21 is more than zero, you may be liable for the alternative minimum tax. See Form 6251.

22 Subtract line 21 from line 19. Enter here and on Form 1040, line 12 . . . . . .

23 If line 19 shows a loss, enter one of the following amounts:
    (i)   If line 7 is zero or a net gain, enter 50% of line 19,
    (ii) If line 18 is zero or a net gain, enter line 19; or,
    (iii) If line 7 and line 18 are net losses, enter amount on line 7 added to 50% of the amount on line 18 . .

24 Enter here and as a loss on Form 1040, line 12, the smallest of:
    (i)   The amount on line 23;
    (ii) $3,000 ($1,500 if married and filing a separate return); or,
    (iii) Taxable income, as adjusted . . . .

Part IV   Computation of Alternative Tax
(Complete this part if line 20 (or Form 4798, line 8) shows a gain and your tax rate is above 50%. See instructions page 23.)

25 Net short-term gain or (loss) from line 5, from sales or exchanges after June 9, 1981 . . . .

26 Net long-term gain or (loss) from line 16, from sales or exchanges after June 9, 1981 . . . .

27 If line 26 shows a gain, combine line 25 and line 26. If line 26 or this line shows a loss or zero, enter zero
    and do not complete rest of this part . . . .

28 Enter the smaller of line 26 or line 27 . . . .

29 Enter the smaller of line 20 (or Form 4798, line 8) or line 28 . . . . . .

30 Enter your Taxable Income from Form 1040, line 34 . . . .

31 Enter 40% of line 29 . . . .

32 Subtract line 31 from line 30. If line 31 is more than line 30, enter zero . . . .

33 Tax on amount on line 32. ☐ Tax Rate Schedule X, Y, or Z; ☐ Schedule G. (See instructions page 23) . .

34 Enter 20% of line 29 . . . .

35 Add lines 33 and 34. If the result is less than your tax using other methods, enter this amount on Form
    1040, line 35 and check Schedule D box . . . .

Part V   Computation of Post-1969 Capital Loss Carryovers from 1981 to 1982
(Complete this part if the loss on line 23 is more than the loss on line 24)

Section A.—Short-term Capital Loss Carryover

36 Enter loss shown on line 7; if none, enter zero and skip lines 37 through 41—then go to line 42 . . .

37 Enter gain shown on line 18. If that line is blank or shows a loss, enter zero . . . .

38 Reduce any loss on line 36 to the extent of any gain on line 37 . . . .

39 Enter amount shown on line 24 . . . .

40 Enter smaller of line 38 or 39 . . . .

41 Subtract line 40 from line 38. This is your short-term capital loss carryover from 1981 to 1982 . . .

Section B.—Long-term Capital Loss Carryover

42 Subtract line 40 from line 39 (Note: *If you skipped lines 37 through 41, enter amount from line 24)* . . .

43 Enter loss from line 18; if none, enter zero and skip lines 44 through 47 . . . .

44 Enter gain shown on line 7. If that line is blank or shows a loss, enter zero . . . .

45 Reduce any loss on line 43 to the extent of any gain on line 44 . . . .

46 Multiply amount on line 42 by 2 . . . .

47 Subtract line 46 from line 45. This is your long-term capital loss carryover from 1981 to 1982 . . . .

Part VI   Complete this Part Only if You are Electing Out of the Installment Method And are Reporting a Note or Other Obligation at Less Than Full Face Value

☐ Check here if you elect out of the installment method.

Enter the face amount of the note or other obligation ▶ ....

Enter the percentage of valuation of the note or other obligation ▶

If you have both a net long-term capital-loss carryover from a year before 1970 and a 1981 net long-term capital loss, you first use up the pre-1970 loss as a deduction up to the $3,000 of ordinary income on a $1-for-$1 basis.

Stocks and Other Securities

Gains and losses, technically called capital gains and losses, are divided into short-term and long-term capital gains. The dividing line on your '81 return is whether the stocks, other securities, or other capital assets were held for more than one year or for not more than one year. It's important to put your transactions in the proper sections. A gain in the "not more than one year" group will generally pay more than a gain in the "more than one year" group.

Q. My broker's slips on the purchase of my stock showed a gross purchase price of $1,200 and commission of $33, resulting in a total of $1,233. When I sold the stock, the slip showed an amount of $1,209 less state tax of $2, commission of $33, or a net of $1,174. How do I show this on the return?

A. The cost of the stock to you is the total cost $1,233, to which is added the expenses of sale and commission, $33, or $1,266. The gross sale price is $1,209. This will result in a loss of $57.

Note that the $2 state tax is not deducted here. Instead, you should deduct it as a regular tax on Schedule A of Form 1040. (See discussion, pages 83-84.) This can be advantageous since, while only part of the gain is taxable, the full state tax is deductible.

Q. During the year, I received a 10 percent stock dividend. Is this reported as a dividend or as a capital gain?

A. A stock dividend is generally not considered as income and you need not report the receipt.

Q. On another stock, I received a nontaxable 5 percent stock dividend, which I sold for $120. How do I show this?

A. The shares are treated as though you had owned them as long as you owned the original stock. Thus, when filling out Schedule D, you show that you acquired the stock dividend when you acquired the original stock. If this was more than a year before the sale, the transaction goes into the long-term capital gains section. The stock has a sale price of $120, and a cost equal to the cost of the original shares spread over the increased number of shares. Thus if you originally had 100 shares which cost $1,050, your 5-share stock dividend would "cost" $50 ($1,050 ÷ 105 shares x 5 shares).

Q. My shares gave me rights to subscribe to more shares of the company. I sold the rights for $100. Is the $100 taxable as ordinary income or capital gain?

A. The receipt of the rights is not taxable. The sale of the rights is a capital gain. Whether the gain is a long-term or short-term one depends on the time the original stock was held, as in the case of stock dividends.

You don't have to report the full $100 as gain if you don't wish to. You are entitled to treat a portion of the cost of your original stock as the cost of your rights. The breakdown is made on the basis of the value of the rights at the time the stock went ex-rights compared to the value of the stock plus rights. You probably don't have this information but you can check with your broker.

Sale of Your Home

Millions of Americans move every year, upgrade themselves by selling their old homes and buying new ones. Many older persons sell their homes and move into apartments. Because of rising prices, the sale of the old home is often made at a profit. This profit is generally taxable in the same way as a profit realized on the sale of stocks, securities, etc.

However, the tax law recognizes two situations where the gain will not be taxed.

1. The tax can be avoided if you purchase a new home within a specified period of time.

If you sold your old home in 1981, the tax on gain from sale of your old home can be avoided if you bought or buy your replacement home within two years before or after sale of your old residence, and you use the new one as your principal residence during that period. To the extent that your selling price exceeds the purchase price of your new principal residence, your gain is taxable. You also have a two-year period for any sale for which the previous 18-month period had not expired on or before July 20, 1981.

The general rule is that only one sale during a two-year period qualifies for avoiding gain by purchasing a new principal residence. But for sale of a principal residence, there is an exception that allows you to avoid gain on more than one sale of a principal residence in a two-year period if the extra sale or sales are caused by your beginning to work as an employee or self-employed person at a new principal place of work. This exception applies only if your new principal job site is at least 35 miles farther away from your old residence than your old job site, and you met the work requirements that are a prerequisite for being allowed to deduct direct moving expenses, as explained on page 62.

2. If you were 55 before the date of the sale or exchange of your home, then even if you don't replace your home, you can elect to eliminate up to $100,000 of gain on a sale before July 21, 1981, or $125,000 if the sale was made after July 20, 1981, if you owned and used the property as your principal residence for at least 3 out of the 5 years before the sale (if the sale was made before July 26, 1981, a person who was 65 can use 5 out of 8 years instead, if he doesn't qualify under the 3 out of 5 years requirement).

This election is a one-shot lifetime exemption, available to persons aged 55 or more, and allows you to avoid tax on up to $100,000 or $125,000 of profit on a sale, regardless of how high your selling price was.

Because this is a one-shot election that can be used for only one sale, a taxpayer should generally not use it if he plans to buy a new home and can avoid tax on sale of his old home under *1* above.

If a 65-or-older taxpayer sold his home before July 27, 1978, and elected to exempt some of his profit under the special exemption then available for gain he realized on the first $35,000 of adjusted sales price, that does not prevent him from making his new one-shot election where he bought another home which he again sold at a profit in 1981.

Form 2119 may be used to report the sale and replacement of your personal residence. It is also used to report the one-shot election by individuals aged 55 or over.

Q. I had lived in my home for 20 years but had rented it during the year before I sold it. Since I am over 55, can I still qualify to use the $100,000 or $125,000 exemption?

A. Yes. The sole requirement is that you meet the three-out-of-five-year test (or the five-out-of-eight-year test if you are over 65 at the date of sale made before July 26, 1981).

Q. Last year my firm shifted me to another state and I had to sell my home at a loss of $1,000. Can I deduct the loss?

A. No. The tax law doesn't permit any deduction for losses incurred in personal transactions such as the sale of a home, personally used cars, boats, etc. However, you have to pay tax on any gains from such transactions.

Note, however, that some of your expenses connected with selling your old and buying your new house may qualify for deduction as moving expenses. (See page 62.)

Q. My home cost me $30,000 in 1969. I sold it last June for $130,000. What tax is due?

A. That depends. If you didn't buy another house and don't expect to soon, *and* if you (or your spouse, where the house was jointly owned and you are filing a joint return) were 55 or over before the sale date, you can elect to eliminate the tax on the complete $100,000 gain since the gain wasn't over $100,000.

If you and your spouse were less than 55 years old, you owe a tax on the $100,000 profit. But this $100,000 is not fully taxable. It is a long-term capital gain. As such, show the transaction under that part of Schedule D.

If you buy a new home for $130,000 or more within 18 months of your sale of your old home, no tax at all will be due regardless of your age. The next question explains this.

Q. The home for which I paid $12,000 in 1969 I sold for $46,000 last year. Just before the sale I spent $1,000 in painting the house so as to spruce it up for sale. I then bought a new house for $45,000. Must I pay tax on the $34,000 profit even though I have no cash profit on the whole deal?

A. No. The special relief provision which applies to all taxpayers regardless of age waives the tax if you put money equal to the sale price into a new house within 18 months after or before the sale of your old one. You must, though, use the residence as your principal residence within the same period. (Two years, if you constructed the home.)

To the extent that you don't put an amount equal to the sale price ($46,000) less the fix-up expenses ($1,000), or $45,000, into a new house, you must pay a tax on the gain. Since you used the $45,000 for your new house, you owe no tax.

A special tax break that you might easily overlook is that fix-up expenses to make your house salable (papering, painting, etc.) can reduce your taxable profit—under certain conditions—if incurred within 90 days before the contract to sell the house and paid within 30 days after the sale. These expenses must be nondeductible in computing income and must not be capital expenditures. Also note that while these fixing-up expenses cut your reportable gain, they don't enter into the computation of the actual profit.

Q. My home cost me $50,000 in 1974. I sold it in August of 1981 for $100,000 and I moved into a rental apartment. I do not intend to buy another house. What tax is due?

A. That depends. If you and your spouse were each under age 55 when you sold the house, you have realized a $50,000 long-term capital gain that you must report on Schedule D. If your house was jointly owned with your spouse and you file a joint return, then if either of you was 55 or over before you sold the house, you can elect to eliminate tax completely on your $50,000 profit.

Q. How do I compute whether I reinvested the sale price in a new home?

A. You compare the so-called adjusted sale price with the purchase price. The adjusted sale price is the selling price of your old home less commissions, expenses of advertising for sale, cost of preparing the deed and other legal fees, and fix-up expenses (such as redecorating discussed in the preceding question) for work performed on the residence to make it more salable.

Here is a table showing how the taxable gain is determined under various conditions:

Your old house cost	You sold at	Commissions were*	Fix-up costs were	You buy or build at	Your taxed gain on sale is
$20,000	$30,000	$1,500	$1,000	$30,000	$ 0
20,000	30,000	1,500	1,000	28,000	0
20,000	30,000	1,500	1,000	27,000	500
20,000	30,000	1,500	1,000	21,000	6,500
20,000	23,000	1,150	1,000	19,000	1,850
20,000	20,000	1,000	1,000	28,000	1,000 loss*

*non deductible

Q. In 1962 I sold my home for $12,000 and bought another for $15,000. I didn't report the profit because of the repurchase. In '81 I sold my newest home for $80,000 and bought another for $80,000. Can I also avoid paying tax on this gain?

A. Yes. You can sell and replace your house as many times as you wish without paying tax on the profits under this rule *except* that you can't do it more than once within any two-year period.

Q. I swapped my old residence as part payment on a new one. Can I still avoid tax on the "gain"?

A. Normally, an exchange of this type is taxable. However, if the cost of the new residence is greater than the sale price of the old, you qualify for the tax saving allowed when a new home is purchased.

Assume that your old home cost $30,000 and there is a mortgage of $15,000. In 1981 you bought a new home for $80,000 and the broker accepted your old home as a trade-in, allowing you $60,000 less the mortgage of $15,000, or $45,000. You placed a $35,000 mortgage on the new home. Since you invested more than the sale price of your old home in the new one, there is no present gain.

Q. I bought a new residence and immediately made about $4,000 of improvements. Does the cost of the new residence include these improvements?

I paid commissions and legal fees too in acquiring the property. Are these also part of the cost of the new residence?

A. "Yes" to both.

Q. I sold my old home and moved into a cooperative apartment. Can the apartment qualify so as to eliminate the gain on the old home?

A. Yes. If you use the apartment as your principal residence. Even such unusual homes as a trailer or houseboat can qualify.

Q. I owned a summer home, which I sold at a $15,000 profit. I put more than the selling price into buying a new summer home. Do I have to report the profit?

A. Yes. The special tax break both for replacing a home and the exemption for houses sold by persons 55 or over applies only to the sale of a principal residence. Since the principal residence is your "winter" home, the sale of your summer home is taxable.

Q. I inherited a residence worth about $60,000. Since I no longer needed my old residence, I sold it for $40,000, realizing a profit of $15,000. Do I have to report the profit?

A. Yes, if you were not at least 55 when you sold your house. The acquisition of a new residence by gift or inheritance is not viewed as the reinvestment of the sale price of the old residence.

However, if you were 55 or older when you sold your house, you may be able to avoid tax on your profit by making the election discussed on page 43.

Q. I owned an old home that I sold at a profit. I purchased a new home, which was put in my wife's name. Does this bar me from avoiding tax on the sale, since the new home wasn't purchased in my name?

A. No. You can still eliminate the profit. The only requirement is that you must agree to an allocation of the basis (cost) of the new residence.

Q. I sold my old home for $80,000, all cash. This represented a profit to me of $12,000. I purchased my new home within six months for $85,000, but I used only $8,000 in cash. A first mortgage made up the difference. Do I still pay no tax even though I have an extra $72,000 in cash?

A. Yes, the $12,000 is not taxable. The cost of your new home is $85,000, even though you paid only $8,000 in cash. But remember that if you ever sell your new home, the profit or loss is figured as though you paid $73,000 (cost $85,000 less $12,000 gain not taxed on sale of old house).

Q. I owned a two-family house for more than 10 years. I occupied half. I sold the house for $90,000, realizing a profit of $50,000, and purchased another two-family house for $105,000. Do I exclude the full $50,000 profit?

A. No. While you have sold your residence, you have also sold a piece of rental property. Since half the house was your residence, only half is exempt because you purchased a new residence (half of new $105,000 home). But half of the house was rented, and therefore $25,000 is taxable.

This qualifies as a long-term capital gain and should be reported on Schedule D.

Q. Does the fact that I was already over 65 when I sold my house in 1981 bar me from electing to exclude my entire $60,000 profit?

A. No. As long as you were 55 or over when you sold it, it doesn't matter how old you actually were. In fact, for a sale made before July 26, 1981, a person 65 or over when he sold it has an even better chance to qualify for the election. Persons who are 55 or over but not yet 65 when they sell must have owned and used their house as a principal residence for at least 3 out of the last 5 years before the sale. But if a person 65 or older can't meet this 3-out-of-5 year requirement, he can nevertheless make the election if he owned and used his house as a principal residence for at least 5 out of the last 8 years.

For example, suppose you moved out of your house in order to let your daughter and her husband live in it. Three years later you sold the house, in June, 1981. This means that you did not own and use the house as your principal residence for 3 out of the last 5 years. If you were not 65 or over at the time of the sale, you couldn't make the election to exempt all the profit on the sale. But if you were 65 or over you could make the election, because you did own and use the house as your principal residence for 5 out of the last 8 years (the 5 years before you moved out in favor of your daughter) and made the sale before July 26, 1981. (See page 43.)

Q. In 1981, my wife and I sold our jointly owned house for a profit of $120,000. Can I elect to exclude $60,000 and my wife also elect to exclude $60,000?

A. No. You, as a married couple, are allowed only one election between you. If you make the election to exclude up to $100,000 of your $120,000 profit, your wife can't make any election.

Even if you buy and sell another house at a future time, neither you nor your wife will be able to make an election for that house.

Sale of Real Estate

Many Americans dabble in real estate; many persons buy acreage and sell it off as lots. In general, the individual who buys a piece of property and sells it when it goes up in price has a long-term capital gain (assuming that he has held it for more than twelve months). You'll run into a question about whether you're in the business of buying and selling real estate only when you have frequent sales. But unless you feel that you are in the real-estate business, it's advisable to claim the gains as capital gains. And if an examining agent does question your claims, consult a professional tax adviser.

Q. I bought several acres five years ago with the thought of building a summer home. I never got around to it, and last year sold the land for a $30,000 profit. Is this a long-term capital gain?

A. Yes. You clearly did not go into the business of buying and selling lots.

Q. I purchased five lots a number of years ago with the thought that they would go up in value. Last year I sold them to three individuals at a profit of $20,000. Is this a capital gain?

A. Yes. You are clearly within the bounds.

Condemnations and Involuntary Exchanges

If any of your property has been taken from you through theft, flood, other casualty, or through condemnation, you may have a deductible loss in the case of a casualty loss, or an ordinary or capital loss in the case of a condemnation. However, sometimes you may collect more from insurance coverage or condemnation awards than the property cost you.

Normally, this excess would be taxed as though you had sold the property at a profit. But the tax law recognizes the inequity of taxing you on this "profit" and therefore does not tax the gain if you:

1. Bought for an amount equal to the proceeds other property similar or related in service or use, or replace real property used in your trade or business or held for investment with other real estate used in your trade or business or held for investment, *and*:

2. Make the replacement in the period beginning with the date the property was damaged or destroyed, or you were first notified of the threat or imminence of requisition or condemnation, and ending two years after the close of the first tax year in which any part of the gain is realized.

Q. I sold my rental property at a profit after the Health Department ruled it unsafe. I bought another piece of rental property shortly thereafter. Can I avoid reporting the gain?

A. No. This type of threat doesn't qualify as a sale under a threat of condemnation.

Q. My home was taken by condemnation, and I received $45,000, of which $15,000 is profit. I intend to replace the home by an even more expensive one. Can I avoid any tax on the gain?

A. Yes. You can avoid the tax under the involuntary conversion rules. However, you can also elect to treat the gain as though a sale were made and defer the profit under the rules covering the sale of a residence and the repurchase of a new one discussed on page 43.

The right to treat the conversion as a sale applies *only* to residences converted as a result of seizure, requisition, condemnation, or their threat or imminence. Involuntary conversion by fire, storm, or other casualty, where the insurance proceeds exceed the cost, must be treated as an involuntary conversion.

Generally, either alternative will result in the same tax avoidance.

Q. My home, which cost $15,000, was destroyed by fire. I received $40,000 in fire-insurance proceeds. Since I am 67 years old, I plan to rent a home or apartment. Do I have to pay tax on the $25,000 profit?

A. No. Since you are 55 or over, you can elect to treat the destruction as a sale and not pay any tax on the gain under the election discussed on page 43.

TAX TIP: Do You Dabble in the Market?

You may wonder whether you handled your stock-market transactions to your best advantage. While it's too late to do anything about your past transactions, keep the following hints in mind for '82.

If you want to sell stock or bonds on which you have a profit, try to pick those which you have held for more than one year. These are called long-term capital gains, while profit on stock held for one year or less is called short-term capital gain. Taking a long-term gain will generally cut your tax on the profit, compared to the tax you would have to pay on the same profit from the sale of stock or bonds you held for one year or less.

On the other hand, if you expect to sell stock at *a loss,* your general goal is to sell before you hold it over one year. That will generally give you the best tax results.

Here are two other pointers:

1. If you purchase such investment-oriented publications as *Barrons, Forbes, The Wall Street Journal,* etc., don't overlook claiming the expenses as an itemized deduction. Such more general publications as *The New York Times* and *Fortune,* which also contain considerable financial information, were considered by the IRS to be an investment expense, for a large investor.

2. If you sold stock or securities at a gain in the closing days of 1981 and payment wasn't received (the settlement date) until '82, you can either (a) defer the gain until 1982, or (b) include the gain in your '81 return. The reason is that the sale is an instalment sale which gives you the choice.

Q. I owned vacant real property on which I planned to build a warehouse. However, before I could build, the land was condemned. I used the proceeds to buy property that contained a garage and service station. Can I avoid tax on the profit I made on the condemnation?

A. Yes. Since you held the original real property for investment and replaced it with a like kind of real property, the gain need not be reported—assuming you used an amount equal to the proceeds to acquire the new property.

Q. My rental property was subject to a mortgage of $5,000. I received $35,000 of condemnation proceeds for the property, of which $5,000 was used to pay off the mortgage. I invested the remaining $30,000 in a like kind of property. Do I have to pay tax on the $5,000 profit I realized on the proceeds?

A. Your proceeds are considered to be $35,000. The amount paid on the mortgage is not considered to be a reinvestment of the proceeds. Since you only invested $30,000 of the $35,000 proceeds, the $5,000 is taxable.

Q. I realized a $20,000 gain when my property was condemned. I received $55,000 for the property and bought like property for $53,000. Is the full $20,000 gain taxable since I didn't invest the full proceeds?

A. No. The entire gain is not taxable. The gain is taxable only to the extent that you did *not* invest the proceeds. Since you "held out" $2,000 ($55,000 less $53,000), your gain taxed is $2,000.

Q. Part of my farm property was condemned. I received a condemnation award of $20,000 plus $5,000 for severance damages. How do I handle the $5,000 severance-damage award?

A. The $5,000 is to be applied as follows:

1. The proportionate share of expenses of securing the award.

2. The full amount of any special assessment levied for benefits to the remaining real estate and withheld from the award.

3. Any expenses of restoring the property left to its former use.

4. Any amount of the $5,000 left reduces the cost of the remaining property.

5. If the amount in *4* exceeds the cost, you have a taxable gain.

Q. My rental property was condemned and I used the proceeds to buy stocks. Can I put a mortgage on my home for the amount of the proceeds and buy other rental property so as to avoid paying tax on the gain?

A. Yes. If you can still do this within the time limit. You do *not* have to use the identical proceeds from the old property.

Q. When I was notified by the City Council of their intention to obtain my business property by negotiation or condemnation, I bought property of like kind. I paid more for the new property than I received for the old. Does the fact that I acquired the new property before the old was condemned mean that the gain is taxable?

A. No. Since you acquired the replacement property after you were first notified of the threat of condemnation, the property qualifies as barring the gain from taxation.

Q. How do I report the involuntary conversion? Can I ignore the whole deal if I replace the property in the time period?

A. The procedure is as follows:

1. If you want to have the gain taxed, because, say, you have offsetting losses, report the gain as you would any taxable gain. That is, report it as a sale of a capital asset, ordinary asset, etc.

If in the next year or so you decide that you would have been better off to have deferred the gain, though, you can change your mind. You can then file a refund claim on Form 1040X indicating that you reported the gain and that you now wish to change your election and be taxed only to the extent of the unexpended proceeds, if any.

2. If you don't want to pay on any gain, attach a statement to your return showing: (a) the gain on the conversion, (b) the amount realized, and (c) the amount of gain, if any, reported. Also give details on the replacement property and the purchase price and show that you are making the election. If you did not spend an amount at least equal to the proceeds on replacement property and you do not intend to, the difference represents taxable gain. Of course, if you spent at least as much as the proceeds, you exclude the full gain.

If you haven't replaced your property by the time the return is filed, you can still make the election. Attach a statement showing all the facts, including your gain. State that you elect to replace the property within the required period. When you later replace the property, attach a statement to the return for the year of replacement giving the detailed information. If you don't replace the property within the time limit, or don't spend the full amount, you will have to file an amended return for the year of conversion showing the correct tax.

Deferred-Payment Sales without Adequate Interest

Most sales made with payments to be spread over a period of years provide for interest on the unpaid balance. However, if the arrangement doesn't provide for the buyer to pay interest of at least 6 percent where the sale was made on or before July 1, 1981, or 9 percent on a later sale, the law treats part of the sale price as interest regardless of whether or not the sale is reported on the instalment basis.

Where this is true, and the sale was made for a price of over $3,000, part of the sale price is considered to include interest of 7 percent or 10 percent, depending on whether the sale was pre-July 1, 1981, or post-June 30, 1981. Adjusting for a hypothetical 7 or 10 percent interest can be a complicated procedure that can affect the amount to be included in income and whether you qualify for the instalment basis.

If you have made this type of sale, contact a professional advisor to aid you in preparing your return.

Deferred-Payment Sales on the Instalment Method

If you sell property at a profit, normally you would have to pay tax on the entire profit in the year of your sale, even though you didn't receive the full amount of cash in that year.

But you are permitted to spread the tax on your profit over the years it takes you to receive the full amount of cash, *if* part or all of the sales price is deferred to a post-1981 year.

If you sell at a loss, the loss is *not* spread over the years, regardless of how much cash you receive in the first year. The full loss is treated as realized in the year of the sale.

If you made a deferred-payment sale at a profit, you will automatically be treated as reporting the profit in proportion to the instalment payments as you receive them, unless you elect not to have the instalment reporting apply to a particular deferred-payment sale. If you elect out and report a note or other obligation at less than full face value, check the box and furnish the information required by Part VI, Page 2 of Schedule D.

Q. I sold some real estate for $20,000 in May, 1981. It cost me $15,000. I received a $5,000 down payment with annual payments of $5,000 to be made in each of the next three years, plus interest. How much do I report this year?

A. You can, of course, report your entire $5,000 profit. But since part of the payment of the sales price is deferred until after 1981, you have the right to report on the instalment basis.

To do this, you figure out what your percent of profit was on the sale. Since you made $5,000 on a $20,000 sale, your percent of profit is 25 percent. Each dollar you receive is therefore considered to be 25 percent profit. Since you received $5,000 in cash in 1981, 25 percent of that, or $1,250, is the taxable profit you would report on the instalment basis for 1981.

In future years, 25 percent of each principal payment received will be taxable in the year received.

Q. I sold my farm last year and qualify to use the instalment basis. However, because of some bad investment, I have enough capital losses to cut the farm gain substantially. Do I have to use the instalment basis?

A. No. If you find it better to report the full profit, go ahead.

Q. In 1980 I received $250 for an option on a sale I made in 1981. Do I include the $250 as part of the cash received in 1981, the year of sale?

A. Yes.

Q. I sold some property that cost me $7,000 for $10,000—$4,000 in cash plus $6,000 in 10-percent notes of the individual purchaser. The notes are worth about $5,000 if I tried to sell them. Since I don't want to use the instalment basis, how do I compute the profit?

A. You value the notes at their fair market value, which means that your taxable profit is $2,000 (the $4,000 in cash plus $5,000 worth of notes which you received, less cost of $7,000). You elect not to report on the instalment basis and instead report your entire $2,000 profit.

But when the notes are paid off to you, one-sixth of each payment to you will be taxed at that time as ordinary income. This represents the difference between the $6,000 face value and the $5,000 fair market value you reported when you figured the profit.

Line 13: Taxable Part of Capital-Gain Distributions Not Reported on Schedule D

The taxable part of capital-gain distributions that are not reported on Schedule D (as explained on page 36) are entered at line 13.

Line 14: Supplemental Gains or Losses

Any net gain or loss from Supplemental Schedule of Gains and Losses, Form 4797, is entered at Line 14.

Line 15: Fully Taxable Pensions and Annuities Not Reported on Line 16

Fully taxable pensions are reported here at line 15.

(If you received a lump-sum distribution from a qualified pension or profit-sharing plan on termination of your employment, you may be eligible to figure your tax on that lump sum in a special, favorable way. For this special computation, you should use the special form provided by the IRS.)

Line 16: Other Pensions and Annuities

The total amount of pensions and annuities other than fully taxable ones reported on line 15 is shown on line 16a. The taxable portion of this amount is shown on line 16b. To compute the taxable portion, use the IRS Worksheet on the right:

1a. Enter your cost . . . . _____

b. Cost recovered in prior years . . _____

c. Subtract line 1b from line 1a . . _____

2. Amount received this year. Also, enter this amount on Form 1040, line 16a . . . . _____

3. Amount on line 2 that is not taxable (but not more than line 1c) . . . . _____

4. Taxable part (subtract line 3 from line 2). Enter here and on Form 1040, line 16b . . . . _____

(Keep a copy of this worksheet for your records)

Note: If you had more than one pension or annuity that is not fully taxable, figure the taxable part of each separately. Enter the total of the taxable parts on Form 1040, line 16b.

If you cannot recover your cost within 3 years, you must use special rules to report your pension or annuity income. For more details, please get **Publication 575.** If you must use this method, enter the amount you received this year on line 16a. Enter the taxable part on line 16b.

SCHEDULE E
(Form 1040)
Department of the Treasury
Internal Revenue Service

Supplemental Income Schedule

(From rents and royalties, partnerships, estates and trusts, etc.)
▶ Attach to Form 1040. ▶ See Instructions for Schedule E (Form 1040).

OMB No. 1545–0074

1981
15

Name(s) as shown on Form 1040 | Your social security number

Part I   Rent and Royalty Income or Loss.

1 Are any of the expenses listed below for a vacation home or similar dwelling rented to others (see Instructions)? .   ☐ Yes ☐ No

2 If you checked "Yes" to question 1, did you or a member of your family occupy the vacation home or similar dwelling for more than 14 days during the tax year? . . . .   ☐ Yes ☐ No

Rental and Royalty Income (describe property in Part V)		Properties A		B		C		Totals	
3 a Rents received								**3**	
b Royalties received									
Rental and Royalty Expenses									
4 Advertising	4								
5 Auto and travel	5								
6 Cleaning and maintenance . . .	6								
7 Commissions	7								
8 Insurance	8								
9 Interest	9								
10 Legal and other professional fees . .	10								
11 Repairs	11								
12 Supplies	12								
13 Taxes (do NOT include Windfall Profit Tax, see Part III, line 35)	13								
14 Utilities	14								
15 Wages and salaries	15								
16 Other (list) ▶									
17 Total deductions (add lines 4 through 16)	17							17	
18 Depreciation expense (see Instructions), or Depletion (attach computation)	18							18	
19 Total (add lines 17 and 18)	19								
20 Income or (loss) from rental or royalty properties (subtract line 19 from line 3a (rents) or 3b (royalties))	20								

21 Add properties with profits on line 20, and enter total profits here . . . . | 21 | |

22 Add properties with losses on line 20, and enter total (losses) here . . . . | 22 | (   ) |

23 Combine amounts on lines 21 and 22, and enter net profit or (loss) here . . . . | 23 | |

24 Net farm rental profit or (loss) from Form 4835, line 50 . . . . | 24 | |

25 Total rental or royalty income or (loss). Combine amounts on lines 23 and 24. Enter here and include in line 37 on page 2 . . . . | 25 | |

For Paperwork Reduction Act Notice, see Form 1040 Instructions.

343–062–1

Line 17: Rents and Royalties, Partnerships, Estates, or Trusts, etc.

We are now moving to separate Schedule E, which is a catchall for income from rents and royalties, and income or losses from partnerships, estates or trusts, and small-business corporations. These are all detailed in separate Schedule E, Supplemental Income Schedule, and you include the total on line 17 of Form 1040.

Don't forget to write your name at the top of separate Schedule E, together with your Social Security number.

Rents and Royalties

First answer questions 1 and 2 of Part I.

If your rental activity is an investment for you rather than your business, then you use Part I to report your rent or royalty income and the expenses of earning that income for each property.

If all your rental property was placed in service before 1981, then use Part V on Page 2 of Schedule E to compute the depreciation for each property.

If you placed any rental property in service after 1980, then you must use Form 4562 to compute the depreciation for all of your properties. See page 129 for the post-1980 depreciation rules.

Part V Depreciation Claimed in Part I.—Complete only if property was placed in service before January 1, 1981. For more space, use Form 4562. If you placed any property in service after December 31, 1980, use Form 4562 for all property; do NOT complete Part V.

(a) Description and location of property	(b) Date acquired	(c) Cost or other basis	(d) Depreciation allowed or allowable in prior years	(e) Depreciation method	(f) Life or rate	(g) Depreciation for this year
Property A						
Totals (Property A)						
Property B						
Totals (Property B)						
Property C						
Totals (Property C)						

Form **4562**	**Depreciation**	OMB No. 1545–0172

(Rev. September 1981)
Department of the Treasury
Internal Revenue Service

▶ See separate instructions.
▶ Attach this form to your return.

Expires 12/31/82

Name(s) as shown on return	Identifying number

▶ Generally, you must use the Accelerated Cost Recovery System of depreciation (ACRS) for all assets you placed in service after December 31, 1980. Report these assets in Part I, lines 1(a) through 1(f).

▶ You may elect to exclude certain property. Report this property in Part I, line 2.

▶ Use Part II for assets you placed in service before January 1, 1981, and certain other assets for which you cannot use ACRS.

▶ Filers of Schedule C (Form 1040), Schedule E (Form 1040) and Form 4835 should see the instructions for those forms before completing Form 4562.

Part I   Assets placed in service after December 31, 1980

A. Class of property	B. Date placed in service	C. Cost or other basis	D. Recovery period	E. Method of figuring depreciation	F. Percentage	G. Deduction for this year
1 Accelerated Cost Recovery System (ACRS) (See instructions for grouping assets):						
(a) 3-year property						
(b) 5-year property						
(c) 10-year property						
(d) 15-year public utility property						
(e) 15-year real property—low-income housing						
(f) 15-year real property other than low-income housing						
2 Property subject to section 168(e) (2) election (see instructions):......						
3 Totals (add amounts in columns C and G) . . .						

4 Depreciation from Part II, line 3 . . . .

5 Total (add column G, lines 3 and 4). Enter this amount on the depreciation expense line (where it applies) of your return . . . .

See Paperwork Reduction Act Notice on page 1 of the separate instructions.   343–168–1   Form **4562** (Rev. 9–81)

Form 4562 (Rev. 9–81)

Part II Assets placed in service before January 1, 1981 and other assets not qualifying for ACRS

A. Description of property	B. Date acquired	C. Cost or other basis	D. Depreciation allowed or allowable in earlier years	E. Method of figuring depreciation	F. Life or rate	G. Depreciation for this year
1 Class Life Asset Depreciation Range (CLADR) System Depreciation . . . . ▶						
2 Other depreciation (for grouping assets, see instructions for Part II):						
Buildings						
Furniture and fixtures . .						
Transportation equipment						
Machinery and other equipment						
Other (specify)...................						

3 Total (add amounts in column G). Enter here and in Part I, line 4 . . . .

Q. I require my tenants to leave one month's rent as security with me in addition to the current month's rent. Do I report the security as income when I receive it?

A. That depends. If your renting arrangements call for that security payment to be applied as rent sometime during the lease, then it's income to you the year you get it, even if it won't be applied to rent until some later year. For example, if you leased an apartment for $400 a month in 1981 on a two-year lease and collected $400 for the first month and $400 security to be applied to the last month in 1982, that $400 of security is taxable in your 1981 income. But if you took the $400 of security merely to protect yourself against possible damage and had to give it back if you didn't use it for damages, then it would be income only when you used it. Thus, in the example above, if you took the second $400 as security against damage, and not as rent payment for the last month of the lease, and you spend $200 of that amount for repairs in 1981, you would report that $200 as 1981 income. You would also have a $200 repair expense.

Q. When I rented an apartment in December 1981 I required the tenant to pay me immediately the $400-a-month rent for three months—December 1981, January and February 1982. Do I report the $800 for January and February which I received in 1981 on my 1981 or 1982 return?

A. Your 1981 return. You report advance rent in the year it is paid to you.

Q. My tenant wanted to break his lease last year because he wanted to move to another neighborhood. I charged him rent for two extra months as a condition for letting him off the lease. How do I treat these payments?

A. Even though you were paid by your tenant for not living in your apartment, that amount is rent and you pay taxes on it.

Q. I rent a house to my brother for only $150 a month although the normal rental value to any stranger would be at least $400 a month. Does this affect the amount of expense I can deduct on my rental property?

A. Yes. You can deduct your depreciation and other expenses only up to the amount of rent you take in. Also, if you permit someone—say, a dependent parent—to use your property rent-free, and if he rents out part of it, you have to include that rent in your return.

Q. What kinds of repairs to my rental property can I deduct?

A. Generally those that simply restore your rental property without adding to its value or useful life. This would include such common expenses as repainting, repapering, fixing a leak in the roof, repairing defective plumbing and wiring, etc.

But those expenses which add to the value or useful life of your property are considered capital expenditures. You add these outlays to the cost of the property which you are depreciating and take depreciation deductions for these outlays instead of deducting them immediately in full as a repair. Examples are the cost of a new room, new furnace, new bathroom fixtures, new lighting fixtures, etc.

Q. What do I deduct as other expenses of my rental property?

A. Fire insurance, liability insurance, janitor service, water, fuel, taxes, mortgage interest, etc. But remember that taxes or assessments for paving, sewer, or other local improvements are not immediately deductible as expenses. These must be added to the cost of property.

Q. My brother and I are equal owners of the property we rent out, but I paid almost all the expenses in 1981. Can I deduct what I paid?

A. No. You can deduct only your proportionate share of the total expenses—which is one-half—even though you paid more.

Q. I own a two-family house. I live in half of it and rent the other half. How do I handle the expenses?

A. In Schedule E, Part II, you can deduct half of the depreciation, repairs, taxes, interest, and other expenses you pay on the entire property. Then you deduct interest and taxes for the half of the house you use, on separate Schedule A of Form 1040 if you are itemizing your actual deductions.

Any repairs and other expenses such as painting, which you do for the tenant's rented half of your property, are deductible in full in Schedule E, Part II. But similar expenses for your half of the house aren't deductible at all.

Q. I am taking the flat standard deduction instead of itemizing my deductions on separate Schedule A. Can I nevertheless deduct depreciation, repairs, and other expenses from my rent income?

A. Yes. You can deduct these from your rent income in getting a net figure on Schedule E, Part I, even if you are not itemizing deductions on separate Schedule A.

Q. I receive royalty payments on a book and on an oil investment. Do I report them on Schedule E, Part I?

A. Yes. You report here your royalties from books, stories, plays, trademarks, formulas; as well as from coal, oil, gas, timber, and other natural resources.

The patents and copyrights that produce royalties may be subject to amortization, if you paid for them. The royalties from natural resources may be subject to depletion, which serves approximately the same purpose as depreciation or amortization does for other property.

Schedule E (Form 1040) 1981   Page 2

| **Part II** | **Income or Losses from Partnerships, Estates or Trusts, or Small Business Corporations** |

If you report a loss below, do you have amounts invested in that activity for which you are not "at risk" (see Instructions)? ☐ Yes ☐ No
If "Yes," and your loss exceeded your amount "at risk," did you limit your loss to your amount "at risk"? . . . . . ☐ Yes ☐ No

	(a) Name	(b) Employer identification number	(c) Net loss (see instructions for "at risk" limitations)	(d) Net income
Partnerships	....	....	....	....
	....	....	....	....
	....	....	....	....

26 Add amounts in columns (c) and (d) and enter here . . . . **26** (_____)
27 Combine amounts in columns (c) and (d), line 26, and enter net income or (loss) **27**
28 Additional first-year depreciation from 1980/1981 fiscal-year partnerships. Enter amount from Form 1065, Schedule K–1, line 2, but not more than $2,000 ($4,000 if a joint return) . . . **28** (_____)
29 Total partnership income or (loss). Combine lines 27 and 28. Enter here and include in line 37 . **29**

Estates or Trusts	....	....	....	....
	....	....	....	....

30 Add amounts in columns (c) and (d) and enter here . . . . **30** (_____)
31 Total estate or trust income or (loss). Combine amounts in columns (c) and (d), line 30. Enter here and include in line 37 . . . . **31**

Small Business Corporations	....	....	....	....
	....	....	....	....

32 Add amounts in columns (c) and (d) and enter here . . . . **32** (_____)
33 Total small business corporation income or (loss). Combine amounts in columns (c) and (d), line 32. Enter here and include in line 37 . . . . **33**

| **Part III** | **Windfall Profit Tax Summary** |

34 Windfall Profit Tax Credit or Refund received in 1981 (see Instructions) **34**
35 Windfall Profit Tax withheld in 1981 (see Instructions) . . . . **35** (_____)
36 Combine amounts on lines 34 and 35. Enter here and include in line 37 . . . . **36**

| **Part IV** | **Summary** |

37 TOTAL income or (loss). Combine lines 25, 29, 31, 33, and 36. Enter here and on Form 1040, line 17 . ▶ **37**
38 Farmers and fishermen: Enter your share of gross farming and fishing income applicable to Parts I and II **38**

Income or Losses from Partnerships, Estates or Trusts, or Small Business Corporations

Part II of Schedule E covers income or loss from any partnership in which you are a partner or from an estate or trust of which you are a beneficiary. This is also the place to show any income (whether distributed or not) or loss from small-business corporations which have elected treatment under Subchapter S of the Internal Revenue Code. We are assuming that, in these complicated tax setups, you have professional advice to guide you.

You now total the income (or losses) of lines 25, 29, 31, 33 and 36 of Part III and also include this figure on line 17, form 1040.

Line 18: Farm Income or Loss

If you are a farmer, enter at line 18 of Form 1040 your profit or loss from farming as shown on separate Schedule F. This book is designed to help the wage-earner, salaried worker, and nonfarm businessperson, and therefore omits Schedule F.

Line 19: Unemployment Compensation

Unemployment compensation may be taxable to you if your adjusted gross income, including the unemployment benefits, exceeds $25,000 if you are married filing jointly, or $20,000 if you are not in this category. Here is the IRS official worksheet for figuring out whether any part of your unemployment insurance received during 1981, shown on line 19a, is taxable. The taxable portion, if any, is entered at line 19b.

To see if any of the unemployment compensation is taxable, fill in the following worksheet:

Check only one box

☐ **A.** Single—enter $20,000 on line 8 below.

☐ **B.** Married filing a joint return—enter $25,000 on line 8 below.

☐ **C.** Married not filing a joint return and lived with your spouse at any time during the year—enter –0– on line 8 below.

☐ **D.** Married not filing a joint return and DID NOT live with your spouse at any time during the year—enter $20,000 on line 8 below.

1. Total unemployment compensation from Form(s) 1099–UC . . _____
2. If you received an overpayment of unemployment compensation in 1981 and repaid it in 1981, enter the repayment here. Also write "repayment" and the amount you repaid in the margin of Form 1040 to the left of line 19a . . . . _____
3. Subtract line 2 from line 1 . . _____

4. Enter the total of the amounts on Form 1040, lines 7, 8e through 18, and 20 (do not include any unemployment compensation in this figure) . . . _____
5. Add lines 3 and 4 . . . . . _____
6. Enter the total of the amounts shown on Form 1040, lines 22 through 27 and 29 . . . . . _____
7. Subtract line 6 from line 5 . . _____
8. Enter { $20,000 if you checked box A or D, or $25,000 if you checked box B, or –0– if you checked box C } . _____
9. Subtract line 8 from line 7. If zero or less, stop here and enter –0– on Form 1040, line 19b . _____
10. Enter one-half (50%) of the amount on line 9 . . . . . _____
11. Taxable unemployment compensation. Enter the amount from line 3 or line 10, whichever is smaller. Also enter on Form 1040, line 19b. . . . . . _____

TAX TIP: Vacation-Home Expenses

Record and still mounting numbers of Americans across the U.S. own vacation homes which they use personally part of the time and rent out part of the time. You have a relatively simple rule for determining how much of your home maintenance and depreciation expenses you can deduct (in addition, of course, to deducting the entire total of your mortgage interest and property taxes).

If you, the owner, use your vacation home for more than two weeks or more than 10 percent of the rental time, whichever is the longer period, your deduction for maintenance and depreciation allocable to the rental period is limited to the amount of your rental income reduced by the property taxes and interest allocable to the rental period. The expenses allocable to the period are the same percentage of total expenses as the rental period is to the period of total use by the owner and the lessee.

For instance, if you use your vacation home for one month and lease it to a tenant for two months, then two-thirds of your various maintenance expenses, depreciation interest and taxes would be allocable to the rental period and one-third to your personal use.

These limitations on your deductions for maintenance and depreciation don't apply if your rental income gives you a profit for the entire year.

Also, if you rent out for less than 15 days a year, then you don't report either the rental income or the maintenance and depreciation expenses allocable to this brief rental period.

To illustrate how the rule works, say you own a vacation home that you use personally in June and rent out in July and August for $3,000. Your total annual costs for this home are: interest on a mortgage $1,200; property taxes $600; maintenance $600; utilities $300. A full year's depreciation is $1,200.

You have used the home for a longer period than the personal-use period specified in the rules because the month of June is longer than two weeks and longer than 10 percent of the two-month rental period. Your allocable deductions are limited as explained in the previous paragraphs.

Your gross rental of $3,000 for July and August is reduced by two-thirds of the $1,800 of property taxes and mortgage interest that is allocable to the rental period, or $1,200. That limits your maintenance and depreciation deductions to no more than $1,800.

Here, your maintenance expenses and depreciation total $2,100 ($600 plus $300 plus $1,200) of which two-thirds, or $1,400, is allocable to the rental period. Since

$1,400 doesn't exceed the $1,800 limit, you can deduct the $1,400. (If the allocable maintenance and depreciation had exceeded $1,800, you could have deducted only $1,800.) In addition to the $1,400 deduction, you also can deduct the full $1,800 of property taxes and interest, which always are deductible in full.

TAX TIP: Renting Out Your Home or Summer Home for Short Time Can Give Tax-Free Income

There are tough special rules limiting deductions for depreciation and maintenance expenses incurred where an owner's residence or vacation home is rented out for part of the year. But there is a special provision that can permit an owner to rent out his property for up to a two-week period during the year and have the entire gross rents treated as tax-free.

The law provides that when an owner's dwelling is rented for less than 15 days during the year, the entire gross rents are exempt. Of course, no deductions will then be allowed for maintenance expenses or depreciation.

If your home is in an area where some sporting, political, or other kind of event will send rents skyrocketing for a short period, the tax-free nature of the rents could be an incentive for renting out part or all of your home.

Line 20: Other Income

This is a catchall line for listing any other kinds of miscellaneous income. Line 20 is for any other type of miscellaneous income (for which you must state the nature and source of the income). You report your self-employment income on Schedule C or Schedule F, and Schedule SE, if applicable.

Where employees receive reimbursement from their employers in excess of their employee expenses, the excess reimbursement is entered at line 20 as income from other sources.

Before filling out this part, make sure that the income is taxable. While you may consider the receipts as income, that doesn't make them taxable. However, in general, your income will be taxable unless expressly exempt.

Q. I received $30 in jury fees in 1981. Are these taxable?

A. Yes.

Q. In addition to receiving a fee for my jury duty, I was also paid a mileage allowance to cover the cost of using my car to get from home to the courthouse and back. Is this mileage allowance also part of my income?

A. The Treasury said it was, but the Tax Court held that it wasn't income.

Q. I bought a new car in 1981 and received a rebate from the auto manufacturer. Is this taxable income?

A. No. The usual manufacturer's rebate given to the public to stimulate the sales of cars in the then-depressed market is not income, but merely reduces your cost of the car.

Q. I paid $10 for lottery tickets and won $1,000. Do I have to report the $990 "profit"?

A. Yes. If you bought losing tickets during the year, then if you itemize your deductions, you can deduct the cost of your losing tickets, but not more than the amount of your lottery and other gambling winnings.

Q. My lodge ran a raffle, which I won. The prize included merchandise that had a retail value of $1,000. Do I include the retail value?

A. The rule is that you include the winnings at their *fair market value.* It isn't clear whether this means retail selling price. It's advisable to claim a value less than its retail price, especially if you didn't particularly want the items for yourself.

Q. I won several items of merchandise on a television quiz program. Are these also taxed?

A. Yes. The rules applying to raffle winnings also cover winnings on TV or radio quizzes, door prizes, etc.

Q. During 1981 my husband died and I received $10,000 on his life-insurance policy. Isn't this exempt?

A. Yes. The proceeds of life insurance paid because of the death of the insured are not taxable except when the policy was previously transferred for a valuable consideration.

Q. During 1981, I received gifts of $200 from members of my family. Do I have to include the $200?

A. No. Gifts are not taxable income.

Q. As a result of the death of one of my relatives, I received a bequest of $5,000. Is this taxable?

A. No. Bequests or inheritances are not subject to income tax.

Q. My endowment policy matured and I received $2,500. Is this also exempt?

A. No, since it wasn't paid because of the death of the insured. However, you are taxed only on the excess of the $2,500 over the cost of the policy to you. This is generally the total of your premiums less any dividends used to reduce the premiums and less any previous payments received.

Q. My husband died in 1981 and his firm gave me a death benefit of $4,000. Is this additional salary which I must include in income?

A. No. Payments made to the beneficiaries of a deceased employee by an employer because of the employee's death are exempt up to $5,000. However, this does not apply to any amount which your husband had a right to receive had he lived.

Q. I received $3,800 in 1981 in Social Security benefits. How much of this is taxable?

A. None. Social Security benefits are exempt whether received because of age, disability, or as a dependent of a qualified worker.

Q. During 1981 I was unemployed for several weeks and received $500 in unemployment-insurance payments from the state. Is this taxable?

A. In general, if your unemployment benefits plus other adjusted gross income exceed $25,000 if you are married filing jointly (without dollar limit if you file separately), or $20,000 in the case of all other individuals, part of your unemployment insurance may be taxable. (See line 20.)

Q. I received $1,500 in 1981 under a so-called guaranteed-annual-wage plan. The payments were received from a company-financed supplemental-unemployment-benefit fund. Is this amount exempt?

A. No. These payments are taxable.

Q. While unemployed in 1981 I received unemployment benefits of $1,250 from my union. Do I include these payments in income?

A. The Treasury says you include these as well as strike and lockout benefits.

While the Supreme Court upheld a lower-court decision treating strike benefits paid by a union to a nonunion striker as nontaxable gifts, this was an unusual case for several reasons and has not been followed in the more usual situation.

Q. I receive various payments from a child-placing agency as a foster parent. How do I report these payments?

A. If you are paid by a nonprofit child-placing agency for food, shelter, clothing, medical expenses, etc., for the child, you report as income any amount by which the reimbursement exceeds your expenses. To the extent that you are not reimbursed for such expenses and pay them out of your own pocket, you deduct the unreimbursed portion as a charitable contribution if you take itemized deductions.

If you also receive compensation for your service as a foster parent in addition to reimbursement for expenses, you report as income the entire amount you receive in excess of your expenses. Any unreimbursed expenses you pay out of your own pocket are deductible as business expenses.

Q. I received $800 in public-assistance payments in 1981. Are these taxable?

A. No.

Q. I received a $750 scholarship. Must this be included in income?

A. No. A scholarship at an eductional institution that has a regular faculty, curriculum, and a regularly organized body of students in attendance is generally exempt.

Q. I received a $500 fellowship, which requires me to teach a few hours a week. Is this exempt?

A. No. You generally can't exclude amounts received for teaching, research, or other services even though the award is designated as a fellowship or scholarship. There is an exception, though, if you are a candidate for a degree and the part-time employment is required of all candidates for the degree.

Q. I received $200 to cover my teaching expenses in connection with my scholarship. Is this also tax-free?

A. Yes, if the expenses were necessary to carry out the purpose of the scholarship, and you actually spent the money for that purpose.

Q. After my graduation, I was given a $5,000 fellowship to do research. Is this exempt?

A. If you are not a candidate for a degree, your exemption is limited to $300 times the number of months for which you received the grant during 1981. However, you can also exclude any amounts received for travel, etc.

There is an overall limitation of 36 months for a taxpayer.

In addition, in order to be exempt when you are not working for a degree, the grant must come from the United States or a state, territory, or possession, or a political subdivision, or the District of Columbia, or from a nonprofit organization operated exclusively for religious, charitable, scientific, testing for public safety, literary, or educational purposes, or for the prevention of cruelty to children or animals, and must not be conditioned on coming to work for the grantor.

Q. As a student nurse, I received Public Health Service awards. Are these taxable?

A. No. They are treated as scholarship grants.

Q. As an intern in a hospital, I received $10,000. Is this a fellowship grant which is not taxable?

A. This type of payment to interns and residents has been held by IRS and various court decisions to be taxable.

Q. I receive benefits paid by the Veterans Administration. Are these tax-exempt?

A. Yes.

Q. I have an accident-and-health policy for which I pay the full premiums. I was out sick during 1981 and under the policy I received $800. Is this $800 taxable?

A. No.

Q. Under an insurance policy that I own, I received $20,000 for the loss of the use of an arm in an accident. Is this taxable?

A. No. Payments received for a permanent loss, or the loss of the use of a member or function of the body, or for permanent disfigurement, are not taxed.

Q. I sued for and was paid damages for an injury to me. Is this income exempt?

A. Yes.

Q. I received $500 in 1981 under the state's workmen's-compensation act. Is this exempt?

A. Yes. Payments for personal injuries or sickness under a workmen's-compensation act are exempt.

Q. I received $200 under the state's workmen's-compensation act, but I had to turn this in to my employer, who paid me my regular salary. Does this mean I lose the benefit of exemption on the $200?

A. No. You claim $200 of your pay as representing tax-exempt workmen's compensation.

Q. Under my employer's health plan, he pays employees a certain amount of the actual medical expenses which they incur for themselves, their wives, and their dependents. He reimbursed me for part of the medical expenses I incurred for myself, my wife, my dependent daughter, and my dependent mother. Is this reimbursement income to me?

A. No. It's tax-exempt. But you'll have to reduce your deductible medical expenses by this reimbursement. Or, if you deducted the medical expenses in a previous year, the reimbursement you receive from the employer this year is taxable to you.

Q. I had hospital expenses during the year for which I collected from two health-insurance policies. My total insurance payments came to more than my actual hospital expenses. Is the amount of insurance payments over my actual hospital expenses exempt?

A. Yes, says the Treasury, if you paid the premiums on both policies. But to the extent that the excess is allocable to insurance paid by your employer, the excess is taxable income. For instance, suppose your hospital expenses were $800 and you collected $500 on a health-insurance policy for which you pay and another $500 from a health-insurance coverage provided by your employer. The $200 in excess of your $800 actual expense is attributable 50 percent to your employer's coverage ($500 of the total $1000 collected). Here the Treasury says you report $100 of your excess insurance (50 percent of $200) as taxable income. The other $100 of excess insurance is exempt.

Q. My fire insurance policy provides for a special payment to cover additional living expenses in case my home should be destroyed by fire. Would that special payment be tax exempt?

A. Yes, if they are above-normal living expenses of you and members of your household resulting from destruction of your principal residence.

TAX TIP: Which Unemployment Benefits Are Exempt and Which Are Not?

The following unemployment benefits are exempt from income tax, so you don't include them in your income, *except as explained at line 19* (see page 56):

Payments made by a state from the Federal Unemployment Trust Fund, or under the Railroad Unemployment Insurance Act; public-assistance or welfare-benefit payments such as Aid to Dependent Children; payments made by state welfare agencies to participants in work-retraining programs if they are not greater than public welfare benefits the participants would otherwise receive; amounts received from a voluntary unemployment fund established privately or by a union, up to the amount the worker contributed but payments received in excess of a worker's personal contribution are taxable; welfare payments in cash, food, or other items that are not directly attributable to services performed; veterans' benefits for education, training, or subsistence from Veterans Administration.

The following kinds of unemployment benefits *are not* exempt from income tax, so you must include them in your income:

Payments from a company-financed supplemental unemployment fund, or similar amounts paid by a former employer; union benefits paid to members from regular dues set aside for this purpose; wages guaranteed under a collective-bargaining agreement for periods of unemployment; severance pay and lump-sum payments for cancellation of employment contracts; payments received for services performed in a state welfare-agency work-relief program.

KEYNOTE: Barter Transactions

The IRS is concerned about the failure of individuals to report income when they exchange their services for the service of other individuals. One evidence of this concern is a Revenue Ruling that dealt with the following situations:

Situation 1. In return for personal legal services performed by a lawyer for a house painter, the house painter painted the lawyer's personal residence. Both the lawyer and the house painter were members of a barter club made up entirely of professional or trade persons. The club actually furnishes its members with a directory of members and the services they provide. Members contact each other directly and negotiate the value of the services to be performed.

IRS ruled that members of the barter club must include in income the value of the services they receive in exchange for the services they perform. The lawyer must therefore include in his gross income the fair market value of the services performed by the house painter, and the house painter must include in his gross income the value of the services performed by the lawyer.

Situation 2. The owner of an apartment building received a work of art created by a professional artist in return for the rent-free use of an apartment for six months by the artist. The IRS ruled that the owner of the building must include in his income the fair market value of the work of art, and the artist must include in his gross income the fair rental value of the apartment.

Thus, if you made barter deals, the IRS will be looking for income to be reported.

Other Income Which Isn't Taxable

Allowances received from husband, parent, etc.; auto-manufacturer and dealer rebates to customers; board and lodging furnished by employer on his premises for his convenience; commissions advanced on drawing account as a loan which must be repaid; damages for personal injuries; employer's payments under employee's health-and-accident-insurance plan; gifts; group accident-and health-insurance premiums paid by employer; group life-insurance premiums paid by employer (when policy is straight term) up to $50,000 of coverage; household allowance, husbands and wives; increase in value of property (not realized by sale, etc.); inheritances; life insurance—dividends on unmatured policies and proceeds on death of insured; living quarters for officers and personnel, armed forces; principal of repaid loans; parents' allowances to children; pensions to soldiers' widows; supper money received from employer, according to old Treasury ruling; assistance payments made on behalf of mortgagors to mortgagees under contracts entered into by the Department of Housing and Urban Development (Section 235 of the National Housing Act).

Servicemen: Allowances for quarters, subsistence, and uniforms; disability pay; family allowance paid by government; mustering-out pay. All other lump-sum payments are ordinarily taxable.

Veterans: Autos received by disabled veterans; benefits paid by Veterans Administration; disability allowances and pensions; family allowances paid by government; government insurance proceeds and dividends; pensions (but retirement pay is taxable); readjustment payments; specially designed homes granted to paraplegic veterans.

TAX TIP: *Medicare Benefits and Premiums for Elderly*

There are two types of insurance coverage under Medicare:

1. *Hospital* benefits for all persons over 65.
2. *Doctor bills*, which is available only for those who paid the monthly premiums for coverage.

Hospital benefits are never included in the individual's income. Doctor-bill benefits are also generally not included in the individual's income, *except* to the extent that the benefits are attributable to (and up to the amount of) monthly premiums that were deducted as a medical expense for earlier years.

The monthly premiums paid for doctor-bill coverage qualify as deductible medical-insurance payments.

In determining whether anyone contributed more than half of the elderly individual's support for purposes of claiming him as a dependent, both the hospital and the doctor benefits are excluded in figuring support.

Neither the hospital nor the doctor-bill payments have any bearing in figuring an individual retirement credit because they aren't considered to be pension or annuities.

Line 21: Total Income

Put the total of lines 7 through 20 on line 21.

ADJUSTMENTS TO INCOME

Adjustments to Income (See Instructions on page 11)					
	22 Moving expense (attach Form 3903 or 3903F)	22			
	23 Employee business expenses (attach Form 2106) . . .	23			
	24 Payments to an IRA (enter code from page 11 ....) .	24			
	25 Payments to a Keogh (H.R. 10) retirement plan	25			
	26 Interest penalty on early withdrawal of savings	26			
	27 Alimony paid	27			
	28 Disability income exclusion (attach Form 2440)	28			
	29 Other adjustments—see page 12 ▶ _____	29			
	30 Total adjustments. Add lines 22 through 29 . . . . ▶		30		

KEYNOTE: Adjustments to Income

On lines 22-30 of Form 1040, you take certain deductions which are allowed, regardless of whether you itemize your personal deductions on separate Schedule A or use the flat standard deduction instead of itemized personal deductions.

These deductions are called adjustments and consist of moving expenses (Form 3903 or Form 3903F), employee business expenses (Form 2106 or statement), payments to a Keogh (H.R. 10) retirement plan, payments to an individual retirement arrangement (IRA), the forfeited-interest penalty for premature withdrawal of a term deposit, alimony paid, and disability-income exclusion and other adjustments. Each adjustment is computed separately and the total of each of the eight adjustments is entered at the appropriate line (22 through 29). These separate lines are then totaled in line 30. Each adjustment is now explained separately, beginning with moving expenses.

Line 22: Moving Expenses

The first category of deductible adjustments is moving expenses, on line 22.

Reasonable moving expenses paid by an *employee* or *self-employed person* in connection with employment are deductible if they meet the complicated requirements described below. I will give you the highlights of these rules here, but if you then think you are entitled to some moving-expense deductions, make your claim for this deduction on Form 3903, which you get from your local Internal Revenue Service office.

There are two main types of deductible moving expenses, (1) *direct* and (2) *indirect.* The chief difference between them is that there is no dollar limit on the amount of deduction for reasonable *direct* moving expenses, while there are dollar limits on the amount you can deduct for *indirect* expenses.

Direct moving expenses include (1) the cost of moving household goods and personal effects (including crating and packing) from the old to the new residence, plus (2) the transportation expenses of the taxpayer and his family (including meals and lodging) while traveling from the old to the new residence.

Indirect moving expenses include:

1. If an employee has already obtained employment at his new job site, or if a self-employed person has already made substantial arrangements to begin working at the new site, the cost of any round trips (including meals and lodging) made by the taxpayer and the members of his household principally to find a new residence.

2. Cost of meals and lodging for the taxpayer and members of his household during the period of 30 consecutive days after getting the new employment and while occupying temporary quarters (whether still looking for, or waiting to move into, a new residence).

3. Costs of selling old and buying new residence, or terminating old lease, including attorneys' fees, escrow fees, appraisal fees, real-estate-agent commissions, title costs, and "points" paid for services. (To the extent that you deduct these house-selling expenses as moving expenses, you can't use them to reduce any profit from sale of your old residence.)

Direct moving expenses can be deducted only if (1) the employee or self-employed person moves to a new principal job site that's at least 35 miles farther from the old residence than the old job site was; and (2) during the 12-month period after arriving at the new job location the employee is a full-time employee for at least 39 weeks; or if a self-employed person moves, he performs full-time services for at least 78 weeks within a 24-month period following arrival at his new work location. There are exceptions to these 39- and 78-week requirements in case of disability, discharge, etc.

Indirect moving expenses are deductible only if they meet both of the requirements listed above for deducting direct moving expense, but the *amount* of deduction for *indirect* expenses is limited as follows: (1) no more than $1,500 in total for trips to find a new house before moving and for temporary living expenses at the new job location; (2) no more than $3,000 for the expenses of selling, buying, or leasing a residence, *less* the amount allowed under (1).

Any reimbursement for moving expenses received by an employee or self-employed person must be reported in income. The recipient then deducts the moving expenses he is entitled to under the rules that I have summarized above.

When to Deduct the Moving Expense

The individual must deduct the qualified moving expenses in the year he pays or incurs them. *If he has already met the 39- or 78-week requirements* (which I explained above) by the April 15, 1982 date for filing his 1981 tax return, there's no problem. He deducts his qualified 1981 moving expenses on his 1981 return. *If he hasn't yet met the 39- or 78-week requirement* by April 15, 1982, but there is still time left within the 12- or 24-month period to meet the requirement, then he can do one of the following two things: (1) He can deduct the 1981 expenses on his 1981 return. But if he thereafter fails to meet the requirement on time, he will have to report the same amount as income on his 1982 (or '83 if self-employed) return. Or (2) he can hold off taking the deduction on his 1981 return, wait until he meets the requirement, then file an amended return for 1981 claiming the deduction.

Where you use your own car for deductible moving expenses, you can figure your actual costs or instead figure your costs at a flat nine cents a mile.

Any part of the moving expenses paid for by your employer must be shown on line 7, Form 1040, as part of wages, etc. Your employer should give you Form 4782 and include the amount on your Form W-2.

Line 23: Employee Business Expenses

The next class of deductible adjustments includes various kinds of employee business expenses on line 23.

You can deduct certain business expenses that were not paid by your employer. Travel, transportation (but not commuting to and from work), and meals and lodging are deductible on line 23 by using Form 2106, even if you don't itemize your deductions on Schedule A. All other business expenses such as union or professional dues, tools, uniforms, materials, and telephone calls can only be deducted if you itemize deductions on Schedule A at lines 31-32. Outside salespersons claim their business expenses on line 23 by using Form 2106.

Any reimbursements or expense allowances you receive from your employer for expenses you pay or incur for travel, transportation, entertainment, and other ordinary and necessary business expenses in connection with your employment must be reported by you on Form 2106, or in a statement attached to your return, unless your employer requires you to account to him for these expenses.

If the reimbursements exceed the expenses, you enter the excess of reimbursement at line 20 of Form 1040, under "Other Income." If the deductible expenses exceed the reimbursements, here's how you deduct them: Any excess of travel expenses away from home overnight, transportation expenses, and all business expenses incurred by an outside salesman are included here as an adjustment. To the extent that the excess consists of other unreimbursed employee expenses, it is deductible only on line 31 of separate Schedule A under "Miscellaneous Deductions," but only if you are itemizing your deductions rather than using the standard deduction.

If you account to your employer for your expenses on his behalf, you don't have to include the reimbursement or allowance he gave you as income in your return, and of course you don't deduct the expenses for which you were reimbursed. However, if your reimbursements or allowances exceeded your expenses, you must include the excess as income on line 20 of Form 1040 under "Other Income."

Q. My employer pays me an expense allowance while I travel on business for him, but my actual expenses are less than the allowance I received, and I give my employer a full accounting of my actual expenses. How do I handle this?

A. Report the excess of your expense allowance over your actual expenses at line 20 of Form 1040, under "Other Income." You don't have to report the expense allowance you receive to the extent it was used for employee expenses for which you accounted to your employer.

Q. I spent $200 to entertain several customers for my employer. I gave him a voucher explaining how I spent the money and he reimbursed me. Do I deduct the $200 I spent?

A. No, you don't include the $200 reimbursement as income, nor do you deduct your $200 expense.

Q. My employer requires me to give him a voucher for expenses. Is this an "accounting" to my employer?

A. Accounting to your employer means that you must give him an expense account or other written statement showing the business nature and amounts of your expenses, broken down into broad categories such as transportation, meals and lodging while away from home overnight, entertainment, and other business expenses.

Also, your employer must require the following detailed information from you for:

Travel expenses—Date, place and cost of travel; number of days away from home overnight; itemized listing of total costs incurred for meals, lodging, cab fares, telephone, etc., plus receipts for large expenditures.

Entertainment expenses—Identify the persons entertained by name, title, or otherwise, so that it establishes the business nature of the expense; place, nature and cost of the entertainment; reason why it was necessary.

Your written voucher or other statement should be subject to examination and approval by someone directly or indirectly responsible to your employer for proper checking of expense accounts. You shouldn't be in a position to approve your own account.

If your employer's accounting procedures and requirements are not adequate, the Treasury may call on you for information about your expense account even though you accounted for your reimbursed expenses.

Q. What about mileage and per diem allowances in lieu of subsistence, and similar fixed allowances for ordinary and necessary expenses on behalf of the employer? Do I have to account to my employer for these in order to qualify under the rule that says I don't have to report reimbursed expenses for which I accounted to my employer?

A. If the fixed amount he pays you is in accordance with a reasonable business practice which the Internal Revenue Service approves, that in itself is considered an accounting to your employer. You don't have to submit anything to him in writing.

The Internal Revenue Service says that it approves any fixed allowance as reasonable if it meets the following tests: For travel (including meals and lodging) and transportation within the continental U.S., any fixed mileage allowance not exceeding 20 cents a mile and/or a per diem allowance in lieu of subsistence not over the greater of $44 a day or the U. S. government per diem for that locality. This assumes you can prove the time, place, and business purpose of the travel. The $44 per diem doesn't cover the cost of taxis, phones, and telegrams. These can be deducted in addition to the $44 per day.

Any fixed allowances over the established amounts will not be considered automatically accounted for to your employer unless he has had these allowances specifically approved by the Internal Revenue Service.

Q. I charge many of my expenses as a salesman through credit cards that are paid directly by my employer. Are these considered reimbursements for which I must account, although no money passes from my employer to me?

A. Yes. The amounts paid by your employer directly or *indirectly* for expenses you incur on his behalf are considered reimbursement. These credit charges which you incur and he pays are in the class of indirect reimbursements. If you don't account for them to your employer, you must report them as explained above.

Q. I work as a salesman for my father. Can I also avoid reporting the details of my expense reimbursement and my expense outlays as a salesman by accounting for these expenses to my father?

A. You can, but it won't help you as much as it will other salesmen. The Treasury says that when the employee is *related* to the employer in certain ways, then even if the employee accounts for reimbursed expenses and doesn't show the reimbursement or itemize the expenses on his return, it may call on him for the supporting information. The Treasury wouldn't do this if you were an unrelated employee.

This rule applies if you are an employee of a brother, sister, husband, wife, father, grandfather, child, grandchild, or corporation of which you own, directly or indirectly, more than 50 percent of the value of the stock.

Q. What about expenses I incur as an employee on behalf of my employer for which I don't have to account? For example, my employer gives me certain weekly allowances for entertaining customers, etc., and doesn't require me to tell him how I spend it.

A. You must attach to your return a statement showing the following information: your occupation, the total expense allowances received from your employer (direct and indirect), the number of days you were away from home on business, and your expenses as an employee—broken into such broad categories as transportation, meals and lodging while away from home overnight, entertainment, and other business expenses.

Q. The expense account I get from my employer doesn't cover all my expenses. I account to my employer for all my expenses, and I want to deduct the expenses I pay out of my own pocket. Can I limit my detailed reporting of expenses on my attached statement just to the part I pay without reimbursement?

A. If you want to deduct any unreimbursed employee expense, no matter how small the amount, you must attach to your return exactly the same kind of statement described in the preceding answer. In other words, you must show all reimbursements to you and all credit charges to your employer, even though properly accounted for, and all expenses.

In this case, you may find it wiser to forget a deduction for your unreimbursed-expense outlay—assuming it isn't too great an amount. By omitting this deduction, you can avoid giving details on your reimbursed expenses.

Q. I am an outside salesman. Where do I deduct my expenses for which I don't account?

A. If you have a full-time job soliciting business for your employer away from his place of business, you are an outside salesman. And outside salesmen can deduct all their ordinary and necessary business expenses, except meals, on Form 2106 as part of the adjustments deductible on line 23 of Form 1040. This is so even if you don't itemize your other deductions and you use the optional standard deduction. The cost of meals is deductible only if eaten away from home overnight on business. This deduction is also taken here.

Q. I am an insurance debit agent. Am I an outside salesman?

A. No.

Q. My job is to make deliveries as well as sell. Am I an outside salesman?

A. You are not if your principal job is to make deliveries or perform a service of some kind.

MINI-GUIDE: Your Guide to Expense-Account Deductions

To be deductible, your business entertainment expenses must not only be "ordinary and necessary," but *also* be either (1) *"directly related"* to the active conduct of your trade or business *or* (2) *"associated with"* the active conduct of your trade or business, if the entertainment directly precedes or follows a business discussion.

Grasp this vital point immediately: *The "directly related" test is exceedingly tough and you should concentrate on qualifying your entertainment deductions under the "associated with" test.*

You'll find, I believe, that *90 percent or more of your business entertainment will be deductible, despite the tough rules,* if you plan properly to come under the "associated with" test.

Here's the key to the deduction. Make sure that you had a "substantial" and "bona fide" business discussion with your customer, prospect, client, etc., directly before or after the entertainment. You need not have clinched an actual deal at this discussion as long as you look for some possibility of income or other benefit from the discussion. This rule holds whether your aim is to build up a new business contact or whether you want only to encourage the continuation of an existing business relationship.

How close together must the entertainment and discussion be? The Treasury says it's all right if they took place the same day. It's even willing to accept entertainment the evening before or after the day of the business discussion if your business associates have come from out of town.

With a worthwhile business discussion directly before or after the entertainment, you have qualified your entertainment for deduction under the "associated with" test—regardless of how noisy the entertainment was, regardless of the fact that you didn't discuss any business whatsoever during the entertainment, etc.

This underlines the main practical reason why you shouldn't try to rely on the "directly related" test for your business entertainment expense deductions. That test requires you to engage actively in a business discussion *during the entertainment period itself.* The Treasury points out, and understandably, that night clubs, theatres, sporting events, and social cocktail gatherings are highly unlikely spots for the necessary discussions. To avoid any hassles over this aspect, it makes much more sense, if possible, to come under the "associated with" test.

If you are a businessman who couldn't get in a substantial business meeting before or after the entertainment, here's what the Treasury insists you must show in order to deduct your entertainment outlays as a "directly related" expense:

1. You had more than a general expectation of deriving income, or other specific business benefits (excluding goodwill), at some indefinite future time, *and*:

2. You engaged in business during the period of entertainment, *and*:

3. The principal character of the combined business and entertainment was the transaction of business.

Quiet Meals

You should have no trouble in deducting the cost of taking your business associates, customers, clients, etc., to lunch, dinner, breakfast, or cocktails.

This is the so-called "quiet business meal," which is officially exempt from the strict expense-account rules. Two things are required to insure deduction of a quiet business meal.

First, *the person whose tab you picked up must have a business relationship to you* which shows that you were entertaining him for business, not social, reasons. For instance, if you show that he was an actual or prospective customer or client, supplier, employee, agent, partner, or professional advisor, that will do.

Here are Treasury examples of business associates who may be entertained:

A manufacturer of products can entertain his retailers.

A salesman can buy lunch for a purchasing agent of a prospective customer.

A life-insurance agent can buy lunch for a client.

A new hotel or theatrical production can wine or dine business representatives and civic leaders.

Second, *you must have had your meal and drinks* in a restaurant, hotel dining room, eating club, cocktail lounge, or similar place *where there were no noisy or distracting influences such as a floor show.* That's where the "quiet" comes from in the quiet-business-meal rule, and most eating places will meet this test.

Once you have had this quiet business meal set up, *you don't even have to have discussed business at the meal* in order to deduct the cost.

Let me repeat, you can actually *talk about anything* other than business and still get your deduction. That's how liberal this rule is. Also, the Internal Revenue Service Commissioner says that you can deduct the full cost of your own meal as well (except when the meals begin to add up to substantial amounts for yourself).

One warning: The Treasury doesn't like the "reciprocal" meal game—governed by the unwritten rule that two or more business associates take turns in picking up their daily lunch check so that their lunches are deductible all year long. This is considered an abuse of the quiet-business-meal rule which the Treasury will try to stop.

Combined Business-Pleasure Trip

The rule here depends on whether your trip is in the U. S. or abroad.

If it is in the U. S., the entire *transportation* cost of the combined business-pleasure trip (including meals while actually traveling) is deductible if you took the trip *primarily* for *business* reasons.

If it is outside the U. S. and lasts for a week or less, or if it is for more than a week but your personal activities take up less than 25 percent of the total trip, then you can deduct your entire transportation costs if the trip was primarily for business.

But if the combined business-pleasure trip is *outside* the U. S. and the total trip lasted more than one week *and* 25 percent or more of the total trip time was for personal activities, then the traveler's expense deduction for his travel costs is limited in proportion to the time spent on business. For instance, suppose you flew to London, spent half of your trip time on business there and half in Paris relaxing. If the trip lasted more than a week, you could theoretically deduct only half your round-trip plane fare instead of the full amount as before.

But the Treasury has adopted such liberal rules for applying this rule that most of the business travelers described above *will still get a deduction for the full fare* instead of only half.

This is because the Treasury says it will let you, a business traveler, deduct your *entire* transportation expense *even if* your trip outside the U. S. lasted more than a week and 25 percent or more was for personal reasons, if either (1) you didn't have substantial control over arranging the business trip, or (2) getting a chance at a personal vacation wasn't a major consideration in your decision to make the trip. *Either one is enough to get the full deduction.*

To make this rule even more liberal, the Treasury will automatically consider you to lack substantial control over your business trip if you traveled for your employer under a reimbursement or other expense-allowance arrangement.

There's just one limit on this very favorable automatic consideration. It doesn't apply to employees owning over 10 percent of their employer corporation's stock, or who are otherwise related to the employer or who are "managing executives" of their employer firms. For this purpose a "managing executive" is an employee who can decide whether he needs to make a business trip without anyone else in the firm really able to say "no" to him.

If you are a managing executive or an over-10-percent stockholder, or an employee otherwise related to your employer, you don't necessarily have to shave down your travel deduction on trips outside the U. S. under the one-week—25-percent rule. The Treasury simply says that you aren't *automatically* entitled to the full deductions if your employer reimbursed you for a business trip, as other employees would be. But if you can *prove* that you either didn't have the substantial control *or* that enjoying a vacation wasn't a major consideration in deciding on the trip, you too can deduct your entire round-trip transportation costs, even if you were away more than one week and spent 25 percent or more of the time on vacation.

Business Gifts

Deductions for business gifts to individuals generally are limited to $25 per donee each year. This covers business gifts which you make to your customers, your business associates, your clients, your employees (except that the employee limit is $400 for gifts recognizing length of service, safety achievements or productivity), and any others for whom you could properly deduct business gifts.

This will not prevent you from making gifts as large as you wish, but it limits your income-tax deduction to no more than $25 for each person to whom you made business gifts during the year.

The $25 limit is figured by what the gift cost you, not what it's worth to the person to whom you gave it.

Club Dues

Dues you paid to country clubs, golf clubs, athletic clubs, hunting and fishing clubs—in fact, to any social or athletic club—must meet two tests in order to be deductible.

First, you, the taxpayer, must have used the club primarily, meaning more than 50 percent of the time, for the furtherance of your business.

Second, if the club was used over 50 percent for your business purposes, you can deduct only that portion of your dues "directly related" to the active conduct of your business. Basically, the idea is that you had to talk serious business with your client or customer, not just have a general goodwill discussion, in order to qualify as "directly related." There's one important exception to this, explained below.

If you treated your business associate or customer or client to lunch or dinner in the club's restaurant or dining room, *you come under the famous "quiet meal" rule*, which doesn't even require that you actually discuss business at the meal. This rule not only entitles you to deduct the cost of the meal and drinks, but it also entitles you to treat the meal as a "directly related" expense for which you can deduct an allocable portion of your club dues (assuming you used the club more than 50 percent for business over the entire year).

Dues paid to Kiwanis, Lions, Rotary, Civilian, or other business clubs, or to bar, medical, or other professional organizations need not meet the tough tests for deduction. They are deductible if they qualify as ordinary and necessary business expenses, as they generally will.

Wives

In at least *one very common situation, the cost of entertaining spouses will definitely be deductible.* (Here is the exact wording of official Treasury Questions and Answers 27 and 28, which permits the deduction.)

"*27. Question:* If a taxpayer entertains a business customer under circumstances where the cost of entertaining the customer is an ordinary and necessary business expense and is not disallowed under the new rules, and the customer's wife joins the taxpayer and the customer during the entertainment because it is impractical under the circumstances to entertain the customer without his wife, is the cost of entertaining the customer's wife deductible as an ordinary and necessary business expense?

"*Answer:* Yes. Such a case might arise, for example, if the customer was from out of town and had his wife traveling with him.

"*28. Question:* Assuming the same facts as in the preceding question and answer, but, in addition the taxpayer's wife joins them during the entertainment because the customer's wife was present, would the cost of entertainment allocable to the taxpayer's wife be considered an ordinary and necessary expense?

"*Answer:* Yes."

Q. My boss regularly sends me on errands to pick up items for the office. Do I have to treat these as reimbursed expenses?

A. No. Even if you don't account for them to your employer, you don't include as income the reimbursement or deduct as expenses the outlays for office expenses, errand expenses, and other incidental expenses for your employer for which you are reimbursed.

Q. I paid an employment agency the fee for placing me in a new job. After I had worked for a while, my employer reimbursed me for the fee I paid. Is this taxable to me?

A. Yes. Not only is it taxable income, but your employer must also withhold income tax and payroll taxes from the reimbursement. You, of course, can deduct your payment of the agency fee you paid. (The net result is to cut down your take-home pay by the payroll and withholding taxes your employer has to take out of your reimbursement.)

Q. My job requires me to wear special clothing. Can I deduct the cost of buying and maintaining these clothes?

A. The Treasury feels that the cost of maintenance of work clothing is generally a personal expense and therefore, not deductible. But if your job specifically requires special apparel or equipment as a condition of your employment, and they aren't adaptable to general or continued use in place of ordinary clothing, you can deduct the cost and maintenance of these items.

Unless you are reimbursed for these expenses, you can deduct them on line 31 of separate Schedule A, under "Miscellaneous Deductions," only if you itemize your deductions.

The Treasury allows deductions for special apparel and equipment required by police officers, firemen, letter carriers, nurses, and ballplayers. Also deductible are uniforms worn by transportation employees (rail, bus, air, etc.) if used solely on the job. But they are not deductible if snap buttons come off the uniforms, enabling them to be put to general use. Theatrical clothing and accessories used by professional musicians and entertainers also are deductible if used only on their jobs.

The white caps, shirts, jackets, and overalls (and regular work shoes) worn by painters aren't deductible even if the union requires you to wear them. Also, blue work clothes worn by a welder at his foreman's request aren't deductible.

Protective clothing required on certain jobs—such as safety shoes and helmets—or work gloves, oil clothes, and rubber boots such as those worn by commercial fishermen are deductible.

Q. Is my service uniform deductible?

A. Not if you are on full-time active duty in the armed forces. But if you are a reservist and are legally limited to wearing your uniform only while performing reserve duties, you can deduct the cost, to the extent it isn't reimbursed, at line 31, separate Schedule A, if you itemize your deductions. You must reduce your deduction by any nontaxable allowance you receive for uniforms.

Q. Can I deduct tools, union dues, etc.?

A. Yes. You can deduct small tools and supplies, union dues related to your job, fees to an employment agency for getting your job, subscriptions to professional journals related to your business or profession, and the cost of periodic physical exams required by your employer to show that you are fit to hold your job.

If unreimbursed, you deduct these expenses at line 30 or 31, separate Schedule A, if you itemize your deductions.

Nondeductible Employee Expenses

The following expenses incurred by employees are nondeductible:

Cost of commuting to and from work, entertainment expenses not required by your job, bar-exam fees and incidental expenses of securing admission to the bar, accounting-certificate fees, medical and dental license fees, and campaign expenses.

KEYNOTE: *The Employee's Office-at-Home Deduction*

If you are an employee who performs part of your job in your house or apartment, it's likely that you are barred from deducting any part of your house or apartment expenses as office-at-home expenses.

What causes the trouble is that you cannot get any deduction at all for an office at home unless you use it for one of the specific business purposes listed below.

1. As your principal place of business; or:

2. As a place of business used by your patients, clients, or customers in meeting or dealing with you in the normal course of your trade or business. (There are also several other purposes, but of a much more limited nature.)

If you are an employee, your business purpose in using your home for either *1* or *2* above must be "for the convenience of your employer."

If you are an outside salesman or other employee who works away from your employer's office location and you are expected by your employer to work out of your own home and keep your own necessary business records, you should have no difficulty in meeting these provisions of the new rules.

But even if you use your office-at-home for one of these acceptable purposes, you cannot take a deduction unless you meet two or more requirements.

Specifically, to deduct a portion of your home expenses (other than your normal deductions for interest and taxes), you must use a portion of your residence both on a *regular basis* and *exclusively* for one of the acceptable purposes.

The IRS claims that in order to qualify, an office-at-home must be a room or an area separated from the rest of the room. But the Tax Court held that a separate undivided portion of a room can qualify. Thus where a college professor had part of his bedroom furnished with a desk, chair, two file cabinets, and three bookcases, where he did his college related work, this part of the bedroom could qualify as a "portion of his home." But the court warned that where there is no physical separation, the court would be more critical in determining whether there was really a separate though unmarked area.

Which Expenses Are Deductible?

If the employee qualifies for an office-at-home deduc-

tion, he can deduct an allocable portion of his rent, gas, electricity, etc. Depreciation can be deducted for the portion of a house used for office-at-home purposes. Purely personal expenses aren't included in the expenses that can be allocated.

How Are the Expenses Allocated?

Since the room or other portion of your home must be used exclusively for business purposes, the allocation must presumably be made solely on a *space* basis. Get the proportion of the *space* used regularly for office purposes to the total area of the house or apartment. For example, if the room used as an office is 100 square feet out of an apartment totaling 1,000 square feet, the allocation is 10 percent of the allocable expenses. Thus, if the total allocable expenses came to $1,000, 10 percent or $100 would be allocable to the office-at-home. Any other reasonable allocation method is probably acceptable.

Can You Have More Than One Principal Place of Business?

Suppose you have a principal place of business in some office or professional building and also use space at home to run a sideline business. IRS had contended that while your office-at-home may be the principal place of business of your sideline operation, it can't qualify as your principal place of business because you can only have *one* principal place of business. For you, your principal place of business can therefore only be where you carry on your regular business.

But the Tax Court disagrees and holds that you can have a principal place of business for each of your several businesses. It had the case of a doctor who regularly worked a 40-hour week at a hospital, and also used a room at home to run his real-estate rental properties. The court allowed him to deduct his office-at-home expenses because the room at home was his principal place of business as the owner of the rental-property business.

The Treasury has indicated that it intends to change its view to conform to the Tax Court decision that an individual may have more than one principal place of business, if he is engaged in several businesses.

TAX TIP: Expense-Account Records to Protect Your Deduction

You can lose your deduction for your travel and entertainment expenses unless you kept the kinds of records required by the Treasury. Here, then, is the information you need in order to make your expense-account deductions stand up.

For Traveling Expenses:

Cost, including transportation, meals and lodging, and incidentals such as telephone and telegraph, etc.;

Time, including departure and return date for each trip, and the number of days away from home spent on business;

Place or places of travel, by name of city, town, etc.

Business reason for trip, or nature of the business benefit derived or expected to be derived as a result of travel to each place.

For Entertainment Expenses in General:

Cost;

Time, including date;

Place or places, including name, address, or location and description of the entertainment, such as dinner or theater, if not otherwise apparent;

Business purpose, including business reason or nature of the business benefit derived or expected to be derived, from the entertainment, and the nature of any business discussion or activity. (For "quiet business meals," nature of business discussion or activity is not required);

Business relationship of each person entertained for whom a deduction is claimed, including name or title, occupation, or other designation which shows business relationship to you. If you think you can later recall the person's title, occupation, etc., keeping the name will be enough. You can give an examining agent the additional information.

If the entertainment directly precedes or follows a substantial and bona fide business discussion, you must also have the following information in addition to what is generally required:

Time, including date and length of business discussion;

Place of the discussion;

Business purpose, including nature of the discussion and business reason for the entertainment, or nature of business benefit derived or expected to be derived from the entertainment.

Business relationship, including identification of those participating in the business discussion.

Here is how you should have kept the information which you collected:

When should you write down the information? Daily. If you waited beyond a day—say until the end of a week—to write up the week's expense account, the Treasury may not accept your records as accurate.

What form should your record take? An account book, diary, statement of expense, or any similar record which shows the necessary facts. If you kept this up currently, you then could transcribe the information to whatever weekly, monthly, or other summary expense-account statement your employer or client may want. Play it safe by keeping your original daily sheets.

What other supporting proof must you keep? Every hotel, motel, or other lodging expense while away from home on business must be supported by a receipt, paid bill, etc., *regardless of amount.* Every separate expense account item of $25 or more will also have to be supported by a receipt, with one exception. The exception is for $25 or more spent on transportation if receipts aren't generally given by the transportation company. Thus you don't need a receipt to support payment for rail or bus travel, since those companies don't generally give receipts. But plane fares of $25 or more require receipts, since air passengers are given receipts.

Keep this in mind. A check made out to a payee won't by itself be accepted as proof of an expense deduction. You will need an itemized bill plus the check, or a receipted bill.

TAX TIP: How to Reduce Expense-Account Record-Keeping

You can reduce your record-keeping by entering into an arrangement with your employer to reimburse you for your business travel at the rate of 20 cents per mile plus a subsistence allowance for travel away from home. This allowance is to be not more than the greater of $44 per day or the maximum per diem allowed by the federal government in the locality in which you travel. The $44 or higher per diem doesn't cover the cost of taxis, phones, and telegrams. These can be deducted in addition to the $44-per-day amount. The daily-allowance rule is limited to employees who are not related to their employers and

who don't own more than 10 percent of their employer company's stock. The 20 cents per mile allowance can be used by all employees.

If your employer gives you a per diem allowance or a reimbursement arrangement not exceeding $44 or higher per diem, and a mileage allowance not over 20 cents per mile, while traveling away from home on business, and reasonably limits it to ordinary and necessary business expenses, all you have to keep are records of time, place, and business purpose of your travel. You won't have to prove the *specific amount* spent for different items and you won't have to keep hotel and motel receipts. And very important, you won't have to show either the allowance or your expenses on your tax return.

Under such a reimbursement arrangement, the Treasury expects the employer to maintain an adequate internal audit control over the employee's expense account, such as requiring approval and verification by some other responsible person. Also, the allowances will have to be based on some reasonably accurate estimates of travel costs, including variances in different localities, etc. In other words, the employer can't give a blanket $44 allowance for daily travel expenses in places where they are unlikely to run over $15 a day.

The $44-per-day ceiling under this Treasury rule may be higher if the U.S. government authorizes a higher per diem allowance in any particular locality for its own employees. IRS will then accept that higher ceiling for private business travel allowances.

The allowance of up to 20 cents a mile for travel doesn't include tolls and parking fees. Your employer can give you a separate allowance for tolls and fees in addition to your mileage allowance.

Both the mileage allowance for tolls and parking fees can be given to an employee who has local transportation expenses connected with his job. They are not limited to employees who travel on business away from home.

There is one "catch" in this rule. The Treasury insists that any excess of allowance over actual expenses will be taxable income to the employee. This means that if a Treasury agent ever claims that an employee spent less than his allowance, about the only safe way for the employee to prove otherwise is to keep the precise records that the Treasury says he doesn't have to keep under the per-diem-and-mileage-allowance rule. So, despite the seeming liberality of this regulation, it may nevertheless pay to keep all the required records if you feel that an agent may ever question whether you actually spent your entire allowance.

Travel and Transportation Expenses

Travel and transportation expenses that are ordinary and necessary to your business or employment are deductible.

If you are an employee and your employer does not reimburse you for these necessary expenses (or if he reimburses you but doesn't require you to account for them), you show these itemized deductions on Form 2106 or a separate schedule attached to the return and treat your net amount as the adjustment.

If you are self-employed—that is, if you operate as an individual proprietor—you deduct your necessary travel and transportation expenses on separate Schedule C, at line 29.

In either case, you should have the necessary supporting records to back up your deductions.

Q. What are the different items I can deduct as travel expenses?

A. The Treasury limits the meaning of traveling expenses to the reasonable and necessary expenses of traveling away from home on behalf of your business or employment. Within this limit, you can include your plane, rail, bus or taxi fares, automobile transportation costs, baggage charges, costs of transporting sample cases, display material, etc., cost of meals and lodging if away from home overnight, and reasonable tips incident to any of these expenses.

Q. While I am away on business trips I spend money entertaining business contacts. Is this deductible as a traveling expense?

A. No. These bills may be deductible as entertainment expenses (see pages 65-67) but they aren't part of your traveling expenses.

Q. While I am away from home on business trips I have cleaning and laundry expenses. Are these part of my deductible traveling expenses?

A. Yes.

Q. What does the Treasury mean when it says I must be away from "home?"

A. For purposes of deducting traveling expenses, your home is your place of business or employment, or your station or post of duty, regardless of where your family lives. For example, you may live with your family in Philadelphia but work in Washington, D.C. On weekdays you stay at a Washington hotel and eat your meals in various Washington restaurants. Every weekend you return to your family in Philadelphia. The Treasury says your tax home is Washington, not Philadelphia. Your weekend traveling is for family, not business, purposes. Therefore you can't deduct any of your expenses of traveling, meals, or lodging.

However, a number of courts have disagreed with the Treasury and hold that a taxpayer's "home" for purposes of deducting traveling expenses away from home is his residence.

Q. I work out of a building located at one edge of a large city. When I'm assigned to jobs at the opposite side of the city, I sometimes stay over until the job is finished. Am I away from my business home when I go to these jobs?

A. No. Your tax home is not a particular building or property. It's the entire city or general area in which your employment or business is located.

Q. I really have two places of employment each year. Do I get any deductions when I travel from one to the other?

A. Yes. If you regularly work in two or more separate areas, your tax home is where your principal business or employment is located. You are considered away from home when you are away from your area of principal business or employment even while you are working at your minor place of business or employment.

Which of your several places of work is your principal place of employment depends on such factors as time spent in each area, how active you are in each area, and how much you earn in each area. For example, you live in St. Louis, where you have a seasonal job at which you earn $9,500 for 9 months of the year. During the other 3 months of the year you work at Miami Beach, where you earn $3,000. St. Louis is your principal place of employment and your tax home because you spend most of your time and earn most of your money there. You can deduct all your traveling expenses to and at Miami Beach, including cost of meals and lodging.

Q. Can I ever be considered traveling away from home while I am in the same city as my family?

A. Yes. Your family may be living in San Francisco while you have taken a job that requires you to live in San Diego, where you have room and board. If your employer assigns you to work in San Francisco two months a year, you'll be considered away from your tax home even though you are with your family in San Francisco. You'll be able to deduct your fare to and from San Franciso and that part of your family's living costs covering your meals and lodging while you are working in San Francisco.

Q. I have an assignment in a city away from the place where I generally work. I don't know how long this job will last. Can I deduct my meals and lodging as traveling expenses away from home while I'm on this job?

A. The Treasury says that if your job at the new location is for an indefinite period—that is, you can't foresee that it will end within a fixed and reasonably short period—the new location becomes your new tax home and you can't deduct the expenses of travel, meals, and lodging while there. But if your work away from your regular location is strictly temporary—you can tell it will end within a fixed and reasonably short period—you are away from home while on the temporary job and can deduct travel, meals, and lodging. You're supposed to decide whether the job is temporary or indefinite at the time you begin the work away from your regular place of work.

Q. I'm a strictly transient worker without any fixed home or place of work. Can I deduct all of my traveling expenses.

A. No. You can't deduct any, because each place you work in turn becomes your principal place of business and your tax home. So you're never away from home for tax purposes.

Q. What is meant by requiring me to be "away from home overnight"?

A. Of course, if your business trips take you away from home for more than a day, you have no problem here. But no deduction for meals and lodging expenses away from home is allowed unless your duties require you to be away from the general area of your tax home overnight, or for a period substantially longer than an ordinary day's work and long enough to require relief from duty in order to let you sleep; not just to permit you to relax or eat. You may meet these tests even if you aren't away from home for a full 24 hours and even if you aren't away from home during the normal sleeping hours from evening to morning.

For example, a bus driver leaves his home station at 8 A.M. and returns about 12 midnight. He reaches his turnaround point at about 2 P.M., where he is given four hours for necessary sleep before starting his return trip at 6 P.M. This driver is away from home overnight and can deduct the cost of meals and lodging at his turnaround point.

On the other hand, a trucker leaves his terminal at 6 P.M. and returns at 9 A.M. next morning. He is given 2 hours off at his turnaround point to relax and eat. He is not away from home overnight and can't deduct the cost of his meals at the turnaround point.

You can't deduct your meal expenses if you merely nap in your car, no matter how long your day's trip may be. The Tax Court says that the required sleep or rest must be of the type which would ordinarily add to a traveler's expense.

Q. What if I took my wife along on that business convention trip to New York, driving in my own automobile?

A. You couldn't deduct the portion of the traveling expenses attributable to her travel, meals, and lodging, unless she was needed by you for a business purpose. Having her perform such incidental services as typing notes for you, helping entertain customers, etc., isn't a good enough business purpose.

You could deduct the total cost of operating your car to and from New York as a traveling expense even though your wife shared the trip. If you paid $70 a day for a double room while in New York and a single room would have cost $60, you could deduct only $60 a day for your hotel room. If you had come with your wife by train, plane, or bus, you could deduct only a full fare for yourself.

Q. I took a trip to find a new plant for my business. Is this a travel expense away from home?

A. No. If you are in business for yourself, the cost of looking for a new location or a new plant or branch is not a deductible expense. You add your outlays to the cost of the new property.

Q. When I am away on business trips, I often use taxis to get to my customers. Are these cab fares deductible as traveling expenses away from home?

A. Yes.

Q. Can I deduct as traveling expenses the cab and bus fares in getting from the air terminal to my hotel on business trips and from my hotel back to the air terminal?

A. Yes. The same holds for cab and bus fares from rail or bus terminals to and from your hotel when you are on a business trip.

Q. While I was away from home on a temporary job assignment, I came home for several visits. Are any of my visiting expenses deductible?

A. Your original cost to reach your temporary job and your expense to get home after finishing it are deductible. So are the meals and lodging, even on your days off, in the city of your temporary assignment. But on your visit home before the temporary job was finished, you cannot deduct the cost of your meals and lodging at home. Your traveling expenses for the visit (including any meals and lodging en route) home and back to the temporary assignment are deductible up to (but no more than) the amount you would have paid for meals and lodging if you had remained at your temporary assignment instead of coming home for the visit. And if you retain your hotel room while home on the visit, your visiting travel-expense deduction can't be more than what you would have paid for meals had you remained at your temporary job location.

Q. What about my transportation expenses while I'm not traveling away from home overnight?

A. These expenses, including air, rail, bus, taxi, subway fares, tips, etc. are deductible—even if not incurred while traveling away from home overnight—to the extent the transportation is directly attributable to the actual conduct of your business or employment.

Q. Can I deduct my daily commuting expenses from Yonkers to New York, where I work?

A. No. Expenses for commuting from your residence to your place of business, which is your tax home, are not deductible. It makes no difference that you may have to commute from a very long distance, or that you may go into a different part of your working area every day.

Q. I work at several different places within the city every day. Can I deduct the transportation cost of getting from one place to the other?

A. Yes. This is so whether you go from one place to the other for the same employer or for different employers. But you can deduct only the cost of going directly from one place of work to the next. If for personal reasons you use a more expensive, indirect route, you can deduct only the transportation cost of the direct route.

Q. I use an automobile exclusively in my business. Can I deduct all the costs of operation?

A. Yes. If you are in business, you deduct the cost of your automobile operation on line 10, separate Schedule C.

Q. I am an employee. My job requires me to use a car exclusively for work. Can I deduct the entire cost of operation?

A. Yes. The place for deducting these costs is on Form 2106 and attach it to Form 1040.

Q. What is included in the cost of operation of an automobile?

A. Costs of gasoline, oil, repairs, garage rent, insurance, depreciation, taxes, licenses, etc.

Q. I use my car for both business and personal use. How do I figure my deductible operating costs?

A. If you use your car on business for some time during every month of the year, you have a relatively simple procedure: Find what percentage of your driving mileage is business mileage. For example, your business mileage may be 45 percent of the total. You can deduct 45 percent of your operating costs. Use Form 2106 to make the actual computations.

If you have no business travel at all during one or more months, then you start your figuring by disregarding both the expenses and the mileage in those months.

Next you total the expenses for all those months in which you did have business travel. You can deduct that percentage of your total car expenses in these months which your business travel is of your business and personal travel in these months.

The basis (cost) of the car for depreciation is multiplied by the same percentage. You then figure a tentative depreciation on this basis. To get your depreciation deduction, you multiply the tentative figure by the number of months in which there was business use and divide by 12.

Use Form 2106 for this more difficult computation.

However, certain costs are fully deductible if you itemize your personal deductions, regardless of whether you use your car for personal or business purposes. These expenses include interest on money borrowed to buy the car or on auto loans.

Q. If I use a passenger automobile wholly or partly for business travel, must I itemize my business travel expense or can I deduct a flat amount per mile for automobile business travel?

A. You have a choice. If you prefer, you can deduct your itemized, actual auto expenses allocable to business use, including gas, oil, taxes on gas and oil, insurance, license tags, sales tax on purchase of car and interest paid in connection with purchase of car, and depreciation. Or, *instead* of listing all these itemized deductions, you can take an optional deduction based on a flat 20 cents a mile for the first 15,000 miles of business travel and 11 cents a mile over that. You can also deduct parking fees and tolls in addition to the flat mileage allowance plus sales tax if you bought the car during the year, plus any interest you paid during the year in connection with purchase of your car.

You can't use this flat optional mileage deduction if you have depreciated your car under a "speedy" depreciation method or have deducted 20 percent first-year depreciation.

Even if your employer gives you a mileage reimbursement that is less than the 20 cents or 11 cents a mile optional deduction, you can use the 20 cents or 11 cents a mile optional deduction as long as you "reflect" your actual reimbursement (meaning presumably that you include the reimbursement in your income) in your return.

One suggestion: The 20/11-cent mileage allowance of IRS does *not* reflect the full rise in gasoline, insurance, and all other car costs. So make a careful check of your actual car costs, including depreciation. These may add up to a considerably higher deduction than the IRS allowance.

One warning: With respect to such auto expenses incurred after 1979, the automobile is considered to have a useful life of 60,000 miles of business use at the 20 cents per mile rate, regardless of the age of the vehicle or years of use. After 60,000 miles of use at the maximum 20 cents per mile rate, the rate for business travel will be limited to only 11 cents per mile.

Q. I am a member of a car pool of employees who drive to and from work. How are the expenses and contributions treated?

A. The costs of operating the cars are not deductible. Amounts received from fellow passengers must be reported as income only to the extent they exceed expenses.

Q. I paid a fine for a traffic violation while driving my car on business. Is it deductible?

A. No. Fines and penalties for violation of traffic laws or other laws or regulations aren't deductible.

TAX TIP: *Deduction for Driving to Work with Tools*

A taxpayer is allowed to deduct only those clearly *additional* driving expenses that he incurs because he needs to transport his tools to work. He has to show exactly how much additional it costs to carry his tools along, above the cost of going the same way without tools.

For example, a taxpayer paid $2 a day to get to and from work by public transportation before he had to carry tools to and from work. After he had to carry tools, he spent $3 a day in driving his car and another $5 a days as rent for a trailer in which to carry the tools. Under the additional expense test he is allowed to deduct $5, which is the additional expense for carrying the tools. He can't deduct the extra $1 that it costs to drive himself by car as against the cost of public transportation.

TAX TIP: *How to Boost Deductions for Cars Used for Both Business and Pleasure*

In figuring your deduction for expenses of a car used for both business and pleasure, the Treasury rules require that you ignore both the expenses and the mileage of any month during which you have no business travel at all. This rule enables you to jack up your deductions if you can time your expenses and business trips properly. The key is to pay for your nonrecurring car expenses, such as tires, repairs, insurance, etc., in months during which you have at least some business travel rather than in any month during which you have no business travel at all. The reason is that you can't deduct any expense at all if you incur and pay it in a month during which you had no business travel. Thus, if you are unlucky enough to require a major repair in a month during which you ordinarily might have no business travel, try to get at least one day of business travel into that month. This will permit you to deduct at least some part of the repair expense.

TAX TIP: *Did You Buy a Car for Business Use during 1981?*

If you are an employee or self-employed, and bought a car in 1981 for use on your job (not for commuting) or business, you are entitled to an investment credit on the purchase. This credit is allowed as a direct reduction of your 1981 tax.

Under the new 1981 Tax Law rules, you are entitled to an investment tax credit of 6 percent of the purchase price (cost) of the car. Thus, if you paid $8,500 for the car at any time during 1981, you should claim a credit of $510 on line 41 of Form 1040 and attach Form 3468. This is not just a deduction from your income. It is a direct reduction of your tax.

In addition, the law allows a depreciation deduction for your car equal to 25 percent of the cost. When you add this deduction to your other deductible expenses of using the car, such as gas, repairs, etc., you may wind up with a larger deduction by claiming your actual expenses than by taking the 20/11-cent flat mileage allowance for business auto travel.

Line 24: Payments to an Individual Retirement Arrangement (IRA)

Individuals who made contributions to an Individual Retirement Arrangement (IRA) in 1981 enter the allowable deduction on line 24. You must attach Form 5329 only if you owe tax on excess contributions, premature distributions, or undistributed IRA funds.

You may include payments made to your IRA on or before the due date of the return (including any extensions). But don't include any early 1981 payments that you previously deducted on your 1980 return.

Enter the number which identifies your situation in the code space on line 24.

One individual IRA **1**
Two individual IRAs **2**
One individual IRA and spousal IRA **3**
One SEP **4**
Two SEPs **5**
One individual IRA and one SEP **6**

"SEP" refers to IRA account payments made for you by your employer as a "simplified employee pension."

TAX TIP: *Self-employed (Keogh) and Individual Retirement Plans (IRAs) Attractive*

Individuals who have self-employment income from a business, profession, service operation, etc., and individuals who are not covered by any regular retirement plan, such as an employee whose employer has no qualified retirement plan, can set up their own tax-deductible retirement plan. They can deduct the amounts they pay into such plans and will not report any income from the plans until the later years when they retire and receive payments from these plans. Self-employed persons use the so-called Keogh (or H.R. 10) plan.

For 1981, you can contribute and deduct up to 15 percent of your earned income, up to a maximum contribution of $7,500. Thus if you set aside $2,000, because that's 15 percent of your self-employment income, you can deduct the full $2,000.

There is also a special defined-benefit Keogh plan which can permit higher contributions and deductions.

A person who is not covered by any regular retirement plan can contribute up to 15 percent of his earned income (but the contribution can't exceed $1,500 a year) to a tax-deductible Individual Retirement Arrangement which may be in the form of an account with a bank, an annuity, a special bond, etc. These Arrangements are commonly referred to as IRAs.

You may also be able to raise your maximum deductible contribution from $1,500 to $1,750 if your spouse is not employed. Check with your bank, etc., as to how you can take advantage of this higher contribution.

Remember that you have until April 15, 1982, to contribute to your existing Keogh plan for a deduction on your 1981 return. You have until April 15, 1982, to set up and contribute to an IRA plan for a deduction on your 1981 return.

For 1982, much more liberal rules apply to both Keogh and IRA plans, as explained at page 12.

Line 25: Payments to a Keogh (H.R. 10) Retirement Plan

This type of adjustment is for payments for self-employed persons to self-employment retirement plans.

If you are a self-employed individual proprietor or partner who has made contributions to a qualified retirement plan for yourself, you enter the deductible portion of your contribution on line 25.

You will also have to file Form 5500-K *as a separate* *return* on or before the last day of the 7th month following the end of the plan year unless you, as the sole proprietor, are the only person who ever participated in your Keogh plan. In that case you don't file a Form 5500-K.

If you are a partner in a partnership covered by a Keogh plan, you don't personally have to file a Form 5500-K.

Line 26: Forfeited-Interest Penalty for Premature Withdrawal of Term Account

If you forfeited a certain amount of interest because you made a premature withdrawal from a time savings account in '81, line 26 is where you deduct this forfeited interest penalty. Because this is classified as an "adjustment," you deduct this here even though you otherwise use the standard deduction instead of itemizing your personal deductions.

Remember to include as interest in line 8a any portion of the forfeited interest that was earned in 1981.

Line 27: Alimony

The tax treatment of alimony and separate-maintenance payments depends on whether they are classified as periodic or other than periodic.

Periodic payments are deductible by the husband (or wife, if she's the one who has to pay alimony) and taxable to the wife (or husband if he receives them) if they are divorced or legally separated and the payments are (1) required by the divorce or separation decree or by a written instrument incident to the decree, (2) in discharge of a legal obligation based on the marital relationship, and (3) paid after the decree.

Payments that are not periodic are neither deductible nor taxable.

However, payments which are designated in the decree or agreement for the support of minor children are not deductible as alimony by the husband or taxable to the wife or ex-wife. But the child-support payments are considered as paid by the husband in determining who is entitled to the dependency deduction for a child. If the decree or agreement doesn't specify a fixed amount as child support, the entire payment is alimony, deductible by the husband and taxable to the wife. If a decree or agreement provides for both child-support and alimony payments and the full payments are not made, the payments are first viewed as being made for child support.

If the husband pays deductible alimony, he deducts it on line 27. The wife should report this same amount as alimony on line 10.

When the total amount of alimony you have to pay is specified in the decree, instrument or agreement, the instalment payments you make don't qualify as periodic alimony, with the following exceptions:

If you have to pay for 10 years or less, the payments will be considered periodic if they are subject to being stopped before the end of the payout period by contingencies such as the wife's death, remarriage, etc.

If you have to pay for more than 10 years, each year's payments received by the wife are periodic to the extent they don't exceed 10 percent of the total of alimony which is specified. For example, if the decree required you to pay your wife $6,000 a year for 5 years and then $2,000 a year for the next 10 years, the total would be $50,000. During the first 5 years, you would deduct and your wife would be taxable on only $5,000 of the $6,000 payment (10 percent of $50,000 is the limit) while $2,000 a year would be deductible and taxable in the next 10 years.

Q. The state court described my alimony payments as made in payment for property rights. Does this disqualify them as periodic payments?

A. Not necessarily. If they are periodic in all other respects and are made in discharge of your legal obligation to support your wife, they will be treated as periodic for tax purposes despite the state court's description of them. If they are in fact in payment of property rights, they can't qualify as periodic payments.

Q. Under my divorce arrangements, I must pay my wife $500 a month for herself and the support of my two minor children. Must I divide the payments between those to my ex-wife and those for my children?

A. No. Unless the agreement specifically fixes the amounts paid for the support of the children, you can deduct the full payment to your ex-wife.

Q. I entered into an out-of-court separation agreement with my wife requiring me to make periodic payments to her. Can I deduct these payments after entering into the agreement, and must my wife report them in her income?

A. Yes, only if you entered into the agreement in writing after August 16, 1954, and you don't file a joint return with your wife. Even if you made the agreement before August 17, 1954, if you alter it in writing in any material way after August 16, 1954, the payments made after the alteration can qualify as periodic payments.

Q. I have been ordered by a court to make support payments to my wife although we are not yet divorced or legally separated. Are these periodic payments which are deductible by me and taxable to my wife?

A. Yes—if the payments are made because of the marital relationship, and the payments qualify in all other respects as periodic.

Q. My divorce decree required me to pay my ex-wife a lump-sum settlement. Is this deductible by me and taxable to my wife?

A. No. It can't qualify as a periodic payment.

Q. I have to pay my ex-wife's medical expenses under our divorce decree. Can these qualify as periodic payments?

A. Yes, if they are periodic in all other respects. You can deduct them, and your ex-wife reports them in her income. But she can include them in her medical expenses, to the extent deductible, if she itemizes her deductions on Schedule A.

Q. I had to put some of my securities in trust to pay my alimony obligations to my ex-wife. What about the payments made from the trust income to her?

A. The payments to her from trust income aren't taxable to you, nor are they deductible by you. Your ex-wife must report them in income.

Q. Under the divorce decree, a part of my alimony payments must be paid by my ex-wife for real-estate taxes, property insurance, and current utility expenses on a residence owned jointly by me and my ex-wife. Is this part deductible by me and taxable to my wife?

A. Yes.

Q. A portion of the alimony I must pay is earmarked by the divorce decree for payment by my ex-wife toward principal and interest on a mortgage covering the residence which we jointly own and on which we're both principal obligors. How is the portion of alimony treated?

A. It isn't deductible by you or taxable to your wife.

Q. I made an additional payment to my ex-wife after she remarried although it wasn't required by the decree. Can I deduct this?

A. No, and your wife doesn't report it as income because you made the payment without legal obligation.

Q. I was required by the divorce decree to repay my ex-wife some money she had loaned me during our marriage. Can I treat this as deductible alimony?

A. No. The payment of the loan arises out of a debtor-creditor relationship, not out of the marital relationship.

Q. Can I deduct the fees I paid for lawyers when my wife sued me for divorce?

A. You can deduct only that portion of your legal fee which you may have paid for *tax advice* in connection with the divorce.

Q. As part of my alimony agreement I must pay the mortgage principal and interest payments due on an old home which we still jointly own. Can I deduct these payments as alimony?

A. Not in full. If you and your ex-wife own the house either as tenants in common, or joint tenancy, or tenants by the entirety with the survivor taking clear title, then 50 percent of the principal and interest payments are deductible as alimony (assuming they otherwise qualify). You can also deduct the remaining 50 percent of the *interest* payments as interest.

Q. I had to pay an attorney to help me collect alimony payments from my ex-husband. These are periodic payments which I must include in my income. Can I deduct my legal expenses in collecting my alimony?

A. Yes.

Line 28: Disability Income Exclusion

You report your full disability pension on line 7 of Form 1040. On line 28, you are allowed to exclude up to $100 a week of disability income if you were under 65 on December 31, 1981, and retired on permanent and total disability and had not reached mandatory retirement age on January 1, 1981, but this exclusion is subject to limitations which you compute on Form 2240 and attach.

Line 29: Other Adjustments

This line is used only for the following items which have very limited application: excess foreign living expenses, forestration/reforestation amortization and repayment of Sub-pay under the Trade Act of 1974.

Line 30: Total Adjustments

Add up the adjustments at lines 22 through 29 and enter the total at line 30.

ADJUSTED GROSS INCOME

| Adjusted Gross Income | 31 Adjusted gross income. Subtract line 30 from line 21. If this line is less than $10,000, see "Earned Income Credit" (line 57) on page 15 of Instructions. If you want IRS to figure your tax, see page 3 of Instructions .... ▶ | 31 | |

Line 31: Adjusted Gross Income

Subtract line 30 from line 21 and show the difference in line 32a. If the amount on line 31 is less than $10,000, you may be eligible to claim an Earned Income Credit. (See discussion on page 21.)

TAX COMPUTATION

Form 1040 (1981)   Page 2

Tax Computation
(See Instructions on page 12)

32a Amount from line 31 (adjusted gross income) .... | 32a |

32b If you do not itemize deductions, enter zero .... } | 32b |
If you itemize, complete Schedule A (Form 1040) and enter the amount from Schedule A, line 41 ...

Caution: If you have unearned income and can be claimed as a dependent on your parent's return, check here ▶ ☐ and see page 12 of the Instructions. Also see page 12 of the Instructions if:
- You are married filing a separate return and your spouse itemizes deductions, OR
- You file Form 4563, OR
- You are a dual-status alien.

32c Subtract line 32b from line 32a .... | 32c |

33 Multiply $1,000 by the total number of exemptions claimed on Form 1040, line 6e .. | 33 |

34 Taxable Income. Subtract line 33 from line 32c .... | 34 |

35 Tax. Enter tax here and check if from ☐ Tax Table, ☐ Tax Rate Schedule X, Y, or Z, ☐ Schedule D, ☐ Schedule G, or ☐ Form 4726 .... | 35 |

36 Additional Taxes. (See page 13 of Instructions.) Enter here and check if from ☐ Form 4970, } ☐ Form 4972, ☐ Form 5544, or ☐ Section 72(m)(5) penalty tax .... | 36 |

37 Total. Add lines 35 and 36 .... ▶ | 37 |

Line 32b: Itemized Deductions

You are ready now to move into the next big section on deductions, which, if properly completed, will cut your tax bill to the absolute legal minimum. The total of these deductions is shown at line 32b. Here are your guidelines for deciding whether you should itemize your deductions or rely on the flat standard deduction. If you are:

1. Married filing jointly or a qualifying widow(er) with dependent child, you should itemize if your itemized deductions are more than $3,400.

2. Married filing separately, you should itemize if your itemized deductions are more than $1,700.

3. Single or unmarried head of household, you should itemize if your deductions are more $2,300.

However, if you are in one of the following groups, you *must* itemize your deductions and complete Schedule A even though they total less than the amounts shown above for your filing status.

a. You are married filing a separate return and your spouse itemizes deductions (unless your spouse falls into category *b* below).

b. You can be claimed as a dependent on your parent's return and you have $1,000 or more of interest, dividends, or other unearned income and less than $2,300 of earned income if you are single (less than $1,700 of earned income if you are married filing a separate return). But you don't have to itemize if you know that your earned income is more than your itemized deductions.

c. You elect to exclude income from sources in United States possessions, or:

d. You are a dual-status alien.

If you have decided to or must itemize your deductions, at this point turn to separate Schedule A, Itemized Deductions.

We caution you here that it is extremely important that you itemize your deductions and total them with utmost care to make sure that you don't cheat yourself by settling for the flat standard deduction.

For obviously, if you can deduct more than the standard deduction, you'll save on taxes.

Note: The complete Schedule A is reproduced in the chapter "Other Federal Forms and Schedules."

Schedules A&B (Form 1040)
Department of the Treasury
Internal Revenue Service

Schedule A—Itemized Deductions

(Schedule B is on back)

▶ Attach to Form 1040.   ▶ See Instructions for Schedules A and B (Form 1040).

OMB No. 1545-0074

1981
07

Name(s) as shown on Form 1040

Your social security number

Medical and Dental Expenses (Do not include expenses reimbursed or paid by others.) *(See page 17 of Instructions.)*

1 One-half (but not more than $150) of insurance premiums you paid for medical care. (Be sure to include in line 10 below.) ▶

2 Medicine and drugs . . .

3 Enter 1% of Form 1040, line 31 . . .

4 Subtract line 3 from line 2. If line 3 is more than line 2, enter zero . . . . .

5 Balance of insurance premiums for medical care not entered on line 1 . . . .

6 Other medical and dental expenses:

a Doctors, dentists, nurses, etc. . . . .

b Hospitals . . . .

c Transportation . . . .

d Other (itemize—include hearing aids, dentures, eyeglasses, etc.) ▶ ....

----

7 Total (add lines 4 through 6d) . . . .

8 Enter 3% of Form 1040, line 31 . . .

9 Subtract line 8 from line 7. If line 8 is more than line 7, enter zero . . . . .

10 Total medical and dental expenses (add lines 1 and 9). Enter here and on line 33 . ▶

Medical Expenses

Before you start to fill out this section, note that it is really a two-part computation. You can deduct one half of any medical-care insurance premiums up to $150 per year. But your other medical expenses, including the balance of your medical-care insurance premiums, are deductible only to the extent that they total more than 3 percent of your adjusted gross income on line 31, Form 1040. And for this computation, your medicine and drugs must first be reduced by 1 percent of your adjusted gross income on line 31, Form 1040.

Thus, if it is obvious that your medical expenses are going to be less than the 3 percent of your adjusted gross income on line 31, there is no need to complete the entire schedule. In that case, merely complete line 1, Schedule A (if any), and line 10.

You can deduct your medical and dental expenses only to the extent they exceed 3 percent of your income on line 31, Form 1040 (your adjusted gross income). Medicines and drugs are part of your medical expenses only to the extent they exceed 1 percent of your income on line 31, Form 1040.

Premiums paid for medical-care insurance are deductible under a special rule on line 1. Regardless of how much your other medical expenses are, you can deduct as an itemized expense *one-half* of the premiums you pay for medical care insurance up to $300 of premiums a year. For example, if you paid $200 of premiums for medical insurance during 1981, you can deduct $100 as an itemized expense regardless of what your other medical expenses add up to. If your premiums were $300 or more, you can deduct $150. The part of the premiums you don't deduct under this special rule is entered at line 5 and becomes part of your other medical expenses. For instance, if your premiums were $200, you deduct $100 under this special-deduction rule on line 1 and you enter the other $100 on line 5.

Premiums for accident and health insurance covering risks other than medical care are not deductible at all. They aren't deductible under the special insurance-premium deduction or under the general medical-expense rules. Thus you get no deductions for premiums covering insurance against loss of income, indemnity for accidental death, loss of eyes, limbs, etc. The kind of medical insurance for which premiums are deductible covers hospital bills, doctor bills, etc.; also the monthly payments for Medicare coverage of doctor bills (but not the hospital-insurance tax included as part of your Social Security tax payment).

You don't have to list separately the payments you made to various doctors and dentists. Add together all such payments you made in '81 and enter the total figure at line 6a. But be sure to keep your own record of these separate payments in case your return is examined and IRS asks you for proof of the total figure on line 6a.

You don't have to list separately the payments you made to any hospital or hospitals. Just add up all such payments you made in '81 and enter the total figure at line 6b. But just as in the case of payments to doctors, keep your own records of payments to hospitals in case IRS asks you for proof if your return is examined.

All other medical expenses should be separately itemized under line 6c.

Enter the total amount at line 10 and again at line 33.

Here is a list of generally deductible medical expenses:

In order to qualify as a medical expense, the payments must be made for the diagnosis, care, mitigation, treatment, or prevention of disease, or for the purpose of affecting any structure or function of the body or for insurance that constitutes medical care for you, your spouse, or dependent. These expenses generally qualify: ambulance hire, artificial limbs, artificial teeth, chiropodists, chiropractors, Christian Science practitioners, crutches, dental care, dentists, diagnostic services, doctors, eyeglasses, guide dogs (for the blind or deaf) and their maintenance, hearing aids and their component parts, hospital care, insurance premiums for hospitalization and medical care, laboratory services, meals and lodging furnished by a hospital or similar institution incident to medical care, medicines prescribed and nonprescribed; nurses (including nurses' board paid by you), nursing services including those rendered by a practical nurse, optometrists, osteopaths, physicians, podiatrists, psychologists, psychiatrists; special equipment such as wheelchairs, special food or beverages prescribed solely for treatment of an illness; surgeons, transportation primarily for and essential to medical care, therapy, X-ray services, cosmetic surgery.

Of course, you can't deduct medical expenses for which you were reimbursed from insurance or otherwise during the year, including Medicare benefits and supplementary Medicare benefits. This is so whether or not reimbursement was made directly to you or to the doctor, hospital, etc.

Q. My wife and myself each pay medical-insurance premiums of more than $300. Can we deduct double the $150 limit?

A. Yes, if you file *separate* returns. But if you are like the vast majority of couples who file *joint* returns, you can deduct only $150 on your joint return.

Q. My medical-insurance policy covers only the cost of prescription drugs. Does this qualify as medical-insurance premiums?

A. Yes.

Q. I carry insurance against loss of or damage to my contact lenses. Does this qualify as medical-insurance premiums?

A. Yes.

Q. I used my credit cards to pay certain medical expenses in 1981, but I didn't pay the credit-card company until '82. In which year can I deduct the medical expenses?

A. IRS says in '81. When you use a credit card you are, in effect, borrowing the money and making the medical-expense payment.

Q. I have an insurance policy that pays me a flat $100 per week while I am ill and not working. Does this qualify as medical insurance?

A. No—since it doesn't cover medical-care expenses. The premiums can't be deducted under either the insurance-premium rule or as a regular medical-expense deduction.

Q. I spent $600 in unreimbursed doctor and hospital bills last year in connection with my wife's broken leg. Unreimbursed medicines and drugs ran another $80. I earn $6,000. How much of a deduction can I take?

A. $440. Here is how you figure it: Your medicine and drug bill of $80 must be reduced by $60 (1 percent of $6,000). This leaves $20 to be added to your $600 doctor and hospital bills, to give total medical expenses of $620. Now this in turn must be reduced by $180 (3 percent of $6,000).

TAX TIP: Important Medical-Expense Rules

The medical-expense deduction rules are as follows:

1. There is no top limit on the amount of medical expenses that may be deducted in a taxable year.

2. Premiums on accident and health insurance policies are deductible only to the extent the insurance covers medical expenses, such as hospital bills, doctor bills, prescription drugs, etc. They are not deductible to the extent the insurance provides reimbursement for inability to work, for loss of compensation, for loss of eyes, limbs, etc.

3. Premiums for accident and health insurance which cover medical expenses are given special treatment as an itemized deduction. One-half of these premiums, up to $300 of such premiums in a year, are deductible, regardless of whether the taxpayer's other medical expenses exceed 3 percent of his adjusted gross income. For instance, if you buy hospital and doctor-bill insurance that costs you $200 a year, you can deduct $100 regardless of your other medical expenses. If it costs you $300 a year you can deduct $150, but if it costs you $400, you can't deduct more than the limit, which is half of $300, or no more than $150. The part of the premium which you don't deduct under this special rule is added onto your other medical expenses. Thus, if your premium is $200 a year, you take an itemized deduction of $100 under this special rule and add the other $100 to your other medical expenses which have to meet the 3-percent wastage rule before you get a deduction for them.

4. You can include medical and dental bills not only for yourself and your spouse, but also bills you paid for:

• All dependents you list on your return; and:

• Any person (such as a child or parent) that you could have listed as a dependent on your return if that person did not have $1,000 or more income or did not file a joint return. For example, you may have contributed more than half of the support for your mother, but you cannot list her as a dependent because she received $1,000 in gross income during the year. In part of your support was the payment of medical bills for her, you can include that part in your medical expenses.

5. Don't overlook the fact that the payments for Social Security Medicare B insurance, which is either deducted from your benefits or paid by you directly, constitute medical-insurance premiums which can be treated as described above.

Q. I know that medical expenses cover doctor and hospital bills. But are there other expenses that qualify as medical expenses?

A. Yes. There are many expenses which taxpayers often overlook. For instance, cost of laboratory tests, X rays and examination; dental services including X rays and straightening teeth; eyeglasses and hearing aids; crutches, wheelchairs, autoettes, braces, elastic stockings, medical and surgical appliances, artificial teeth and limbs; seeing-eye dogs; special instruction in speech and lip-reading for a deaf person; special mattress and bedboard for arthritis; amounts paid directly or withheld by your employer as your contribution to group hospital and medical plans such as Blue Cross, etc.; cab fares and other traveling to and from doctor's office; cost of hand controls and other equipment specially adapted to permit a physically handicapped individual to operate his car have also been allowed; cost of whiskey to relieve angina pain and special ulcer food, if prescribed by a doctor and if not *in place* of normal diet; cost of meals and lodgings while at a hotel after an operation because of lack of space in the hospital, where the taxpayer was advised by his doctor not to return home; cost of modifying auto so that individual confined to wheelchair could have his chair and himself placed in car; cost of special phone equipment enabling deaf person to communicate; 75 percent of cost of household help for a semi-invalid who was unable to care for herself. But the cost of a high-protein, moderate-fat, and low-carbohydrate diet prescribed by a doctor, or a special diet for a diabetic, is not deductible where it is a substitute for a normal diet. But the Tax Court says that the *additional cost* of special foods and beverages over the cost of a normal diet, where prescribed by a physician for alleviation or treatment of an illness, is deductible as a medical expense. Medical expenses include all costs incurred to prevent or cure an illness during the taxable year.

Birth-control expenditures are also deductible as medical expenses. The medical expenses include cost of birth-control pills bought under a doctor's prescription, legal vasectomy, and cost of legal abortion.

Q. Can I deduct my own car expenses in traveling to and from my doctor's office?

A. Yes. The Treasury says that it will permit a medical-expense deduction of 9 cents per mile. Thus, if you wish, merely take your figure of miles driven for medical purposes and multiply by 9 cents. Thus, if you drove 1,200 miles during '81 for medical purposes, you can deduct $108 as medical expenses. Note that if you wish to claim your actual car expenses, you can't include depreciation on your car as a medical expense.

Q. Are my general drug purchases deductible as medical expenses?

A. Toothpaste and toothbrushes are not, nor are female-hygiene supplies, toiletries, shaving creams and lotions, cosmetics used for ordinary cosmetic purposes, deodorants, hand lotions, or face creams.

Vitamins and minerals prescribed by a doctor to alleviate pain or suffering and not solely to satisfy nutritional requirements are a medical expense.

Q. Is laetrile considered a medicine or drug that is deductible as a medical expense?

A. The answer depends on whether sale and use of laetrile is legal in the locality where it is purchased on prescription by a physician. If such sale and use are legal, laetrile qualifies as a medicine or drug; if not, then the cost of laetrile doesn't qualify as a medical expense.

Q. What medical expenses in connection with having a baby are deductible?

A. You can deduct for these expenses: doctor bills, including use of delivery room, X rays, etc.; dentist bills, registered nurse, laboratory tests; special equipment and supplies, such as invalid chairs, arches; "stork service," such as ambulance to and from hospital; travel expenses essential to getting medical care; medical treatments such as blood transfusion. But note that you *cannot* claim the cost of maternity clothing or antiseptic diaper service. Nor can you deduct the cost of a practical nurse to care for a healthy baby, even one whose mother died in childbirth.

Q. I had to install an air conditioner in my bedroom because of an allergy which I have. Is this deductible?

A. Yes—even if the equipment is attached to your house, as long as it is detachable. You will need a doctor's statement that the air conditioner is primarily installed to relieve your breathing. If you can meet this test you can deduct the cost (less salvage value, if any) of the equipment, and also the operating expenses, such as electricity.

Q. What about swimming pools, central air conditioning, home elevators or inclinators, bedrooms or bathrooms added to lower floor, oil burner replacing coal burner, etc., which are recommended as part of medical care?

A. These are deductible even though they represent a permanent improvement to the property or improve the value of the property, subject to the following limits:

To the extent that the expenditure adds to the value of the house, no medical expense deduction is allowed. Thus, if you have to spend $1,500 on air conditioning your home for medical reasons and the value of the house is increased by $1,000, you can only deduct $500 ($1,500 less $1,000).

IRS has claimed that the deduction is further limited to the minimum amount necessary to accomplish the medical goal and doesn't extend to the cost of a luxury-type version of the improvement. While the Tax Court has said that it knew of no rules limiting a medical expense to the cheapest form of treatment, a higher court has held that at least where a capital-expenditure type of medical expense such as a swimming pool is involved, the deductible amount is limited to the minimum reasonable costs of a functionally adequate pool.

Q. On recommendation of my doctor, I installed a central air-conditioning system in '81 which I deducted as a recommended medical expense. Can I also deduct the cost of operating the air conditioner in '81 for medical reasons?

A. Yes, you can. The Treasury says that if a capital expenditure qualifies as a medical expense, the cost of operating or maintaining the facility also qualifies as a medical expense as long as the medical reason for the capital expenditure exists.

Q. A cardiac specialist prescribed a reclining chair to give me maximum rest for my cardiac condition. Is the chair a medical expense?

A. Yes, if its only purpose is to help your ailment and the chair isn't used generally as an article of furniture.

Q. Are the costs of various kinds of birth control deductible as medical expenses?

A. Yes. The cost of birth-control pills bought by a woman for personal use under her physician's prescription, the cost of a legal vasectomy for a man, and the cost of a legal abortion for a woman all qualify as deductible medical expenses.

Q. My doctor recommended that I take a trip to a warmer climate for my general health. Is the cost of my trip a medical expense?

A. The Treasury says you can't deduct the expenses of a trip taken for a change of environment, improvement of morale, or a general improvement in health. But if your doctor prescribes a trip to a warm climate for the purpose of alleviating your specific chronic ailment, the cost of your trip is a deductible medical expense. The cost of your meals and lodging is not, unless part of your hospital bill.

Q. I had to take my child to the clinic for special treatment. Are my traveling expenses deductible as medical expenses?

A. Yes.

Q. I had to pay a nurse to accompany my wife to a clinic for special treatment in order to give her necessary injections, etc., during the trip. Are the nurse's traveling expenses also deductible as medical expenses?

A. Yes.

Q. My physician recommended that I should have an air cleaner in the house because I was allergic to household dust. If I buy an ordinary vacuum cleaner to remove dust from the air, can I deduct the cost as a medical expense?

A. IRS says you can't deduct the cost as a medical expense, because your physician didn't specify that you should use a vacuum cleaner as an air cleaner. For the vacuum cleaner to qualify as a medical expense you would need proof, such as a medical prescription, that you bought it primarily for medical care, that you wouldn't have bought it but for your allergy, and so on.

Q. Can I deduct my YMCA gym dues as a medical expense?

A. No. What you pay to keep your general mental and physical health isn't a medical expense unless related to alleviation of some particular disease or defect. That's why steam baths, health clubs, vacations, etc., aren't medical expenses.

Q. Because my wife's physical ailment made it impossible for her to perform household duties, our doctor recommended that we hire domestic help to take over the household jobs. Is the cost of this help a medical expense?

A. No.

Q. I live alone and had a heart attack. On my doctor's advice I hired a live-in worker to call for help in the event of another attack. Can I deduct part or all of her wages?

A. No. This is not considered a medical expense.

Q. My son is undergoing psychiatric treatment for a disturbed condition. Are the psychiatrist's fees deductible as medical expenses?

A. Yes, because the psychiatric care is primarily for the purpose of alleviating a mental illness or defect. But these fees would not be deductible if paid by a student because he had to undergo analysis as part of his training.

Q. I spent over $400 for a course at a treatment center to break my smoking habit. Since this was at the recommendation of my doctor, can I treat the expense as a medical expense?

A. No. Unlike similar costs for treatment at a drug-abuse center or to break an alcohol habit by attending meetings of Alcoholics Anonymous, which are deductible, IRS contends that smoking is not a recognized disease. Thus the course is merely beneficial to your general health and well-being, not deductible.

Q. I enrolled in a weight-reduction program at my doctor's advice. Can I deduct the cost?

A. Not unless the program was recommended because of a specific condition requiring you to lose weight.

Otherwise IRS treats this as merely improving your general health.

Q. Is the cost of keeping my father in an old-age home a medical expense?

A. Only that portion of the cost which is for medical or nursing care is a medical expense. The rest of the cost, such as for meals and lodging, is not. If he was kept in a nursing home principally for medical reasons, then even the cost of meals and lodging would be deductible.

Q. I pay a monthly life-care fee to a retirement home, where I live. Can I treat any part of this fee as a medical expense?

A. You can treat as a medical expense that specific portion of the fee which covers the cost of providing medical care for you. You find out what the portion is from the home, on the basis of its experience.

Q. Can I deduct the cost of keeping a handicapped child in a special school?

A. Yes, if the chief reason for sending him there is to use the institution's resources for alleviating his condition. Thus, the cost for a blind child to attend a school for teaching braille, or for a deaf child to attend a school that teaches lip-reading, or for a mentally retarded child's special education, training, and treatment in an institution are medical expenses. This includes the cost of meals, lodging, and ordinary education furnished by the institution, in addition to specialized care. It also includes the cost of the parents' trips to and from the institution if their visits are an essential part of the child's therapy and medical management.

If you have to pay for remedial reading courses because of brain damage to a child, this cost may also be deducted as a medical expense.

Q. Are amounts which I paid to maintain a child in a halfway house, including room and board, considered medical payments?

A. IRS says yes, where the halfway house offers transitional care to help a child adjust from life in a mental hospital to life in the community.

Q. Can I deduct medical care paid a nonprofessional?

A. Yes, the Treasury says that medical care is determined by the nature of the services rendered, not by the experience, qualifications, or title of the person rendering the services. Thus, the cost of physical therapy required for medical purposes was deductible even though performed by a nonprofessional.

Q. Am I limited to deducting medical expenses only for my wife and my dependents?

A. No. You may also deduct medical expenses paid for any person who could have been your dependent if it weren't for the fact that his income was $1,000 or more.

TAX TIP: Handle Support Payments for Your Parents to Get Maximum Tax Break

If your parents have heavy medical expenses, which are being wasted taxwise because of their low or no-tax burden, it can pay for you to pay the bills. This can be done even though you could have been reimbursed if you had asked for it. The result can be a three-way tax break for you if your payment of their medical expenses plus other support payments you make to them add up to more than half their total support for the year. This permits you to claim the medical expenses you pay for them. Second, you may be able to claim a dependency on their income. Third, this may also qualify you, if unmarried, to use the lower head-of-household tax rates in figuring your tax.

For example, you may furnish more than half your father's support, but his income of $1,500 from dividends and interest bars you from claiming the $1,000 dependency deduction for him. If you pay a doctor for his care, you may claim that as your medical expense even though your father is not technically your dependent.

Q. Are funeral and burial costs medical expenses?
A. No.

Q. My group hospitalization insurance paid some of my medical expenses during the year. Does this affect my medical-expense deduction?
A. Yes. You must reduce your total medical expenses for the year by medical-expense reimbursement received from your group health program, medical insurance, or other sources. (You don't reduce your medical expenses by reimbursement for loss of earnings or by damages for personal injuries.) For example, if you had $600 of medical expenses and group health coverage paid $200 for your medical expenses during the year, you would have $400 of net medical expenses.

Q. I had several large medical bills in 1981 which I will pay in 1982. Can I deduct the expenses for 1981?
A. No—only the expenses actually paid in 1981 can be deducted. Your 1982 payments of 1981 expenses will have to wait until you file in 1983.

If you are again faced with this situation, you may save money on taxes by borrowing to pay your medical expenses. You then take a medical-expense deduction even though you don't repay your loan until the following year. And you can deduct the interest paid on the loan, too.

Q. At the end of December, I paid the hospital an advance payment covering the room for the first week of January. Can I deduct the payment?
A. Payment in the current year for medical services to be furnished in a later year is generally not deductible. But IRS ruled in connection with a prepaid lump-sum care fee to a retirement home, and an advance payment for lifetime care of a handicapped child, that such prepayment is deductible in the year prepaid because there was a contractual obligation by the taxpayer in that year to make the advance payment in order to obtain the future medical services.

Q. I have an accident-and-health policy, which paid me $100 a week for loss of earnings while out sick for three weeks. Must I consider the $300 I received from the insurance company as a reduction of my medical expenses of $275?
A. No. You can claim the $275 in full as a medical expense (subject, of course, to the 3-percent limitation). Since the $300 was not received as a direct payment for medical expenses, it does not reduce the medical expenses.

If you paid the premiums on the policy, you also need not include the $300 in income.

Q. I am blind and have to pay for a specially trained dog to help me. Are these expenses deductible as medical expenses?
A. Yes.

Q. Because of a duplication of health-insurance policies, I received $700 under one policy and $500 under another, for medical expenses which cost me only $900. Is the excess $300 taxable income?
A. That depends on who paid the premiums. If you paid them, the entire $300 is exempt. If your employer paid for the policies, the $300 is taxable. If you paid for one and your employer paid for the other, the excess $300 is taxable to the extent applicable to the employer's premiums.

Taxes

The taxes you can deduct are state and local income taxes, personal-property and real-property taxes, general sales taxes, and those taxes paid in connection with a business or for the production of income.

State and local taxes on gasoline, diesel fuel, and other motor fuels can't be deducted as an itemized nonbusiness tax deduction. They are deductible only if the gasoline, etc., is used in business or investment activities.

Thus, state transfer taxes or gasoline taxes can be deducted only if they are paid in connection with a business or a transaction entered into for the production of income. State transfer taxes paid on the sale of stock or securities, like the New York State tax on stock transfers, can be deducted since the sale of the stock was made for the production of income. If you have paid such a state transfer tax, describe it and list the amount on line 15 and identify it and include in "Total taxes" at line 16.

You may not deduct any federal taxes as taxes. However, the federal excise taxes on sales of various items, services, or transactions carried on for business or profit can be deducted as a business cost of the particular item, service, or transaction. Thus, if you have telephone bills in connection with a business or property held for income, you can deduct the full bill, including the federal

Taxes *(See page 18 of Instructions.)*

11	State and local income		
12	Real estate		
13 a	General sales (see sales tax tables)		
b	General sales on motor vehicles		
14	Personal property		
15	Other (itemize) ▶		
16	Total taxes (add lines 11 through 15). Enter here and on line 34 ▶		

excise tax, as a business expense. If you have a personal home phone, the federal excise tax is not deductible.

A tax may be deducted on the appropriate line under "taxes." But if it is incurred in connection with a business or transaction entered into for profit, it is deducted at the pertinent place. This would be on Separate Schedule C for a business, or on separate Schedule E, Part I, for rental property.

Enter the total amount at line 16 and again at line 34.

KEYNOTE: Which Taxes Are Deductible?

Here is a list of the most common taxes that *may* or *may not* be deducted, if not incurred in connection with a business:

Deductible:
State stock-transfer taxes if in connection with sale of stock
Real-estate taxes
Personal-property taxes
State and local income taxes
General sales taxes
Foreign income taxes (but note that they can be used as credit)
Employee contributions to the Rhode Island Temporary Disability Fund, and to state disability funds in California, New York, and New Jersey

Nondeductible:
Auto inspection fees, license and registration fees, except to the extent based on the value of the car
Social Security taxes withheld from your pay
Railroad retirement taxes withheld from your pay
Water bills
Assessment for local benefits (streets, sidewalks, sewers, trash collection, etc.). But these are deductible if made for the purpose of repair or maintenance or to meet interest charges, or by certain special taxing districts.
Federal income, gift, or estate taxes
Federal self-employment taxes

State inheritance, legacy, or succession taxes
Dog tags
Hunting licenses
Marriage licenses
Federal excise taxes on telephone, transportation, gasoline, tobacco, wine, distilled spirits, etc.
Poll taxes
Customs duties
Employment taxes paid on domestics
Title fees
Foreign personal-property, sales, and gas taxes
Occupancy taxes
Local admission taxes
Local cigarette and tobacco taxes
Local alcohol-beverage taxes
Parking meter charges
Fines
Water bills, sewage, and other service charges assessed against your home are not taxes but rather nondeductible personal expenses. But if they are assessed against your business or rental property you can deduct them as business expenses.
State or local gasoline taxes (unless car was used in business or investment activity)
State transfer taxes *not* incurred in business or in the production of income. Thus, transfer taxes on sale of residence are added to cost or subtracted from sales price.

Q. I live in New York State, where the state and New York City withhold their income taxes from my pay. Do I deduct the withholding taxes, and when?

A. Since the taxes are state or local income taxes, they are deductible. When your employer withholds the taxes, you are considered to have paid the taxes and can deduct them. Therefore, you claim a deduction for the taxes withheld from your pay during 1981, plus, of course, any taxes you paid directly.

Q. Can I deduct taxes if I use the standard deduction instead of itemizing my personal deductions?

A. That depends on the kind of taxes. Taxes incurred in connection with a business or business property, other than state income taxes, can be deducted. These are shown in separate Schedule C. Taxes incurred in connection with property producing rents or royalties are deductible in separate Schedule E, Part II.

Taxes against any other income-producing property, and all other deductible taxes which aren't connected with business, can only be shown here if you itemize your deductions. Therefore, no deduction is allowed for these if you use the standard deduction.

Q. My mother owns her own home. To help her make both ends meet, I pay her real-estate taxes. Can I deduct the taxes?

A. No. While real-estate taxes are deductible, they are deductible only if they are imposed on you or your property. No deduction is allowed for any taxes that are not yours.

Q. My wife owns our home, but I pay the real-estate taxes. Does this mean that since I pay someone else's taxes I forfeit the deduction?

A. Not if you file a joint return with your wife. In that case the deduction is allowed, since you and your wife, in effect, become one taxpayer. However, if separate returns are filed, you will lose the deduction.

Q. I purchased a cooperative apartment (or a home in a cooperative housing project). Can I deduct my share of the taxes and interest?

A. Yes.

Q. How do I figure my sales tax deductions, since I don't keep a record of all my taxable purchases?

A. In the IRS instruction booklet that you received with your return is a series of tables labeled "State Sales Tax Tables." If your state has a sales tax, use the table for your state. The official chart is designed to allow sales-tax deductions depending upon the income and family size of the taxpayer. But the definition of income as used here is not only your income on line 31, Form 1040, but also includes other receipts which are not subject to tax at all. The official IRS table points out that nontaxable receipts include such items as Social Security, veterans' and Railroad Retirement benefits, workmen's compensation,

untaxed portion of long-term capital gains, unemployment compensation, dividends exclusion, disability-income exclusion, and public-assistance payments. But in addition, IRS has informally indicated that it also includes gifts, inheritance, prizes, awards, and nontaxable insurance proceeds.

Run down the chart to the figure opposite the income and under the Family Size (persons in your family). That will give you the amount of state sales tax which you can deduct on line 13a.

You can also add to the sales tax derived from the official tables any sales tax paid on the purchase of (1) a boat, airplane, home (including mobile or prefabricated home), or materials you bought to build a new home, if the tax rate was the same as the general sales-tax rate and the seller stated the tax separately from the price but included it in the total amount you paid, and (2) a car, motorcycle, motor home, or truck (except in Vermont, or West Virginia, on sales before 6/1/81 where the deduction is limited to the amount of sales tax paid at the general sales-tax rate). Also check footnotes for your state in the official tables. These can show that you are entitled to add still more to your sales tax because of certain local sales taxes.

If you can prove that you paid more sales taxes than the chart shows you are entitled to, you can claim the larger amount.

Q. My mortgage provides for monthly payments to a bank for real-estate taxes. Do I deduct the monthly payments set aside for taxes?

A. No. You deduct the actual tax payments made for you by the bank during 1981. This should approximate the monthly payments, but need not always be the same.

Q. When I bought my house, I paid a state property-transfer tax, a county real-estate transfer tax, and a county recordation tax. Can I deduct all of these as state and local real property taxes?

A. You can't deduct any of these, because they don't qualify as either real property taxes or general sales taxes. They are all transfer taxes, which are not on the list of deductible taxes unless they are paid in connection with business.

Q. Are my auto license and auto inspection fees deductible as taxes?

A. No, except to the extent the license fees are based on the value of the car. To this extent they are deductible as personal-property taxes. To the extent an auto is used for business or income producing purposes, both fees are deductible as taxes.

Q. I sold my home on October 31, 1981, after paying $900 real-estate taxes for the period July 1 to December 31, 1981. Can I deduct the $900?

A. No. You deduct only about $400, since you only

owned the house for two-thirds of the time for which the taxes were paid. Taxes were paid for a six-month period, while you only held the property for four months.

The buyer of your property can deduct the remaining $500 even though you paid the taxes.

Q. I received dividends on Canadian stock from which the Canadian corporation withheld a tax. Can I deduct the tax withheld?

A. Yes. However, you also have an option to treat the tax withheld in a manner similar to that allowed for federal income taxes withheld by Uncle Sam. You report the full dividend in income, compute your regular tax, and then claim a credit on line 42, page 2, Form 1040. This credit often can be more advantageous than taking a deduction, since a credit is allowed against your tax. A deduction merely reduces your taxable income subject to tax.

If you use the credit method, fill out and file Form 1116 with your return.

Q. I received a tax rebate on my home. How do I treat this?

A. You reduce the real estate taxes on your home by the amount of the rebate. If the rebate exceeds your tax, the excess is income.

Q. As a tenant, I received part of the landlord's tax rebate. Do I have to include this in my income?

A. No. It is viewed as a rent rebate. Since no deduction is allowed for rent, the reduction is not taxable.

Q. Can I deduct the taxes I paid on cigarettes?

A. No federal or local cigarette taxes can be deducted.

Q. I understand that most of my liquor cost goes for taxes. Can I deduct a fraction of my liquor bills as taxes?

A. No, except for any general sales tax.

TAX TIP: *Mortgage Points on Buying House*

If you were one of the millions of persons who bought a home in 1981, you may have had to pay points on your mortgage. That is, while your mortgage principal was $50,000, you actually received only $48,000. The missing $2,000 is known as "points." You may or may not be able to deduct the full $2,000 as an interest expense. Here are the rules:

IRS says that points paid in lieu of specified service charges in connection with a loan (such as a Veterans Administration loan) are not deductible as interest. Also, such points are not part of the cost of buying a house.

But points that are paid for a conventional loan over and above service charges for the loan are deductible as interest.

Points in the nature of interest would generally not be allowed as an immediate deduction but would instead be deductible over the term of the mortgage. But if points are generally charged in the geographic area where the loan on the home is made, you can take an immediate deduction for the number of points that are generally charged in your area.

If you sold a house, raised the mortgage, and paid the points, the points aren't interest. They merely reduce the selling price.

Q. I qualified for mortgage assistance payments from the U. S. under Sec. 235 of the National Housing Act. I know that I don't have to include those payments as income, but can I also deduct the payment to the extent it covers mortgage interest and real estate taxes on my home?

A. You can't deduct the mortgage interest to the extent the Department of Housing and Urban Development makes assistance payments with respect to your mortgage. But these assistance payments don't reduce your deduction for property taxes that you pay.

Interest Deductions

Any interest that you pay on a debt of yours is deductible regardless of how, why, and to whom the debt is owed. There is no limit on the amount you can deduct, and the interest is deductible whether you pay it in connection with your business or personal activities.

Interest on your business loans or on rental property loans is deductible on separate Schedule C or Schedule E, Part II, whichever is applicable. Interest on personal loans is deductible on line 19, Schedule A.

Don't overlook interest deductions on your credit purchases. The extra expense of things you buy on credit plans may be in part deductible as interest.

Interest Expense (See page 18 of Instructions.)		
17 Home mortgage		
18 Credit and charge cards		
19 Other (itemize) ▶		
20 Total interest expense (add lines 17 through 19). Enter here and on line 35 ▶		

Interest also includes such payments as "points" if you are a buyer, mortgage prepayment penalty, finance charges separately stated, bank credit-plan interest, note discount interest, and redeemable ground rents in certain states.

Excess investment interest. Where interest is paid on borrowed money used for investment purposes, and the interest paid exceeds the investment income by more than $10,000, the excess is disallowed. Higher-bracket taxpayers in these circumstances should consult their professional advisors.

Borrowings to buy tax-exempts. Interest paid on borrowings to purchase or carry tax-exempt obligations is not deductible. This also applies to interest paid on indebtedness incurred to purchase or carry stock of a mutual fund from which you receive exempt-interest dividends.

Q. Can I deduct interest if I don't itemize my deductions?

A. Yes—if the interest was paid in connection with a regular business activity or rental property, you can deduct it in addition to the flat standard deduction. You report this interest as a deduction on Schedule C or Schedule E, Part II, whichever is applicable.

Other interest is not deductible if you don't itemize your deductions.

Q. I borrowed $10,000 on my home to use in my business. Can I deduct the $900 interest as a business expense in addition to the flat standard deductions?

A. Yes. While the mortgage was placed on a nonbusiness asset—your home—the money was used in your business. It's the use made of the money, and not the property used to secure the loan, which determines whether the interest is incurred for a business or personal reason.

Q. I own a two-family house. Half is rented to a tenant; the other half I occupy. How do I treat the $900 interest I paid on the mortgage?

A. Half of the interest is viewed as applicable to the half rented to the tenant. Therefore, $450 is deducted on Schedule E, Part II, and this is allowed even though you use the flat standard deduction.

The other $450 is deducted under regular deductions on line 19, Schedule A. If you use the optional deduction, though, you will not be allowed this $450.

Q. The mortgage on my house is held by a bank, to which I pay $600 per month. Can I deduct this amount as interest?

A. No. The $600 per month probably covers the interest on your mortgage, principal payments, real-estate taxes, and insurance. Usually the bank sends you a statement showing the breakdown of the amount paid. If you haven't received this, ask for it.

After you receive the breakdown, you can deduct the amount you paid for interest, and the amount for taxes (see pages 83-86). The amounts paid against principal and for insurance are not deductible.

Q. I live in a cooperative apartment. Can I deduct a portion of my rent?

A. If you are a tenant-stockholder, you can deduct a portion of the interest (and taxes) paid by the cooperative corporation. The cooperative should furnish you with a breakdown showing how much this is.

Q. I was late paying my real-estate taxes and had to pay $30 in interest and penalties. Can I deduct the $30?

A. You can deduct the interest payments, but *not* the penalty. Thus, if the interest was $20 and the penalty $10, you can deduct $20.

Q. I had to pay $400 additional tax on my 1978 income tax, plus $80 in interest. I know I can't deduct the $400, but is this interest deductible?

A. Yes. All interest is deductible. But note that this interest is "personal" interest, which can't be deducted if you use the flat standard deduction. The Treasury claims that this is true even though the additional interest related to business income.

Q. I borrowed $500 from the bank last year on which I paid no interest. It just gave me $480 and I paid back $500 in instalments. Do I have any deduction?

A. Yes. The $20 discount is interest. Loan interest often is deducted in advance as discount rather than added as interest.

Q. I borrowed $1,000 from my bank in December last year and they "charged" me $75 in interest by giving me only $925. Can I deduct the $75?

A. Yes, but not for last year. You deduct the $75 only when you pay the note, which will be this year.

Q. Can I deduct the entire amount of the finance charge on my oil-company credit card as interest?

A. Yes.

Q. I have charge accounts where they charge me a

finance charge if I'm late in making payments. Can I deduct the finance charges as interest?

A. Yes. IRS says that where the store finance charge is only added if payment isn't timely made, is not a fixed charge, and is based on the unpaid balance and computed monthly, it constitutes interest because it's paid solely for the privilege of deferring payment. Prepayment charges for prepayment by a retail customer under a retail instalment contract are also classified as a deductible interest.

Q. I borrowed $3,000 on my life-insurance policy. The company collected the interest by adding to my loan. Can I deduct the $180 interest on the loan?

A. No. Only interest *paid* can be deducted. The fact that $180 was added to your loan isn't considered as your payment.

If you pay the interest by a separate check this year, you can claim the deduction. It might be wise to do this even if you have to borrow from someone else to get the money.

Q. At the end of December 1981, I paid the January 1982 interest instalment due on my mortgage. Can I deduct the interest even though it was not due?

A. If the January interest instalment covered the period of December 1981, the answer is yes. If the January instalment is interest for the month of January 1982, your prepayment in December 1981 is not deductible in 1981. The general rule is that interest paid in one year which is allocable to a period in the following year can only be deducted in the following year.

Charitable Contributions

The tax law permits you to deduct your charitable contributions up to a specified maximum.

Add up all the cash charitable contributions you made in '81. Except if you gave a cash contribution of $3,000 or more to any one organization, enter the total of all your

cash contributions at line 21a. Those of you who gave cash contributions of $3,000 or more to any one organization, show these separately for each such organization at line 21b.

The total of all contributions you made other than in cash is entered at line 22. List the kind of property you gave and the name of the organization to which you gave it.

If you made any contributions in property, you must submit with the return a description of the property, the date you gave it, and your method of valuation, except for securities. For any gift of property valued at more than $200 and for any gift of ordinary income or capital-gain property, you must explain any conditions attached to the gift, the way you obtained the property, and the cost or other basis of the property to you if owned by you for less than five years, or if you must reduce the contribution by any ordinary income or capital gain that would have resulted if you had sold the property at its fair market value. You are also expected to attach a signed copy of an appraisal. Enter the total of such contributions on line 22.

Line 23 is for those individuals who contributed more than the allowable maximum contributions in past years and therefore have a carryover of the excess to this year.

Enter on line 24 of this block the total of lines 21a-23, and again at line 36.

Q. Just how much can I deduct as charitable contributions?

A. You can, of course, deduct only the amounts which you actually pay. The overall limitation on what can be deducted—which affects few of us—is: No person can deduct more than 50 percent of his adjusted gross income. Contributions to almost any qualified public charitable, religious, or educational organizations and to the U.S., state, or local governments are deductible up to 50 percent of your adjusted gross income. But contributions to such organizations which do not normally receive a substantial part of their support from governmental bodies or the general public, such as private charitable foundations, are deductible only up to 20 percent of the taxpayer's adjusted gross income.

The general 50 percent ceiling drops to 30 percent for gifts of appreciated long-term capital-gains property.

Q. I agreed to give my church $700, but paid the pledge with stock that cost me $300 but was worth $700. Do I have to report the $400 profit?

A. You don't have to report the profit. But the amount of your charitable deduction may be cut to $300, depending on how long you held the stock before you gave it to the charity. The rule is that your profit can't be included as part of the contribution deduction where the profit would have been a short-term capital gain (or ordinary income) if you had sold the stock on the day you contributed it. Thus, if you had held that stock for one year or less, your contribution deduction would be only $300 and you would have no taxable profit. But if you had

Contributions (See page 19 of Instructions.)		
21 a Cash contributions (If you gave $3,000 or more to any one organization, report those contributions on line 21b) .		
b Cash contributions totaling $3,000 or more to any one organization (show to whom you gave and how much you gave) ▶		
22 Other than cash (see page 19 of Instructions for required statement)		
23 Carryover from prior years		
24 **Total contributions (add lines 21a through 23).** Enter here and on line 36 ▶		

held the stock for more than one year before giving it to the charity, your profit would have been long-term and you can deduct the full $700 and report no taxable profit.

Q. I run a small dry-goods store. I gave the local charitable organization merchandise that cost me $1,000 but which I normally would sell for $1,750. How do I handle this?

A. If the merchandise was contributed out of current purchases, you get no contribution deduction. You will automatically get an equivalent $1,000 deduction because the item will not be reported in your closing inventory. As I explained in the previous answer, since you would have realized ordinary income if you had sold the property, the profit can't be included as part of your contribution or other deduction.

Q. I pledged $500 to my church in December but didn't send the money until January 1982. Can I deduct the contribution for '81?

A. No. A charitable contribution is deductible only when paid. You will have to wait until you file your '82 return to claim the January payment.

Q. I mailed my $200 contribution on the last day, December 31. But the charity didn't cash the check until January. Can I claim the deduction for '81?

A. Yes. When you drop a check into the mails in a properly addressed and stamped envelope, you are considered to have paid the contribution.

Q. I gave $300 to a friend in need. Can I deduct this?

A. No. Contributions can only be deducted if made to a corporation, trust, community chest, fund, or foundation operated exclusively for purposes that are charitable, religious, educational, scientific, literary, or for the prevention of cruelty to children or animals. And the organization must be organized or created in the U.S.

Direct contributions to individuals can't qualify.

Q. I donated $200 to our local community to build a wing on the public library. Does this qualify?

A. Yes. Gifts to or for the use of a state, a territory, the United States or a political subdivision are deductible if made for exclusively public purposes.

Q. My fraternal lodge maintains a home for aged members. During the year I contributed $45 to the home. Does this qualify?

TAX TIP: *How Do Your Deductions Compare?*

If you're in the $10,000-to-$20,000 income bracket and if in 1981 you gave around $577 to various charities, you had about $885 of medical expenses, and you paid out roughly $2,286 for interest, your deductions for these items will match the average amounts being deducted by other taxpayers in your income class.

The chances are, therefore, that if and when a tax agent checks your return, he'll pass by your deductions without questioning them. You're taking off what has been calculated as typical amounts; your deductions appear reasonable.

If, though, your deductions are far above the totals you've just read, you're asking for a second look—and should your return be selected for an audit, you can bet you'll get it.

We assume that the reason you have bought this book is that you're a normal taxpayer trying to figure out how you can get your maximum deductions and pay a minimum tax without breaking the law or inviting a session with a Treasury sleuth.

Thus, we think you'll find it of considerable aid to know how the deductions you take compare with the averages for others in your income bracket. The table below is your guide.

And so the deductions mount as the income brackets mount. But comparisons in the rarefied income brackets aren't of practical concern to many of us.

Now, what do these comparisons mean to you? In addition to showing you how you compare, they flash two points:

• If you are claiming deductions well above the averages, presumably you're honest about it, but your chances of being questioned are decidedly enhanced, simply by the fact that you stand out. Be prepared with ample proof to back your claims.

• If you're claiming deductions well below the averages, presumably you're spending less than other taxpayers in your bracket. Or perhaps you're overlooking some deductions and this guide may jog you into hard thinking.

But note that these averages do not entitle you to deduct the average if you did not actually spend that much. You can only deduct what you actually spent for these expenses.

Adjusted gross income in thousands of dollars

	10—20	20—30	30—40	40—50	50—75	75—100	100 up
Medical expenses	$885	$570	$518	$514	$662	$820	$1,223
Taxes	1,292	1,868	2,526	3,327	4,562	6,565	13,409
Contributions	577	617	795	1,115	1,566	2,569	8,958
Interest	2,286	2,685	3,110	3,609	4,709	6,615	11,896

A. Yes. Gifts to a domestic fraternal society operating under the lodge system are deductible if to be used exclusively for religious, charitable, etc., purposes.

But note that you can't deduct contributions that are to be used to pay sickness or burial expense of members.

Q. **During the year, I attend about 5 movie and theater benefits for my local church or other charitable organizations. The tickets cost me about $200. Can I deduct the $200?**

A. You can't deduct the full $200. However, you can claim a charitable contribution for the excess of the $200 over the regular price for the tickets. Thus, if the regular price plus tax was $140, you can claim a $60 deduction.

Q. **I often buy raffles sold by my local church or charitable organization. Can I deduct the cost?**

A. No. You have merely paid for a chance to win a prize.

Q. **Are only contributions by cash or check deductible?**

A. No. You can take a deduction for the value of any property you gave to a charitable, religious, educational, etc., organization. For example, if you gave clothing, household articles, supplies, etc., to a charitable organization, the value of these things can generally be deducted.

However, in connection with these gifts of clothing, household articles, paintings, etc. (tangible personal property), note that if the property is worth more than it cost you, then 40 percent of that increase in value can't be deducted *if* the charity, etc., plans to resell it and not use it for its exempt purposes.

Also note that if you would have realized ordinary income or short-term capital gain from selling rather than giving the property as a contribution, then no part of the appreciation in value is deductible as part of the contribution.

Q. **How do I value old clothes, used furniture, drapes, etc., that I gave to my church? I probably couldn't get more than $25 from a used-clothes dealer, but if I had to replace them, they could run to $100 even in their present condition.**

A. The Treasury generally takes the view that it's the $25 the dealer would pay you, not how much it would cost you to replace them in their used condition. But some cases have allowed a deduction for the $100 that an ultimate consumer would have to pay, rather than a dealer; this is roughly your replacement cost. So if you aren't afraid of a Treasury battle, you might claim the $100; otherwise you would deduct only $25.

Again, if you would have realized a profit from selling this property, see the answers in the previous questions.

Q. **My child goes to parochial school and I gave the church $1,500 in lieu of tuition. Is this deductible?**

A. The Treasury claims that this amount is considered as tuition or in lieu of tuition and therefore not deductible.

Q. **During the year, I donated blood twice to a local community hospital. Can the value of the blood be deducted?**

A. IRS says no.

Q. **I spent over a month of the time as a voluntary nonpaid nurse in the local community hospital. I conservatively figure that my time was worth at least $600 and plan to claim this as a contribution. Am I right?**

A. No. The value of your time or services is not considered a charitable contribution.

Q. **As a volunteer nurse at a local hospital, I must wear a uniform, which I buy myself. Can this be deducted?**

A. Yes. The costs of uniforms which have no general utility and are required apparel while performing donated services are deductible.

Q. **I purchased $500 worth of bonds issued by my church to help finance a new building. Can I deduct the $500.**

A. No. A contribution isn't a contribution if you receive a consideration in return.

But if you contribute the bonds at a later date, you can claim a deduction.

Q. **I paid a $200 membership fee in joining my church. Is this deductible?**

A. Yes. Dues, membership fees, initiation fees, or assessments paid to a church, synagogue or other religious organization can be deducted. But similar payments to veterans' organizations, lodges, fraternal organizations, and country clubs are not deductible.

Q. **I pay $20 a year to a nonprofit cemetery company for the care of my parents' graves. Can I claim this as a deductible contribution?**

A. No. A contribution for the care of a particular lot or mausoleum crypt does not qualify. However, if a contribution is made to the nonprofit cemetery company that is irrevocably dedicated to the perpetual care of the cemetery as a whole, it is deductible.

Q. **A charitable organization ran a picnic in order to raise funds. I paid $20 for a box lunch that wasn't worth more than $5. Can I deduct the $15 "overpayment"?**

A. Yes. If you pay more than fair market value for goods, merchandise, property, services, etc., the overpayment can be claimed as a charitable contribution—assuming that the proceeds go to the organization.

Q. In connection with my free work for a charitable organization, I have to be away from home overnight. It cost me $250 during the year for meals and lodging while away from home. Can I claim this as a contribution to the organization?

A. Yes.

Q. In order for me to do voluntary work for a charitable organization, I had to hire a babysitter to care for my baby. Can I deduct the expense as a charitable contribution?

A. No.

TAX TIP: Use of Car in Connection with Charitable Work

If *you* use *your* car in connection with volunteer work for a religious, charitable, or educational organization, you can claim a charitable deduction for the cost of gas, oil, etc. But you can't claim a deduction for depreciation and insurance on your car.

Determining the actual gas, oil, repair, etc. costs applicable to the charitable use of the car can be a difficult problem. But IRS says that if you wish, you can use a quick and easy rule of thumb:

Merely determine the mileage that you used the car for charitable purposes and multiply that by 9 cents a mile. IRS will accept the result as a deductible charitable expense.

Thus, if you calculate that you drove your car 1,700 miles in connection with charitable work during '81, you can deduct $153 (9 cents times 1,700 miles), as a charitable contribution.

Any parking fees and tolls attributable to the charitable travel can be added to this mileage allowance.

TAX TIP: Back Up Your Checks to Charity

A canceled check made out to a church, school, or other charitable organization is not automatic proof of a charitable contribution deduction. Here's why:

Many payments made to charitable, religious, or educational organizations are used for noncharitable, etc., purposes. These amounts are not deductible even though paid to a church, school, etc.

For example, charitable organizations organize and sell tickets to benefit theatrical performances, sightseeing trips, tours, etc. The deductible charitable contribution for these events is not the face amount of the check, but only the excess of the amount paid over the fair market value of what the contributor gets. Thus if you pay $100 for benefit tickets that are normally worth $50, your contribution deduction is only $50; if you pay $2,500 for an all-expense trip worth $1,500, only $1,000 is deductible.

The Treasury may ask a contributor whose return is being examined to back up his deduction by furnishing a statement from the charitable organization showing the date, purpose, and amount of the contribution.

If you received any receipts or other evidence of a contribution from your charitable organization showing that it was a bona fide contribution, keep these records. They may save you a headache later on.

Make List of Contributions of Clothing, Furniture, Etc.

If you give contributions of used furniture, clothing, books, etc., make sure to get and keep a detailed receipted record of what you gave. If you can also get a valuation from the charity, do so. If you do not keep these records, an examining agent may bar or reduce the deductions.

Did You Use Your Credit Cards to Make a Contribution?

IRS says you are considered as having made the contribution when you "charged" the contribution, not when you paid the credit company.

Casualty or Theft Loss(es) *(You must attach Form 4684 if line 29 is $1,000 or more, OR if certain other situations apply.) (See page 19 of Instructions.)*

25 Loss before reimbursement		
26 Insurance or other reimbursement you received or expect to receive		
27 Subtract line 26 from line 25. If line 26 is more than line 25, enter zero . . .		
28 Enter $100 or amount from line 27, whichever is smaller		
29 Total casualty or theft loss(es) (subtract line 28 from line 27). Enter here and on line 37 ▶		

Losses from Accidents, Fires, Storm, or Other Casualty

Losses you suffer as the result of a sudden, unexpected, or unusual destructive force, such as an automobile collision, fire, flood, storm, drought, hurricane, or similar event are deductible at lines 25–29 of Schedule A. Similarly, a loss from a theft is deductible.

However, the amount of the loss from each casualty must be reduced by $100 to get the deductible amount as shown on line 29. This $100 reduction does not apply to business or income-producing property. Any loss attributable to the business or income-producing property is deductible in full.

The $100 reduction applies to the entire loss from each casualty, not to each item of property lost. And if you file a joint return with your spouse, there is only one $100 reduction against the entire loss of property of you and your spouse because of the casualty. If you had more than one casualty, omit lines 25 through 28. Instead, prepare on a separate sheet of paper a schedule for each casualty, using the information on lines 25 through 29 for each casualty. Total the net losses for each casualty, enter the total at line 29, and write in the margin to the right of line 29 "Multiple losses, see attachment."

Examples of losses which qualify and which do not.
You can deduct for losses from:
1. Fire.
2. Storm, such as heavy rain, freezing, winds, etc.
3. Automobile accidents that are caused by faulty driving of either driver, provided that the collision wasn't caused by your willful negligence, such as drunken driving.
4. Theft or embezzlement losses.
5. Mine cave-in damage to your property.
6. Vandalism.
7. Damages to trees or shrubs by storm.
8. Bursting hot-water boiler.
9. Freezing of water pipes. However, a loss in a business building has not been allowed.
10. Earthquake damages.
11. Damage through pressure of ice jam.
12. Cracking of walls, etc., caused by weakening of building foundations due to shrinkage of subsoil in drought. Note that the IRS takes the position that property damage resulting from drought is not a deductible casualty loss, except if incurred with respect to a trade of business or a transaction entered into for profit.
13. Damage through unusually heavy blasting in nearby quarry.
14. Damage to a car by a child—such as the breaking of the car starter by a child pressing on it while the motor is running.
15. Damage to septic tank and waterlines by accidental plowing.
16. Casualty losses to property of a minor dependent child's belongings. However, once the child reaches majority, the parent can't claim a deduction even if the child is still a dependent.
17. Pine beetle loss.
You cannot deduct for losses from:
1. Mislaid or lost property.
2. Misrepresentation by the seller. This is not considered a theft.
3. Expenses of taking care of personal injuries.
4. Cost of temporary lights, fuel, moving, or rental of temporary quarters.
5. Breakage of glassware, dishes, etc., by yourself, your maid, or your pets.
6. Drop in value because of fear of future storms, floods, etc.
7. Drying up of well through prolonged lack of rain, or hot summer, not amounting to drought.
8. Loss of property through confiscation by foreign government.
9. Damage from rats.
10. Gradual erosion.
11. Unexplained settling of house.
12. Cave-in of partially completed oil well.
13. Damage to land caused by seismograph explorations.
14. Inadvertent throwing away of jewelry.
15. Dropping watch or eyeglasses.
16. Disappearance of valuable dog.
17. Disappearance of clothing and baggage in transit.
18. Moth and carpet-beetle damage.
19. Auto breakdowns.
20. Termite damage.
21. Tree disease. Loss caused by disease is not viewed as sudden enough to qualify as a casualty even though the disease may be transmitted by insects. This applies to such diseases as Dutch Elm and "lethal yellowing" for coconut palm trees. However, a loss caused by insects, such as pine-beetle loss, can be deducted where sudden enough.
22. Drought. The IRS takes the view that generally a drought loss is not a casualty loss unless incurred with respect to a trade or business or a transaction entered into for profit. However, the Tax Court has allowed a drought loss for personal losses where the drought was of record

severity and the plants and shrubs were dead within a few months.

The IRS says you are to use and attach Form 4684 if (1) you had a net casualty or theft loss of $1,000 or more (after subtracting any reimbursement and the $100 limitation), (2) you had more than one casualty or theft, (3) you had more than one item lost or damaged by casualty or theft, (4) your casualty or theft involved trade, business, or income-producing property, or (5) you had a gain from casualty or thefts.

TAX TIP: If You Were Hit by Hurricanes, Floods, Drought, or Other Disasters

Hurricanes and other natural disasters, such as fires, storms, floods, etc., caused fantastic amounts of damage to homes and business properties in 1981. If you were involved, make sure you take the maximum deductions allowed under the law for losses you suffered. See the questions and answers giving you guides on this.

While the tax law permits you to deduct losses caused by casualties, a deduction of this type is normally a "red flag" for an examining agent. He is going to ask you to back up any casualty-loss deduction which you claim.

Therefore, be prepared to show:

1. The nature of the casualty and when it occurred (or, in the case of theft, when it was discovered);

2. That the loss was the direct result of the casualty (or, in the case of theft, that the property was actually stolen);

3. That you were the owner of the property;

4. The cost or other basis of the property, evidenced by purchase contract, deed, etc. (improvements should be supported by checks, receipts, etc.);

5. Depreciation allowed or allowable, if any;

6. Value before and after casualty; and

7. The amount of insurance or other compensation received or recoverable.

Get a written appraisal by an experienced and reliable appraiser, if possible.

And if you have any photographs or your property showing the condition before and after the damage, make sure you keep them to back up your claim.

How to Compute Your Loss

Your loss is the value before the casualty less the value afterward—but this loss may not be greater than the cost, or depreciated cost, of the property. From this figure, deduct at line 26 any insurance or other compensation received or recoverable because of the damage. If the property is nonbusiness or nonincome-producing property, the net loss computed above must be reduced by $100.

Q. My summer cottage was destroyed by fire. It cost me $8,500 but was worth $23,000 before the fire. Afterward it was worth only $9,000. I collected $5,000 from the insurance company. How do I compute my loss?

A. Using the formula I described above:

The value before the fire was	$23,000
The value after the fire was	9,000
Drop in value	$14,000
Limited to cost (basis) of	8,500
Insurance recovered	5,000
Loss	$ 3,500
Less $100 because property is personal (not business or income-producing)	100
Deductible loss	$ 3,400

Q. My daughter's bike, which I had just bought for $95, was stolen. I reported the theft to the police but it wasn't recovered. Can I deduct the $95?

A. No. While the loss qualified as a casualty loss, no deduction is allowed because the loss did not exceed $100.

Q. My automobile was in an accident and it cost me $450 to fix up the damages. Can I deduct the $450 repair bill less the $100 reduction?

A. The cost of repairing, replacing, or cleaning up after a casualty is considered by IRS not to be deductible as such. However, if these expenses don't improve the property but just bring the property back to its condition before the casualty, the costs may be used to measure the casualty loss. In your case, this rule will probably permit the $450 to represent a measure of the drop in value. Then reduce this by $100 to get your $350 deduction. But note that if the repairs did not restore your car to its precasualty condition, you can measure your loss deduction by the drop in value of your car if that is larger than the cost of the repairs; to do this you must prove that the repairs did not restore the car to its preaccident condition.

Q. I carry a $100-deductible insurance policy. My car had over $400 of damage in an accident, but all I paid to

have the damage repaired was $100. How much can I claim as a casualty loss?

A. Nothing. Your actual loss after reimbursement by the insurance company was only $100. The $100 reduction required by the tax law will bar any deduction if you used the car only for pleasure. If the car was used solely for business, you can deduct the $100 loss. If it was used half for business, $50 can be claimed as a deduction.

Q. My car was totally wrecked in an accident and I received its "Blue Book" value from my insurance company. Since it would have cost me much more to replace it, can I claim a casualty loss for the difference?

A. You may have to fight for it, but you will have the Tax Court's backing if you can prove the replacement cost by reference to the cost of a similar car. The court takes the view that the Blue Book value doesn't bar you from claiming a higher value and deducting as a casualty loss the excess over "Blue Book" value.

Q. A heavy rainstorm flooded the basement of my store and severely damaged a good deal of merchandise. I had to throw out $5,000 of merchandise (at my cost), which was uninsured. Can I deduct the $5,000?

A. Yes, you can deduct the $5,000. However, if you use inventories in determining your cost of goods sold, as almost surely you do, this $5,000 loss will automatically be reflected through a reduction in your closing inventory. If you want to show the $5,000 separately as a casualty loss, you will have to make a credit entry to purchases, reducing that figure. This will prevent a duplication of the loss. Since this is business property, the $100 flat deduction does not apply.

Q. Assume that I had recovered $2,000 in insurance. How would I handle the insurance recovery?

A. That would depend on how you handled the loss. If you let the closing inventory show the loss, the insurance proceeds would have to be included in income. If you showed the loss of $5,000 separately, after cutting your purchases by the same amount, the insurance proceeds would reduce the $5,000 casualty loss to $3,000.

Q. A heavy snowstorm did considerable damage to my home. I have filed a claim with the insurance company but haven't yet been paid. Do I take the full casualty loss this year and include the insurance next year?

A. No. Even though you don't receive the insurance until next year, you must reduce your casualty loss by the estimated amount of recoverable insurance or other recoverable compensation.

If your estimate is substantially incorrect, you will have to file an amended return or refund claim.

Q. My home was badly damaged by a flood last year and my employer gave me $1,000 to help me rehabilitate my house. Do I have to reduce my loss by the $1,000?

A. Yes. Amounts received from an employer or from disaster-relief agencies, in the form of cash or property, in order to restore or rehabilitate property lost or damaged in a casualty, reduce the amount of the deductible loss.

Q. In this same disaster, I received food and other forms of subsistence. Do I have to reduce my loss by the value of this aid?

A. No. These are treated as tax-free gifts.

Q. I had a theft of $400, which was covered by insurance, but I didn't make any claim for fear of losing coverage or having my premiums increased. Can I deduct the $400, less the $100 exclusion?

A. The IRS and a district court say no. But the Tax Court holds that you can, even though you could have received insurance to cover your loss if you had filed a claim with your insurance company.

Q. It cost me $100 to have my property appraised in connection with determining my casualty-loss deduction. Can I deduct the $100?

A. Yes. Appraisal fees can be deducted as an expense of preparing your tax return. These expenses are not subject to the $100 reduction.

Show the costs of proving that you had a property loss,

TAX TIP: *If Your Property Damage Resulted from an Event Labeled as a Disaster by the President*

Many 1981 storms, floods, etc., were classified as disasters by the President. If your property suffered uninsured damage from such a disaster, you can choose to deduct your loss either on your 1981 return or your 1980 return. Therefore, check to see whether you would save more

taxes by claiming a refund on your 1980 return than by deducting the loss on your 1981 return. If you would, file a refund claim for 1980 no later than April 15, 1982. You can do this by filing a refund claim on Form 1040X.

such as your appraisal fees or the cost of photos, etc., on line 31 rather than adding them to your casualty loss.

Q. Many valuable trees on my property were damaged as a result of insect attack. Can I deduct a casualty loss?

A. IRS had originally barred any such loss deduction. But the Tax Court had permitted such loss to be deducted where pine trees were destroyed by pine-beetle infestation over a period of 30 days. As a result, IRS has agreed to the deduction where the loss happens very suddenly, in its example within 10 days.

Q. My property was damaged by an overflow of a nearby river. In addition to the damage caused by the water, I had to spend $1,000 to erect a dike to prevent future flooding. Is this part of my casualty loss?

A. No. While you may consider this a loss due to the flooding, the tax law views it as a capital improvement.

Q. A sudden freeze killed a number of my shrubs. It cost me $475 to replace them. However, since the original shrubs cost me nothing, am I barred from deducting any loss?

A. No. Orchards, trees, and shrubs in connection with nonbusiness property are viewed as part of the entire property. When you have a casualty loss on these items, you must compute the value of the entire property before and after the loss. This loss is limited to the basis of the entire property, not the basis of the shrubs.

Q. Last year an old family heirloom was stolen. While its value was only about $300, it was worth considerably more than that to me because of its sentimental value. Can I claim, say, $800 for the heirloom?

A. No. The casualty loss must be based on intrinsic and not sentimental value.

Q. I accidentally hit another car. Damages to my car were $450, but it cost me $650 to repair his car since it was my fault. Do I claim $1,100 as the casualty loss less $100?

A. No. You can claim only $350 ($450 minus $100). No deduction is allowed for damages to the other person's car. Nor could you claim any deduction if you had to pay for personal injuries incurred.

Q. Can banged-up fenders to my pleasure car that resulted from my misjudging my garage doors be claimed as a casualty loss?

A. Yes—to the extent that the loss exceeds $100.

Q. I accidentally dropped my wife's engagement ring into the kitchen sink and made junk out of it by turning on the garbage-disposal unit. Can I deduct this as a casualty loss?

A. Yes. The Treasury agrees that casualty losses include the ordinary everyday, domestic household mishaps.

Q. A storm damaged my house last year but I haven't repaired it yet. Do I claim the loss now or wait until I fix it up?

A. The loss must be claimed when the casualty occurred, not when you fix it up.

Q. I checked my special silverware and discovered that it had been stolen. However, the theft could have occurred in either 1980 or 1981. In which year do I claim the loss?

A. Theft losses are claimed in the year you discover the loss. Therefore, you deduct your loss in 1981.

Q. Because of faulty construction by the builder, my house is worth less than I paid for it. I can't collect for the damage, but can I claim a casualty loss?

A. No. IRS says that this is not a casualty.

Miscellaneous Deductions	(See page 19 of Instructions.)		
30 a Union dues			
b Tax return preparation fee			
31 Other (itemize) ▶			
32 Total miscellaneous deductions (add lines 30a through 31). Enter here and on line 38 . . . . ▶			

Miscellaneous Deductions

The last category under Itemized Deductions, called "Miscellaneous Deductions," includes line 30a for union dues, line 30b for tax return preparation fee, and line 31, a catchall section, for "other." These are discussed on the following pages. Certain unreimbursed employee expenses are deductible at this point. These are discussed under Adjustments for Employee Business Expenses on page 63.

Enter the total at line 32 and again at line 38.

Here Are Some Other Items You Can Deduct:

Service charges paid to union by a nonunion employee; attorneys' fees for collecting alimony or separate-maintenance payments that are taxable income to you; ordinary and necessary costs of producing or collecting income or of managing property held for producing or collecting income or of managing property held for production of income—such as the costs of: tax advice, safe-deposit box for holding taxable securities, investment counsel, custodian fees, clerical help, and office rent.

You can also deduct here dues to professional organizations and chambers of commerce, subscriptions to professional journals, amounts you paid in '81 to have your tax returns prepared, and any other expenses paid to produce or collect income or to manage or protect your property held for producing income.

Q. I incurred various expenses while seeking employment. Where do I deduct these expenses on Form 1040?

A. Any travel and transportation expenses incurred in seeking your new employment are deducted at line 24 on Form 1040, whether you use the flat standard deduction or itemized deductions.

But any expenses you incurred for typing, printing, and mailing resumes are deductible only if you itemize your deductions. These expenses would come under other deductions. You can't deduct these expenses at all if you use the flat standard deduction.

Bad Debts

If you have a loan outstanding that became worthless in 1981, you can deduct the loss. However, generally the loss will have to be treated as a short-term capital loss to be shown in Schedule D, unless the debt is a business bad debt which was originally created or acquired in your trade or business. In this case, the debt is to be deducted in Schedule C.

If the loan was made to a child or another relative, you will have to show that the loan was a legally collectible debt and not a gift, which is not deductible.

Q. I loaned $500 to my son to help him pay part of his tuition. He hasn't been able to get a job and I can't collect the amount. Can I claim the $500 as a bad debt?

A. It's highly questionable. The Treasury generally presumes that loans to children are gifts.

Q. A loan to a business acquaintance became worthless in 1980. However, I neglected to claim it as a deduction in that year. Can I claim this loss in 1981?

A. No. A bad debt can only be deducted for the year that it became worthless.

Q. I loaned $1,000 to a friend several years ago. He hasn't been able to repay the loan and there is no sense in suing, since I can't collect. Can I claim the $1,000 as a bad debt?

A. The question isn't easy to answer. To be claimed as worthless, a debt must not only be uncollectible now but also appear to be uncollectible at any time in the future. While the failure to sue isn't crucial, you will have to submit persuasive evidence that your friend will not be able to pay in the future. You will also have to show that the debt wasn't worthless before '81.

Q. I report on the cash basis. I loaned an individual $1,000 in 1980 at interest. He went bankrupt in 1981 and I haven't collected my $1,000 or $150 in interest. Can I deduct the $1,150?

A. No. While you can deduct the $1,000, you can't claim the $150 in accrued interest, since you didn't include this in your income or lay out the money.

Here Are Some Expenses You Can't Deduct:

Attorneys' fees paid to get a divorce or to prepare a will, to get a property settlement in a divorce, or to get appointed as a trustee or for legal help for personal matters; premiums you pay on your life insurance; commuting expenses; car-pool expenses; repairs to your home; repayment of your debts; insurance, including fire, property damage, etc., to your home; bridge and road tolls on personal trips; rent for your apartment or home; union assessments for accident, death, and sick benefits; expenses of producing tax-exempt income, such as safe-deposit-box costs for storing your tax-exempt bonds; costs of midday meals and meals while working overtime; entertaining friends.

You Can't Take Losses For:

Sale of your home, furniture, autos, etc., used for personal purposes; lost or misplaced cash or property; gambling losses that exceed your gambling gains.

TAX TIP : *Expenses of Visiting Your Broker*

Note that if you dabble in the market and travel to your broker's office to consult with him, the Tax Court says you can deduct your carfare to and from your broker. If you haven't kept a detailed record of your trips, a reasonable estimate can be deducted. But you can't deduct the fare to a broker if you go to his office primarily for tape-watching and not for consultation.

TAX TIP: Cost of Hunting for a Job

IRS says that you can deduct the cost of seeking new employment in your *same* trade or business, regardless of whether you get the new job. But you can't deduct the cost of seeking employment in a *different* trade or business, even if you get the job. Thus, if you paid an employment-agency fee for getting a new job in the same trade, you can deduct the fee. But if you paid a similar fee to get a job in a new trade or business, you can't deduct the fee.

A person who seeks employment for the first time can't deduct the cost of securing a job, because he or she is entering a new trade or business.

Education Expenses

You can deduct expenses for education if incurred primarily for either of the following reasons:

1. To maintain or improve the skills required in your trade or business or in performing the duties of your present employment, or:

2. To meet the specific requirements of your employer, or requirements of law or regulations, for keeping your present salary, status, or employment.

You can't deduct expenses for education if your primary purpose for incurring them is any of the following:

1. To get a new position.

2. To get a general education.

3. To meet the minimum requirements to qualify for or to establish a trade or business.

Q. Can I deduct education expenses even though I am an individual proprietor, not an employee?

A. Yes, even if you are an individual proprietor or a partner, you can deduct education expenses that maintain or improve skills required in your trade or business. Generally, these costs will be deductible if it's customary for other established members of your trade or business to get the education to maintain or improve skills required in your trade or business. But it isn't absolutely necessary that you be able to prove this in order to uphold your own education.

Q. Must I be forced in some way to take the education in order to be able to deduct the expenses?

A. Not necessarily. You can deduct the education expenses even if you voluntarily decide they will help you maintain or improve skills required in your trade or business, or your present job.

Q. I teach art in a high school. I am taking courses that will qualify me to teach mathematics. In the future I also expect to take courses that will qualify me to be a principal. Can I deduct the cost of the courses I am taking to qualify as a math teacher? Will I also be able to deduct the costs of training to qualify as a principal, when I take those courses?

A. Yes to both questions.

Q. I am a permanent teacher. The board of education regulations require us to take certain courses every two years in order to hold our jobs as permanent teachers. The courses also qualify us for automatic salary increases. Can I deduct the cost of these courses?

A. Yes, because you took them primarily to hold onto your present job.

Q. I taught school in early '81 and I then left to take courses full time to qualify for a better teaching job. Can I deduct my education expenses even though I was not teaching during the time I went to school?

A. IRS says you deduct these expenses if you were away from school on a leave of absence. But if you ended your previous school connection without a leave of absence, IRS and some courts say that you can't deduct your expenses of educating yourself for a better job. Another court says that you can deduct these expenses even though you completely ended your connection with the school where you taught. So, if you aren't afraid of an IRS battle, claim the deductions in either case.

Q. I am a public accountant. In order to qualify for the CPA examination I had to take some extra college courses. Are these deductible?

A. No, because these expenses are intended to meet the minimum requirements to become a CPA.

Q. I own a TV, radio, and phonograph repair shop, in which the bulk of my work is on TV. Because of the many new developments in hi-fi and stereo, I took special courses to catch up. Are my expenses deductible?

A. Yes, because they are primarily to maintain and improve the skills required in your trade.

Q. I am a physician who has a general practice. I took courses to qualify myself as a surgeon. Are these deductible?

A. Yes. The Treasury permits a doctor to deduct the costs of qualifying for a specialty within the medical field.

Q. Do educational expenses include laboratory fees, books, etc., in addition to tuition?

A. Yes.

Q. Is the cost of a correspondence-school course deductible if it meets all other requirements?

A. Yes.

Q. In order to attend college for the purpose of taking the courses needed to hold my job, I had to travel to another city. Are my travel expenses deductible?

A. If your education expenses qualify for deduction, then your cost of travel, meals, and lodging while away from home are also deductible if incurred primarily to take the courses. Any part of your expenses incurred in purely personal activity, such as sightseeing, social visits, etc., would not be deductible.

Q. I voluntarily took courses in '81 which I felt would help my chances of promotion by improving my skills. This year, 1982, I was actually promoted in the same type of work. Can I claim the costs as education expenses?

A. Yes. The Tax Court held that a person, such as you, who took courses to go up the business ladder from a lower-level store manager to a higher-level store manager was not going into a new trade or business.

Q. Can I deduct my costs of commuting to the school where I take courses?

A. No. This applies whether you take the courses in your home city or in a distant city. The cost of going from your permanent or temporary residence to the school is a nondeductible commuting expense.

Q. How do I take my deduction for deductible education expenses?

A. If you are an employee and itemize your deductions, then you deduct your unreimbursed education expenses (those for which your employer didn't pay you) on separate Schedule A, under "Miscellaneous Deductions" on line 31. Any money you spent on deductible travel, meals, or lodging in getting your deductible education should be shown on Form 2106 as deductible adjustments are totaled at line 23, Form 1040. These travel, meal, and lodging expenses are deductible regardless of whether you itemize your deductions on separate Schedule A or take the flat standard deduction.

Every employee should attach a statement to his return explaining his deduction and stating the relationship of the education to the duties of his employment. Treasury Form 2106 can be used for this purpose.

If you are a self-employed person, you should take your deductible education expenses and any deductible travel, meal, and lodging outlays on separate Schedule C. You too should attach a statement to your return explaining your deduction and showing the relationship of the education to your trade, business, or profession.

TAX TIP: *Teachers' Travel Expenses*

Teachers who travel, especially during a sabbatical leave, have a good chance of deducting their travel expense as an educational expense. Formerly, travel was generally considered personal in nature and not deductible. But the Treasury has eased up on this strict view.

It says that if the travel is directly related to the teacher's job, the expense can be deductible even though it may also be of the broadening, cultural type which is generally considered to yield personal satisfaction. Thus, if a French teacher, while on sabbatical leave granted for the purpose of travel, journeys through France in order to improve his knowledge of the French language, the expenses of his travel (including transportation and expenses necessarily incurred for meals and lodging), are deductible if he can show that the itinerary was chosen and the major portion of his activities during the trip were undertaken for the primary purpose of maintaining and improving his skills in the use and teaching of the French language, and that the places visited and his activities were of a nature calculated to result in actual or potential benefit to him in his position as a teacher in French. This would be so even though his activities while traveling may consist largely of visiting French schools and families, attending motion pictures, plays, or lectures in the French language, and the like. Similarly, an art teacher was allowed to deduct her travel expenses on a European trip taken in order to look at many of the great works of art which were the subject matter of her teaching. A history teacher who visited France during the summer vacation was likewise allowed a deduction where she visited places of professional interest to her.

But the travel must be directly related to the teaching position to be deductible. Thus, while the trip described above could be deductible by a French or history teacher, it couldn't be by a math teacher. A math teacher would have to show that the trip was directly related to his or her teaching of math and was expected to be of actual or potential benefit to him or her on the job.

These expenses would presumably be deductible as part of the Adjustments on line 23 of Form 1040.

TAX TIP: *Deducting the Costs of Qualifying for a "Specialty"*

The Treasury permits business and professional persons to deduct the costs of qualifying for a "specialty" within their field. Thus, a doctor engaged in general practice may deduct the expenses of training to specialize in some particular field of medicine. The training for a new specialty can be on a full-time basis if the taxpayer continues his or her business on a part-time basis. Thus, a dentist who returned to dental school on a full-time basis for postgraduate study in orthodontics was allowed to deduct his school costs while he continued his general dental practice on a part-time basis.

TAX TIP: *Correcting Oversights on Your 1980 Return*

Did you overlook any deductions when you prepared your '80 return? You don't have to take the attitude that it's now too late. The Treasury has made it easy for individuals to correct their earlier returns. You don't need any detailed legal "red tape." Just get Form 1040X from your local Director of Internal Revenue, fill it out, and file it. The form is a simple, one-sheet form, which merely asks for the change that would cancel the error. And the fact that you file this correction won't automatically cause your return to be examined. The Treasury indicates that your original return plus the correction you file on Form 1040X will be chosen and reviewed by the IRS in the same way as if you had filed a correct return originally.

Summary of Itemized Deductions
(See page 20 of Instructions.) **A**

33 Total medical and dental—from line 10 .

34 Total taxes—from line 16 . . . . .

35 Total interest—from line 20 . . . .

36 Total contributions—from line 24 . . .

37 Total casualty or theft loss(es)—from line 29 .

38 Total miscellaneous—from line 32 . .

39 Add lines 33 through 38 . . . . .

40 If you checked Form 1040, Filing Status box:
  2 or 5, enter $3,400 . . . . }
  1 or 4, enter $2,300 . . . . } . . .
  3, enter $1,700 . . . . . }

41 **Subtract line 40 from line 39. Enter here and on Form 1040, line 32b. (If line 40 is more than line 39, see the Instructions for line 41 on page 20.) . . . . . ▶**

Summary of Itemized Deductions

Add up all your deductions and enter the total on line 39.

Because the flat standard deduction is built into the Tax Tables and Tax Rate Schedules, it is first necessary to reduce the total of your itemized deductions by the amount of the flat standard deduction allocable to your filing status in order to avoid giving you the benefit of both the flat standard deduction and your itemized deductions. Therefore, you enter at line 40 of Schedule A the amount of the flat standard deduction allocable to your filing status. You then subtract line 40 from the total of your itemized deductions at line 39 and enter the difference on line 32b of Form 1040.

If line 40 is larger than line 39, you should not have itemized your deductions. Discard Schedule A and merely enter zero at line 41 and at line 32b of Form 1040, *unless* you are in one of the four groups I listed on page 78, who *must* use itemized deductions.

If you are in one of the four groups, then if line 40 is larger than line 39, don't enter any figure on 32b. Instead, fill out the IRS Worksheet below in order to arrive at the figure that you will enter at line 32c.

Worksheet

1 Enter the amount from Form 1040, line 32a . . . .

2 If you checked Form 1040, Filing Status Box:
  2 or 5, enter $3,400 . . . . }
  1 or 4, enter $2,300 . . . . }
  3, enter $1,700 . . . . . . }

3 Enter the amount from Schedule A, line 39 . . . .
  Caution: If you can be claimed as a dependent on your parents' return, be sure you check the box below line 32b of Form 1040.

4 Subtract line 3 from line 2 . . .

5 **Add lines 1 and 4.** Enter here and on Form 1040, line 32c. (Leave Form 1040, line 32b blank. Disregard the instruction to subtract line 32b from line 32a. Follow the rest of the instructions for Form 1040, line 32c).

Lines 32c–37: Figuring Your Tax

Subtract the amount on line 32b from the amount on line 32a and show the difference on line 32c. On line 33, you enter $1,000 times the number of exemptions you claimed on line 6e of Form 1040. For example, if you entered 5 on line 6e, you would enter $5,000 on line 33. You then subtract the amount on line 33 from that on line 32c and show the difference on line 34. This is your "taxable income."

If your taxable income at line 34 is under $5,000 *and* you don't use the alternative tax on Schedule D, or income averaging on Schedule G, or the 50 percent maximum tax on personal service income on Form 4726, then you must obtain your tax from the official IRS 1981 Tax Table (reproduced on pages 139-145) and enter the tax figure at line 35. The table automatically takes into consideration the zero bracket amount (standard deduction) and the 1.25 percent tax credit for '81.

For example, if your taxable income at line 34 is $26,175 and you are married, filing jointly, your tax will be in the income bracket $26,150-$26,200 under the column "married filing jointly." Your tax would be $4,946, which you would enter at line 35.

If your taxable income is $50,000 or more, or—regardless of amount of taxable income—you use the alternative tax on Schedule D, or income averaging on Schedule G, or the 50 percent maximum tax on Form 4726, you must compute your tax on your taxable income using the 1981 Tax Rate Schedules, instead of obtaining your tax from the IRS Tax Table. The tax obtained this way is generally to be reduced by the 1.25 percent tax credit for '81. This reduction is computed on an IRS Worksheet shown on page 146 of this book, alongside the 1981 Tax Rate Schedules. The reduced amount obtained on the Worksheet is entered on line 35.

For those who use Schedule G, the 1.25 percent tax reduction credit is taken in the process of arriving at the tax on this form. The 1.25 percent tax reduction credit is not allowed against the 50 percent maximum tax of Form 4726.

Line 36 is used by those relatively few taxpayers who have additional tax from accumulation distributions from trusts, etc.

Bring your tax from lines 35 and 36 down to line 37.

Married Persons Living Apart

Even though you are married, you can file as a single person, or a head of household, and get lower tax rates, if you meet all the following:

1. You file a separate return;

2. You paid more than half the cost to keep up your home for 1981;

3. Your spouse did not live with you at any time during 1981, and

4. For over 6 months of 1981, your home was the principal residence of your child or stepchild whom you can claim as a dependent.

Head of Household

A "head of household" pays lower taxes than other single persons on the same income.

In order to qualify as "head of household" you must be unmarried or legally separated under a decree of divorce or separate maintenance (including certain married persons who live apart and certain abandoned spouses) on December 31, 1981, and you must meet the following tests:

1. You paid more than half the cost of keeping up a home that was the main home of your father or mother, whom you can claim as a dependent. (You did not have to live with that parent.)

2. You paid more than half the cost of keeping up your home, which (except for temporary absences for vacation or school) was lived in all year by one of the following persons:

a. Your unmarried child, grandchild, foster child, or stepchild. (This person did not have to be your dependent.)

b. Any other person listed below whom you can claim as a dependent. However, this person does not qualify you if he or she is your dependent under a multiple-support agreement where two or more taxpayers supported the relative and no one gave more than half the support.

Grandparent
Brother
Sister
Stepbrother
Stepsister
Stepmother
Stepfather
Mother-in-law
Father-in-law
Brother-in-law
Sister-in-law
Son-in-law
Daughter-in-law
If related by blood:
  Uncle
  Aunt
  Nephew
  Niece

A person who is married to a nonresident alien may also be able to qualify as a head of household.

Q. How does the rule work for a mother or father?

A. First, your parent must qualify as your dependent. Next, your parent must live in a home that you maintain. But you don't have to live in the same household as your parent in order to qualify as the head of a household. You can set your parent up in a separate apartment, hotel room, etc.

Thus, it is important for you to make sure that at least one of your parents qualifies as a dependent. For example, if you contribute $3,000 toward supporting your widowed mother in her own apartment and she uses her own $3,000 of Social Security for the same purpose, you are neither contributing more than half the cost of maintaining the household nor are you furnishing more than half of your mother's support. Thus, she doesn't qualify as your dependent.

By giving her $1 more a year, you can accomplish two tax savings. You make her a dependent, entitling you to a $1,000 deduction. And if your $3,001 is used for costs of maintaining the household (see above) you are also obviously contributing more than half her household costs and you thereby qualify for the lower head-of-household rates.

Q. I pay to keep my parent in a home for the aged. Does this qualify as a household that I maintain for him?

A. The Treasury says that you do not qualify because you don't provide more than half the cost of maintaining the rest home for the parent. But the Tax Court took a more practical approach and permitted the head-of-household classification. So if you aren't afraid of a fight, claim the head-of-household tax classification in this situation.

If you keep your parent in a separate apartment or hotel room, even the Treasury will recognize your right to head-of-household rates.

Q. How does the rule work for my unmarried child, grandchild, or stepchild?

A. Your unmarried child, grandchild, or stepchild does not have to be your dependent in order to qualify you as a head of household, but your unmarried child, grandchild, or stepchild can't live in a home apart from you. You must maintain a household that is the principal residence of both you and your unmarried child, grandparent, or stepchild.

Q. How does the rule work for other relatives, such as a married child or a brother, uncle, etc.?

A. These persons must be your dependents and live with you in your household in order for you to qualify as a head of household.

Q. I kept my widowed mother in an apartment until she died in February 1980. Am I eligible for head of household computation?

A. Yes. If the person who qualifies you as a head of household either died or was born during 1980, you are eligible as a head of household so long as you maintained the principal residence for her or him during the entire part of 1980 that she or he was alive.

Q. In figuring out whether I furnish more than half the cost of maintaining a household, what items can I include?

A. You include the following expenses in the cost of maintaining a household: property taxes, mortgage interest, rents, utility charges, upkeep and repairs, property insurance, domestic help, and food eaten on the premises.

You can't include: clothing, education, vacations, life insurance, medical care, or the value of any services rendered by you or any other members of your household. Nor can you include the rental value of a home that you own and which is used as the household.

Certain Recent Widows and Widowers

A widow or a widower whose spouse died during either 1979 or 1980 may be able to use the rate used by married persons filing joint returns. To qualify, the widow or widower must have been eligible to file a joint income-tax return with the deceased spouse in the year the spouse died, even if a joint return wasn't actually filed.

Also, the widow or widower mustn't have remarried and must furnish over half the cost of maintaining his or her home, which is also the principal residence of a son, stepson, daughter, or stepdaughter for whom a dependence exemption can be claimed. In determining whether you paid over half the costs, the tests are the same as those set out for a head of household.

Here's how the tax rates work out. For 1980, when your husband died, you were entitled to file a joint return to get full income splitting. For the next two years after his death, 1981 and 1982, while you are supporting the child, you can still get full income-splitting rates as a qualified widow. For 1983 and the years following, during which you are supporting the child, you will get head-of-household rates. (See page 100.) And if and when you remarry, you qualify for full income splitting again.

Once you have determined which classification applies to you, you simply find your tax on the appropriate Tax Table or compute it, if so required, and enter the tax on line 35.

TAX TIP: Income Averaging

Before you complete your return, don't fail to make this important checkup. It may save you considerable tax money. If you qualify, part of your '81 income (your averageable income) is, *in effect,* taxed as if it is spread over 5 years, thus giving you the benefit of lower tax rates.

Dig out your Forms 1040 for 1977, 1978, 1979, and 1980. Copy the figure shown on line 34 of each return. (If you filed a Form 1040A for 1977 and for 1978, use the figure shown on line 10 for those years. If you filed a Form 1040A for 1979 and/or 1980, use the figure on line 11.) Subtract from each year's figure the number of your total exemptions times $750 for '77 and '78, and times $1,000 for '79 and '80. This gives you the taxable income for each of those years. After that, add together the net amounts for each year, divide by 4, and multiply by 120 percent. If your 1981 taxable income exceeds that figure by $3,000 or more, you can use income averaging.

Income averaging can save you tax money. But it involves a somewhat complicated computation, and it may be advisable to consult a professional adviser if you qualify for income averaging.

Q. My taxable incomes for 1977—1980 are as follows: $7,500, $8,000, $9,500, $12,000. My 1981 taxable income is $20,000. How do I figure whether I can use income averaging?

A. Add up the four figures, which gives you $37,000. Divided by four equals $9,250; multiplied by 120 percent brings the amount to $11,100. Since your '81 taxable income of $20,000 is more than $3,000 in excess of $11,000, you qualify for income averaging.

CREDITS

Credits (See Instructions on page 13)						
	38	Credit for contributions to candidates for public office . . .	38			
	39	Credit for the elderly (attach Schedules R&RP)	39			
	40	Credit for child and dependent care expenses (attach Form 2441) .	40			
	41	Investment credit (attach Form 3468)	41			
	42	Foreign tax credit (attach Form 1116)	42			
	43	Work incentive (WIN) credit (attach Form 4874)	43			
	44	Jobs credit (attach Form 5884)	44			
	45	Residential energy credit (attach Form 5695)	45			
	46	Total credits. Add lines 38 through 45		46		
	47	Balance. Subtract line 46 from line 37 and enter difference (but not less than zero) . ▶		47		

Line 38: Credit for Political Contributions

You can take a direct credit against your tax at line 38, Form 1040, for qualified political contributions.

Here is how the credit works: A credit is allowed at line 38, Form 1040, for one-half of the amount of qualified political contributions you made in 1981 up to $200 of contributions by married persons filing joint returns. This means that the maximum credit allowed on a joint return is limited to no more than $100 for political contributions of $200 or more during 1981. On other returns, this limit on the amount of credit that you can take is $50 for contributions of $100 or more. In no event can your credit be larger than your tax.

You can take the credit for your qualified political contributions regardless of whether you itemize your personal deductions or take the standard deduction. Each dollar of credit will cut your tax due (or increase your refund) by one dollar.

What are qualified political contributions? These include contributions or gifts that you made during '81 to (1) any candidates for federal, state, or local elective public office; (2) any committee organized to influence the nomination or election of such candidates; (3) the national, state or local committees of a national political party.

Line 39: Credit for the Elderly

If you or your spouse are 65 or over, you may be entitled to a credit against your tax in an amount equal to 15 percent of a specified amount as shown on Schedule R. But you can't qualify for this credit and shouldn't bother with filling out Schedule R if you are a married couple who are both 65 or over and have an adjusted gross income (line 32a Form 1040) over $17,500, or over $15,000 if only one of you is 65 or over, and over $12,500 if you are single and 65 or over, or over $8,750 if you are married filing separately, 65 or over, and have not lived with your spouse at any time during 1981. You are also barred from this credit if your Social Security or Railroad Retirement Act pension or annuity or other pensions excludable from income exceeds the maximum amounts shown on Schedule R, line 1, for your status. The credit can be taken for a nonresident alien married to a U.S. citizen or resident who chooses to file a joint return and be taxed on worldwide income.

Because of the rise in Social Security benefit payments, relatively few persons who receive Social Security monthly payments will be eligible for the credit. The maximum possible credit is $3,750 if married with both spouses over 65, and $2,500 for a single person over 65, less the Social Security payments. Most Social Security benefit payments will exceed these limits and kill the credit.

Furthermore, if your income is low enough so that you will have no tax to pay, the credit for the elderly will be of no use to you because it can only be applied to reduce any income tax that you would otherwise have to pay. For example, if you are a married couple who are both over 65, you will definitely have no tax to pay unless your gross income is at least over $7,400.

If you do qualify for the credit, then check the appropriate box and place the amount shown for the box on line 1 of Schedule R.

On line 2a, show the total you received from pensions and annuities that are not taxed. (Do not include amounts received from worker's compensation, insurance, damages, etc., for injury or sickness.) Include payments received from: Social Security (include Medicare premiums); Railroad Retirement (but not supplemental annuities); veterans' pensions (but not military disability pensions).

On line 2e, enter half of your adjusted gross income (line 32a, Form 1040) in excess of $7,500 if you are single, in excess of $10,000 if you are married and filing jointly, and in excess of $5,000 if you are married and filing separately and have not lived with your spouse at any time during the taxable year.

On line 3, add the amounts on lines 2a and e.

On line 4, subtract line 3 from line 1. If line 3 is larger than line 1, don't file this schedule. If the amount on line 1 exceeds the figure on line 3, enter the excess here.

On line 5, enter 15 percent of line 4.

On line 6, show the amount of tax on line 37 of Form 1040.

On line 7, the credit for the elderly is the smaller of the amounts of line 5 and 6. Enter this same figure at line 39 of Form 1040.

Q. Both my husband and I are over 65. Our adjusted gross income is $9,000 and our total Social Security payments are $3,600. How much credit can we claim?

A. The maximum amount on which you could have claimed credit is $3,750, but you must subtract from this the $3,600 of Social Security payments that you received. This leaves you with only $150 on which to take the 15 percent credit. Your credit thus comes to $22.50, which you can use to reduce your income taxes.

Q. We received $8,000 of dividends and interest during the year plus $2,800 of Social Security payments. We are both over 65. Does this mean that we can take a 15 percent credit for the elderly on $950 ($3,750 minus $2,800) which will give us a credit of $142.50?

A. Not quite. Your regular tax on your entire income will come to only $81. Therefore, your credit will be limited to only $81.

Certain taxpayers under 65 who receive income under a public retirement system can also qualify for a 15 percent credit. If you qualify, you must fill out Schedule RP.

If you or your spouse are 65 or over and one of you can use the new credit for the elderly while the other qualifies with a pension from a public retirement system, you and your wife can elect to use either credit.

Community-Property States

You should disregard community-property laws in figuring the credit for the elderly on Schedule RP. (Community-property states are: Arizona, California, Idaho, Louisiana, Nevada, New Mexico, Texas, and Washington.) The total of all taxable and nontaxable income should be entered in the column for the spouse who received it.

Schedules R & RP
(Form 1040)
Department of the Treasury
Internal Revenue Service

Credit for the Elderly
▶ See Instructions for Schedules R and RP.
▶ Attach to Form 1040. ▶ Schedule RP is on back.

OMB No. 1545-0074
1981
21

Name(s) as shown on Form 1040

Your social security number

Please Note: *IRS will figure your Credit for the Elderly and compute your tax. Please see "IRS Will Figure Your Tax and Some of Your Credits" on page 3 of the Form 1040 instructions and complete the applicable lines on Form 1040 and Schedule R or RP.*

Should You Use Schedule R or RP?

If you are:	And were:	Use Schedule:
Single	▶ 65 or over	R
	▶ under 65 and had income from a public retirement system	RP
Married, filing separate return [1]	▶ 65 or over (unless joining in the election to use Schedule RP with your spouse who is under 65 and had income from a public retirement system)	R
	▶ under 65 and had income from a public retirement system (unless your spouse is 65 or over and does not join in the election to use Schedule RP)	RP
Married, filing joint return	▶ both 65 or over	R
	▶ one 65 or over, and one under 65 with no income or income other than from a public retirement system	R
	▶ both under 65 and one or both had income from a public retirement system . .	RP
	▶ one 65 or over, and one under 65 with income from a public retirement system .	R or RP [2]

[1] You can take the credit on a separate return ONLY if you and your spouse lived apart for the whole year. See "Purpose" in Schedules R&RP instructions for limitation.

[2] Figure your credit on both schedules to see which gives you more credit.

Schedule R   **Credit for the Elderly—For People 65 or Over**
If you received nontaxable pensions (social security, etc.) of $3,750 or more or your adjusted gross income (Form 1040, line 32a) was $17,500 or more, you cannot take the credit for the elderly. Do not file this schedule.

Filing Status and Age (check only one box)		
A ☐	Single, 65 or over	
B ☐	Married filing joint return, only one spouse 65 or over	
C ☐	Married filing joint return, both 65 or over	
D ☐	Married filing separate return, 65 or over, and did not live with spouse at any time in 1981	**R**

1 Enter: { $2,500 if you checked box A or B . . . . }
         { $3,750 if you checked box C . . . . }
         { $1,875 if you checked box D . . . . }
  1

2 a Enter amounts you received as pensions or annuities under the Social Security Act or under the Railroad Retirement Acts (but not supplemental annuities), and certain other exclusions from gross income (see instructions). **If none, enter zero** **2a**

  b Enter amount from Form 1040, line 32a . .   **2b**

  c Enter: { $7,500 if you checked box A . . . }
         { $10,000 if you checked box B or C . } ·   **2c**
         { $5,000 if you checked box D . . . }

  d Subtract line 2c from 2b. If line 2c is more than line 2b, enter zero **2d**

  e Enter one-half (½) of line 2d **2e**

3 Add lines 2a and 2e. (If line 3 is the same or more than line 1, you cannot take the credit; do not file this schedule. If line 3 is less than line 1, go on to line 4.) **3**

4 Subtract line 3 from line 1 . . . .   **4**

5 Multiply line 4 by 15% (.15) **5**

6 Enter amount of tax from Form 1040, line 37. (If this amount is zero, you cannot take the credit; do not file this schedule.) **6**

7 Enter the amount from line 5 or line 6, above, whichever is less. This is your **Credit for the Elderly.** Enter the same amount on Form 1040, line 39 . . . . ▶   **7**

For Paperwork Reduction Act Notice, see Form 1040 Instructions.

343-065-1

Schedules R&RP (Form 1040) 1981

OMB No. 1545-0074

Name(s) as shown on Form 1040	Your social security number

Schedule RP	Credit for the Elderly—For People Under 65 Who Had Pension or Annuity Income from a Public Retirement System	**21**

If you are under 72 and received nontaxable pensions (social security, etc.) of $2,500 or more or your earned income (salaries, wages, etc.) was $3,950 or more, you cannot take the credit for the elderly. Do not file this schedule.

Name(s) of public retirement system(s)

RP

Filing Status and Age (check only one box)

A ☐ Single, under 65

B ☐ Married filing joint return, one spouse is under 65, and that person had income from a public retirement system. (If you checked this box and had community property income, see Community Property Income on page 26 of the instructions.)

C ☐ Married filing joint return, both under 65. (If you checked this box and had community property income, see Community Property Income on page 26 of the instructions.)

D ☐ Married filing separate return, under 65, and did not live with your spouse at any time in 1981.

E ☐ Married filing separate return, 65 or over, did not live with your spouse at any time in 1981, and you are joining with your spouse in electing to use Schedule RP.

Column (b)—Fill out column (b) whether you file a separate or joint return.

Column (a)—Fill out column (a) if you file a joint return. Use it only to show amounts for:
- The wife, if both of you were under 65, or
- The spouse who was 65 or over.

		(a)	(b)
1 Enter:	{ $2,500 if you checked box A . . . . ⎫ $3,750 if you checked box B or C. Allocate this amount between you and your spouse, but do not enter more than $2,500 for either of you. It will generally be to your benefit to allocate the greater amount to the spouse with more retirement income . . $1,875 if you checked box D or box E . . . . ⎭ } **1**		
2 Enter:			
a Amounts you received as pensions or annuities under the Social Security Act or under the Railroad Retirement Acts (but not supplemental annuities), and certain other exclusions from gross income (see instructions). **If none, enter zero** **2a**			
b Earned income such as wages, salaries, fees, etc. you received (does not apply to people 72 or over). (See page 26 of instructions for definition of earned income.):			
(i) If you are under 62, enter earned income that is over $900 . . . . **2b(i)**			
(ii) If you are 62 or over but under 72, enter an amount that you will figure as follows: If earned income is $1,200 or less, enter zero . . . . . If earned income is over $1,200 but not over $1,700, enter one-half of the amount over $1,200 . . . If earned income is over $1,700, enter the amount over $1,450 . . . . } **2b(ii)**			
3 Add lines 2a and 2b **3**			
4 Subtract line 3 from line 1. (If the result for either column is more than zero, go on. If the result for either column is zero or less, do not complete the rest of the lines in that column. If the result for both columns is zero or less, you cannot take the credit; do not file this schedule.) **4**			
5 Retirement income:			
a If under 65— Enter only income from pensions and annuities under public retirement systems (e.g. Federal, State Governments, etc.) that you received as a result of your services or services of your spouse that you reported as income. Do not enter social security, railroad retirement or certain other payments reported on line 2a **5a**			
b If 65 or over— Enter total of pensions and annuities, interest, dividends, proceeds of retirement bonds, and amounts you received from individual retirement arrangements and individual retirement annuities that you reported as income, and gross rents from: Schedule E, Part I, columns A–C, line 3a. Also include your share of gross rents from partnerships and your share of taxable rents from estates and trusts **5b**			
6 Enter amount from line 4 or line 5, whichever is less. **6**			

7 Add amounts in columns (a) and (b) of line 6. Enter total here . . . . ▶ **7**

8 Multiply line 7 by 15% (.15) **8**

9 Enter amount of tax from Form 1040, line 37. (If this amount is zero, you cannot take the credit; do not file this schedule.) **9**

10 Enter the amount from line 8 or line 9, above, whichever is **less**. This is your **Credit for the Elderly.** Enter the same amount on Form 1040, line 39 . . . . ▶ **10**

For Paperwork Reduction Act Notice, see Form 1040 Instructions. ☆ U.S. GOVERNMENT PRINTING OFFICE : 1981—O-343-065

343-065-1

Line 40: Credit for Child and Dependent Care Expenses

An important credit is allowed on line 40 for certain child and dependent care expenses necessary to enable you to go to work. The credit can be as much as $400 if you have one qualifying individual in your household and $800 if you have more than one qualifying individual. Note that this is a credit that directly reduces your taxes instead of a deduction that simply reduces your taxable income.

Who can obtain the credit: You can if you furnish more than half the cost of maintaining a household which includes one or more of the following qualifying individuals, and you incur employment-related expenses that enable you to be gainfully employed.

The qualifying individuals must fall into one of the following categories:

1. A person who is under 15 (14 or younger) and for whom you are entitled to a dependence deduction (your own child or other dependent) or would be entitled to a dependence exemption but for the fact that this individual has $1,000 or more of income, *or:*

2. A dependent of yours who is physically or mentally incapable of caring for himself, for example your ill parent (the fact that you can't claim a dependency exemption for this individual because he has income of $1,000 or more is immaterial), *or:*

3. Your wife (or husband) if she (or he) is physically or mentally incapable of caring for herself (or himself).

Amount of credit. The credit is 20 percent of up to $2,000 of your employment-related expenses paid during the year ($400 maximum credit) if there is one qualifying individual in your household, and 20 percent of up to $4,000 ($800 maximum credit) if there are two or more qualifying individuals.

What are employment-related expenses. The 20 percent credit can be claimed on the following expenses if incurred to enable you to be gainfully employed. The expenses must be incurred while gainfully employed for yourself or others or in the active search for gainful employment. But unpaid volunteer work for a nominal salary does not qualify.

1. Expenses for household services such as for a maid, and housekeeper, but not for gardeners, chauffeurs, or bartenders.

2. Expenses for care for a dependent child under 15. These would also include certain out-of-household expenses such as costs of a day-care center or cost of leaving a child in another person's home. And you can't take a credit on expenses incurred for a child's education in the first or higher grades. Thus, fees paid to nursery or kindergarten schools up to $200 a month, etc., as out-of-household expenses would be eligible for credit.

Your employment-related expenses can't exceed your earned income if you are unmarried at the end of the year, or the *lesser* of your or your spouse's earned income if you are married at the end of the year. But if one spouse is a full-time student or a disabled spouse, then for each month of full-time study or disability, that spouse is considered to have earned income of $166.66 if there is one qualifying person (who can be the spouse if disabled), and $333 if there are two or more qualifying persons (one of whom may be the spouse if disabled).

You can claim a credit for payment to the following relatives as qualifying employment-related expenses, but only if neither you nor your spouse can claim the relative as a dependent:

1. Your son or daughter, or their children.

2. Your stepson or stepdaughter.

3. Your brother, sister, stepbrother, or stepsister.

4. Your father or mother or an ancestor of either.

5. Your stepfather or stepmother.

6. A son or daughter of your brother or sister.

7. A brother or sister of your father or mother.

8. A son-in-law, daughter-in-law, father-in-law, mother-in-law, brother-in-law, or sister-in-law of the taxpayer.

9. A dependent who has his principal place of abode in your home and is a member of the taxpayer's household.

Special rules for married and divorced individuals. If you are married and living together, you can get the credit if you file a joint return.

If you are married and living apart, you can claim the credit on your separate return only if you maintain a household for which you furnish half the cost for the year, which is the principal place of abode of your child or other qualifying individual for more than half the year, and from which home your spouse is absent for the last six months of the year.

If you are divorced or legally separated and want to claim the credit for your under-15-year-old child, the child must receive more than half of his support from both you and your spouse, he must be in your or your spouse's custody for more than half the year, and you are the parent who has had custody of the child for the longer period. You do not have to be able to claim the child as a dependent.

| Form **2441**
Department of the Treasury
Internal Revenue Service | **Credit for Child and Dependent Care Expenses**
▶ Attach to Form 1040.
▶ See Instructions below. | OMB No. 1545–0068
1981
26 |

Name(s) as shown on Form 1040

Your social security number

1 See the definition for "qualifying person" in the instructions. Then read the instructions for line 1.

(d) During 1981, the person lived with you for:

(a) Name of qualifying person	(b) Date of birth	(c) Relationship	Months	Days

2 Persons or organizations who cared for those listed on line 1. See the instructions for line 2.

(a) Name and address (If more space is needed, attach schedule)	(b) Social security number, if applicable	(c) Relationship, if any	(d) Period of care From Month—Day	To Month—Day	(e) Amount of 1981 expenses (include those not paid during the year)

To Figure Your Credit, You MUST Complete ALL Lines That Apply

3 Add the amounts in column 2(e) **3**

4 Enter $2,000 ($4,000 if you listed two or more names in line 1) or amount on line 3, whichever is less . . . **4**

5 Earned income (wages, salaries, tips, etc.). See the instructions for line 5. An entry MUST be made on this line.

   (a) If unmarried at end of 1981, enter your earned income . . . .

   (b) If married at end of 1981, enter:

      (1) Your earned income . . . $ _____ | Enter the lesser

      (2) Your spouse's earned income $ _____ | of b(1) or b(2) . . ▶ **5**

6 Enter the amount on line 4 or line 5, whichever is less **6**

7 Amount on line 6 paid during 1981. An entry MUST be made on this line . . . . ▶ **7**

8 Child and dependent child care expenses for 1980 paid in 1981. See instructions for line 8 . . . **8**

9 Add amounts on lines 7 and 8 . . . . **9**

10 Multiply line 9 by 20 percent **10**

11 Limitation:

   a Enter tax from Form 1040, line 37 . . . . **11a**

   b Enter total of lines 38, 39, and 41 through 43 of Form 1040 . . **11b**

   c Subtract line 11b from line 11a (if line 11b is more than line 11a, enter zero) **11c**

12 Credit for child and dependent care expenses. Enter the smaller of line 10 or line 11c here and on Form 1040, line 40 . **12**

13 If payments listed on line 2 were made to an individual, complete the following:

Yes | No

   (a) If you paid $50 or more in a calendar quarter to an individual, were the services performed in your home? . . . .

   (b) If "Yes," have you filed appropriate wage tax returns on wages for services in your home (see instructions for line 13)? . . . . .

   (c) If answer to (b) is "Yes," enter your employer identification number . . . . . . ▶

Paperwork Reduction Act Notice.—The Paperwork Reduction Act of 1980 says we must tell you why we are collecting this information, how we will use it, and whether you have to give it to us. We ask for the information to carry out the Internal Revenue laws of the United States. We need it to ensure that you are complying with these laws and to allow us to figure and collect the right amount of tax. You are required to give us this information.

General Instructions

If you or your spouse worked or looked for work, and you spent money to care for a qualifying person, this form might save you tax.

What is the Child and Dependent Care Expenses Credit?—This is a credit you can take against your tax if you paid someone to care for your child or dependent so that you could work or look for work. You can also take the credit if you paid someone to care for your spouse. The instructions that follow list tests that must be met to take the credit. If you need more information,

please get **Publication 503**, Child and Disabled Dependent Care.

For purposes of this credit, we have defined some of the terms used here. Refer to these when you read the instructions.

Definitions

A qualifying person can be:

● Any person under age 15 whom you list as a dependent. (If you are divorced, legally separated, or separated under a written agreement, please see the Child Custody Test in the instructions.)

● Your spouse who is mentally or physically not able to care for himself or herself.

● Any person not able to care for himself or herself whom you can list as a dependent, or could list as a dependent except that he or she had income of $1,000 or more.

A relative is your child, stepchild, mother, father, grandparent, brother, sister, grandchild, uncle, aunt, nephew, niece, stepmother, stepfather, stepbrother, stepsister, mother-in-law, father-in-law, brother-in-law, sister-in-law, son-in-law, and daugh-

ter-in-law. A cousin is not a relative for purpose of this credit.

A full-time student is one who was enrolled in a school for the number of hours or classes that is considered full time. The student must have been enrolled at least 5 months during 1981.

What Are Child and Dependent Care Expenses?

These expenses are the amounts you paid for household services and care of the qualifying person.

Household Services.—These are services performed by a cook, housekeeper, governess, maid, cleaning person, babysitter, etc. The services must have been needed to care for the qualifying person as well as run the home. For example, if you paid for the services of a maid or a cook, the services must have also been for the benefit of the qualifying person.

Care of the Qualifying Person.—Care includes cost of services for the well-being and protection of the qualifying person.

(Continued on back)

343-157-1

Care does not include expenses for food and clothes. If you paid for care that included these items and you cannot separate their cost, take the total payment.

Example: You paid a nursery school to care for your child and the school gave the child lunch. Since you cannot separate the cost of the lunch from the cost of the care, you can take all of the amount that you paid to the school.

This example would not apply if you had school costs for a child in the first grade or above because these costs cannot be counted in figuring the credit.

You can count care provided outside your home if the care was for your dependent under age 15.

You can claim medical expenses you paid for the qualifying person if you paid them so you could work or look for work. If you itemized deductions, you may want to take all or part of these expenses on Schedule A. For example, if you can't take all of the medical expenses on Form 2441 because your costs for care have reached the limit ($2,000 or $4,000), you can take the rest of the medical expenses on Schedule A. If you show all of the medical expenses on Schedule A, you cannot take on Form 2441 that part you could not deduct on Schedule A because of the 3-percent limit.

To Take This Credit.—You must file Form 1040, not Form 1040A, and you must meet all of the tests listed below.

(1) You paid for child and dependent care so you (and your spouse if you were married) could work or look for work.

(2) One or more qualifying persons lived in your home.

(3) You (and your spouse if you were married) paid more than half the cost of keeping up your home. This cost includes rent; mortgage interest; utility charges; maintenance and repairs; property taxes and property insurance; and food costs (but not dining out).

(4) You must file a joint return if you were married. There are two exceptions to this rule. You can file a separate return if:

(a) You were legally separated; or

(b) You were living apart and:

• The qualifying person lived in your home for more than 6 months; and

• You paid more than half the cost of keeping up your home; and

• Your spouse did not live in your home during the last 6 months of your tax year.

(5) You paid someone, other than your spouse or a person for whom you could claim a dependency exemption, to care for the qualifying person.

You are allowed to pay a relative, including a grandparent, who was not your dependent. If the relative is your child, he or she must also have been 19 or over by the end of the year.

Child Custody Test.—If you were divorced, legally separated, or separated under a written agreement, your child is a qualifying person if you had custody for the longer period during 1981. The child must also have:

• Received over half of his or her support from the parents, and

• Been in the custody of one or both parents for more than half of 1981, and

• Been under 15, or physically or mentally unable to care for himself or herself.

Credit Limit.—The credit is generally 20% of the amount you paid someone to care for the qualifying person. The most

you can figure the credit on is $2,000 a year for one qualifying person ($4,000 for two or more).

Line-by-Line Instructions

Line 1.—*In column (a)* list the name of each qualifying person who was cared for during 1981 so you could work or look for work. In column (b) show the date of birth of each person. In column (c) show that person's relationship to you (for example: son or daughter). In column (d) show the number of months and days each person lived in your home during 1981. Count only the times when the person was qualified.

Line 2.—*In column (a)* show the name and address of the person or organization who cared for each qualifying person. If you listed a person who was your employee and who provided the care in your home, then in column (b) enter that person's social security number. Leave column (b) blank if the person: was not your employee; was self-employed; was an employee of an organization or a partnership; or did not provide the care in your home.

In column (c) write none if the person who provided the care was not related to you. If the care was provided by a relative, show the relationship to you. See definition of relative on the front of the form.

In column (d) show the period of time each person or organization provided care.

In column (e) list the amount of your 1981 expenses including those not paid during the year.

Line 3.—Add the amounts in column 2(e) and enter the total.

Line 4.—Enter $2,000 ($4,000 if more than one person is listed on line 1) or the amount on line 3, whichever is less.

Line 5.—This line is used to figure your *earned income.* Generally, you can figure earned income using steps (a) through (c). If you are unmarried, enter your amounts from Form 1040 when they are needed for the steps below. If you are married, each spouse's earned income will have to be figured separately and without regard to community property laws.

(a) Enter one spouse's income from Form 1040, line 7 . . . _____

(b) Enter the same spouse's net profit or (loss) from Schedule C or Schedule F (Form 1040) if applicable _____

(c) Combine amounts on lines (a) and (b). (If the result is zero or less, enter zero.) . . . _____

If you are unmarried, enter the amount from (c) on line 5. If you are married, enter the amount from (c) on line 5(b)(1) and go back and figure your spouse's earned income using steps (a) through (c). Enter your spouse's earned income from (c) on line 5(b)(2). Enter the lesser of line 5(b)(1) or line 5(b)(2) on line 5.

If your spouse was a full-time student or not able to care for himself or herself, use the greater of your spouse's monthly earned income or $166 ($333 if you listed two qualifying persons on line 1(a)) to determine his or her total income for the year.

If, in the same month, both you and your spouse were full-time students and did not work, you cannot use any amount paid that month to figure the credit. The same ap-

plies to a couple who did not work because neither was capable of self-care.

Line 6.—Enter the amount from line 4 or line 5, whichever is smaller.

Line 7.—How much of the amount on line 6 did you pay in 1981? Enter this amount on line 7. Do not list any amounts for 1981 that you did not pay until 1982.

Line 8.—If you had child and dependent care expenses for 1980 that you did not pay until 1981, add them and enter the total on this line. Be sure the total is not over your 1980 limit. Attach a sheet similar to the example below, showing how you figured the amount you are carrying over to 1981.

Example: In 1980 you had child care expenses of $2,100 for your 12-year-old son. For one child, you were limited to $2,000. Of the $2,100, you paid $1,800 in 1980 and $300 in 1981. Your spouse's earned income of $5,000 was less than your earned income. You would be allowed to figure a credit on $200 in 1981, as follows:

(1) 1980 child care expenses paid in 1980 . $1,800

(2) 1980 child care expenses paid in 1981 . $\underline{\quad 300}$

(3) Total 2,100

(4) Limit for one qualifying person . . . 2,000

(5) Earned income reported in 1980 . . . 5,000

(6) Smaller of line 3, 4, or 5 2,000

(7) Subtract child care expenses on which credit was figured in 1980 1,800

(8) 1980 child care expenses carried over for credit this year (1981) . . . . . $ 200

Line 9.—Add lines 7 and 8 and enter the total on line 9.

Line 10.—Multiply the amount on line 9 by 20% and enter the result on line 10.

Line 11.—Your credit for child and dependent care expenses cannot be more than your tax after subtracting certain credits. To figure the allowable credit, enter your tax from Form 1040, line 37, on line 11a. Add the amounts, if any, you entered on Form 1040, lines 38, 39, and 41 through 43. Enter the total of these lines on line 11b. Subtract line 11b from 11a and enter the difference on line 11c. If line 11b is more than line 11a, enter zero on line 11c.

Line 12.—Enter the smaller of line 10 or 11c on this line and Form 1040, line 40. This is your credit for child and dependent care expenses.

Line 13.—On line 13(a), check the yes box if you paid cash wages to an employee for household services. Check the no box if you did not. In general, if you paid cash wages of $50 or more in a calendar quarter for household services to a person such as a cook, housekeeper, governess, maid, cleaning person, babysitter, etc., you must file an employment tax return. If you are not sure whether you should file an employment tax return, ask the Internal Revenue Service or get Form 942, Employer's Quarterly Tax Return for Household Employees. **Note:** *You should file a Form 940, Employer's Annual Federal Unemployment Tax Return, for 1981 by February 1, 1982, if you paid cash wages of $1,000 or more for household services in any calendar quarter in 1980 or 1981.*

On line 13(b), check the yes box if you have filed appropriate wage tax returns. Check the no box if you have not.

On line 13(c), enter your employer identification number if you checked the yes box on line 13(b).

TAX TIP: *You Can Get a Child-Care Credit for Payments to Your Parent*

If you qualify for the special 20-percent credit for employment-related expenses for the care of one or more of your children under the age of 15, you can claim a credit for payments made during 1981 to your parents to care for your children—if your parents are not your dependents. The credit has been expanded for 1982, as explained under "More Tax Breaks for Individuals in '82," beginning on page 14. If you haven't already done so in 1982, consider giving your parents income by paying them to care for your children in order to allow you to go to work. You then can also claim a credit against your income tax. Caution: This will not work, however, if your parent is your dependent.

Q. I am a widow with a 4-year-old child. In order to get a job, I put him into a nursery school. Is the full cost of the nursery school the basis on which I can figure the credit?

A. Yes, you include even that part of the school fee which covers the cost of lunch. This assumes that the expenses on which you claim credit don't exceed the $2,000 maximum for one qualifying child.

Q. I am a working widow and I employ a maid to care for my apartment while my 14- and 16-year-old children attend high school. Can I count as the basis for the child-care credit only the portion of my household expenses allocable to my 14-year-old?

A. No. When you incur maid services within your household that covers both dependent children under 15 and older children, you don't have to divide the cost of the maid services between the qualifying children under 15 and the other children. You count the entire cost of the maid service in figuring the amount of your child-care expenses.

Q. Should my child or dependent care payments also qualify as a medical expense? How should I handle it?

A. You can treat it either way, whichever is better for you, but you can't take both the credit and the deduction for the same amount of expense. If you take a credit for the child or dependent care expense, then any portion that exceeds the maximum allowable employment-related expenses on which the 20-percent credit is computed, you can count in with your medical expenses. But if you take these expenses as medical deductions, then any portion of these expenses that isn't deductible because of the 3-percent wastage rule can't be counted as child or dependent care expenses on which the credit is computed.

Q. I am a single woman, and my invalid mother lives with me. In order to be free to work, I hire a practical nurse who cares for my mother while I'm at work. Is the nurse's salary a household expense on which the credit is allowed?

A. Yes.

Q. I am a widow who was able to shift from a part-time to a full-time job by transferring my 9-year-old child from a short-session public school to a private school. Are the school fees child-care expense on which the credit is figured?

A. No, since the payment is for education above the kindergarten level (first or higher).

Q. Both my husband and I work full time. We paid a maid $400 a month in 1981 to care for our house and keep an eye on our 13-year-old son, who now goes to high school. Can we treat the entire $4,800 as employment-related expenses on which the credit is allowed? Our salaries and other income total $30,000.

A. Since you have one qualifying individual, your son, your credit is only 20 percent of $2,000, or $400. The size of your income is immaterial.

Q. Am I gainfully employed when I am out of work and looking for a new job?

A. Yes, if you're actively looking for a job.

Q. I paid to place my child in a nursery school so that I could finish my education and training courses. Are my payments part of my employment-related expenses?

A. No. Continuing education and training courses are not gainful employment.

Q. My wife is physically incapable of caring for herself, and I have to hire a practical nurse to care for her while I am at work. Can I treat the expense as employment-related expenses entitled to the credit?

A. Yes, but note that even though your disabled wife earned no income, the law considered her to have earnings of $166.66 per month in order to avoid the earned-income limitation that would otherwise reduce your credit.

Q. My child became 15 on July 1, 1981. What about my child-care expenses?

A. You can treat only the amounts paid before July 1 as qualifying expenses.

Q. I paid a niece to care for my 7-year-old child while I, a widow, went to work. Do these expenses qualify for the credit?

A. Yes, so long as your niece is not your dependent.

Q. Both my wife and I work full time. We paid a maid to keep house so that both of us can work. Can we figure the credit on the payments for the household services even though we have no children?

A. No, you can't. In order to be allowed the credit you must have a dependent child under 15, or another disabled dependent.

Q. Both my wife and I work full time. We paid $300 per month to keep one child in nursery school. We also paid $150 a month for part-time help to keep house while our 14-year-old goes to school. Can we treat the entire payments as qualifying for the credit?

A. Since you have two qualifying individuals, you can take credit on up to $4,000 of employment-related expenses. Your actual expenses totaled $5,400 for the year but your credit is limited to 20 percent of $4,000, or $800.

Q. I leave my child to be cared for at my parent's home and I pay her. Does the payment qualify for the credit?

A. The answer is yes, so long as your parent can't be claimed as your dependent.

Q. I am divorced and work only part time. While at work I paid a person to care for my child, whom I support. Can I take credit against these expenses up to the $2,000 limit?

A. Yes. It is not necessary to work full time in order to qualify for the credit.

Q. I work full time while my husband goes to medical school. I paid $3,000 in 1981 for a person to care for my 4-year-old while I am at work. Does the $3,000 qualify for credit?

A. Yes, up to the $2,000 limit. While your husband earns no money, the law considers him to be earning $166.66 per month so that the $2,000 limit on which you claim the 20-percent credit of $400 is not reduced.

Q. I have a live-in housekeeper for my young child in order to enable me to go work. Can I include the cost of her meals and lodging in addition to her wages as part of my child-care expenses for which I receive a credit?

A. Her meal costs are includable, but IRS says her lodging costs are generally not includable except where you make out-of-pocket payments for her lodging in addition to your normal household expenses. An example of the exception would be where you move to an apartment with an added bedroom for the use of your live-in housekeeper.

Q. I hire a housekeeper to care for my young child during the day so that I can go to work. I was absent from work for two months because of illness, during which time my employer continued paying my regular salary. Even though I was not working during those two months, I kept the housekeeper on for my child. Is there any question whether the payments to the housekeeper qualify as subject to the credit?

A. Yes. IRS says the payments made during the months you were away from work due to illness don't qualify, because payments didn't enable you to be gainfully employed during that period.

Line 41: Investment Credit

The investment credit is, in effect, a tax rebate given to you on the purchase of depreciable tangible personal property such as autos, equipment, furniture, etc., used in a business or for the production of income.

But instead of giving you the rebate in cash, the Treasury lets you take the credit as a *direct reduction of the tax you owe on your return*. Thus, if your 1981 tax is $1,500 and your credit is $200, you will send the Internal Revenue Service only $1,300.

The credit does *not* reduce the cost of your asset in figuring depreciation. For property placed in service in 1981, the amount of the credit is 6 percent for property such as autos, which is considered depreciable over 3

years, or 10 percent for machinery and equipment which is depreciable over 5 years. (See page 129.)

Q. I am a salesman who uses my car to see customers as part of my job. I bought a new $8,000 car in 1981. Can I claim an $800 credit?

A. Since you use the car for business (job) you can claim the credit. However, the amount depends on the recovery period of your car. Since an auto is depreciable over 3 years under the '81 Act, you claim a credit of 6 percent, or $480.

The investment credit computed on separate Form 3468 is entered on line 41.

Line 42: Foreign Tax Credit

This line is for the few taxpayers who have credits for foreign income taxes. If you claim a credit for foreign income taxes, attach Form 1116. You may claim this credit only if you itemize your deductions.

Line 43: Work Incentive Credit

In claiming either one of these credits, fill out and attach Form 4874 to Form 1040. The Work-Incentive Credit may be taken by taxpayers who employ participants in the Federal Work Incentive (WIN) program.

Line 44: Job Credit

The job credit is available on line 44 to certain business employers who increase their work force by hiring additional employees.

Line 45: Residential Energy Credits

You can claim on your 1981 return on line 45 for expenditures on your principal residence during 1981 for items listed below. In order to get the energy credits, you must be the first to use the item and you must expect to use it for at least three years for property subject to a 15-percent credit, five years for property subject to the 40-percent credit.

But if you took an energy tax credit for pre-'81 expenditures, you can only claim the credit for '81 energy-saving expenditures to the extent that you haven't already used up your maximum credit below. Make sure you take full advantage of this government subsidy. Use Form 5695 to figure your credit and attach it to your return.

Insulation and Other Energy-Saving Costs. You are allowed a 15-percent credit on the first $2,000 of qualifying expenditures. For this purpose, you have made such an expenditure in the year in which the original installation of the item is completed, regardless of the year in which you actually pay for it. But the credit can't exceed your tax for '81. However, any excess can be carried over.

The expenditures must be made on or in your principal residence, the construction of which was substantially completed before April 20, 1977, *and* for the following items:

Insulation. This is defined as any item specifically and primarily designed to reduce, when installed in or on a dwelling or water heater, the heat loss or gain of the dwelling or water heater.

Other Energy-Conserving Component. This means any item (other than insulation) which is:

1. A furnace replacement burner designed to achieve a reduction in the amount of fuel consumed as a result of increased combustion efficiency.

2. A device for modifying flue openings designed to increase the efficiency of operation of the heating system.

3. An electrical or mechanical furnace-ignition system that replaces a gas pilot light.

4. A storm or thermal window or door for the exterior of the dwelling.

5. A thermostat with an automatic setback.

6. Caulking or weatherstripping of an exterior door or window.

7. A meter that shows the cost of energy used.

But you can't get credit for the following items:

1. Carpeting.

2. Drapes.

3. Wood paneling.

4. Exterior siding.

5. Heat pump (both air and water).

6. Wood- or peat-burning stoves.

7. Fluorescent replacement lighting system.

8. Hydrogen-fueled residential equipment.

9. Replacement of boilers and furnaces.

10. Expenditures for a swimming pool used as an energy storage medium.

Note that both owners and renters can get this credit. If you own stock in a cooperative housing association or are a member of a condominium management association, you are also entitled to the credit.

Installation of Solar, Wind, or Geothermal Energy Equipment

For '81, you are entitled to a credit of 40 percent on up to $10,000 of qualifying expenditures made in years beginning after '79, or $4,000. For pre-'80 years, you were only allowed a credit for 30 percent of the first $2,000 and 20 percent of the next $8,000 of qualifying expenditures made on or after April 20, 1977, through December 31, 1979.

Any qualifying expenditures made before '80 reduce the $10,000 expenditure limit for post-'79 years. Thus, if you spent $6,000 in '78-'79 and had no qualifying expenditure for 1980, you can only claim the 40 percent on an additional $4,000 of qualifying expenditures for '81.

Here, too, an expenditure is considered made in the year in which the original installation is completed, regardless of the year in which you actually pay for it. There is one exception to this. If these expenditures are made in connection with construction or reconstruction of a dwelling, they are considered as made by you in the year in which you first use the dwelling as your principal residence.

The credit is allowed only up to the amount of your '81 tax. No refund is allowed for any credit above your tax, but a carryover is allowed for unused credit. The credit is allowed with respect to existing, newly constructed, and reconstructed principal residences. Owners, renters, etc., as described above, can use the credits. The expenditure has to have been made for installations in connection with the principal residence for these items:

1. Solar-energy equipment, including both "passive" and "active" solar systems. Expenditures for solar panels installed as roofs or parts of roofs after '79 qualify even though they are structural components of the dwellings.

2. Wind energy equipment.

3. Equipment using geothermal energy.

Expenditures for the labor costs of drilling a geothermal well after '79 qualify so long as they haven't been deducted as intangible drilling costs.

Solar- and geothermal-energy property may be used to heat or cool your residence (or provide hot water). Expenditures in '81 include expenditures for property used to produce electricity for use in a residence.

Solar energy property includes such items as collectors, rockbeds, and heat exchangers that transforms sunlight into heat or electricity. Geothermal energy property includes equipment that distributes the natural heat in rocks and water. Wind energy property uses wind to produce energy in any form (generally electricity) for residential purposes.

IRS is given the right to add a list of equipment items which rely on "renewable energy resources." So keep an eye on possible new approved items added by IRS.

Note: The above credits are one-shot credits. That means that if you have already taken the maximum credits in previous years, you can't get any further credit for insulation, etc., in '81. But if you didn't use up the maximum, you can claim additional credit in '81.

Q. I spent $600 in 1979 on installing storm windows, for which I claimed a credit of $90. In 1980, I insulated my house at a cost of $2,000. How much of a credit can I claim?

A. Since you used up $600 of your total $2,000 of allowable energy-savings expenditures in 1979, you can only claim a 15 percent credit on your 1980 return on the remaining $1,400, or $210.

TAX TIP: *Important Points to Note on Energy Credit*

Note that the above limits apply to *each* principal residence you own. (You can have only one principal residence at a time). Thus, the credit can be multiplied by the number of principal residences in which you lived during '81 and in which you made the appropriate investments. For instance, if you sold your principal residence in May '81 and purchased another in June, you can claim up to the maximum amount on each residence for which you made the investments.

Also Important: Unlike other expenses, which you must have paid in '81 to get the deduction in '81, you need not have paid the energy cost in '81. The law says that you are treated as having paid the cost of the energy-conservation item when the original installation of the item is completed. Thus, if the installation was completed on your home in '81 but was not paid for until 1982, you still can claim the credit for '81. If the item was a renewable-energy-source property made in connection with the construction or reconstruction of your home, you are treated as having paid the expense when you began original use of the dwelling.

Your principal residence is the place in the U.S. where you and your family live—whether you own or rent it. This includes a condominium or cooperative apartment, but it does not include a summer or vacation home.

Line 46: Total Credits

Show the total amounts on lines 38 through 45 on line 46.

Line 47: Balance

Subtract the amount on line 46 from line 37 to obtain the amount on line 47, but not less than zero.

OTHER TAXES

Other Taxes (Including Advance EIC Payments)	48	Self-employment tax (attach Schedule SE)	48		
	49a	Minimum tax. Attach Form 4625 and check here ▶ ☐	49a		
	49b	Alternative minimum tax. Attach Form 6251 and check here ▶ ☐	49b		
	50	Tax from recomputing prior-year investment credit (attach Form 4255)	50		
	51a	Social security (FICA) tax on tip income not reported to employer (attach Form 4137) . .	51a		
	51b	Uncollected employee FICA and RRTA tax on tips (from Form W–2)	51b		
	52	Tax on an IRA (attach Form 5329)	52		
	53	Advance earned income credit (EIC) payments received (from Form W–2)	53		
06	54	**Total tax.** Add lines 47 through 53 . . . . ▶	54		

Line 48: Self-Employment Tax

Refer to the calculation of your self-employment tax if you are self-employed, on separate Schedule SE. (See page 136.)

Line 49: Minimum Tax

The 15 percent minimum tax applies only to those individuals who have such items as intangible drilling expenses, accelerated depreciation, etc. This minimum tax is shown at line 49a. Long-term capital gains are not subject to this tax but are subject to the alternative minimum tax below.

The alternative minimum tax computed on Form 6251 applies to relatively few individuals and is entered at line 49b. This tax may apply to you if you have long-term capital gain, and/or itemized deductions (other than medical expenses, casualty losses and state and local taxes) that exceed 60 percent of your adjusted gross income on line 32a of Form 1040, reduced by the same deductions. The tax is computed by first adding back to your taxable income the untaxed 60 percent of your long-term capital gain and the excess itemized deductions. You reduce this total by $20,000 and then apply tax rates ranging from 10 percent to 20 percent. If this tax is higher than your regular tax, you pay the higher amount.

Form 6251 contains the details of this tax which will not affect the vast majority of persons.

Line 50: Tax from Recomputing Prior-Year Investment Credit

Enter here any credit you must pay back as a result of selling or otherwise disposing of property on which you previously took an investment credit.

Line 51: FICA Tax on Tip Income Not Reported to Employer and Uncollected FICA and RRTA Tax on Tips

These are self-explanatory.

Line 52: Tax on an IRA

At this line you enter any additional tax due because you contributed more than allowed to your Individual Retirement Arrangement.

Line 53: Advance Earned Income Credit Payments Received

If you received an advance earned-income-credit payment from your employer, which will be shown on your Form W-2, you enter the amount on line 53.

Line 54: Balance

At line 54 total any entries you made on lines 47 through 53.

PAYMENTS

Payments			55	
	55	Total Federal income tax withheld	55	
Attach Forms W-2, W-2G, and W-2P to front.	56	1981 estimated tax payments and amount applied from 1980 return .	56	
	57	Earned income credit. If line 32a is under $10,000, see page 15 of Instructions	57	
	58	Amount paid with Form 4868	58	
	59	Excess FICA and RRTA tax withheld (two or more employers)	59	
	60	Credit for Federal tax on special fuels and oils (attach Form 4136 or 4136–T)	60	
	61	Regulated Investment Company credit (attach Form 2439)	61	
	62	Total. Add lines 55 through 61 . . . . ▶	62	

Line 55: Total Federal Income Tax Withheld

The amount withheld from your wages is entered here as a reduction of the tax due. The figure here is taken from the Forms W-2 received from your employers. Remember to attach Copy B of Form W-2 which your employer gave you to the front of your return together with any Forms W-2G and W-2P.

Line 56: 1981 Estimated Tax Payments and Amount Applied from 1980 Return

If you filed a declaration of estimated tax for 1981, enter here the payments you made or the credits you took for any 1980 overpayments.

To see if you can take the Earned Income Credit, complete Form 1040 through line 32a, and answer the questions below.

	Yes	No
1. Is the amount you listed on Form 1040, line 32a, less than $10,000?	☐	☐
2. Did you receive any wages, salaries, tips, or other earned income (see "What is Earned Income?" on this page)?	☐	☐
3. Did you have a child (see **Note 1** below) who lived with you in the same principal residence in the U.S. during all of 1981?	☐	☐

4. If you checked Filing Status box 2 or box 5 on Form 1040, did you claim your child as a dependent on Form 1040, line 6c? **OR**

If you checked Filing Status box 4 on Form 1040 and your child was **married** for 1981, did you claim that child as a dependent on Form 1040, line 6c? **OR**   ☐ ☐

If you checked Filing Status box 4 on Form 1040 and your child was **unmarried** for 1981, did you enter that child's name on Form 1040, line 4 (or 6c if you claimed that child as a dependent)?

Note 1—For this purpose, the word **child** means:

● Your son or daughter.
● Your stepchild, adopted child, or a child placed with you by an authorized placement agency for legal adoption (even if the child became your stepchild or adopted child, or was placed with you, during the year).
● Any other child whom you cared for as your own child for the whole year, unless the child's natural or adoptive parents provided more than half of the support for that year.

If you answered NO to any question, you can't take the earned income credit. Do not fill in the worksheet. Instead write "NO" on line 57 of Form 1040.

If you answered YES to all the questions, you **may** be able to take the credit. Use the Earned Income Credit Worksheet to figure the amount of any credit.

Note 2—If you expect to answer **YES** to all of the above questions for 1982 and want to receive advance payments of the credit, file Form W–5 with your employer.

Earned Income Credit Worksheet

To figure your credit, follow the instructions below.

1. Enter the amount from Form 1040, line 7, plus any other compensation from your employer, regardless of whether it is taxable. Include disability pensions but **do not** include other pensions or annuities.	$
2. If you were self-employed, enter the amount, even if a loss, from Schedule SE, line 13. If you have self-employment income that you reported on line 1 above, do not include it here. (Clergy and religious workers, see **Publication 517**)	
3. Earned income. Add lines 1 and 2. However, if line 2 is a loss, subtract line 2 from line 1. If the amount on line 3 is $0 or less, do not complete the rest of this worksheet; you cannot take the credit. If it is more than zero, complete 4 and either 5 or 6 below.	
4. Adjusted gross income. Enter the amount from Form 1040, line 32a.	
5. If line 4 above is $6,000 or less, use the amount from line 3 above to find your credit in the table on page 41. Enter the credit here and on Form 1040, line 57.	
6. If line 4 above is over $6,000: a. First find the amount from line 3 above in the table on page 41 and enter the credit for that amount here. $............... b. Then find the amount from line 4 in the table and enter the credit for that amount here. $............... c. Enter the amount from line 6a or 6b, whichever is smaller, here and on Form 1040, line 57.	$

Do NOT file this worksheet with your return—Keep it for your tax records

Line 57

Earned Income Credit

What Does the Earned Income Credit Do?

The earned income credit helps many taxpayers who have incomes under $10,000. If you can take the earned income credit, you can subtract it from tax you owe or get a refund even if you had no tax withheld from your pay. The credit can go as high as $500.

What Is Earned Income?

In most cases, you had earned income if you worked last year.

Earned income includes:

● wages, salaries, and tips.
● anything else of value (money, goods, or services) you get from your employer for services you performed regardless of whether it is taxable.

Note: *The following are examples of amounts received from your employer that must be included in line 1 of the worksheet—*

a. Housing allowance (or rental value of a parsonage) for members of the clergy.
b. Meals and lodging.
c. Disability pensions which qualify for exclusion on Form 2440.
● earnings from self-employment—this is usually the amount shown on Schedule SE (Form 1040), line 13.

Earned income does not include items such as interest, dividends, social security payments, welfare benefits, veterans' benefits, workmen's compensation or unemployment compensation (insurance).

Who Can't Take the Earned Income Credit?

You can't take the credit if:

● your income is $10,000 or more; or
● you are single (Filing Status Box 1); or
● you are married filing a separate return (Filing Status Box 3); or
● you are entitled to file Form 2555 to exclude income earned overseas or claim excess foreign living expenses; or
● you are entitled to file Form 4563 to exclude income earned from sources in U.S. possessions.

If you can take the credit, enter on line 57 the credit from line 5 or line 6c of this worksheet, whichever applies.

Line 57: Earned Income Credit

At this line, you take the earned income credit if you are eligible for it. See page 21 for a complete explanation of who is eligible and how the credit is compiled. In order to claim this credit, be sure to enter the child's name at line 4 or 6c of Form 1040.

Line 58: Amount Paid with Form 4868

This is the amount you paid with an application for an automatic two-month extension of time to file your '79 Form 1040.

Line 59: Excess FICA and RRTA Tax Withheld

If you worked for more than one employer during 1981, and together these employers paid you more than $29,700 in wages during 1981, then they may have withheld too much Social Security (FICA) tax, or Railroad Retirement (RRTA) tax, or a combination of both FICA and RRTA taxes. If the total of these taxes withheld from you exceeded $1,975.05 for 1981, then you credit the excess against your 1981 income tax, by entering it on line 59.

If you file a joint return with your spouse and he or she also worked for two or more employers during 1981, you figure whether any excess amount was withheld from him or her and apply that also against your 1981 income tax. But you must figure his or her excess separately from yours. You do not combine your withheld taxes with his or hers to determine whether an excess was withheld.

If any of your employers withheld more than $1,975.05 in your Social Security taxes, be sure to ask your employer to refund the excess. You can't claim credit for this on your return.

TAX TIP: *Asking for an Automatic Extension to File Your Return*

If you can't file your '81 return on time, you can get an automatic two-month extension to June 15, 1982, by filing Form 4868. However, this does not give you an extension to *pay* your '81 tax. Therefore you must pay what you expect to be the balance of your '81 tax at the same time that you file Form 4868 for an extension to file your return.

If with Form 4868 you drastically underpay the amount still due on your '81 tax, and you have reason to know that it is a drastic underpayment, IRS will disregard your Form 4868 and you will be penalized for not filing on time. This happened to one taxpayer who showed no tax payments due when he filed his Form 4868 even though he had ample evidence that he had a substantial tax liability.

Note also that if the balance due on your final '81 tax is more than 10 percent of your total tax on line 54 of Form 1040, you will be hit with a 0.5 percent-per-month late-payment penalty unless you can show reasonable cause for not paying the tax on time.

Note that an extension of time to file your '81 return gives you extra time to make a contribution to an existing or new IRA or to a Keogh plan already set up in '81, and to have the contributions deductible for '81.

Line 60: Credit for Federal Tax on Special Fuels and Oils

This line is used to obtain a credit for federal gasoline and lubricating-oil taxes paid for nonhighway use on a farm or for a motorboat, plane, etc. If you claim a refund here, file Form 4136 with your return. This form is supplied with your instruction booklet.

Line 61: Regulated Investment Company Credit

If you have received notice from your mutual fund on Form 2439 that you are entitled to a tax credit, show the amount by attaching Copy B of Form 2439.

Line 62: Total

Enter the total lines 55 to 61 at line 62.

REFUND OR BALANCE DUE

Refund or Balance Due	63 If line 62 is larger than line 54, enter amount **OVERPAID** . . . . ▶	63	
	64 Amount of line 63 to be **REFUNDED TO YOU** . . . . ▶	64	
	65 Amount of line 63 to be applied to your 1982 estimated tax . . . ▶	65	
	66 If line 54 is larger than line 62, enter **BALANCE DUE.** Attach check or money order for full amount payable to "Internal Revenue Service." Write your social security number and "1981 Form 1040" on it. ▶ (Check ▶ ☐ if Form 2210 (2210F) is attached. See page 16 of Instructions.) ▶ $	66	

Line 63: Refund

If the total of the tax that was withheld from your pay, plus what you paid with your declaration of estimated tax, plus the other credits, is more than the tax that you have computed to be due, you enter on this line 63 the amount of your overpayment. This line is the basis for your refund claim.

If your refund claim is $1 or less, the government will refund it only if you specifically ask for it.

Lines 64—65: Amount to Be Refunded to You and Amount to Be Applied to Your 1982 Estimated Tax

Here you indicate to the government the amount you want refunded or credited to your 1982 estimated tax.

Line 66: Balance Due

The amounts of tax that were withheld from your pay, that you paid on a declaration of estimated tax, etc., may add up to more or less than the tax that you now have computed you owe.

If the tax that was withheld from you, the amount paid with your declaration, etc., is less than the tax you have computed, then you enter the balance of the tax due on this line.

If you owe the government money, you must pay the entire amount owed with this return. There is no provision for instalment payment. In hardship cases, though, you may be able to obtain an extension by applying on the proper form for this aid at the Internal Revenue Service. Make your check or money order payable to Internal Revenue Service and write your Social Security number and "1981 Form 1040" on the check or money order.

If you owe less than $1, forget it. The government will forgive you for this.

If your 1981 withheld income taxes plus your 1981 estimated tax payments totaled less than 80 percent of your 1981 tax as shown on line 54 of Form 1040 (less any minimum tax and certain other taxes listed on Form 2210) you may be subject to a penalty for underpayment of estimated tax. There are four exceptions that will excuse you from the penalty for underpayment that otherwise would apply under the general rule. To determine whether you are subject to the penalty, or whether the exceptions protect you from the penalty, fill out Form 2210. This Form provides detailed explanations of the four exceptions. Check the box if you attach Form 2210 to your return.

TAX TIP: Don't Overlook Your 1982 Declaration of Estimated Tax!

Some taxpayers, in addition to filing your income tax return for 1981, will simultaneously also have to file a declaration of estimated tax for 1982.

You will have to file this declaration and make the necessary instalment payment:

1. If you reasonably expect that your gross income from sources other than wages subject to withholding (such as dividends, interest, etc.), will exceed $500 in '82.

2. Or if your gross income is expected to exceed:

    a. $20,000, assuming you are a single person, a head of household, a surviving wife or husband, or a married individual entitled to file a joint declaration, but only if your husband or wife doesn't receive any wages.

    b. $10,000, assuming you are a married individual entitled to file a joint return where both you and your husband (or wife) receive wages.

    c. $5,000, assuming you are a married person not entitled to file a joint declaration.

But note that no declaration is necessary, regardless of whether you meet the above tests, if your estimated tax is reasonably expected to be less than $200. The size or nature of your income is immaterial. Thus, if you expect to have more than $500 in dividends in '82 but your withholding on your wages is expected to cover all but $195 of your total tax, you don't have to file a declaration.

If you have to file an estimate, but you fail to estimate your tax and pay as much as you should, you may have to pay a penalty. But there are several "safety zone" methods of estimating your 1982 tax which can protect you against the penalty even if you do underestimate your 1982 tax.

You are required to estimate your tax to within 80 percent of the actual tax that will be due—and even if you pay up in full with your final tax return, the law requires you to explain why you shouldn't be penalized for underpayment. You would be excused, though, if you correctly used one of the "safety zone" methods in figuring your estimated tax even if that produced less than 80 percent of your final tax.

A way to cut down your estimated-tax payments is to have your withholding tax increased by your employer. You can do this by giving up your exemptions for withholding-tax purposes. Or if you want even more tax withheld, you may enter into a special withholding agreement with your employer for this purpose.

And in any year when it seems clear that you will be subject to a penalty for having underpaid your estimated tax during the year, you can cut the penalty by having your employer boost your withheld taxes before the end of the year.

KEYNOTE: Common Errors

Before you file your return, make sure that you have not made any of the following errors. The Treasury says these are common ones.
- Failure to attach Forms W-2.
- Incomplete address or incorrect Social Security number.
- Failure to check correct blocks indicating filing status.

- Incorrect checking of blocks for personal exemptions or listing of dependents.
- Incomplete listing of itemized deductions.
- Listing income, deduction, or tax items on wrong line.
- Failure to sign return.

TAX TIP: What Are the Chances of Your Return Being Audited?

On a straight statistical basis, they are as follows, based on 100 returns filed and adjusted gross income.

If you weren't in business:

Under $10,000	1.14
$10,000 under $50,000	2.46
$50,000 and over	8.74

If you were in business:

Under $10,000	3.18
$10,000 under $30,000	1.79
$30,000 and over	4.79

Thus, if you filed a nonbusiness Form 1040, your chances of audit are very low. They are 1.14 out of 100, or 114 out of 10,000 returns filed.

SIGNING

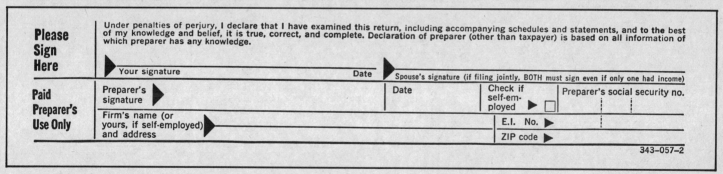

Don't forget that both of you must sign the form if you are filing a joint return. This is so even if your spouse had no income in 1981.

SCHEDULE C
(Form 1040)
Department of the Treasury
Internal Revenue Service

Profit or (Loss) From Business or Profession
(Sole Proprietorship)
Partnerships, Joint Ventures, etc., Must File Form 1065.
► Attach to Form 1040 or Form 1041.   ► See Instructions for Schedule C (Form 1040).

OMB. No. 1545–0074

1981
08

Name of proprietor

Social security number of proprietor

A Main business activity (see Instructions) ►   ; product ►

B Business name ►

C Employer identification number

D Business address (number and street) ►
City, State and ZIP Code ►

E Accounting method: **(1)** ☐ Cash   **(2)** ☐ Accrual   **(3)** ☐ Other (specify) ►

C

F Method(s) used to value closing inventory:
(1) ☐ Cost   **(2)** ☐ Lower of cost or market   **(3)** ☐ Other (if other, attach explanation)

	Yes	No

G Was there any major change in determining quantities, costs, or valuations between opening and closing inventory? . .
If "Yes," attach explanation.

H Did you deduct expenses for an office in your home? . . . .

Part I Income

1 a Gross receipts or sales	**1a**		
b Returns and allowances	**1b**		
c Balance (subtract line 1b from line 1a)	**1c**		
2 Cost of goods sold and/or operations (Schedule C–1, line 8)	**2**		
3 Gross profit (subtract line 2 from line 1c)	**3**		
4 a Windfall Profit Tax Credit or Refund received in 1981 (see Instructions)	**4a**		
b Other income (attach schedule)	**4b**		
5 Total income (add lines 3, 4a, and 4b) . . . . ►	**5**		

Part II Deductions

6 Advertising	**29 a** Wages . .	
7 Amortization	**b** Jobs credit	
8 Bad debts from sales or services .	**c** WIN credit	
9 Bank service charges	**d** Total credits	
10 Car and truck expenses	**e** Subtract line 29d from 29a .	
11 Commissions	**30** Windfall Profit Tax withheld in	
12 Depletion	1981	
13 Depreciation (see Instructions) .	**31** Other expenses (specify):	
14 Dues and publications . . .	**a**	
15 Employee benefit programs . .	**b**	
16 Freight (not included on Schedule C–1) .	**c**	
17 Insurance	**d**	
18 Interest on business indebtedness	**e**	
19 Laundry and cleaning	**f**	
20 Legal and professional services .	**g**	
21 Office supplies and postage . . .	**h**	
22 Pension and profit-sharing plans .	**i**	
23 Rent on business property . . .	**j**	
24 Repairs	**k**	
25 Supplies (not included on Schedule C–1) .	**l**	
26 Taxes (do not include Windfall Profit Tax, see line 30)	**m**	
27 Travel and entertainment . . .	**n**	
	o	
28 Utilities and telephone	**p**	

32 Total deductions (add amounts in columns for lines 6 through 31p) . . . . ►   **32**

33 Net profit or (loss) (subtract line 32 from line 5). If a profit, enter on Form 1040, line 11, and on Schedule SE, Part II, line 5a (or Form 1041, line 6). If a loss, go on to line 34 . . . . .   **33**

34 If you have a loss, do you have amounts for which you are not "at risk" in this business (see Instructions)? . . ☐ **Yes** ☐ **No**
If you checked "No," enter the loss on Form 1040, line 11, and on Schedule SE, Part II, line 5a (or Form 1041, line 6).

For Paperwork Reduction Act Notice, see Form 1040 Instructions.

343–060–1

SCHEDULE C–1.—Cost of Goods Sold and/or Operations (See Schedule C Instructions for Part I, line 2)

1 Inventory at beginning of year (if different from last year's closing inventory, attach explanation) .	**1**	
2 a Purchases **2a**		
b Cost of items withdrawn for personal use **2b**		
c Balance (subtract line 2b from line 2a)	**2c**	
3 Cost of labor (do not include salary paid to yourself)	**3**	
4 Materials and supplies	**4**	
5 Other costs (attach schedule)	**5**	
6 Add lines 1, 2c, and 3 through 5	**6**	
7 Inventory at end of year	**7**	
8 Cost of goods sold and/or operations (subtract line 7 from line 6). Enter here and on Part I, line 2 . ▶	**8**	

SCHEDULE C–2.—Depreciation (See Schedule C Instructions for line 13)

Complete Schedule C–2 if you claim depreciation **ONLY** for assets placed in service before January 1, 1981. If you need more space, use Form 4562. If you claim a deduction for any assets placed in service after December 31, 1980, use Form 4562 to figure your total deduction for all assets; do **NOT** complete Schedule C–2.

Description of property (a)	Date acquired (b)	Cost or other basis (c)	Depreciation allowed or allowable in prior years (d)	Method of computing depreciation (e)	Life or rate (f)	Depreciation for this year (g)
1 Depreciation (see Instructions):						
2 Totals					**2**	
3 Depreciation claimed in Schedule C–1					**3**	
4 **Balance** (subtract line 3 from line 2). Enter here and on Part II, line 13 . . . . ▶					**4**	

SCHEDULE C–3.—Expense Account Information (See Schedule C Instructions for Schedule C–3)

Enter information for yourself and your five highest paid employees. In determining the five highest paid employees, add expense account allowances to the salaries and wages. However, you don't have to provide the information for any employee for whom the combined amount is less than $50,000, or for yourself if your expense account allowance plus line 33, page 1, is less than $50,000.

Name (a)	Expense account (b)	Salaries and wages (c)
Owner		
1		
2		
3		
4		
5		

Did you claim a deduction for expenses connected with:	Yes	No
A Entertainment facility (boat, resort, ranch, etc.)?		
B Living accommodations (except employees on business)?		
C Conventions or meetings you or your employees attended outside the North American area? (see Instructions) . . .		
D Employees' families at conventions or meetings?		
If "Yes," were any of these conventions or meetings outside the North American area?		
E Vacations for employees or their families not reported on Form W–2?		

Schedule C, Profit or (Loss) from Business or Profession

SCHEDULE C
(Form 1040)
Department of the Treasury
Internal Revenue Service

Profit or (Loss) From Business or Profession
(Sole Proprietorship)
Partnerships, Joint Ventures, etc., Must File Form 1065.
▶ Attach to Form 1040 or Form 1041.   ▶ See Instructions for Schedule C (Form 1040).

OMB. No. 1545–0074

1981
08

Name of proprietor | Social security number of proprietor

A Main business activity (see Instructions) ▶ _____ ; product ▶

B Business name ▶ _____ | **C** Employer identification number

D Business address (number and street) ▶ ....
City, State and ZIP Code ▶

E Accounting method: **(1)** ☐ Cash   **(2)** ☐ Accrual   **(3)** ☐ Other (specify) ▶ ....

F Method(s) used to value closing inventory:
(1) ☐ Cost   **(2)** ☐ Lower of cost or market   **(3)** ☐ Other (if other, attach explanation)

	Yes	No

G Was there any major change in determining quantities, costs, or valuations between opening and closing inventory? . .
If "Yes," attach explanation.
H Did you deduct expenses for an office in your home? . . . .

If you are in business for yourself or practice a profession as a sole proprietorship, you must complete separate Schedule C.

You use Schedule C to group all your business income and then carry over this figure to line 11 on page 1, Form 1040 and to Schedule SE, Part II, line 5a.

If you are using the flat standard deduction, make sure that all your business expenses are shown on Schedule C rather than on separate Schedule A. The reason is that you may deduct business expenses in addition to the optional deduction, while you may not deduct the items in separate Schedule A in addition to the optional deduction.

In any case, it's exceedingly important that you compute your business income correctly. Your self-employment tax and Social Security benefits are based on your business income.

You should find supplying the information on the top of Schedule C no problem. The only point to note is that if you deal in several lines or are engaged in both manufacturing and wholesaling, or wholesaling and

retailing, your "Main Business Activity" will be the product or service that accounts for the largest percentage of your total receipts. Describe your business as "retail hardware"; "wholesale tobacco"; "services—legal"; "manufacturing—furniture," etc.

Use your home address only if you actually conduct the business from your home. Show a street address instead of a box number.

Also show the method of accounting that you use by checking the box for cash, accrual, or other. Also answer the questions at G and H.

Q. I run a farm as a hobby and in 1981 I had a small loss. Do I use Schedule C or Schedule F?

A. Neither. A hobby doesn't qualify as a trade or business. Therefore, you have to include the hobby income in your return Form 1040 but you can deduct expenses only to the amount of your income. In practical words, your losses aren't deductible.

Part I   Income

1 a Gross receipts or sales	**1a**	
b Returns and allowances	**1b**	
c Balance (subtract line 1b from line 1a)	**1c**	
2 Cost of goods sold and/or operations (Schedule C–1, line 8)	**2**	
3 Gross profit (subtract line 2 from line 1c)	**3**	
4 a Windfall Profit Tax Credit or Refund received in 1981 (see Instructions)	**4a**	
b Other income (attach schedule)	**4b**	
5 Total income (add lines 3, 4a, and 4b) . . . . ▶	**5**	

Schedule C, Part I, Line 1: Gross Receipts Less Allowances, Rebates, and Returns

Q. This is my first year in business. Some of the bills I sent out for merchandise are still unpaid. Do I include these in my receipts, or only the cash I received during the year?

A. As this is your first year, you can choose your accounting method—usually the cash or the accrual method. The cash-basis taxpayer generally reports his income as he is paid. The accrual-basis taxpayer generally reports his income as he gets a right to it, even though it hasn't yet been paid to him. If you are in the business of selling merchandise, you will have to use inventories and the accrual method for computing purchases and sales. This means that you will treat the unpaid bills as part of this year's receipts.

Q. At the end of the year, I had a number of orders on hand and the merchandise was completed and ready for shipment. Since I am on the accrual basis, do I include the selling price of this merchandise in my receipts?

A. No. Even if you are on the accrual basis, you aren't considered to have a right to receive payment until the sale is completed. Since this generally happens only when title to your merchandise passes, you don't have to pick up the receipts until you ship your merchandise.

Q. I am on the cash basis and received $1,200 in checks on December 30, which I couldn't deposit until January 1982. Are these includable?

A. Yes. As long as the checks don't bounce, you are viewed as having the income on receipt of the checks. The fact that you didn't deposit the checks is immaterial.

Q. One of my clients paid me in advance in December 1981 for work that I performed in January 1982. Do I include the income in 1981's return even though I earned the pay in 1982?

A. Yes, if you are on the cash basis, no, if on the accrual basis. The Treasury says that an accrual-basis taxpayer who receives advance payment for services that are to be performed by the end of the next year includes it in income in the year it is earned.

Q. I had about $20,000 of receivables outstanding at December 31. I know that because of a 2-percent cash discount taken by most of my accounts, I'll only receive about $19,600. Can I reduce my receipts on the accrual basis by the estimated discounts?

A. No. While you are on firm grounds from an accounting viewpoint, you cannot set up a reserve for tax purposes. The view is that the expense for the cash discount doesn't accrue until the payment is made.

Q. In 1981 I started to sell merchandise on the instalment basis. Do I treat these sales the same way as my regular retail sales—that is, pick up the full profit when I make the sale?

A. Yes, if you wish. However, it will usually be more advantageous to you if you use the instalment basis in reporting these sales. Under this method, you report the gross profit only as your instalment receivables are paid—a method that will substantially lighten your capital requirements.

Here is how this works. Assume you sold $20,000 of merchandise during the year on the instalment basis. Your gross profit was 45 percent, and at December 31 your outstanding instalment receivables were $14,000. If you don't use the instalment basis, your receipts will include the full $9,000 of gross profits (45 percent of $20,000). But if you elect to report on the instalment basis, all you include in your 1981 return is 45 percent of the $6,000 you actually received on your instalment sales, or $2,700. You don't have to pay any tax on the gross profit on the $14,000 of your as-yet-unpaid receivables.

Schedule C, Part I, Line 2: Cost of Goods Sold and/or Operations

If you produce, buy, or sell merchandise, you must fill in Schedule C-1. If you are in a business that doesn't involve the sale of merchandise, you can ignore these lines, which don't apply.

The purpose of the computation here is to determine the cost of the merchandise that you sold. Since this represents merely a return of your own money, you can deduct these costs in arriving at your taxable income.

Schedule C (Form 1040) 1981   Page **2**

SCHEDULE C–1.—Cost of Goods Sold and/or Operations (See Schedule C Instructions for Part I, line 2)

1 Inventory at beginning of year (if different from last year's closing inventory, attach explanation) . | **1**
2 a Purchases . . . . | **2a**
   b Cost of items withdrawn for personal use . . . . . . | **2b**
   c Balance (subtract line 2b from line 2a) . . . . | **2c**
3 Cost of labor (do not include salary paid to yourself) . . . . | **3**
4 Materials and supplies . . . . | **4**
5 Other costs (attach schedule) . . . . | **5**
6 Add lines 1, 2c, and 3 through 5 . . . . | **6**
7 Inventory at end of year . . . . | **7**
8 Cost of goods sold and/or operations (subtract line 7 from line 6). Enter here and on Part I, line 2 . ▶ | **8**

Schedule C-1, Line 1: Inventory

Q. I began business this year. What figure do I enter as the inventory at the beginning of the year (line 1)?

A. Since you had no inventory on hand, you leave this line blank.

Q. Is there a fast way of getting the opening inventory figure? I'd like to avoid digging out my last year's inventory sheets, which I've filed away.

A. Yes, there is. All you have to do is enter on line 1, Schedule C-1, the same figure you entered on your 1980 return as the closing inventory. If you use a figure different from the closing '80 inventory, you must attach a statement explaining the difference.

Schedule C-1, Line 2: Purchases

Q. Is my merchandise-purchase figure the total of what I paid for merchandise during 1981?

A. No. It is the total of bills for merchandise purchased during 1981 regardless of whether these bills have been paid or not. Under the accrual method, just as you report the total sales in your receipts even though you haven't received payment, you also include your bills in "Purchases" even though you haven't yet paid them. In other words, when you are on the accrual method, you use it for both sales and purchases.

Q. In my small retail store, I help myself to whatever merchandise my family needs. Does this have to be taken into account anywhere?

A. Yes, it does—right on this same line. Since you took the merchandise for your personal use, you can't claim a deduction for its cost. The actual purchases shown on the first blank space must be reduced by the cost of your personal merchandise, which is entered in the second blank space on this line.

Q. How do I arrive at the amount of the merchandise I took for personal use? I don't keep any records of these withdrawals.

A. Estimate as well as you can the cost of the merchandise you withdrew for this purpose.

Schedule C-1, Line 3: Cost of Labor

The labor referred to here is any compensation paid in connection with the production, manufacture, etc., of the merchandise. Thus, if you are in a retail or wholesale business, ignore this line and show your labor costs on line 29a of Part II.

Schedule C-1, Line 4: Materials and Supplies

This line is for material and supplies used in a manufacturing enterprise where the items become a part of the manufactured product. A retail or wholesale business shows these expenses on line 25, Schedule C.

Schedule C-1, Line 5: Other Costs

Like all the other lines in this section, this one is generally aimed at manufacturing companies and can be virtually ignored by retail, wholesale, or other non-manufacturing businesses. A manufacturing concern shows here such costs as depreciation on machinery or equipment used in manufacturing, containers and packages that become part of the finished product, and manufacturing overhead expenses. You explain the amount entered on this line and attach a schedule.

Q. I'm a small wholesaler and spent $5,252 in freight bills to get my merchandise into place. Where do I deduct these?

A. You show them on this line. This is one of the exceptions where this line must be used by nonmanufacturers.

Schedule C-1, Line 6: Add

Just arithmetic.

Schedule C-1, Line 7: Inventory at End of Year

Your inventory at the end of the year is, in effect, additional income, since it reduces your costs. Be careful, therefore, to price and value your inventory correctly.

Q. What do I include in my inventory?

A. All the goods you are holding on hand at the end of the year for sale, or raw materials that will physically become a part of the merchandise you intend to sell.

Q. I had goods in my place at the end of the year which I hadn't paid for, and other goods that were left on consignment. Do I include these here?

A. Do not include the merchandise on consignment, since you don't own it. Do include the merchandise that you haven't paid for in your inventory, since you own it even though you haven't yet paid for it.

In listing your inventory, be sure that every item is represented by a bill that you have entered as part of your purchases for this year or a prior year (if the merchandise is that old). If you include in your inventory any goods for which a bill wasn't entered this year, you are needlessly increasing your income by the cost of that item.

You can easily make this tax error if you don't enter your year-end bills in the proper year. For instance, maybe you received merchandise during December but didn't get some of the bills until January. Your failure to treat the bills as December purchases will distort your income—to your disadvantage.

Q. How do I price the goods in my inventory?

A. If you have been in business for a while, you have adopted a method of valuation such as cost; cost or market, whichever is lower; etc. You must continue whatever method you have been using.

If you haven't had inventories before, you can choose whatever method is acceptable. You will probably wish to use the most common method—cost or market, whichever is lower. This means that in valuing each item in your inventory, you use the cost to you of the item or the market value of the item, whichever is lower. The market value is what it would cost you to replace the item at the end of the year.

Even if the price of your goods hasn't dropped, it's still advisable to select the cost-or-market method. If prices do drop in a succeeding year, you will be able to take advantage of the drop.

Q. What do I do with "seconds"?

A. Goods that are unsalable at normal prices or unsalable in the normal way because of damage, imperfections, shop wear, changes of style, odd or broken lots, or other similar changes are to be valued at selling price less your direct cost of disposing of them. The selling price is the price at which the goods were offered for sale within 30 days after the end of the year.

Q. Is the cost of my goods the invoice price?

A. Ordinarily, the cost is the invoice price minus trade discounts. However, add to the cost any freight, cartage, or other expenses involved in getting your merchandise to your place of business.

Schedule C-1, Line 8: Cost of Goods Sold and/or Operations

Your cost of goods sold and/or operations is line 6 less line 7.

Schedule C, Part I, Line 3: Gross Profit

Enter the amount from line 8 of Schedule C-1 at line 2 of Part I and subtract from line 1. This gives you the gross profit at line 3.

Schedule C, Part I, Line 4: Other Income

At line 4a enter any Windfall Profit Tax Credit or Refund, and at 4b any other miscellaneous income. Attach a schedule explaining this income.

Schedule C, Part I, Line 5: Total Income

At line 5 you total your gross profit and any other income at line 4.

Part II Deductions

6 Advertising	29 a Wages
7 Amortization	b Jobs credit
8 Bad debts from sales or services	c WIN credit
9 Bank service charges	d Total credits
10 Car and truck expenses	e Subtract line 29d from 29a
11 Commissions	30 Windfall Profit Tax withheld in 1981
12 Depletion	31 Other expenses (specify):
13 Depreciation (see Instructions)	a
14 Dues and publications	b
15 Employee benefit programs	c
16 Freight (not included on Schedule C-1)	d
17 Insurance	e
18 Interest on business indebtedness	f
19 Laundry and cleaning	g
20 Legal and professional services	h
21 Office supplies and postage	i
22 Pension and profit-sharing plans	j
23 Rent on business property	k
24 Repairs	l
25 Supplies (not included on Schedule C-1)	m
26 Taxes (do not include Windfall Profit Tax, see line 30)	n
27 Travel and entertainment	o
28 Utilities and telephone	p

32 Total deductions (add amounts in columns for lines 6 through 31p) ▶ | 32

33 Net profit or (loss) (subtract line 32 from line 5). If a profit, enter on Form 1040, line 11, and on Schedule SE, Part II, line 5a (or Form 1041, line 6). If a loss, go on to line 34. | 33

34 If you have a loss, do you have amounts for which you are not "at risk" in this business (see Instructions)? ☐ Yes ☐ No
If you checked "No," enter the loss on Form 1040, line 11, and on Schedule SE, Part II, line 5a (or Form 1041, line 6).

For Paperwork Reduction Act Notice, see Form 1040 Instructions.   343-060-1

Deductions

Most of the deductions are self-explanatory. Some of the key items are explained below.

Schedule C, Part II, Line 7: Amortization

You use this line only if you incurred expenditures for pollution-control facilities, research or experimentation, trade name, trademark, and so on.

Schedule C, Part II, Line 8: Bad Debts

You include here losses from business bad debts. However, these losses are limited to loss of your capital or losses of items which were previously included in income as a result of prior sales, services, loans, etc. You can't deduct losses from sales, professional services, rents, interest, etc., if you did not include the income from them either in current or past years.

You can deduct bad debts by writing them off in the year they became bad in whole or part, or by adding to a reserve for bad debts. If you have previously used either method, you must continue to use the same method. However, if you are filing a return for the first time, you may use whichever method you wish.

Q. A corporate bond for $1,000, which I bought several years ago, went bad this year. Do I deduct this bad debt here?

A. No. This isn't viewed as bad debt but rather as a loss similar to that which you might suffer by selling stock for less than cost. When you own corporate bonds or debentures and they become worthless, you have a capital loss.

Q. One of my customers owes me $1,500 for merchandise that I sold to him and on which I reported the profit. However, he is far past due and the likelihood is that I'll never collect more than about $700. Can I deduct $800?

A. Yes—if you write off the $800 on your books. If you are using the reserve method, you can accomplish the same deduction by increasing the reserve to take care of the doubtful account. This assumes that the reserve isn't already large enough to take care of the bad debt.

Q. In 1979, I wrote off $1,000 of bad debts. In 1981, I collected $750 on account of these written-off debts. Do I include this in income this year or correct my 1979 return?

A. Include the debt in income this year. There is only one exception that could permit you to eliminate the $750 from income. If the write-off deduction in 1979 didn't actually reduce your tax in 1979—for instance, because your taxable income was less than your exemptions—you don't have to include the recovery in income.

Schedule C, Part II, Line 12: Depletion of Mines, Oil and Gas Wells, Timber, etc.

This line is for people who have investments in natural resources. The ordinary small-business man who doesn't fall into this group can ignore this line.

Schedule C, Part II, Line 13: Depreciation

SCHEDULE C-2.—Depreciation (See Schedule C Instructions for line 13)

Complete Schedule C-2 if you claim depreciation **ONLY** for assets placed in service before January 1, 1981. If you need more space, use Form 4562. If you claim a deduction for any assets placed in service after December 31, 1980, use Form 4562 to figure your total deduction for all assets; do **NOT** complete Schedule C-2.

Description of property (a)	Date acquired (b)	Cost or other basis (c)	Depreciation allowed or allowable in prior years (d)	Method of computing depreciation (e)	Life or rate (f)	Depreciation for this year (g)
1 Depreciation (see Instructions):						
2 Totals					**2**	
3 Depreciation claimed in Schedule C-1					**3**	
4 Balance (subtract line 3 from line 2). Enter here and on Part II, line 13 . . . . ▶					**4**	

KEYNOTE: *Property Depreciation Rules*

There are two sets of depreciation rules, depending on whether the particular depreciable property was placed in service before 1981 or during 1981.

1. Property placed in service during 1981:

Every business person or owner of income-producing property who placed in service in 1981 either machinery and equipment, furniture, etc., or real property used in his business or income-producing activity, has a completely new set of depreciation and investment-credit rules to operate under as a result of the 1981 Tax Act. There is no longer any need for you to try to estimate the useful life of the asset in order to figure out your annual depreciation deduction.

Basically, here is how the new rules operate for 1981:

If you acquired an auto or light truck in 1981, it is considered to have a useful life of 3 years. *Regardless* of when

during 1981 you purchased the asset, your 1981 depreciation deduction is 25 percent of the cost of the asset. In 1982 you deduct 38 percent and in 1983 37 percent. In addition, you are allowed a 6-percent investment credit.

If you acquired machinery and equipment in 1981, this is considered to have a useful life of 5 years. Regardless of when during 1981 you acquired the asset, you take 1981 depreciation equal to 15 percent of the cost. In addition, you are allowed a 10-percent investment credit.

If in 1981 you acquired business real property, it is considered to have a useful life of 15 years and the depreciation is computed under a 175-percent declining-balance method. For 1981, the depreciation will be computed on the basis of the number of months in service. IRS has yet to explain exactly how. No investment credit is allowed.

If you run into complications it may be necessary to obtain professional help in this area.

Q. I bought a new auto for my business in November 1981 for $10,000. I intend to use the car for five years and then I hope to sell it for about $2,000. How much depreciation can I deduct for 1981?

A. 25 percent of $10,000, or $2,500. And you also can get an investment credit of 6 percent of $10,000, or $600.

2. Property placed in service before 1981:

For such property, you should continue to compute your depreciation deductions under the same methods you used in arriving at your 1980 depreciation deductions. Thus, if you used straight-line depreciation over your anticipated useful life for the property, you continue to use the same depreciation over the same useful life.

If the only property for which you claim depreciation is property you placed in service before 1981, then fill out Schedule C-2 to compute your depreciation. If you claim depreciation for any assets you placed in service after 1980, don't use Schedule C-2. Instead, use Form 4562 (see page 51) to compute depreciation for both the post-'80 property and any pre-'81 property.

Schedule C, Part II, Line 17: Insurance

Enter here the premiums or other costs incurred for business insurance. Note that the premiums paid on life insurance covering the owner are not deductible, regardless of who is the beneficiary.

Schedule C, Part II, Line 18: Interest on Business Indebtedness

You total here all the interest that you paid during the year on indebtedness attributable to your business.

Q. I borrowed $5,000 from the bank during 1981, but they only credited me with $4,850. Can I deduct the $150 discount this year even though I haven't yet paid off the loan?

A. Not if you are on the cash basis. You can deduct the discount (which is really interest) only when you pay the loan.

If you are on the accrual basis, you can deduct the $150 ratably over the period of the loan. Thus, if your loan was for six months and at the end of the year had three months to go, you can deduct half the discount, or $75.

Q. I borrowed $10,000 in July 1981 from my father to help me carry an exceptionally large inventory. I have agreed to pay him 8 percent interest on the loan when I repay it next June. Can I accrue $400 of interest, since I use the accrual basis?

A. Not if you follow through on your plan. If you want to deduct the interest, you will have to pay it by March 15, 1982. This is another instance in which you could be penalized by the tax-avoidance provision outlined below at page 132 under line 29a.

Schedule C, Part II, Line 22: Retirement Plans, Etc., Other Than Your Share

Payments that are deductible because made under a pension, profit-sharing, annuity, or bond-purchase plan for your employees are entered on line 22. But note that any payments made for you, as a self-employed owner, are not to be entered here. They are to be shown on line 25 of Form 1040.

Payments to other employee benefit plans, such as insurance, health, and welfare plans, are entered at line 15.

Schedule C, Part II, Line 23: Rent on Business Property

This line is for the rents paid or accrued for property used in your business. The rent can be on real property or such personal property as machines, tools, trucks, etc. But you can't deduct those rents paid on property to which you will acquire title or in which you are building up equity.

Q. My lease requires me to pay all the expenses on the property for the landlord, including taxes, insurance, etc. Do I report these under the various expenses?

A. No. These expenditures, which you have to pay for the landlord, are additional rent. Report the total of all these expenses plus your regular rental payments as the rent figure.

Schedule C, Part II, Line 24: Repairs

Money you spend repairing equipment, machines, buildings, etc., is deductible if you spend it in connection with property used in your business. Generally, the chief problem is whether the expenditures are repairs, which are immediately deductible in full, or improvements, which are depreciated over the years as part of the cost of the improved property.

Q. I repainted the outside of my building. Is this an immediately deductible repair item, or must it be added to the cost of the building?

A. It is an immediately deductible repair item. Other common repair expenditures are patching and repairing floors, repairing roofs and gutters, mending leaks, etc.

Q. I had a fifteen-year-old building completely reconditioned. I received a variety of small and large bills from various contractors. How do I separate the repairs from the improvements?

A. Because you followed an overall general plan of reconditioning, your entire cost is a capital expenditure, which must be recovered by depreciation deductions. No part of the cost is immediately deductible in full, even though it might have been if it hadn't been part of an overall general reconditioning plan.

Where you spend money for reconditioning, improving, or altering of premises, all expenditures, even though otherwise qualifying as repairs, are merely added to the cost of the property.

Q. In order to install air conditioning, it was necessary for me to rewire my premises. Is this an immediately deductible repair?

A. No. Money you spend for such items as new wiring, new roof, new plumbing, lighting fixtures, strengthening a wall by bricking up windows, etc., is considered spent for improvements.

Q. I purchased tires and tubes for my trucks during the year. I generally have to replace these every year. How do I classify these?

A. As immediately deductible repairs.

Q. Many of my expenses during the year are hard to classify as either repairs or improvements. Can you help me draw the line?

A. It's a difficult line to draw and therefore causes much litigation. The general rule is that a *repair* is an expenditure made to keep property in an ordinarily efficient operating condition. An *improvement* is an expenditure that increases the value of the property, prolongs its life, or makes it adaptable to different use.

Of course, in many cases an expenditure may accomplish both jobs. If there is a question as to whether it's a repair or improvement, you will probably want to resolve the doubt in your own favor.

Schedule C, Part II, Line 26: Taxes on Business and Business Property

All taxes paid or accrued which are directly attributable to your business are shown on this line. Include here property taxes, payroll taxes, and miscellaneous taxes, but you cannot deduct on this line, or on any other, your federal income taxes.

Schedule C, Part II, Line 29a: Wages

Here, enter any compensation paid in your business to employees if you haven't already included it as cost of labor in arriving at cost of goods sold above (line 3 of Schedule C-1). However, don't include any amounts that you paid to yourself.

Q. My son has worked for me after school and during vacations. I paid him what I paid other boys. Can I deduct the $450 salary paid to him?
A. Yes. Your son can be an employee.

Q. My wife also helps out part time, and she has a salary of $250 a week while I draw a salary of $750. Can I deduct her salary here?
A. You can deduct her salary on this line. But you will have to include the same amount on page 1 as income of your wife—unless she files a separate return. And if she files a separate return she will have to show the income on that return.

Q. I give my employees a bonus each Christmas. Are these considered additional salary?
A. Yes. Add them to the regular wages.

Q. The salary for the last week of the year was paid in January. Can I deduct this on the 1981 return?
A. The answer depends on whether you are on the accrual or cash basis. If you are on the accrual basis, the answer is yes. But if you are on the cash basis, you will have to wait until you file your 1982 return to deduct the salary payment. In the future, it may be wise to make out your employees' last week's salary checks a little early and pay them before the end of the year.

Q. I employ my brother at a salary of $2,000 a month. Since my cash position was tight, I haven't paid him two months' salary due for November and December 1981. As an accrual-basis taxpayer, can I deduct the $4,000 due my brother?
A. Yes—but only if you pay your brother by March 15, 1982. If you don't, the deduction will be lost for 1981 and you will never get it.

This is a tricky tax provision designed to prevent tax avoidance by accruing salaries to a close relative and deferring payment for an indefinite time. Otherwise the business could save taxes by the deduction, while the employee would not be taxed. If you are on the accrual basis and owe salaries to a closely related person who is on the cash basis, be sure to pay him by March 15, 1982, if you don't want to lose the deduction forever.

Schedule C, Part II, Line 31: Other Business Expenses

These are the catchall lines for all other business expenses that don't belong on one of the specific lines above. You can deduct here all the other ordinary and necessary expenses directly connected with your trade, business, or profession.

Q. Are there any limits on the amount of business expenses that can be deducted?
A. No. As long as they are business expenses, they can be deducted even though the result is a loss from the business.

Q. Can you give me some examples of other business expenses?
A. Supplies and materials such as office supplies, wrapping paper, etc.; heat, light, and power; traveling expenses; entertainment; postage; stationery; telephone and telegraph; freight and trucking; license fees; advertising.

Q. During 1981, merchandise that cost me $1,200 and which had a retail price of $2,000 was stolen. Do I deduct the $2,000 or the $1,200?
A. In this particular case, you can't take any deduction here at all. The reason is that your closing inventory at line 7 of Schedule C-1 (see page 126) will already have been reduced by the stolen merchandise—since it wasn't on hand at the end of the year. A deduction of the loss would give you a double deduction for the same loss. This obviously you cannot get.

Q. During 1981, a fire completely destroyed a shed used to store my trucks. The shed had a depreciated cost of $10,000 but was worth at least twice that at the time of the fire. Since I had no insurance, can I claim the full loss of value?
A. No. A loss can't be claimed in excess of the depreciated cost of the destroyed or damaged property. Thus, even though you have "lost" $20,000, you can claim only $10,000.

Q. A storm did considerable damage to my building, for which I received $3,000 in insurance. The building had a depreciated cost on my books of $30,000 but was worth $60,000 before the storm. I figure that the actual drop in value because of the storm was $15,000. How do I compute my loss?

A. The Treasury says that your loss is the drop in value ($15,000), but the loss cannot exceed your depreciated cost ($30,000). From this, you deduct the insurance recovery ($3,000). Thus you claim a loss of $12,000.

Q. I had a bad flood loss in December, but the insurance company hasn't yet settled my claim. Do I compute my loss this year, or do I have to wait until next year when I receive the insurance proceeds?

A. Compute your loss for this year by estimating the amount of insurance that you will recover. If you find that the estimate is substantially inaccurate, you should file an amended return correcting your original return.

Q. In 1981, I discovered one of my employees had embezzled $3,500 in 1979. Since the losses took place before 1981, do I file an amended return?

A. No. Deduct the $3,500 for 1981. A theft loss is deductible when the loss is discovered. The fact that the loss took place in an earlier year is immaterial.

Q. I have a one-year lease on my premises plus a 5-year renewal privilege, which I expect to exercise. I modernized the store front at a cost of $10,000. While the front is good for at least 10 years, can I deduct my costs over a shorter period than 10 years because of my lease?

A. Yes. If your lease plus renewal period which you expect to exercise is shorter than the life expectancy of your improvements, you can deduct your costs over the shorter period.

Schedule C, Part II, Line 32: Total Deductions

Just arithmetic.

Schedule C, Line 33: Net Profit or (Loss)

This is just arithmetic. The one key point to note is that if you have a loss here that you can't use to offset other income on Form 1040, you may be able to deduct the unused portion of the loss against your income of 1978-79-80 and possibly get a refund of part or all of the taxes you paid in those years.

Schedule C, Line 34: "At Risk" Provisions

If you incurred your business loss in any business except real estate, there are certain "at risk" provisions that may limit your loss deduction. See page 28 of the official IRS instructions for Form 1040 if you are involved in an "at risk" situation. Then check the "Yes" or "No" box on line 34.

SCHEDULE C-3.—Expense Account Information (See Schedule C Instructions for Schedule C-3)

Enter information for yourself and your five highest paid employees. In determining the five highest paid employees, add expense account allowances to the salaries and wages. However, you don't have to provide the information for any employee for whom the combined amount is less than $50,000, or for yourself if your expense account allowance plus line 33, page 1, is less than $50,000.

Name (a)	Expense account (b)	Salaries and wages (c)	
Owner			
1			
2			
3			
4			
5			

Did you claim a deduction for expenses connected with: | Yes | No
A Entertainment facility (boat, resort, ranch, etc.)? . . . .
B Living accommodations (except employees on business)? . . . .
C Conventions or meetings you or your employees attended outside the North American area? (see Instructions) . . .
D Employees' families at conventions or meetings? . . . .
  If "Yes," were any of these conventions or meetings outside the North American area? . . . .
E Vacations for employees or their families not reported on Form W-2? . . . .

☆ U.S. GOVERNMENT PRINTING OFFICE : 1981—O—343-060

343-060-3

Expense-Account Information

To complete this form, fill out the expense account information asked for. Note that this can be disregarded for yourself, if the amount on line 33, page 1, plus your expense-account allowance, is less than $50,000. And it need not be completed for any employee whose combined salary and wages plus expense account is less than $50,000.

The Treasury says that there is no penalty for not giving the information. "However, if a taxpayer does not furnish the information required, this may lead to an examination of his return."

Expense-account allowances include amounts received as advances or reimbursements, and amounts paid directly by or for the proprietor for expenses incurred by or on behalf of him or his employees. It includes all amounts charged through any type of credit card.

Expense account allowances do not include:
• Goods purchased for resale or use in the employer's business. Thus, the fact that you sign for merchandise, parts, etc., doesn't make the amount a reimbursement expense.
• Minor expenses such as buying office supplies or paying for local transportation in doing errands.
• Fringe benefits such as hospitalization insurance, approved pension trust funds, and unemployment insurance.

TAX TIP: Can You Prove That You Filed Your Return on Time?

Most tax returns that are mailed to the District Director reach their destination promptly with no problems. But suppose that after you mail your return on time, it goes astray in the mail, is mismarked on receipt by the District Director's office, or otherwise shows up late according to the Treasury's records. To avoid a penalty for late filing, you would have to be able to prove that you did file on time. This ordinarily can be a mighty tough job.

To make sure that you don't get caught in this trap, it may pay to mail your returns either certified mail or registered mail with return receipt requested. Or better still, deliver the return by hand and get a receipt from the office (generally the District Director's office will stamp your copy as a receipt).

SCHEDULE SE
(Form 1040)

Department of the Treasury
Internal Revenue Service

Computation of Social Security Self-Employment Tax

▶ See Instructions for Schedule SE (Form 1040).
▶ Attach to Form 1040.

Name of self-employed person (as shown on social security card)	Social security number of self-employed person ▶	

Part I — Computation of Net Earnings from FARM Self-Employment

Regular Method

1 Net profit or (loss) from:		
a Schedule F (Form 1040)	1a	
b Farm partnerships	1b	
2 Net earnings from farm self-employment (add lines 1a and 1b)	2	

Farm Optional Method

3 If gross profits from farming are:		
a Not more than $2,400, enter two-thirds of the gross profits		
b More than $2,400 and the net farm profit is less than $1,600, enter $1,600	3	
4 Enter here and on line 12a, the amount on line 2, or line 3 if you elect the farm optional method .	4	

Part II — Computation of Net Earnings from NONFARM Self-Employment

SE

Regular Method

5 Net profit or (loss) from:		
a Schedule C (Form 1040)	5a	
b Partnerships, joint ventures, etc. (other than farming)	5b	
c Service as a minister, member of a religious order, or a Christian Science practitioner. (Include rental value of parsonage or rental allowance furnished.) If you filed Form 4361 and have not revoked that exemption, check here ▶ ☐ and enter zero on this line	5c	
d Service with a foreign government or international organization	5d	
e Other (specify) ▶ _____	5e	
6 Total (add lines 5a through 5e)	6	
7 Enter adjustments if any (attach statement, see instructions)	7	
8 Adjusted net earnings or (loss) from nonfarm self-employment (line 6, as adjusted by line 7). Enter here and on line 12b. (Note: If the amount on line 8 is less than $1,600, you may wish to use the nonfarm optional method instead. See instructions.)	8	

Nonfarm Optional Method (Use only if your earnings from nonfarm self-employment are less than $1,600 and less than two-thirds of your gross nonfarm profits.)

9 a Maximum amount reportable under both optional methods combined (farm and nonfarm) . .	9a	$1,600	00
b Enter amount from line 3. (If you have no amount on line 3, enter zero.)	9b		
c Balance (subtract line 9b from line 9a)	9c		
10 Enter two-thirds of gross nonfarm profits or $1,600, whichever is smaller	10		
11 Enter here and on line 12b, the amount on line 9c or line 10, whichever is smaller	11		

Part III — Computation of Social Security Self-Employment Tax

12 Net earnings or (loss):			
a From farming (from line 4)	12a		
b From nonfarm (from line 8, or line 11 if you elect to use the Nonfarm Optional Method) . . .	12b		
13 Total net earnings or (loss) from self-employment reported on lines 12a and 12b. (If line 13 is less than $400, you are not subject to self-employment tax. Do not fill in rest of schedule)	13		
14 The largest amount of combined wages and self-employment earnings subject to social security or railroad retirement taxes for 1981 is	14	$29,700	00
15 a Total FICA wages (from Forms W–2) and RRTA compensation	15a		
b Unreported tips subject to FICA tax from Form 4137, line 9 or to RRTA	15b		
c Add lines 15a and 15b	15c		
16 Balance (subtract line 15c from line 14)	16		
17 Self-employment income—line 13 or line 16, whichever is smaller	17		
18 Self-employment tax. (If line 17 is $29,700, enter $2,762.10; if less, multiply the amount on line 17 by .093.) Enter here and on Form 1040, line 48	18		

For Paperwork Reduction Act Notice, see Form 1040 Instructions.

Computation of Self-employment Tax, Schedule SE

This schedule is used to determine your self-employment tax. This tax, while collected with the regular income tax, isn't an income tax. It is the Social Security tax collected from individuals who don't work for a salary or wage or who didn't earn $29,700 from wages and salary but who do have business or certain other income from self-employment. If you are self-employed and Form 1040, line 31, shows that you have less than $10,000 of adjusted gross income, you may wish to complete lines 1 through 13 of Schedule SE even though your self-employment income is less than $400 and you would not have to pay a self-employment tax. That is because you may be eligible for the earned-income credit described on page 21, and if so, including even the small amount of self-employment income in computing the credit can increase your credit. Take care in completing this schedule, for your Social Security benefits may be based on your tax.

If you had a salary or wages of $29,700 or more subject to Social Security taxes, disregard this schedule.

If you had a salary or wages of less than this, but were not self-employed, also disregard this schedule.

Farmers complete Part I and Part III.

Nonfarmers complete Part II and Part III. Most self-employed individuals need only complete lines 5 thru 8 of Part II plus the computations in Part III. Lines 9 thru 11 of Part II are designed for those self-employed individuals with adjusted net earnings from nonfarm self-employment of less than $1,600 who wish to obtain higher Social Security benefits by paying a higher self-employment tax on up to the $1,600. If this election is made, the individual pays tax on ⅔ of his nonfarm gross profits (but on not more than $1,600) rather than his lower net earnings.

To use this election you must be regularly self-employed or regularly a member of a partnership. This requirement is met if you had actual net earnings from self-employment of $400 or more (including your distributive share of the income or loss from any partnership of which you are a member) from trades or businesses (nonfarm and farm) in at least 2 years of the 3 consecutive years immediately preceding the year for which you elect to use the nonfarm option.

The majority of self-employed persons, who use the regular method, compute the self-employment tax as follows.

COMPUTATION OF NET EARNINGS FROM NONFARM SELF-EMPLOYMENT

In Part II of Schedule SE, the lines are used to collect all the possible sources of self-employment income which an individual may have.

Schedule SE, Line 5: Net Profit or (Loss)

Line 5a is merely the amount shown on Schedule C.

Line 5b is used to show the amount of the net earnings from self-employment derived from partnerships, joint ventures, etc. (other than farming). If you are a member of a partnership or joint venture, the figure to be shown here should be picked up from the partnership return filed by that business.

Line 5c is used by members of religious orders and Christian Science practitioners unless they elect not to be covered by Social Security and therefore not to pay the self-employment tax.

Lines 5d and 5e are self-explanatory.

Schedule SE, Line 6: Total Net Earnings or (Loss) from Self-employment

The total of all amounts shown on the five lines 5a through 5e is entered here.

Schedule SE, Line 7: Adjustments

Line 7 is used to eliminate from net earnings: (1) income from the performance of duties by public officials, by an employee or employee representative under Railroad Retirement system, and by most employees; (2) certain payments to retired partners; (3) real-estate rentals; (4) dividends and interest; and (5) property gains and losses.

No deduction is allowed for net operating-loss carryovers or carrybacks, and additional first-year depreciation is added to income. These adjustments are made here and a statement attached explaining them.

Schedule SE, Line 8: Adjusted Net Earnings or (Loss) from Nonfarm Self-employment

The amount on line 6 increased or decreased by the amount on line 7 is entered on line 8.

Schedule SE, Lines 9–11: Nonfarm Optional Method

Individuals who are using the optional method, as explained above, fill out lines 9 thru 11. All others omit these lines and go to Part III.

Schedule SE, Lines 12–13: Net Earnings

All that is necessary to complete lines 12 and 13 is to bring forward the figures from line 4, Part I, and line 8 (or 11) from Part II. These two amounts are totaled and shown on line 13. If line 13 is less than $400, you are not subject to self-employment tax and you do not then fill in the rest of the form.

Schedule SE, Lines 14–16: Maximum Amount Subject to Self-employment Tax

The maximum amount subject to self-employment tax for 1981 is $29,700 less the amount of wages that have already been subject to a deduction for Social Security tax. You'll find the $29,700 maximum already printed on line 14.

You enter on line 15 the amount of any wages for the year which have been subject to Social Security. Your Form W-2 will give you the information.

The difference between $29,700 and the amount on line 15 is then shown on line 16. This is the maximum amount on which self-employment tax is due.

Schedule SE, Line 17: Taxable Self-employment Income

The amount on line 13 or 16, whichever is smaller, is shown here. In brief, you are taxed on the actual self-employment income but not more than the maximum shown on line 16.

Schedule SE, Line 18: Self-employment Tax

The self-employment tax due is .093 of the amount on line 13. If the amount on line 13 is $29,700 enter $2,762.10 here. You also report this on line 48, page 2 of Form 1040, where it is added to the income tax due.

1981 Tax Table

The following official IRS tax tables are used to obtain the tax on taxable income of less than $50,000 on either Form 1040A (line 12) or Form 1040 (line 34).

1981 Tax Table
Based on Taxable Income
For persons with taxable incomes of less than $50,000.

Example: Mr. and Mrs. Brown are filing a joint return. Their taxable income on line 34 is $23,270. First, they find the $23,250-23,300 income line. Next, they find the column for married filing jointly and read down the column. The amount shown where the income line and filing status column meet is $4,082. This is the tax amount they must write on line 35 of their return.

At least	But less than	Single	Married filing jointly *	Married filing separately	Head of a household
			Your tax is—		
23,200	23,250	5,208	4,069	6,438	4,805
23,250	23,300	5,224	4,082	6,462	4,820
23,300	23,350	5,241	4,096	6,486	4,836

If line 34 (taxable income) is— At least	But less than	Single	Married filing jointly *	Married filing separately	Head of a house-hold
			Your tax is—		
0	1,700	0	0	0	0
1,700	1,725	0	0	a2	0
1,725	1,750	0	0	5	0
1,750	1,775	0	0	9	0
1,775	1,800	0	0	12	0
1,800	1,825	0	0	16	0
1,825	1,850	0	0	19	0
1,850	1,875	0	0	22	0
1,875	1,900	0	0	26	0
1,900	1,925	0	0	29	0
1,925	1,950	0	0	33	0
1,950	1,975	0	0	36	0
1,975	2,000	0	0	40	0

2,000

At least	But less than	Single	Married filing jointly *	Married filing separately	Head of a house-hold
2,000	2,025	0	0	43	0
2,025	2,050	0	0	47	0
2,050	2,075	0	0	50	0
2,075	2,100	0	0	54	0
2,100	2,125	0	0	57	0
2,125	2,150	0	0	60	0
2,150	2,175	0	0	64	0
2,175	2,200	0	0	67	0
2,200	2,225	0	0	71	0
2,225	2,250	0	0	74	0
2,250	2,275	0	0	78	0
2,275	2,300	0	0	81	0
2,300	2,325	b2	0	85	b2
2,325	2,350	5	0	88	5
2,350	2,375	9	0	92	9
2,375	2,400	12	0	95	12
2,400	2,425	16	0	99	16
2,425	2,450	19	0	102	19
2,450	2,475	22	0	105	22
2,475	2,500	26	0	109	26
2,500	2,525	29	0	112	29
2,525	2,550	33	0	116	33
2,550	2,575	36	0	119	36
2,575	2,600	40	0	123	40
2,600	2,625	43	0	126	43
2,625	2,650	47	0	130	47
2,650	2,675	50	0	133	50
2,675	2,700	54	0	137	54
2,700	2,725	57	0	140	57
2,725	2,750	60	0	143	60
2,750	2,775	64	0	147	64
2,775	2,800	67	0	151	67
2,800	2,825	71	0	155	71
2,825	2,850	74	0	159	74
2,850	2,875	78	0	163	78
2,875	2,900	81	0	167	81
2,900	2,925	85	0	171	85
2,925	2,950	88	0	175	88
2,950	2,975	92	0	179	92
2,975	3,000	95	0	183	95

3,000

At least	But less than	Single	Married filing jointly *	Married filing separately	Head of a house-hold
3,000	3,050	100	0	189	100
3,050	3,100	107	0	197	107
3,100	3,150	114	0	204	114
3,150	3,200	121	0	212	121
3,200	3,250	128	0	220	128
3,250	3,300	135	0	228	135
3,300	3,350	142	0	236	142
3,350	3,400	149	0	244	149
3,400	3,450	156	c3	252	156
3,450	3,500	164	10	260	162
3,500	3,550	172	17	268	169
3,550	3,600	180	24	276	176
3,600	3,650	188	31	283	183
3,650	3,700	196	38	291	190
3,700	3,750	203	45	299	197
3,750	3,800	211	52	307	204
3,800	3,850	219	59	316	211
3,850	3,900	227	66	324	218
3,900	3,950	235	73	333	225
3,950	4,000	243	79	342	232

4,000

At least	But less than	Single	Married filing jointly *	Married filing separately	Head of a house-hold
4,000	4,050	251	86	351	238
4,050	4,100	259	93	360	245
4,100	4,150	267	100	369	252
4,150	4,200	275	107	378	259
4,200	4,250	282	114	387	266
4,250	4,300	290	121	395	273
4,300	4,350	298	128	404	280
4,350	4,400	306	135	413	287
4,400	4,450	315	142	422	294
4,450	4,500	323	149	431	302
4,500	4,550	332	156	440	310
4,550	4,600	341	162	449	318
4,600	4,650	350	169	458	326
4,650	4,700	359	176	467	334
4,700	4,750	368	183	475	342
4,750	4,800	377	190	484	350
4,800	4,850	386	197	493	357
4,850	4,900	395	204	502	365
4,900	4,950	403	211	511	373
4,950	5,000	412	218	520	381

5,000

At least	But less than	Single	Married filing jointly *	Married filing separately	Head of a house-hold
5,000	5,050	421	225	529	389
5,050	5,100	430	232	538	397
5,100	5,150	439	238	547	405
5,150	5,200	448	245	555	413
5,200	5,250	457	252	564	421
5,250	5,300	466	259	573	429
5,300	5,350	474	266	582	436
5,350	5,400	483	273	591	444
5,400	5,450	492	280	600	452
5,450	5,500	501	287	609	460

At least	But less than	Single	Married filing jointly *	Married filing separately	Head of a house-hold
			Your tax is—		
5,500	5,550	510	294	618	468
5,550	5,600	519	302	627	476
5,600	5,650	528	310	635	484
5,650	5,700	537	318	644	492
5,700	5,750	546	326	653	500
5,750	5,800	554	334	662	508
5,800	5,850	563	342	671	515
5,850	5,900	572	350	680	523
5,900	5,950	581	357	689	531
5,950	6,000	590	365	698	539

6,000

At least	But less than	Single	Married filing jointly *	Married filing separately	Head of a house-hold
6,000	6,050	599	373	709	547
6,050	6,100	608	381	719	555
6,100	6,150	617	389	730	563
6,150	6,200	626	397	740	571
6,200	6,250	634	405	750	579
6,250	6,300	643	413	761	587
6,300	6,350	652	421	771	594
6,350	6,400	661	429	781	602
6,400	6,450	670	436	792	610
6,450	6,500	679	444	802	618
6,500	6,550	688	452	812	627
6,550	6,600	697	460	823	635
6,600	6,650	707	468	833	644
6,650	6,700	716	476	844	653
6,700	6,750	726	484	854	662
6,750	6,800	735	492	864	671
6,800	6,850	744	500	875	680
6,850	6,900	754	508	885	689
6,900	6,950	763	515	895	698
6,950	7,000	772	523	906	707

7,000

At least	But less than	Single	Married filing jointly *	Married filing separately	Head of a house-hold
7,000	7,050	782	531	916	715
7,050	7,100	791	539	927	724
7,100	7,150	801	547	937	733
7,150	7,200	810	555	947	742
7,200	7,250	819	563	958	751
7,250	7,300	829	571	968	760
7,300	7,350	838	579	978	769
7,350	7,400	848	587	989	778
7,400	7,450	857	594	999	787
7,450	7,500	866	602	1,009	795
7,500	7,550	876	610	1,020	804
7,550	7,600	885	618	1,030	813
7,600	7,650	894	627	1,041	822
7,650	7,700	904	635	1,051	831
7,700	7,750	913	644	1,061	840
7,750	7,800	923	653	1,072	849
7,800	7,850	932	662	1,082	858
7,850	7,900	941	671	1,092	867
7,900	7,950	951	680	1,103	875
7,950	8,000	960	689	1,113	884

*This column must also be used by a qualifying widow(er).

Continued on next page

a If your taxable income is exactly $1,700, your tax is zero.
b If your taxable income is exactly $2,300, your tax is zero.
c If your taxable income is exactly $3,400, your tax is zero.

1981 Tax Table (*Continued*)

If line 34 (taxable income) is— At least	But less than	Single	Married filing jointly *	Married filing separately	Head of a household
			Your tax is—		
8,000					
8,000	8,050	969	698	1,124	893
8,050	8,100	979	707	1,136	902
8,100	8,150	988	715	1,148	911
8,150	8,200	998	724	1,160	920
8,200	8,250	1,007	733	1,172	929
8,250	8,300	1,016	742	1,184	938
8,300	8,350	1,026	751	1,195	947
8,350	8,400	1,035	760	1,207	955
8,400	8,450	1,045	769	1,219	964
8,450	8,500	1,054	778	1,231	973
8,500	8,550	1,064	787	1,243	982
8,550	8,600	1,074	795	1,255	991
8,600	8,650	1,085	804	1,266	1,000
8,650	8,700	1,095	813	1,278	1,009
8,700	8,750	1,105	822	1,290	1,019
8,750	8,800	1,116	831	1,302	1,029
8,800	8,850	1,126	840	1,314	1,040
8,850	8,900	1,136	849	1,326	1,051
8,900	8,950	1,147	858	1,338	1,062
8,950	9,000	1,157	867	1,349	1,073
9,000					
9,000	9,050	1,167	875	1,361	1,084
9,050	9,100	1,178	884	1,373	1,095
9,100	9,150	1,188	893	1,385	1,106
9,150	9,200	1,199	902	1,397	1,116
9,200	9,250	1,209	911	1,409	1,127
9,250	9,300	1,219	920	1,421	1,138
9,300	9,350	1,230	929	1,432	1,149
9,350	9,400	1,240	938	1,444	1,160
9,400	9,450	1,250	947	1,456	1,171
9,450	9,500	1,261	955	1,468	1,182
9,500	9,550	1,271	964	1,480	1,192
9,550	9,600	1,282	973	1,492	1,203
9,600	9,650	1,292	982	1,503	1,214
9,650	9,700	1,302	991	1,515	1,225
9,700	9,750	1,313	1,000	1,527	1,236
9,750	9,800	1,323	1,009	1,539	1,247
9,800	9,850	1,333	1,018	1,551	1,258
9,850	9,900	1,344	1,027	1,563	1,268
9,900	9,950	1,354	1,035	1,575	1,279
9,950	10,000	1,364	1,044	1,586	1,290
10,000					
10,000	10,050	1,375	1,053	1,598	1,301
10,050	10,100	1,385	1,062	1,610	1,312
10,100	10,150	1,396	1,071	1,623	1,323
10,150	10,200	1,406	1,080	1,637	1,334
10,200	10,250	1,416	1,089	1,651	1,344
10,250	10,300	1,427	1,098	1,664	1,355
10,300	10,350	1,437	1,106	1,678	1,366
10,350	10,400	1,447	1,115	1,692	1,377
10,400	10,450	1,458	1,124	1,706	1,388
10,450	10,500	1,468	1,133	1,720	1,399
10,500	10,550	1,479	1,142	1,734	1,410
10,550	10,600	1,489	1,151	1,747	1,421
10,600	10,650	1,499	1,160	1,761	1,431
10,650	10,700	1,510	1,169	1,775	1,442
10,700	10,750	1,520	1,178	1,789	1,453
10,750	10,800	1,530	1,186	1,803	1,464
10,800	10,850	1,541	1,195	1,817	1,475
10,850	10,900	1,553	1,204	1,830	1,486
10,900	10,950	1,565	1,213	1,844	1,497
10,950	11,000	1,577	1,222	1,858	1,507
11,000					
11,000	11,050	1,589	1,231	1,872	1,518
11,050	11,100	1,601	1,240	1,886	1,529
11,100	11,150	1,613	1,249	1,899	1,540
11,150	11,200	1,624	1,258	1,913	1,551
11,200	11,250	1,636	1,266	1,927	1,562
11,250	11,300	1,648	1,275	1,941	1,573
11,300	11,350	1,660	1,284	1,955	1,583
11,350	11,400	1,672	1,293	1,969	1,594
11,400	11,450	1,684	1,302	1,982	1,605
11,450	11,500	1,696	1,311	1,996	1,616
11,500	11,550	1,707	1,320	2,010	1,627
11,550	11,600	1,719	1,329	2,024	1,638
11,600	11,650	1,731	1,338	2,038	1,649
11,650	11,700	1,743	1,346	2,052	1,659
11,700	11,750	1,755	1,355	2,065	1,670
11,750	11,800	1,767	1,364	2,079	1,681
11,800	11,850	1,778	1,373	2,093	1,693
11,850	11,900	1,790	1,382	2,107	1,704
11,900	11,950	1,802	1,392	2,121	1,716
11,950	12,000	1,814	1,402	2,134	1,728
12,000					
12,000	12,050	1,826	1,412	2,148	1,740
12,050	12,100	1,838	1,423	2,162	1,752
12,100	12,150	1,850	1,433	2,176	1,764
12,150	12,200	1,861	1,443	2,190	1,776
12,200	12,250	1,873	1,454	2,204	1,787
12,250	12,300	1,885	1,464	2,217	1,799
12,300	12,350	1,897	1,475	2,232	1,811
12,350	12,400	1,909	1,485	2,248	1,823
12,400	12,450	1,921	1,495	2,264	1,835
12,450	12,500	1,933	1,506	2,280	1,847
12,500	12,550	1,944	1,516	2,295	1,858
12,550	12,600	1,956	1,526	2,311	1,870
12,600	12,650	1,968	1,537	2,327	1,882
12,650	12,700	1,980	1,547	2,343	1,894
12,700	12,750	1,992	1,558	2,359	1,906
12,750	12,800	2,004	1,568	2,374	1,918
12,800	12,850	2,015	1,578	2,390	1,930
12,850	12,900	2,027	1,589	2,406	1,941
12,900	12,950	2,040	1,599	2,422	1,953
12,950	13,000	2,053	1,609	2,438	1,965
13,000					
13,000	13,050	2,065	1,620	2,453	1,977
13,050	13,100	2,078	1,630	2,469	1,989
13,100	13,150	2,091	1,640	2,485	2,001
13,150	13,200	2,104	1,651	2,501	2,013
13,200	13,250	2,117	1,661	2,517	2,024
13,250	13,300	2,130	1,672	2,532	2,036
13,300	13,350	2,142	1,682	2,548	2,048
13,350	13,400	2,155	1,692	2,564	2,060
13,400	13,450	2,168	1,703	2,580	2,072
13,450	13,500	2,181	1,713	2,596	2,084
13,500	13,550	2,194	1,723	2,611	2,095
13,550	13,600	2,207	1,734	2,627	2,107
13,600	13,650	2,219	1,744	2,643	2,119
13,650	13,700	2,232	1,755	2,659	2,131
13,700	13,750	2,245	1,765	2,675	2,143
13,750	13,800	2,258	1,775	2,690	2,155
13,800	13,850	2,271	1,786	2,706	2,167
13,850	13,900	2,284	1,796	2,722	2,178
13,900	13,950	2,296	1,806	2,738	2,190
13,950	14,000	2,309	1,817	2,754	2,202
14,000					
14,000	14,050	2,322	1,827	2,769	2,214
14,050	14,100	2,335	1,837	2,785	2,226
14,100	14,150	2,348	1,848	2,801	2,238
14,150	14,200	2,361	1,858	2,817	2,250
14,200	14,250	2,373	1,869	2,833	2,261
14,250	14,300	2,386	1,879	2,848	2,273
14,300	14,350	2,399	1,889	2,864	2,285
14,350	14,400	2,412	1,900	2,880	2,297
14,400	14,450	2,425	1,910	2,896	2,309
14,450	14,500	2,438	1,920	2,912	2,321
14,500	14,550	2,450	1,931	2,927	2,332
14,550	14,600	2,463	1,941	2,943	2,344
14,600	14,650	2,476	1,952	2,959	2,356
14,650	14,700	2,489	1,962	2,975	2,368
14,700	14,750	2,502	1,972	2,991	2,380
14,750	14,800	2,515	1,983	3,006	2,392
14,800	14,850	2,528	1,993	3,022	2,404
14,850	14,900	2,540	2,003	3,038	2,415
14,900	14,950	2,553	2,014	3,054	2,427
14,950	15,000	2,566	2,024	3,071	2,439
15,000					
15,000	15,050	2,580	2,034	3,089	2,451
15,050	15,100	2,595	2,045	3,107	2,464
15,100	15,150	2,609	2,055	3,126	2,477
15,150	15,200	2,624	2,066	3,144	2,490
15,200	15,250	2,639	2,076	3,162	2,503
15,250	15,300	2,654	2,086	3,180	2,516
15,300	15,350	2,669	2,097	3,199	2,528
15,350	15,400	2,684	2,107	3,217	2,541
15,400	15,450	2,698	2,117	3,235	2,554
15,450	15,500	2,713	2,128	3,254	2,567
15,500	15,550	2,728	2,138	3,272	2,580
15,550	15,600	2,743	2,149	3,290	2,593
15,600	15,650	2,758	2,159	3,308	2,606
15,650	15,700	2,772	2,169	3,327	2,618
15,700	15,750	2,787	2,180	3,345	2,631
15,750	15,800	2,802	2,190	3,363	2,644
15,800	15,850	2,817	2,200	3,381	2,657
15,850	15,900	2,832	2,211	3,400	2,670
15,900	15,950	2,846	2,221	3,418	2,683
15,950	16,000	2,861	2,232	3,436	2,695
16,000					
16,000	16,050	2,876	2,243	3,455	2,708
16,050	16,100	2,891	2,254	3,473	2,721
16,100	16,150	2,906	2,266	3,491	2,734
16,150	16,200	2,921	2,278	3,509	2,747
16,200	16,250	2,935	2,290	3,528	2,760

*This column must also be used by a qualifying widow(er).

Continued on next page

1981 Tax Table (Continued)

If line 34 (taxable income) is— At least	But less than	Single	Married filing jointly *	Married filing separately	Head of a household
			Your tax is—		
16,250	16,300	2,950	2,302	3,546	2,772
16,300	16,350	2,965	2,314	3,564	2,785
16,350	16,400	2,980	2,326	3,582	2,798
16,400	16,450	2,995	2,337	3,601	2,811
16,450	16,500	3,009	2,349	3,619	2,824
16,500	16,550	3,024	2,361	3,637	2,837
16,550	16,600	3,039	2,373	3,655	2,849
16,600	16,650	3,054	2,385	3,674	2,862
16,650	16,700	3,069	2,397	3,692	2,875
16,700	16,750	3,083	2,409	3,710	2,888
16,750	16,800	3,098	2,420	3,729	2,901
16,800	16,850	3,113	2,432	3,747	2,914
16,850	16,900	3,128	2,444	3,765	2,926
16,900	16,950	3,143	2,456	3,783	2,939
16,950	17,000	3,158	2,468	3,802	2,952
17,000					
17,000	17,050	3,172	2,480	3,820	2,965
17,050	17,100	3,187	2,491	3,838	2,978
17,100	17,150	3,202	2,503	3,856	2,991
17,150	17,200	3,217	2,515	3,875	3,003
17,200	17,250	3,232	2,527	3,893	3,016
17,250	17,300	3,246	2,539	3,911	3,029
17,300	17,350	3,261	2,551	3,930	3,042
17,350	17,400	3,276	2,563	3,948	3,055
17,400	17,450	3,291	2,574	3,966	3,068
17,450	17,500	3,306	2,586	3,984	3,081
17,500	17,550	3,320	2,598	4,003	3,093
17,550	17,600	3,335	2,610	4,021	3,106
17,600	17,650	3,350	2,622	4,041	3,119
17,650	17,700	3,365	2,634	4,062	3,132
17,700	17,750	3,380	2,646	4,083	3,145
17,750	17,800	3,395	2,657	4,104	3,158
17,800	17,850	3,409	2,669	4,126	3,170
17,850	17,900	3,424	2,681	4,147	3,183
17,900	17,950	3,439	2,693	4,168	3,196
17,950	18,000	3,454	2,705	4,189	3,209
18,000					
18,000	18,050	3,469	2,717	4,210	3,222
18,050	18,100	3,483	2,728	4,232	3,235
18,100	18,150	3,498	2,740	4,253	3,247
18,150	18,200	3,513	2,752	4,274	3,260
18,200	18,250	3,529	2,764	4,295	3,274
18,250	18,300	3,546	2,776	4,317	3,290
18,300	18,350	3,562	2,788	4,338	3,305
18,350	18,400	3,579	2,800	4,359	3,320
18,400	18,450	3,596	2,811	4,380	3,336
18,450	18,500	3,613	2,823	4,402	3,351
18,500	18,550	3,630	2,835	4,423	3,366
18,550	18,600	3,646	2,847	4,444	3,381
18,600	18,650	3,663	2,859	4,465	3,397
18,650	18,700	3,680	2,871	4,486	3,412
18,700	18,750	3,697	2,883	4,508	3,427
18,750	18,800	3,713	2,894	4,529	3,443
18,800	18,850	3,730	2,906	4,550	3,458
18,850	18,900	3,747	2,918	4,571	3,473
18,900	18,950	3,764	2,930	4,593	3,489
18,950	19,000	3,781	2,942	4,614	3,504

If line 34 (taxable income) is— At least	But less than	Single	Married filing jointly *	Married filing separately	Head of a household
			Your tax is—		
19,000					
19,000	19,050	3,797	2,954	4,635	3,519
19,050	19,100	3,814	2,965	4,656	3,535
19,100	19,150	3,831	2,977	4,678	3,550
19,150	19,200	3,848	2,989	4,699	3,565
19,200	19,250	3,865	3,001	4,720	3,580
19,250	19,300	3,881	3,013	4,741	3,596
19,300	19,350	3,898	3,025	4,762	3,611
19,350	19,400	3,915	3,037	4,784	3,626
19,400	19,450	3,932	3,048	4,805	3,642
19,450	19,500	3,949	3,060	4,826	3,657
19,500	19,550	3,965	3,072	4,847	3,672
19,550	19,600	3,982	3,084	4,869	3,688
19,600	19,650	3,999	3,096	4,890	3,703
19,650	19,700	4,016	3,108	4,911	3,718
19,700	19,750	4,032	3,120	4,932	3,733
19,750	19,800	4,049	3,131	4,954	3,749
19,800	19,850	4,066	3,143	4,975	3,764
19,850	19,900	4,083	3,155	4,996	3,779
19,900	19,950	4,100	3,167	5,017	3,795
19,950	20,000	4,116	3,179	5,038	3,810
20,000					
20,000	20,050	4,133	3,191	5,060	3,825
20,050	20,100	4,150	3,202	5,081	3,841
20,100	20,150	4,167	3,214	5,102	3,856
20,150	20,200	4,184	3,226	5,123	3,871
20,200	20,250	4,200	3,239	5,145	3,887
20,250	20,300	4,217	3,253	5,166	3,902
20,300	20,350	4,234	3,267	5,187	3,917
20,350	20,400	4,251	3,280	5,208	3,932
20,400	20,450	4,267	3,294	5,230	3,948
20,450	20,500	4,284	3,308	5,251	3,963
20,500	20,550	4,301	3,322	5,272	3,978
20,550	20,600	4,318	3,336	5,293	3,994
20,600	20,650	4,335	3,350	5,314	4,009
20,650	20,700	4,351	3,363	5,336	4,024
20,700	20,750	4,368	3,377	5,357	4,040
20,750	20,800	4,385	3,391	5,378	4,055
20,800	20,850	4,402	3,405	5,399	4,070
20,850	20,900	4,419	3,419	5,421	4,086
20,900	20,950	4,435	3,433	5,442	4,101
20,950	21,000	4,452	3,446	5,463	4,116
21,000					
21,000	21,050	4,469	3,460	5,484	4,131
21,050	21,100	4,486	3,474	5,506	4,147
21,100	21,150	4,503	3,488	5,527	4,162
21,150	21,200	4,519	3,502	5,548	4,177
21,200	21,250	4,536	3,516	5,569	4,193
21,250	21,300	4,553	3,529	5,590	4,208
21,300	21,350	4,570	3,543	5,612	4,223
21,350	21,400	4,586	3,557	5,633	4,239
21,400	21,450	4,603	3,571	5,654	4,254
21,450	21,500	4,620	3,585	5,675	4,269
21,500	21,550	4,637	3,598	5,697	4,285
21,550	21,600	4,654	3,612	5,718	4,300
21,600	21,650	4,670	3,626	5,739	4,315
21,650	21,700	4,687	3,640	5,760	4,330
21,700	21,750	4,704	3,654	5,782	4,346

If line 34 (taxable income) is— At least	But less than	Single	Married filing jointly *	Married filing separately	Head of a household
			Your tax is—		
21,750	21,800	4,721	3,668	5,803	4,361
21,800	21,850	4,738	3,681	5,824	4,376
21,850	21,900	4,754	3,695	5,845	4,392
21,900	21,950	4,771	3,709	5,866	4,407
21,950	22,000	4,788	3,723	5,888	4,422
22,000					
22,000	22,050	4,805	3,737	5,909	4,438
22,050	22,100	4,821	3,751	5,930	4,453
22,100	22,150	4,838	3,764	5,951	4,468
22,150	22,200	4,855	3,778	5,973	4,483
22,200	22,250	4,872	3,792	5,994	4,499
22,250	22,300	4,889	3,806	6,015	4,514
22,300	22,350	4,905	3,820	6,036	4,529
22,350	22,400	4,922	3,833	6,058	4,545
22,400	22,450	4,939	3,847	6,079	4,560
22,450	22,500	4,956	3,861	6,100	4,575
22,500	22,550	4,973	3,875	6,121	4,591
22,550	22,600	4,989	3,889	6,142	4,606
22,600	22,650	5,006	3,903	6,164	4,621
22,650	22,700	5,023	3,916	6,185	4,637
22,700	22,750	5,040	3,930	6,206	4,652
22,750	22,800	5,056	3,944	6,227	4,667
22,800	22,850	5,073	3,958	6,249	4,682
22,850	22,900	5,090	3,972	6,270	4,698
22,900	22,950	5,107	3,986	6,293	4,713
22,950	23,000	5,124	3,999	6,317	4,728
23,000					
23,000	23,050	5,140	4,013	6,341	4,744
23,050	23,100	5,157	4,027	6,365	4,759
23,100	23,150	5,174	4,041	6,389	4,774
23,150	23,200	5,191	4,055	6,414	4,790
23,200	23,250	5,208	4,069	6,438	4,805
23,250	23,300	5,224	4,082	6,462	4,820
23,300	23,350	5,241	4,096	6,486	4,836
23,350	23,400	5,258	4,110	6,510	4,851
23,400	23,450	5,275	4,124	6,535	4,866
23,450	23,500	5,292	4,138	6,559	4,881
23,500	23,550	5,310	4,151	6,583	4,898
23,550	23,600	5,329	4,165	6,607	4,916
23,600	23,650	5,348	4,179	6,631	4,934
23,650	23,700	5,367	4,193	6,656	4,951
23,700	23,750	5,387	4,207	6,680	4,969
23,750	23,800	5,406	4,221	6,704	4,987
23,800	23,850	5,425	4,234	6,728	5,005
23,850	23,900	5,444	4,248	6,752	5,022
23,900	23,950	5,464	4,262	6,776	5,040
23,950	24,000	5,483	4,276	6,801	5,058
24,000					
24,000	24,050	5,502	4,290	6,825	5,076
24,050	24,100	5,521	4,304	6,849	5,094
24,100	24,150	5,541	4,317	6,873	5,111
24,150	24,200	5,560	4,331	6,897	5,129
24,200	24,250	5,579	4,345	6,922	5,147
24,250	24,300	5,598	4,359	6,946	5,165
24,300	24,350	5,618	4,373	6,970	5,182
24,350	24,400	5,637	4,386	6,994	5,200
24,400	24,450	5,656	4,400	7,018	5,218
24,450	24,500	5,675	4,414	7,043	5,236

*This column must also be used by a qualifying widow(er).

Continued on next page

1981 Tax Table (Continued)

If line 34 (taxable income) is— At least	But less than	Single	Married filing jointly *	Married filing separately	Head of a household
			Your tax is—		
24,500	24,550	5,695	4,428	7,067	5,254
24,550	24,600	5,714	4,442	7,091	5,271
24,600	24,650	5,733	4,457	7,115	5,289
24,650	24,700	5,752	4,472	7,139	5,307
24,700	24,750	5,772	4,488	7,164	5,325
24,750	24,800	5,791	4,504	7,188	5,342
24,800	24,850	5,810	4,520	7,212	5,360
24,850	24,900	5,829	4,536	7,236	5,378
24,900	24,950	5,849	4,551	7,260	5,396
24,950	25,000	5,868	4,567	7,285	5,413
25,000					
25,000	25,050	5,887	4,583	7,309	5,431
25,050	25,100	5,906	4,599	7,333	5,449
25,100	25,150	5,926	4,615	7,357	5,467
25,150	25,200	5,945	4,630	7,381	5,485
25,200	25,250	5,964	4,646	7,406	5,502
25,250	25,300	5,984	4,662	7,430	5,520
25,300	25,350	6,003	4,678	7,454	5,538
25,350	25,400	6,022	4,694	7,478	5,556
25,400	25,450	6,041	4,709	7,502	5,573
25,450	25,500	6,061	4,725	7,526	5,591
25,500	25,550	6,080	4,741	7,551	5,609
25,550	25,600	6,099	4,757	7,575	5,627
25,600	25,650	6,118	4,773	7,599	5,645
25,650	25,700	6,138	4,788	7,623	5,662
25,700	25,750	6,157	4,804	7,647	5,680
25,750	25,800	6,176	4,820	7,672	5,698
25,800	25,850	6,195	4,836	7,696	5,716
25,850	25,900	6,215	4,852	7,720	5,733
25,900	25,950	6,234	4,867	7,744	5,751
25,950	26,000	6,253	4,883	7,768	5,769
26,000					
26,000	26,050	6,272	4,899	7,793	5,787
26,050	26,100	6,292	4,915	7,817	5,805
26,100	26,150	6,311	4,931	7,841	5,822
26,150	26,200	6,330	4,946	7,865	5,840
26,200	26,250	6,349	4,962	7,889	5,858
26,250	26,300	6,369	4,978	7,914	5,876
26,300	26,350	6,388	4,994	7,938	5,893
26,350	26,400	6,407	5,010	7,962	5,911
26,400	26,450	6,426	5,025	7,986	5,929
26,450	26,500	6,446	5,041	8,010	5,947
26,500	26,550	6,465	5,057	8,035	5,965
26,550	26,600	6,484	5,073	8,059	5,982
26,600	26,650	6,503	5,089	8,083	6,000
26,650	26,700	6,523	5,104	8,107	6,018
26,700	26,750	6,542	5,120	8,131	6,036
26,750	26,800	6,561	5,136	8,156	6,053
26,800	26,850	6,580	5,152	8,180	6,071
26,850	26,900	6,600	5,168	8,204	6,089
26,900	26,950	6,619	5,183	8,228	6,107
26,950	27,000	6,638	5,199	8,252	6,124
27,000					
27,000	27,050	6,657	5,215	8,276	6,142
27,050	27,100	6,677	5,231	8,301	6,160
27,100	27,150	6,696	5,247	8,325	6,178
27,150	27,200	6,715	5,262	8,349	6,196
27,200	27,250	6,735	5,278	8,373	6,213

If line 34 (taxable income) is— At least	But less than	Single	Married filing jointly *	Married filing separately	Head of a household
			Your tax is—		
27,250	27,300	6,754	5,294	8,397	6,231
27,300	27,350	6,773	5,310	8,422	6,249
27,350	27,400	6,792	5,326	8,446	6,267
27,400	27,450	6,812	5,341	8,470	6,284
27,450	27,500	6,831	5,357	8,494	6,302
27,500	27,550	6,850	5,373	8,518	6,320
27,550	27,600	6,869	5,389	8,543	6,338
27,600	27,650	6,889	5,405	8,567	6,356
27,650	27,700	6,908	5,420	8,591	6,373
27,700	27,750	6,927	5,436	8,615	6,391
27,750	27,800	6,946	5,452	8,639	6,409
27,800	27,850	6,966	5,468	8,664	6,427
27,850	27,900	6,985	5,484	8,688	6,444
27,900	27,950	7,004	5,499	8,712	6,462
27,950	28,000	7,023	5,515	8,736	6,480
28,000					
28,000	28,050	7,043	5,531	8,760	6,498
28,050	28,100	7,062	5,547	8,785	6,516
28,100	28,150	7,081	5,563	8,809	6,533
28,150	28,200	7,100	5,578	8,833	6,551
28,200	28,250	7,120	5,594	8,857	6,569
28,250	28,300	7,139	5,610	8,881	6,587
28,300	28,350	7,158	5,626	8,906	6,604
28,350	28,400	7,177	5,642	8,930	6,622
28,400	28,450	7,197	5,657	8,954	6,640
28,450	28,500	7,216	5,673	8,978	6,658
28,500	28,550	7,235	5,689	9,002	6,676
28,550	28,600	7,254	5,705	9,026	6,693
28,600	28,650	7,274	5,721	9,051	6,711
28,650	28,700	7,293	5,736	9,075	6,729
28,700	28,750	7,312	5,752	9,099	6,747
28,750	28,800	7,331	5,768	9,123	6,764
28,800	28,850	7,352	5,784	9,147	6,784
28,850	28,900	7,374	5,800	9,172	6,804
28,900	28,950	7,395	5,815	9,196	6,825
28,950	29,000	7,417	5,831	9,220	6,846
29,000					
29,000	29,050	7,439	5,847	9,244	6,867
29,050	29,100	7,461	5,863	9,268	6,887
29,100	29,150	7,482	5,879	9,293	6,908
29,150	29,200	7,504	5,894	9,317	6,929
29,200	29,250	7,526	5,910	9,341	6,950
29,250	29,300	7,547	5,926	9,365	6,970
29,300	29,350	7,569	5,942	9,389	6,991
29,350	29,400	7,591	5,958	9,414	7,012
29,400	29,450	7,613	5,973	9,438	7,032
29,450	29,500	7,634	5,989	9,462	7,053
29,500	29,550	7,656	6,005	9,486	7,074
29,550	29,600	7,678	6,021	9,510	7,095
29,600	29,650	7,700	6,037	9,535	7,115
29,650	29,700	7,721	6,052	9,559	7,136
29,700	29,750	7,743	6,068	9,583	7,157
29,750	29,800	7,765	6,084	9,607	7,178
29,800	29,850	7,786	6,100	9,631	7,198
29,850	29,900	7,808	6,116	9,656	7,219
29,900	29,950	7,830	6,133	9,680	7,240
29,950	30,000	7,852	6,151	9,704	7,261

If line 34 (taxable income) is— At least	But less than	Single	Married filing jointly *	Married filing separately	Head of a household
			Your tax is—		
30,000					
30,000	30,050	7,873	6,169	9,729	7,281
30,050	30,100	7,895	6,187	9,756	7,302
30,100	30,150	7,917	6,206	9,783	7,323
30,150	30,200	7,939	6,224	9,809	7,344
30,200	30,250	7,960	6,242	9,836	7,364
30,250	30,300	7,982	6,261	9,863	7,385
30,300	30,350	8,004	6,279	9,889	7,406
30,350	30,400	8,025	6,297	9,916	7,426
30,400	30,450	8,047	6,315	9,943	7,447
30,450	30,500	8,069	6,334	9,969	7,468
30,500	30,550	8,091	6,352	9,996	7,489
30,550	30,600	8,112	6,370	10,023	7,509
30,600	30,650	8,134	6,388	10,049	7,530
30,650	30,700	8,156	6,407	10,076	7,551
30,700	30,750	8,177	6,425	10,103	7,572
30,750	30,800	8,199	6,443	10,129	7,592
30,800	30,850	8,221	6,461	10,156	7,613
30,850	30,900	8,243	6,480	10,183	7,634
30,900	30,950	8,264	6,498	10,209	7,655
30,950	31,000	8,286	6,516	10,236	7,675
31,000					
31,000	31,050	8,308	6,535	10,263	7,696
31,050	31,100	8,330	6,553	10,289	7,717
31,100	31,150	8,351	6,571	10,316	7,738
31,150	31,200	8,373	6,589	10,343	7,758
31,200	31,250	8,395	6,608	10,369	7,779
31,250	31,300	8,416	6,626	10,396	7,800
31,300	31,350	8,438	6,644	10,423	7,821
31,350	31,400	8,460	6,662	10,449	7,841
31,400	31,450	8,482	6,681	10,476	7,862
31,450	31,500	8,503	6,699	10,503	7,883
31,500	31,550	8,525	6,717	10,529	7,903
31,550	31,600	8,547	6,735	10,556	7,924
31,600	31,650	8,569	6,754	10,583	7,945
31,650	31,700	8,590	6,772	10,609	7,966
31,700	31,750	8,612	6,790	10,636	7,986
31,750	31,800	8,634	6,809	10,663	8,007
31,800	31,850	8,655	6,827	10,689	8,028
31,850	31,900	8,677	6,845	10,716	8,049
31,900	31,950	8,699	6,863	10,743	8,069
31,950	32,000	8,721	6,882	10,769	8,090
32,000					
32,000	32,050	8,742	6,900	10,796	8,111
32,050	32,100	8,764	6,918	10,823	8,132
32,100	32,150	8,786	6,936	10,849	8,152
32,150	32,200	8,808	6,955	10,876	8,173
32,200	32,250	8,829	6,973	10,902	8,194
32,250	32,300	8,851	6,991	10,929	8,215
32,300	32,350	8,873	7,010	10,956	8,235
32,350	32,400	8,894	7,028	10,982	8,256
32,400	32,450	8,916	7,046	11,009	8,277
32,450	32,500	8,938	7,064	11,036	8,297
32,500	32,550	8,960	7,083	11,062	8,318
32,550	32,600	8,981	7,101	11,089	8,339
32,600	32,650	9,003	7,119	11,116	8,360
32,650	32,700	9,025	7,137	11,142	8,380
32,700	32,750	9,046	7,156	11,169	8,401

*This column must also be used by a qualifying widow(er).

Continued on next page

1981 Tax Table (*Continued*)

If line 34 (taxable income) is— At least	But less than	Single	Married filing jointly *	Married filing separately	Head of a house-hold
32,750	32,800	9,068	7,174	11,196	8,422
32,800	32,850	9,090	7,192	11,222	8,443
32,850	32,900	9,112	7,210	11,249	8,463
32,900	32,950	9,133	7,229	11,276	8,484
32,950	33,000	9,155	7,247	11,302	8,505
33,000					
33,000	33,050	9,177	7,265	11,329	8,526
33,050	33,100	9,199	7,284	11,356	8,546
33,100	33,150	9,220	7,302	11,382	8,567
33,150	33,200	9,242	7,320	11,409	8,588
33,200	33,250	9,264	7,338	11,436	8,609
33,250	33,300	9,285	7,357	11,462	8,629
33,300	33,350	9,307	7,375	11,489	8,650
33,350	33,400	9,329	7,393	11,516	8,671
33,400	33,450	9,351	7,411	11,542	8,691
33,450	33,500	9,372	7,430	11,569	8,712
33,500	33,550	9,394	7,448	11,596	8,733
33,550	33,600	9,416	7,466	11,622	8,754
33,600	33,650	9,438	7,485	11,649	8,774
33,650	33,700	9,459	7,503	11,676	8,795
33,700	33,750	9,481	7,521	11,702	8,816
33,750	33,800	9,503	7,539	11,729	8,837
33,800	33,850	9,524	7,558	11,756	8,857
33,850	33,900	9,546	7,576	11,782	8,878
33,900	33,950	9,568	7,594	11,809	8,899
33,950	34,000	9,590	7,612	11,836	8,920
34,000					
34,000	34,050	9,611	7,631	11,862	8,940
34,050	34,100	9,633	7,649	11,889	8,961
34,100	34,150	9,656	7,667	11,916	8,983
34,150	34,200	9,680	7,685	11,942	9,006
34,200	34,250	9,704	7,704	11,969	9,028
34,250	34,300	9,729	7,722	11,996	9,051
34,300	34,350	9,753	7,740	12,022	9,074
34,350	34,400	9,777	7,759	12,049	9,096
34,400	34,450	9,801	7,777	12,076	9,119
34,450	34,500	9,825	7,795	12,102	9,142
34,500	34,550	9,850	7,813	12,129	9,164
34,550	34,600	9,874	7,832	12,156	9,187
34,600	34,650	9,898	7,850	12,182	9,210
34,650	34,700	9,922	7,868	12,209	9,233
34,700	34,750	9,946	7,886	12,236	9,255
34,750	34,800	9,971	7,905	12,262	9,278
34,800	34,850	9,995	7,923	12,289	9,301
34,850	34,900	10,019	7,941	12,316	9,323
34,900	34,950	10,043	7,959	12,342	9,346
34,950	35,000	10,067	7,978	12,369	9,369
35,000					
35,000	35,050	10,092	7,996	12,396	9,392
35,050	35,100	10,116	8,014	12,422	9,414
35,100	35,150	10,140	8,033	12,449	9,437
35,150	35,200	10,164	8,051	12,476	9,460
35,200	35,250	10,188	8,071	12,502	9,482
35,250	35,300	10,212	8,092	12,529	9,505
35,300	35,350	10,237	8,113	12,556	9,528
35,350	35,400	10,261	8,134	12,582	9,551
35,400	35,450	10,285	8,156	12,609	9,573
35,450	35,500	10,309	8,177	12,636	9,596

If line 34 (taxable income) is— At least	But less than	Single	Married filing jointly *	Married filing separately	Head of a house-hold
35,500	35,550	10,333	8,198	12,662	9,619
35,550	35,600	10,358	8,219	12,689	9,641
35,600	35,650	10,382	8,240	12,716	9,664
35,650	35,700	10,406	8,262	12,742	9,687
35,700	35,750	10,430	8,283	12,769	9,710
35,750	35,800	10,454	8,304	12,796	9,732
35,800	35,850	10,479	8,325	12,822	9,755
35,850	35,900	10,503	8,347	12,849	9,778
35,900	35,950	10,527	8,368	12,876	9,800
35,950	36,000	10,551	8,389	12,902	9,823
36,000					
36,000	36,050	10,575	8,410	12,929	9,846
36,050	36,100	10,600	8,432	12,956	9,869
36,100	36,150	10,624	8,453	12,982	9,891
36,150	36,200	10,648	8,474	13,009	9,914
36,200	36,250	10,672	8,495	13,035	9,937
36,250	36,300	10,696	8,516	13,062	9,959
36,300	36,350	10,721	8,538	13,089	9,982
36,350	36,400	10,745	8,559	13,115	10,005
36,400	36,450	10,769	8,580	13,142	10,028
36,450	36,500	10,793	8,601	13,169	10,050
36,500	36,550	10,817	8,623	13,195	10,073
36,550	36,600	10,842	8,644	13,222	10,096
36,600	36,650	10,866	8,665	13,249	10,118
36,650	36,700	10,890	8,686	13,275	10,141
36,700	36,750	10,914	8,708	13,302	10,164
36,750	36,800	10,938	8,729	13,329	10,187
36,800	36,850	10,962	8,750	13,355	10,209
36,850	36,900	10,987	8,771	13,382	10,232
36,900	36,950	11,011	8,792	13,409	10,255
36,950	37,000	11,035	8,814	13,435	10,277
37,000					
37,000	37,050	11,059	8,835	13,462	10,300
37,050	37,100	11,083	8,856	13,489	10,323
37,100	37,150	11,108	8,877	13,515	10,346
37,150	37,200	11,132	8,899	13,542	10,368
37,200	37,250	11,156	8,920	13,569	10,391
37,250	37,300	11,180	8,941	13,595	10,414
37,300	37,350	11,204	8,962	13,622	10,436
37,350	37,400	11,229	8,984	13,649	10,459
37,400	37,450	11,253	9,005	13,675	10,482
37,450	37,500	11,277	9,026	13,702	10,505
37,500	37,550	11,301	9,047	13,729	10,527
37,550	37,600	11,325	9,068	13,755	10,550
37,600	37,650	11,350	9,090	13,782	10,573
37,650	37,700	11,374	9,111	13,809	10,595
37,700	37,750	11,398	9,132	13,835	10,618
37,750	37,800	11,422	9,153	13,862	10,641
37,800	37,850	11,446	9,175	13,889	10,664
37,850	37,900	11,471	9,196	13,915	10,686
37,900	37,950	11,495	9,217	13,942	10,709
37,950	38,000	11,519	9,238	13,969	10,732
38,000					
38,000	38,050	11,543	9,260	13,995	10,754
38,050	38,100	11,567	9,281	14,022	10,777
38,100	38,150	11,592	9,302	14,049	10,800
38,150	38,200	11,616	9,323	14,075	10,823
38,200	38,250	11,640	9,344	14,102	10,845

If line 34 (taxable income) is— At least	But less than	Single	Married filing jointly *	Married filing separately	Head of a house-hold
38,250	38,300	11,664	9,366	14,129	10,868
38,300	38,350	11,688	9,387	14,155	10,891
38,350	38,400	11,712	9,408	14,182	10,913
38,400	38,450	11,737	9,429	14,209	10,936
38,450	38,500	11,761	9,451	14,235	10,959
38,500	38,550	11,785	9,472	14,262	10,981
38,550	38,600	11,809	9,493	14,289	11,004
38,600	38,650	11,833	9,514	14,315	11,027
38,650	38,700	11,858	9,536	14,342	11,050
38,700	38,750	11,882	9,557	14,369	11,072
38,750	38,800	11,906	9,578	14,395	11,095
38,800	38,850	11,930	9,599	14,422	11,118
38,850	38,900	11,954	9,620	14,449	11,140
38,900	38,950	11,979	9,642	14,475	11,163
38,950	39,000	12,003	9,663	14,502	11,186
39,000					
39,000	39,050	12,027	9,684	14,529	11,209
39,050	39,100	12,051	9,705	14,555	11,231
39,100	39,150	12,075	9,727	14,582	11,254
39,150	39,200	12,100	9,748	14,609	11,277
39,200	39,250	12,124	9,769	14,635	11,299
39,250	39,300	12,148	9,790	14,662	11,322
39,300	39,350	12,172	9,812	14,689	11,345
39,350	39,400	12,196	9,833	14,715	11,368
39,400	39,450	12,221	9,854	14,742	11,390
39,450	39,500	12,245	9,875	14,769	11,413
39,500	39,550	12,269	9,896	14,795	11,436
39,550	39,600	12,293	9,918	14,822	11,458
39,600	39,650	12,317	9,939	14,849	11,481
39,650	39,700	12,342	9,960	14,875	11,504
39,700	39,750	12,366	9,981	14,902	11,527
39,750	39,800	12,390	10,003	14,929	11,549
39,800	39,850	12,414	10,024	14,955	11,572
39,850	39,900	12,438	10,045	14,982	11,595
39,900	39,950	12,462	10,066	15,009	11,617
39,950	40,000	12,487	10,088	15,035	11,640
40,000					
40,000	40,050	12,511	10,109	15,062	11,663
40,050	40,100	12,535	10,130	15,089	11,686
40,100	40,150	12,559	10,151	15,115	11,708
40,150	40,200	12,583	10,172	15,142	11,731
40,200	40,250	12,608	10,194	15,168	11,754
40,250	40,300	12,632	10,215	15,195	11,776
40,300	40,350	12,656	10,236	15,222	11,799
40,350	40,400	12,680	10,257	15,248	11,822
40,400	40,450	12,704	10,279	15,275	11,845
40,450	40,500	12,729	10,300	15,302	11,867
40,500	40,550	12,753	10,321	15,328	11,890
40,550	40,600	12,777	10,342	15,355	11,913
40,600	40,650	12,801	10,364	15,382	11,935
40,650	40,700	12,825	10,385	15,408	11,958
40,700	40,750	12,850	10,406	15,435	11,981
40,750	40,800	12,874	10,427	15,462	12,004
40,800	40,850	12,898	10,448	15,488	12,026
40,850	40,900	12,922	10,470	15,515	12,049
40,900	40,950	12,946	10,491	15,542	12,072
40,950	41,000	12,971	10,512	15,568	12,094

*This column must also be used by a qualifying widow(er).

Continued on next page

1981 Tax Table (*Continued*)

If line 34 (taxable income) is— At least	But less than	Single	Married filing jointly *	Married filing separately	Head of a household	If line 34 (taxable income) is— At least	But less than	Single	Married filing jointly *	Married filing separately	Head of a household	If line 34 (taxable income) is— At least	But less than	Single	Married filing jointly *	Married filing separately	Head of a household
41,000						**44,000**						**47,000**					
41,000	41,050	12,995	10,533	15,595	12,117	44,000	44,050	14,596	11,807	17,255	13,480	47,000	47,050	16,225	13,154	19,003	15,026
41,050	41,100	13,019	10,555	15,622	12,140	44,050	44,100	14,623	11,829	17,284	13,503	47,050	47,100	16,253	13,178	19,032	15,053
41,100	41,150	13,043	10,576	15,648	12,163	44,100	44,150	14,650	11,850	17,314	13,525	47,100	47,150	16,280	13,202	19,061	15,080
41,150	41,200	13,067	10,597	15,675	12,185	44,150	44,200	14,677	11,871	17,343	13,548	47,150	47,200	16,307	13,226	19,091	15,106
41,200	41,250	13,092	10,618	15,702	12,208	44,200	44,250	14,705	11,892	17,372	13,571	47,200	47,250	16,334	13,251	19,120	15,133
41,250	41,300	13,116	10,640	15,728	12,231	44,250	44,300	14,732	11,913	17,401	13,593	47,250	47,300	16,361	13,275	19,149	15,160
41,300	41,350	13,140	10,661	15,755	12,253	44,300	44,350	14,759	11,935	17,430	13,616	47,300	47,350	16,388	13,299	19,178	15,186
41,350	41,400	13,164	10,682	15,782	12,276	44,350	44,400	14,786	11,956	17,459	13,639	47,350	47,400	16,415	13,323	19,207	15,213
41,400	41,450	13,188	10,703	15,808	12,299	44,400	44,450	14,813	11,977	17,488	13,662	47,400	47,450	16,443	13,347	19,236	15,240
41,450	41,500	13,213	10,724	15,835	12,322	44,450	44,500	14,840	11,998	17,518	13,684	47,450	47,500	16,470	13,371	19,265	15,266
41,500	41,550	13,238	10,746	15,862	12,344	44,500	44,550	14,868	12,020	17,547	13,707	47,500	47,550	16,497	13,396	19,295	15,293
41,550	41,600	13,265	10,767	15,888	12,367	44,550	44,600	14,895	12,041	17,576	13,730	47,550	47,600	16,524	13,420	19,324	15,320
41,600	41,650	13,292	10,788	15,915	12,390	44,600	44,650	14,922	12,062	17,605	13,752	47,600	47,650	16,551	13,444	19,353	15,346
41,650	41,700	13,320	10,809	15,942	12,412	44,650	44,700	14,949	12,083	17,634	13,775	47,650	47,700	16,578	13,468	19,382	15,373
41,700	41,750	13,347	10,831	15,968	12,435	44,700	44,750	14,976	12,105	17,663	13,800	47,700	47,750	16,606	13,492	19,411	15,400
41,750	41,800	13,374	10,852	15,995	12,458	44,750	44,800	15,003	12,126	17,692	13,826	47,750	47,800	16,633	13,517	19,440	15,426
41,800	41,850	13,401	10,873	16,022	12,481	44,800	44,850	15,030	12,147	17,721	13,853	47,800	47,850	16,660	13,541	19,469	15,453
41,850	41,900	13,428	10,894	16,048	12,503	44,850	44,900	15,058	12,168	17,751	13,880	47,850	47,900	16,687	13,565	19,498	15,480
41,900	41,950	13,455	10,916	16,075	12,526	44,900	44,950	15,085	12,189	17,780	13,906	47,900	47,950	16,714	13,589	19,528	15,506
41,950	42,000	13,483	10,937	16,102	12,549	44,950	45,000	15,112	12,211	17,809	13,933	47,950	48,000	16,741	13,613	19,557	15,533
42,000						**45,000**						**48,000**					
42,000	42,050	13,510	10,958	16,128	12,571	45,000	45,050	15,139	12,232	17,838	13,960	48,000	48,050	16,768	13,638	19,586	15,560
42,050	42,100	13,537	10,979	16,155	12,594	45,050	45,100	15,166	12,253	17,867	13,986	48,050	48,100	16,796	13,662	19,615	15,586
42,100	42,150	13,564	11,001	16,182	12,617	45,100	45,150	15,193	12,274	17,896	14,013	48,100	48,150	16,823	13,686	19,644	15,613
42,150	42,200	13,591	11,022	16,208	12,640	45,150	45,200	15,221	12,296	17,925	14,040	48,150	48,200	16,850	13,710	19,673	15,640
42,200	42,250	13,618	11,043	16,235	12,662	45,200	45,250	15,248	12,317	17,954	14,066	48,200	48,250	16,877	13,734	19,702	15,666
42,250	42,300	13,646	11,064	16,262	12,685	45,250	45,300	15,275	12,338	17,984	14,093	48,250	48,300	16,904	13,759	19,731	15,693
42,300	42,350	13,673	11,085	16,288	12,708	45,300	45,350	15,302	12,359	18,013	14,120	48,300	48,350	16,931	13,783	19,761	15,720
42,350	42,400	13,700	11,107	16,315	12,730	45,350	45,400	15,329	12,381	18,042	14,146	48,350	48,400	16,959	13,807	19,790	15,746
42,400	42,450	13,727	11,128	16,342	12,753	45,400	45,450	15,356	12,402	18,071	14,173	48,400	48,450	16,986	13,831	19,819	15,773
42,450	42,500	13,754	11,149	16,368	12,776	45,450	45,500	15,384	12,423	18,100	14,200	48,450	48,500	17,013	13,855	19,848	15,800
42,500	42,550	13,781	11,170	16,395	12,798	45,500	45,550	15,411	12,444	18,129	14,226	48,500	48,550	17,040	13,880	19,877	15,826
42,550	42,600	13,808	11,192	16,422	12,821	45,550	45,600	15,438	12,465	18,158	14,253	48,550	48,600	17,067	13,904	19,906	15,853
42,600	42,650	13,836	11,213	16,448	12,844	45,600	45,650	15,465	12,487	18,188	14,280	48,600	48,650	17,094	13,928	19,935	15,879
42,650	42,700	13,863	11,234	16,475	12,867	45,650	45,700	15,492	12,508	18,217	14,306	48,650	48,700	17,122	13,952	19,965	15,906
42,700	42,750	13,890	11,255	16,502	12,889	45,700	45,750	15,519	12,529	18,246	14,333	48,700	48,750	17,149	13,976	19,994	15,933
42,750	42,800	13,917	11,277	16,528	12,912	45,750	45,800	15,546	12,550	18,275	14,360	48,750	48,800	17,176	14,001	20,023	15,959
42,800	42,850	13,944	11,298	16,556	12,935	45,800	45,850	15,574	12,573	18,304	14,386	48,800	48,850	17,203	14,025	20,052	15,986
42,850	42,900	13,971	11,319	16,585	12,957	45,850	45,900	15,601	12,597	18,333	14,413	48,850	48,900	17,230	14,049	20,081	16,013
42,900	42,950	13,999	11,340	16,614	12,980	45,900	45,950	15,628	12,621	18,362	14,440	48,900	48,950	17,257	14,073	20,110	16,039
42,950	43,000	14,026	11,361	16,644	13,003	45,950	46,000	15,655	12,646	18,391	14,466	48,950	49,000	17,284	14,097	20,139	16,066
43,000						**46,000**						**49,000**					
43,000	43,050	14,053	11,383	16,673	13,026	46,000	46,050	15,682	12,670	18,421	14,493	49,000	49,050	17,312	14,121	20,168	16,093
43,050	43,100	14,080	11,404	16,702	13,048	46,050	46,100	15,709	12,694	18,450	14,520	49,050	49,100	17,339	14,146	20,198	16,119
43,100	43,150	14,107	11,425	16,731	13,071	46,100	46,150	15,737	12,718	18,479	14,546	49,100	49,150	17,366	14,170	20,227	16,146
43,150	43,200	14,134	11,446	16,760	13,094	46,150	46,200	15,764	12,742	18,508	14,573	49,150	49,200	17,393	14,194	20,256	16,173
43,200	43,250	14,161	11,468	16,789	13,116	46,200	46,250	15,791	12,767	18,537	14,600	49,200	49,250	17,420	14,218	20,285	16,199
43,250	43,300	14,189	11,489	16,818	13,139	46,250	46,300	15,818	12,791	18,566	14,626	49,250	49,300	17,447	14,242	20,314	16,226
43,300	43,350	14,216	11,510	16,847	13,162	46,300	46,350	15,845	12,815	18,595	14,653	49,300	49,350	17,475	14,267	20,343	16,253
43,350	43,400	14,243	11,531	16,877	13,185	46,350	46,400	15,872	12,839	18,624	14,680	49,350	49,400	17,502	14,291	20,372	16,279
43,400	43,450	14,270	11,553	16,906	13,207	46,400	46,450	15,899	12,863	18,654	14,706	49,400	49,450	17,529	14,315	20,402	16,306
43,450	43,500	14,297	11,574	16,935	13,230	46,450	46,500	15,927	12,888	18,683	14,733	49,450	49,500	17,556	14,339	20,431	16,333
43,500	43,550	14,324	11,595	16,964	13,253	46,500	46,550	15,954	12,912	18,712	14,760	49,500	49,550	17,583	14,363	20,460	16,359
43,550	43,600	14,352	11,616	16,993	13,275	46,550	46,600	15,981	12,936	18,741	14,786	49,550	49,600	17,610	14,388	20,489	16,386
43,600	43,650	14,379	11,637	17,022	13,298	46,600	46,650	16,008	12,960	18,770	14,813	49,600	49,650	17,637	14,412	20,518	16,413
43,650	43,700	14,406	11,659	17,051	13,321	46,650	46,700	16,035	12,984	18,799	14,840	49,650	49,700	17,665	14,436	20,547	16,439
43,700	43,750	14,433	11,680	17,081	13,344	46,700	46,750	16,062	13,009	18,828	14,866	49,700	49,750	17,692	14,460	20,576	16,466
43,750	43,800	14,460	11,701	17,110	13,366	46,750	46,800	16,090	13,033	18,858	14,893	49,750	49,800	17,719	14,484	20,605	16,493
43,800	43,850	14,487	11,722	17,139	13,389	46,800	46,850	16,117	13,057	18,887	14,920	49,800	49,850	17,746	14,509	20,635	16,519
43,850	43,900	14,515	11,744	17,168	13,412	46,850	46,900	16,144	13,081	18,916	14,946	49,850	49,900	17,773	14,533	20,664	16,546
43,900	43,950	14,542	11,765	17,197	13,434	46,900	46,950	16,171	13,105	18,945	14,973	49,900	49,950	17,800	14,557	20,693	16,573
43,950	44,000	14,569	11,786	17,226	13,457	46,950	47,000	16,198	13,130	18,974	15,000	49,950	50,000	17,828	14,581	20,722	16,599

*This column must also be used by a qualifying widow(er).

50,000 or over—use tax rate schedules

1981 Tax Rate Schedules
Your zero bracket amount has been built into these Tax Rate Schedules.

Schedule X
Single Taxpayers

Use this schedule if you checked **Filing Status Box 1** on Form 1040—

If the amount on Form 1040, line 34 is: Over—	But not Over—	Enter on line 2 of the worksheet on this page:	of the amount over—
$0	$2,300	—0—	
2,300	3,400	.... 14%	$2,300
3,400	4,400	$154+16%	3,400
4,400	6,500	314+18%	4,400
6,500	8,500	692+19%	6,500
8,500	10,800	1,072+21%	8,500
10,800	12,900	1,555+24%	10,800
12,900	15,000	2,059+26%	12,900
15,000	18,200	2,605+30%	15,000
18,200	23,500	3,565+34%	18,200
23,500	28,800	5,367+39%	23,500
28,800	34,100	7,434+44%	28,800
34,100	41,500	9,766+49%	34,100
41,500	55,300	13,392+55%	41,500
55,300	81,800	20,982+63%	55,300
81,800	108,300	37,677+68%	81,800
108,300	....	55,697+70%	108,300

Schedule Z
Unmarried Heads of Household

(including certain married persons who live apart (and abandoned spouses)—see page 6 of the Instructions)

Use this schedule if you checked **Filing Status Box 4** on Form 1040—

If the amount on Form 1040, line 34 is: Over—	But not Over—	Enter on line 2 of the worksheet on this page:	of the amount over—
$0	$2,300	—0—	
2,300	4,400	.... 14%	$2,300
4,400	6,500	$294+16%	4,400
6,500	8,700	630+18%	6,500
8,700	11,800	1,026+22%	8,700
11,800	15,000	1,708+24%	11,800
15,000	18,200	2,476+26%	15,000
18,200	23,500	3,308+31%	18,200
23,500	28,800	4,951+36%	23,500
28,800	34,100	6,859+42%	28,800
34,100	44,700	9,085+46%	34,100
44,700	60,600	13,961+54%	44,700
60,600	81,800	22,547+59%	60,600
81,800	108,300	35,055+63%	81,800
108,300	161,300	51,750+68%	108,300
161,300	....	87,790+70%	161,300

Schedule Y
Married Taxpayers and Qualifying Widows and Widowers

Married Filing Joint Returns and Qualifying Widows and Widowers

Use this schedule if you checked **Filing Status Box 2 or 5** on Form 1040—

If the amount on Form 1040, line 34 is: Over—	But not over—	Enter on line 2 of the worksheet on this page:	of the amount over—
$0	$3,400	—0—	
3,400	5,500	.... 14%	$3,400
5,500	7,600	$294+16%	5,500
7,600	11,900	630+18%	7,600
11,900	16,000	1,404+21%	11,900
16,000	20,200	2,265+24%	16,000
20,200	24,600	3,273+28%	20,200
24,600	29,900	4,505+32%	24,600
29,900	35,200	6,201+37%	29,900
35,200	45,800	8,162+43%	35,200
45,800	60,000	12,720+49%	45,800
60,000	85,600	19,678+54%	60,000
85,600	109,400	33,502+59%	85,600
109,400	162,400	47,544+64%	109,400
162,400	215,400	81,464+68%	162,400
215,400	....	117,504+70%	215,400

Married Filing Separate Returns

Use this schedule if you checked **Filing Status Box 3** on Form 1040—

If the amount on Form 1040, line 34 is: Over—	But not over—	Enter on line 2 of the worksheet on this page:	of the amount over—
$0	$1,700	—0—	
1,700	2,750	.... 14%	$1,700
2,750	3,800	$147.00+16%	2,750
3,800	5,950	315.00+18%	3,800
5,950	8,000	702.00+21%	5,950
8,000	10,100	1,132.50+24%	8,000
10,100	12,300	1,636.50+28%	10,100
12,300	14,950	2,252.50+32%	12,300
14,950	17,600	3,100.50+37%	14,950
17,600	22,900	4,081.00+43%	17,600
22,900	30,000	6,360.00+49%	22,900
30,000	42,800	9,839.00+54%	30,000
42,800	54,700	16,751.00+59%	42,800
54,700	81,200	23,772.00+64%	54,700
81,200	107,700	40,732.00+68%	81,200
107,700	....	58,752.00+70%	107,700

Caution

You must use the Tax Table instead of these Tax Rate Schedules if your taxable income is less than $50,000 unless you use Form 4726 (maximum tax), Schedule D (alternative tax), or Schedule G (income averaging), to figure your tax. In those cases, even if your taxable income is less than $50,000, use the rate schedules on this page to figure your tax.

Instructions

If you cannot use the Tax Table, figure your tax on the amount on line 34 of Form 1040 by using the appropriate Tax Rate Schedule. Then, unless you use Schedule G or Form 4726, figure your 1981 Rate Reduction Credit (1.25%) on the worksheet below.

Tax Computation Worksheet

(Do not use if you figure your tax on Schedule G or Form 4726.)

1. Taxable income from Form 1040, line 34 . _____
2. Tax on the amount on line 1 from Tax Rate Schedule X, Y, or Z . _____
3. Rate Reduction Credit. Multiply the amount on line 2 by .0125 . . . . . _____
4. Subtract line 3 from line 2. Enter here and on Form 1040, line 35 . . . . _____

Do not file—keep for your records.

Note: *If you use the alternative tax computation on Schedule D (Form 1040), enter the amount from Schedule D, line 32, on line 1 of the worksheet. Complete the worksheet and enter the amount from line 4 of the worksheet on Schedule D, line 33.*

Other Federal Forms and Schedules

1981 Earned Income Credit Table

This is the Earned Income Credit Table in the Form 1040 Instructions. To use the same Table for the Form 1040A Earned Income Credit Worksheet, replace "If line 3 or 4 of the worksheet is—" with "line 1 or 2," and replace "Enter that amount on 5 or 6…" with "line 3 or 4."

1981 Earned Income Credit Table Caution: This is Not a Tax Table

To find your earned income credit: Read down the column titled "If line 3 or 4 of the worksheet is—" and find the appropriate amount from the Earned Income Credit Worksheet on page 15. Read across to the right and find the amount of the earned income credit. Enter that amount on line 5 or 6 of the worksheet, whichever applies.

If line 3 or 4 of the worksheet is—		Your earned income credit is—	If line 3 or 4 of the worksheet is—		Your earned income credit is—	If line 3 or 4 of the worksheet is—		Your earned income credit is—	If line 3 or 4 of the worksheet is—		Your earned income credit is—	If line 3 or 4 of the worksheet is—		Your earned income credit is—
Over	But not over		Over	But not over		Over	But not over		Over	But not over		Over	But not over	
$0	$50	$3	$1,800	$1,850	$183	$3,600	$3,650	$363	$6,350	$6,400	$453	$8,150	$8,200	$228
50	100	8	1,850	1,900	188	3,650	3,700	368	6,400	6,450	447	8,200	8,250	222
100	150	13	1,900	1,950	193	3,700	3,750	373	6,450	6,500	441	8,250	8,300	216
150	200	18	1,950	2,000	198	3,750	3,800	378	6,500	6,550	434	8,300	8,350	209
200	250	23	2,000	2,050	203	3,800	3,850	383	6,550	6,600	428	8,350	8,400	203
250	300	28	2,050	2,100	208	3,850	3,900	388	6,600	6,650	422	8,400	8,450	197
300	350	33	2,100	2,150	213	3,900	3,950	393	6,650	6,700	416	8,450	8,500	191
350	400	38	2,150	2,200	218	3,950	4,000	398	6,700	6,750	409	8,500	8,550	184
400	450	43	2,200	2,250	223	4,000	4,050	403	6,750	6,800	403	8,550	8,600	178
450	500	48	2,250	2,300	228	4,050	4,100	408	6,800	6,850	397	8,600	8,650	172
500	550	53	2,300	2,350	233	4,100	4,150	413	6,850	6,900	391	8,650	8,700	166
550	600	58	2,350	2,400	238	4,150	4,200	418	6,900	6,950	384	8,700	8,750	159
600	650	63	2,400	2,450	243	4,200	4,250	423	6,950	7,000	378	8,750	8,800	153
650	700	68	2,450	2,500	248	4,250	4,300	428	7,000	7,050	372	8,800	8,850	147
700	750	73	2,500	2,550	253	4,300	4,350	433	7,050	7,100	366	8,850	8,900	141
750	800	78	2,550	2,600	258	4,350	4,400	438	7,100	7,150	359	8,900	8,950	134
800	850	83	2,600	2,650	263	4,400	4,450	443	7,150	7,200	353	8,950	9,000	128
850	900	88	2,650	2,700	268	4,450	4,500	448	7,200	7,250	347	9,000	9,050	122
900	950	93	2,700	2,750	273	4,500	4,550	453	7,250	7,300	341	9,050	9,100	116
950	1,000	98	2,750	2,800	278	4,550	4,600	458	7,300	7,350	334	9,100	9,150	109
1,000	1,050	103	2,800	2,850	283	4,600	4,650	463	7,350	7,400	328	9,150	9,200	103
1,050	1,100	108	2,850	2,900	288	4,650	4,700	468	7,400	7,450	322	9,200	9,250	97
1,100	1,150	113	2,900	2,950	293	4,700	4,750	473	7,450	7,500	316	9,250	9,300	91
1,150	1,200	118	2,950	3,000	298	4,750	4,800	478	7,500	7,550	309	9,300	9,350	84
1,200	1,250	123	3,000	3,050	303	4,800	4,850	483	7,550	7,600	303	9,350	9,400	78
1,250	1,300	128	3,050	3,100	308	4,850	4,900	488	7,600	7,650	297	9,400	9,450	72
1,300	1,350	133	3,100	3,150	313	4,900	4,950	493	7,650	7,700	291	9,450	9,500	66
1,350	1,400	138	3,150	3,200	318	4,950	5,000	498	7,700	7,750	284	9,500	9,550	59
1,400	1,450	143	3,200	3,250	323	5,000	6,000	500	7,750	7,800	278	9,550	9,600	53
1,450	1,500	148	3,250	3,300	328	6,000	6,050	497	7,800	7,850	272	9,600	9,650	47
1,500	1,550	153	3,300	3,350	333	6,050	6,100	491	7,850	7,900	266	9,650	9,700	41
1,550	1,600	158	3,350	3,400	338	6,100	6,150	484	7,900	7,950	259	9,700	9,750	34
1,600	1,650	163	3,400	3,450	343	6,150	6,200	478	7,950	8,000	253	9,750	9,800	28
1,650	1,700	168	3,450	3,500	348	6,200	6,250	472	8,000	8,050	247	9,800	9,850	22
1,700	1,750	173	3,500	3,550	353	6,250	6,300	466	8,050	8,100	241	9,850	9,900	16
1,750	1,800	178	3,550	3,600	358	6,300	6,350	459	8,100	8,150	234	9,900	9,950	9
												9,950	9,999	3

Schedules A&B (Form 1040)
Department of the Treasury
Internal Revenue Service

Schedule A—Itemized Deductions
(Schedule B is on back)

▶ Attach to Form 1040. ▶ See Instructions for Schedules A and B (Form 1040).

OMB No. 1545-0074

1981
07

Name(s) as shown on Form 1040 | Your social security number

Medical and Dental Expenses (Do not include expenses reimbursed or paid by others.) (See page 17 of Instructions.)

1 One-half (but not more than $150) of insurance premiums you paid for medical care. (Be sure to include in line 10 below.) . ▶
2 Medicine and drugs .
3 Enter 1% of Form 1040, line 31 . .
4 Subtract line 3 from line 2. If line 3 is more than line 2, enter zero . . . . .
5 Balance of insurance premiums for medical care not entered on line 1 . . . .
6 Other medical and dental expenses:
  a Doctors, dentists, nurses, etc. . . . .
  b Hospitals . . . .
  c Transportation . . . .
  d Other (itemize—include hearing aids, dentures, eyeglasses, etc.) ▶

7 Total (add lines 4 through 6d) . . . .
8 Enter 3% of Form 1040, line 31 . . .
9 Subtract line 8 from line 7. If line 8 is more than line 7, enter zero . . . . .
10 Total medical and dental expenses (add lines 1 and 9). Enter here and on line 33 . ▶

Taxes (See page 18 of Instructions.)

11 State and local income . . . . .
12 Real estate . . . .
13 a General sales (see sales tax tables) .
   b General sales on motor vehicles . .
14 Personal property . . . .
15 Other (itemize) ▶

16 Total taxes (add lines 11 through 15). Enter here and on line 34 . . . . ▶

Interest Expense (See page 18 of Instructions.)

17 Home mortgage . . . .
18 Credit and charge cards . . . . . .
19 Other (itemize) ▶

20 Total interest expense (add lines 17 through 19). Enter here and on line 35 ▶

Contributions (See page 19 of Instructions.)

21 a Cash contributions (If you gave $3,000 or more to any one organization, report those contributions on line 21b) .
   b Cash contributions totaling $3,000 or more to any one organization (show to whom you gave and how much you gave) ▶

22 Other than cash (see page 19 of Instructions for required statement) . . . .
23 Carryover from prior years . . . . .
24 Total contributions (add lines 21a through 23). Enter here and on line 36 ▶

Casualty or Theft Loss(es) (You must attach Form 4684 if line 29 is $1,000 or more, OR if certain other situations apply.) (See page 19 of Instructions.)

25 Loss before reimbursement . . . .
26 Insurance or other reimbursement you received or expect to receive . . .
27 Subtract line 26 from line 25. If line 26 is more than line 25, enter zero . .
28 Enter $100 or amount from line 27, whichever is smaller . . . . . .
29 Total casualty or theft loss(es) (subtract line 28 from line 27). Enter here and on line 37 ▶

Miscellaneous Deductions (See page 19 of Instructions.)

30 a Union dues . . . .
   b Tax return preparation fee . . . .
31 Other (itemize) ▶

32 Total miscellaneous deductions (add lines 30a through 31). Enter here and on line 38 . . . . ▶

Summary of Itemized Deductions (See page 20 of Instructions.)   **A**

33 Total medical and dental—from line 10 .
34 Total taxes—from line 16 . . . . .
35 Total interest—from line 20 . . . .
36 Total contributions—from line 24 . . .
37 Total casualty or theft loss(es)—from line 29 .
38 Total miscellaneous—from line 32 . . .
39 Add lines 33 through 38 . . . . .
40 If you checked Form 1040, Filing Status box:
   2 or 5, enter $3,400 . . . . .
   1 or 4, enter $2,300 . . . . .
   3, enter $1,700 . . . . .
41 Subtract line 40 from line 39. Enter here and on Form 1040, line 32b. (If line 40 is more than line 39, see the Instructions for line 41 on page 20.) . . . . . ▶

For Paperwork Reduction Act Notice, see Form 1040 Instructions.

343-059-1

SCHEDULE G
(Form 1040)
Department of the Treasury
Internal Revenue Service

Income Averaging

▶ See instructions on back.
▶ Attach to Form 1040.

OMB No. 1545-0074

1981
20

Name(s) as shown on Form 1040

Your social security number

Base Period Income and Adjustments	(a) 1980		(b) 1979		(c) 1978		(d) 1977	
1 Enter amount from: Form 1040—line 34 Form 1040A (1977 and 1978)—line 10 Form 1040A (1979 and 1980)—line 11 . .								
2 a Multiply $750 by your total number of exemptions each year, 1977 and 1978 .								
b Multiply $1,000 by your total number of exemptions each year, 1979 and 1980 .								
3 Taxable income (subtract line 2a or 2b from line 1). If less than zero, enter zero . . .								
4 Income earned outside of the United States or within U.S. possessions and excluded under sections 911 and 931								
5 Base period income (add lines 3 and 4) . .								

Computation of Averageable Income

6 Taxable income for 1981 from Form 1040, line 34	6	
7 Certain amounts received by owner-employees subject to a penalty under section 72(m)(5)	7	
8 Subtract line 7 from line 6	8	
9 Excess community income	9	
10 Adjusted taxable income (subtract line 9 from line 8). If less than zero, enter zero	10	
11 Add columns (a) through (d), line 5, and enter here	11		11	
12 Enter 30% of line 11	12	
13 Averageable income (subtract line 12 from line 10)	13	

If line 13 is $3,000 or less, do not complete the rest of this form. You do not qualify for income averaging.

G

Computation of Tax

14 Amount from line 12	14	
15 20% of line 13	15	
16 Total (add lines 14 and 15)	16	
17 Excess community income from line 9	17	
18 Total (add lines 16 and 17)	18	
19 Tax on amount on line 18 (see caution below)	19	
20 Tax on amount on line 16 (see caution below)	20	
21 Tax on amount on line 14 (see caution below)	21	
22 Subtract line 21 from line 20	22	
23 Multiply the amount on line 22 by 4	23	

Note: If no entry was made on line 7 above, skip lines 24 through 26 and go to line 27.

24 Tax on amount on line 6 (see caution below)	24	
25 Tax on amount on line 8 (see caution below)	25	
26 Subtract line 25 from line 24	26	
27 Add lines 19, 23, and 26	27	
28 Multiply line 27 by .0125	28	
29 Tax (subtract line 28 from line 27). Enter here and on Form 1040, line 35 and check Schedule G box . .	29	

Caution: Use Tax Rate Schedule X, Y, or Z from the Form 1040 instructions, but do not use the Tax Computation Worksheet on that page. Do not use the Tax Table.

For Paperwork Reduction Act Notice, see Form 1040 instructions.

343-064-2

Instructions

If your income this year is much greater than the average of your income for the past 4 base period years, you may be able to reduce your tax by income averaging. To see if you qualify, complete lines 1–13 of this schedule. If line 13 is more than $3,000, complete the rest of this schedule to see if you benefit from income averaging.

If you are eligible, and line 29 of this schedule is less than your tax using other methods, you may choose the income averaging method. You must attach this schedule to your Form 1040 to choose the benefits of income averaging. Generally you may make or change this choice anytime within 3 years from the date you filed your return.

A. Requirements.—To be eligible to file Schedule G with Form 1040, you must meet the following requirements:

(1) Citizenship or residence.—You must have been a U.S. citizen or resident for all of 1981. You are not eligible if you were a nonresident alien at any time during the 5 tax years ending with 1981.

(2) Support.—You must have furnished at least 50% of your own support for each of the years 1977 through 1980. In a year in which you were married, you and your spouse must have provided at least 50% of the support of both of you. For the definition of support, see Form 1040 Instructions, page 7.

Exceptions: Disregard the support requirement if any one of the three following situations applies to you:

(1) You were 25 or older before the end of 1981 and were not a full-time student during 4 or more of your tax years which began after you reached 21; or

(2) More than 50% of your 1981 taxable income (line 6) is from work you performed in substantial part during 2 or more of the 4 tax years before 1981; or

(3) You file a joint return for 1981 and your income for 1981 is not more than 25% of the total combined adjusted gross income (line 31, Form 1040).

For definition of full-time student, see Form 1040 Instructions, page 7.

B. Limitations.—In the same year you file Schedule G you may not:

(1) Exclude income from sources outside the United States or within U.S. possessions; or

(2) Use maximum tax to figure the tax on personal service income.

If you income average you may also use the alternative tax. See instructions for Schedule D (Form 1040).

C. Computation of Base Period Income (figure each year separately).—

(1) Use your separate income and deductions for all years if you were unmarried in 1977 through 1981.

(2) Use the combined income and deductions of you and your spouse for a base period year:

● If you are married in 1981, and

● If you file a joint return with your spouse or are a qualifying widow(er) in 1981, and

● If you were not married to any other spouse in that base period year.

(3) If (1) and (2) do not apply, your separate base period income is the largest of the following amounts:

(a) Your separate income and deductions for the base period year;

(b) Half of the base period income from adding your separate income and deductions to the separate income and deductions of your spouse for that base period year;

(c) Half of the base period income from adding your separate income and deductions to your 1981 spouse's separate income and deductions for that base period year.

Note: *If you were married to one spouse in a base period year and are married and file a joint return with a different spouse in 1981, your separate base period income is the larger of (3)(a) or (b) above. Combine the result with your 1981 spouse's separate base period income for that base period year.*

D. Computation of Separate Income and Deductions.—The amount of your separate income and deductions for a base period year is your gross income for that year minus your allowable deductions.

If you filed a joint return for a base period year, your separate deductions are:

(1) For deductions allowable in figuring your adjusted gross income, the sum of those deductions attributable to your gross income; and

(2) For deductions allowable in figuring taxable income (exemptions and itemized deductions), the amount from multiplying the deductions allowable on the joint return by a fraction whose numerator is your adjusted gross income and whose denominator is the combined adjusted gross income on the joint return. However, if 85% or more of the combined adjusted gross income of you and your spouse is attributable to one spouse, all deductions allowable in figuring taxable income are allowable to that spouse.

In figuring your separate taxable income when community property laws apply, you must take into account all of your earned income without regard to the community property laws, or your share of the community earned income under community property laws, whichever is more.

If you must figure your separate taxable income for any of the base period years,

attach a statement showing the computation and the names under which the returns were filed.

Line-by-Line Instructions

Line 1.—If you did not file a return, enter the amount that would otherwise be reportable on the appropriate lines specified in line 1.

Enter any corrected amount in columns (a), (b), (c), and (d) if the amount reported on your return for any of the years was changed by an amended return or by the Internal Revenue Service.

Line 4.—Enter on line 4 for each base period year the income (less any deductions) previously excluded from income because it was earned income from sources outside the United States or from income within U.S. possessions.

Line 6.—Since you can't exclude income under sections 911 or 931 through 934, include in line 6 the amount otherwise excludable.

Line 7.—If you are or were an owner-employee, and received income from a premature or excessive distribution from a Keogh (H.R. 10) plan or trust, enter that income on line 7.

Line 9.—You must make this adjustment if you are married, a resident of a community property State, and file a separate return for 1981. Enter the community earned income you reported minus that part of the income which is attributable to your services. Skip this line if the earned income attributable to your services is more than 50% of your combined community earned income.

Example:

	Attributable to Service of		
Community Earned Income .	John $40,000	Carol $20,000	Total $60,000

(a) John filing a separate return has no adjustment since the amount of earned income attributable to the services of John ($40,000) is more than 50% of the combined community earned income ($30,000).

(b) Carol filing a separate return must include $10,000 in the total for line 9. This is the excess of the community earned income reportable by Carol ($30,000) over the amount of community earned income attributable to Carol's services ($20,000).

Lines 19, 20, 21, 24, and 25.—Figure the tax using Tax Rate Schedule X, Y, or Z from the 1040 instructions, but do not use the Tax Computation Worksheet on that page to reduce your tax by the 1.25% rate reduction credit. Instead, compute the 1.25% rate reduction credit on line 28 after completing line 27.

For more information and a filled-in sample Schedule G, please get **Publication 506,** Income Averaging.

Form **3468**	**Computation of Investment Credit**	OMB. No. 1545-0155
Department of the Treasury Internal Revenue Service	▶ Attach to your tax return. ▶ Use separate Schedule B (Form 3468) to figure your tentative business energy investment credit.	**1981** 27

Name	Identifying number as shown on page 1 of your tax return

Part I — Elections (Check the box(es) below that apply to you (see Instruction D).)

A The corporation elects the basic or basic and matching employee plan percentage under section 48(n)(1) . . . . ☐

B I elect to increase my qualified investment to 100% for certain commuter highway vehicles under section 46(c)(6) . . . . . ☐

C I elect to increase my qualified investment by all qualified progress expenditures made this tax year and all later years . . . . . ☐

Enter total qualified progress expenditures included in column (4), Part II ▶ ....

D I claim full credit on certain ships under section 46(g)(3). (See **Instruction B** for details.) . . . . ☐

Part II — Qualified Investment

Figure your qualified investment in new or used investment credit property acquired or constructed and placed in service during the tax year. The qualified investment for qualified progress expenditures and qualified rehabilitation expenditures is allowed in the tax year the expenditure is incurred or in the case of self-constructed property the year the expenditure is chargable to a capital account for the property.

For certain taxpayers, the basis or cost of property placed in service after February 18, 1981, is limited to the amount the taxpayer is at risk for the property at year end. See Instruction E.

Note: Include your share of investment in property made by a partnership, estate, trust, small business corporation, or lessor.

1 Recovery Property	Line	(1) Recovery Period	(2) Unadjusted Basis	(3) Applicable percentage	(4) Qualified investment (Column 2 × column 3)
New	(a)	3-Year		60	
	(b)	Other		100	
Used	(c)	3-Year		60	
	(d)	Other		100	

2 Total—Add lines 1(a) through 1(d) **2**

3 Nonrecovery Property	Line	(1) Life years	(2) Basis or cost	(3) Applicable percentage	(4) Qualified investment (Column 2 × column 3)
New	(a)	3 or more but less than 5		33⅓	
	(b)	5 or more but less than 7		66⅔	
	(c)	7 or more		100	
Used	(d)	3 or more but less than 5		33⅓	
	(e)	5 or more but less than 7		66⅔	
	(f)	7 or more		100	

4 Total—Add lines 3(a) through 3(f) **4**

5 New commuter highway vehicle—Enter total qualified investment. (See **Instruction D**) . . . **5**

6 Used commuter highway vehicle—Enter total qualified investment. (See **Instruction D**) . . . **6**

7 Qualified rehabilitation expenditures incurred before January 1, 1982, for: (see specific instructions)

(a) Improvements with 5 or more but less than 7 years—Enter 66⅔% of expenditures . . . **7(a)**

(b) Improvements with 7 or more life years—Enter 100% of expenditures . . . . **7(b)**

8 Total qualified investment in 10% property—Add lines 2, 4, 5, 6, 7(a) and 7(b). (See instructions for special limits) . **8**

9 Enter 100% of qualified rehabilitation expenditures incurred after December 31, 1981, for: . .

(a) 30-year old buildings **9a**

(b) 40-year old buildings **9b**

(c) Certified historic structures (Enter the Dept. of Interior assigned project number ....) **9c**

10 Total qualified investment—Add lines 8, 9(a), 9(b), and 9(c). **10**

Part III — Tentative Regular Investment Credit

11 10% of line 8 . . . . **11**

12 15% of line 9(a) **12**

13 20% of line 9(b) **13**

14 25% of line 9(c) **14**

15 Corporations electing the basic or basic and matching employee plan percentage for contributions to tax credit employee stock ownership plans—Check box A above (see **Instruction D**)

(a) Basic 1% credit—Enter 1% of line 10 . . . . **15a**

(b) Matching credit (not more than 0.5%)—Enter allowable percentage times adjusted line 10 (attach schedule) . **15b**

16 Credit from Cooperative—Enter regular investment credit from cooperatives **16**

17 Current year regular investment credit—Add lines 11 through 16 . . . . **17**

18 Carryover of unused credits **18**

19 Carryback of unused credits **19**

20 Tentative regular investment credit—Add lines 17, 18, and 19, enter here and in Part IV, line 21 . **20**

For Paperwork Reduction Act Notice, see page 2.

Form **3468** (1981)

343–160–1

Form 3468 (1981)   Page **2**

Part IV   Tax Liability Limitations

21 Tentative credit from Part III, line 20	**21**	
22 (a) Individuals—Enter amount from Form 1040, line 37, page 2 . . . . }		
(b) Estates and trusts—Enter amount from Form 1041, line 26, page 1 . . . . } .	**22**	
(c) Corporations—Enter amount from Schedule J (Form 1120), line 3, page 3 . . . . . }		
(d) Others—Enter tax before credits from your return . . . . }		

23 (a) Credit for the elderly (individuals only)	**23(a)**	
(b) Foreign tax credit	**23(b)**	
(c) Tax on lump-sum distribution from Form 4972 or Form 5544 .	**23(c)**	
(d) Possessions corporation tax credit (corporations only) . . .	**23(d)**	
(e) Section 72(m)(5) penalty tax (individuals only)	**23(e)**	

24 Total—Add lines 23(a) through 23(e)	**24**	
25 Subtract line 24 from line 22	**25**	
26 (a) Enter smaller of line 25 or $25,000. See instruction for line 26	**26(a)**	
(b) If line 25 is more than line 26(a), and your tax year ends in 1981, enter 80% of the excess (if your tax year ends in 1982, enter 90% of the excess)	**26(b)**	
27 Regular investment credit limitation—Add lines 26(a) and 26(b)	**27**	
28 Allowed regular investment credit—Enter the smaller of line 21 or line 27	**28**	
29 Business energy investment credit limitation—Subtract line 28 from line 25	**29**	
30 Business energy investment credit—Enter amount from line 14 of Schedule B (Form 3468) .	**30**	
31 Allowed business energy investment credit—Enter smaller of line 29 or line 30	**31**	
32 Total allowed regular and business energy investment credit—Add lines 28 and 31. Enter here and on Form 1040, line 41; Schedule J (Form 1120), line 4(b), page 3; or the proper line on other returns	**32**	

343–160–1   ☆ U.S. GOVERNMENT PRINTING OFFICE : 1981—O—343-160

Form **4797**
Department of the Treasury
Internal Revenue Service

Supplemental Schedule of Gains and Losses
(Includes Gains and Losses From Sales or Exchanges of Assets
Used in a Trade or Business and Involuntary Conversions)
To be filed with Form 1040, 1041, 1065, 1120, etc.—See Separate Instructions

OMB No. 1545-0184

1981
31

Name(s) as shown on return | Identifying number

Part I   Sales or Exchanges of Property Used in a Trade or Business, and Involuntary Conversions From Other Than Casualty and Theft—Property Held More Than 1 Year (Except for Certain Livestock)

Note: Use Form 4684 to report involuntary conversions from casualty and theft.
Caution: If you sold property on which you claimed the investment credit, you may be liable for recapture of that credit. See Form 4255 for additional information.

a. Kind of property and description	b. Date acquired (mo., day, yr.)	c. Date sold (mo., day, yr.)	d. Gross sales price minus expense of sale	e. Depreciation allowed (or allowable) since acquisition	f. Cost or other basis, plus improvements	g. LOSS (f minus the sum of d and e)	h. GAIN (d plus e minus f)
1							

2 (a) Gain, if any, from Form 4684, Part II, line 25 . . . . . .

(b) Section 1231 gain from installment sales from Form 6252, line 19 or 27 . . . . .

3 Gain, if any, from line 26, Part III, on back of this form from other than casualty and theft . .

4 Add lines 1 through 3 in column g and column h . . . . ( )

5 Combine line 4, column g and line 4, column h. Enter gain or (loss) here, and on the appropriate line as follows:
  (a) For all except partnership returns:
    (1) If line 5 is a gain, enter the gain as a long-term capital gain on Schedule D (Form 1040, 1120, etc.) that is being filed. See instruction E.
    (2) If line 5 is zero or a loss, enter that amount on line 6.
  (b) For partnership returns: Enter the amount shown on line 5 above, on Schedule K (Form 1065), line 8.

Part II   Ordinary Gains and Losses

a. Kind of property and description	b. Date acquired (mo., day, yr.)	c. Date sold (mo., day, yr.)	d. Gross sales price minus expense of sale	e. Depreciation allowed (or allowable) since acquisition	f. Cost or other basis, plus improvements	g. LOSS (f minus the sum of d and e)	h. GAIN (d plus e minus f)
6 Loss, if any, from line 5(a)(2)							
7 Gain, if any, from line 25, Part III on back of this form							
8 (a) Net gain or (loss) from Form 4684, lines 17 and 24a							
(b) Ordinary gain from installment sales from Form 6252, line 18 or 26							
9 Other ordinary gains and losses (include property held 1 year or less):							

10 Add lines 6 through 9 in column g and column h . . . . ( )

11 Combine line 10, column g and line 10, column h. Enter gain or (loss) here, and on the appropriate line as follows:
  (a) For all except individual returns: Enter the gain or (loss) shown on line 11, on the line provided on the return (Form 1120, etc.) being filed. See instruction F for specific line reference.
  (b) For individual returns:
    (1) If the loss on line 6 includes a loss from Form 4684, Part II, column B(ii), enter that part of the loss here and on line 29 of Schedule A (Form 1040). Identify as from "Form 4797, line 11(b)(1)" . . . . . .
    (2) Redetermine the gain or (loss) on line 11, excluding the loss (if any) entered on line 11(b)(1). Enter here and on Form 1040, line 14 . . . .

Part III   Gain From Disposition of Property Under Sections 1245, 1250, 1251, 1252, 1254, 1255

Skip lines 20 and 21 if there are no dispositions of farm property or farmland, or if this form is filed by a partnership.

12 Description of sections 1245, 1250, 1251, 1252, 1254, and 1255 property:	Date acquired (mo., day, yr.)	Date sold (mo., day, yr.)
(A)		
(B)		
(C)		
(D)		

Part III is continued on page 2.

For Paperwork Reduction Act Notice, see page 1 of separate instructions.

343-177-1

Form **4797** (1981)

Form 4797 (1981)   Page **2**

Relate lines 12(A) through 12(D) to these columns ▶ ▶ ▶	Property (A)	Property (B)	Property (C)	Property (D)
13 Gross sales price minus expense of sale				
14 Cost or other basis				
15 Depreciation (or depletion) allowed (or allowable) . . .				
16 Adjusted basis, subtract line 15 from line 14				
17 Total gain, subtract line 16 from line 13				
18 If section 1245 property:				
(a) Depreciation allowed (or allowable) after applicable date (see instructions)				
(b) Enter smaller of line 17 or 18(a)				
19 If section 1250 property: (If straight line depreciation used, enter zero on line 19(i).)				
(a) Additional depreciation after 12/31/75 (see instructions)				
(b) Applicable percentage times the smaller of line 17 or line 19(a) (see instruction G.4)				
(c) Subtract line 19(a) from line 17. If line 17 is not more than line 19(a), skip lines 19(d) through 19(h) . . .				
(d) Additional depreciation after 12/31/69 and before 1/1/76				
(e) Applicable percentage times the smaller of line 19(c) or 19(d) (see instruction G.4)				
(f) Subtract line 19(d) from line 19(c). If line 19(c) is not more than line 19(d), skip lines 19(g) and 19(h) . .				
(g) Additional depreciation after 12/31/63 and before 1/1/70				
(h) Applicable percentage times the smaller of line 19(f) or 19(g) (see instruction G.4)				
(i) Add lines 19(b), 19(e), and 19(h)				
20 If section 1251 property:				
(a) If farmland, enter soil, water, and land clearing expenses for current year and the four preceding years .				
(b) If farm property other than land, subtract line 18(b) from line 17; if farmland, enter smaller of line 17 or 20(a)				
(c) Excess deductions account (see instruction G.5) . .				
(d) Enter smaller of line 20(b) or 20(c)				
21 If section 1252 property:				
(a) Soil, water, and land clearing expenses made after 12/31/69				
(b) Amount from line 20(d), if none enter zero . . .				
(c) Subtract line 21(b) from line 21(a). If line 21(b) is more than line 21(a), enter zero				
(d) Line 21(c) times applicable percentage (see instruction G.5)				
(e) Subtract line 21(b) from line 17				
(f) Enter smaller of line 21(d) or 21(e)				
22 If section 1254 property:				
(a) Intangible drilling and development costs deducted after 12/31/75 (see instruction G.6)				
(b) Enter smaller of line 17 or 22(a)				
23 If section 1255 property:				
(a) Applicable percentage of payments excluded from income under section 126 (see instruction G.7) . . .				
(b) Enter the smaller of line 17 or 23(a)				

Summary of Part III Gains (Complete Property columns (A) through (D) through line 23(b) before going to line 24)

24 Total gains for all properties (add columns (A) through (D), line 17) . . . . _____

25 Add columns (A) through (D), lines 18(b), 19(i), 20(d), 21(f), 22(b) and 23(b). Enter here and on Part II, line 7 . _____

26 Subtract line 25 from line 24. Enter the portion from casualty and theft on Form 4684, line 19; enter the portion from other than casualty and theft on Form 4797, Part I, line 3 . . . .

Part IV   Complete this Part Only if You are Electing Out of the Installment Method And are Reporting a Note or Other Obligation at Less Than Full Face Value

☐ Check here if you elect out of the installment method.

Enter the face amount of the note or other obligation ▶ _____

Enter the percentage of valuation of the note or other obligation ▶

Form **3903**	**Moving Expense Adjustment**	OMB No. 1545-0062
Department of the Treasury Internal Revenue Service	▶ **Attach to Form 1040.**	**1981**

Name(s) as shown on Form 1040 | Your social security number

(a) What is the distance from your **former** residence to your **new** job location? .... miles

(b) What is the distance from your **former** residence to your **former** job location? .... miles

(c) If the distance in (a) is 35 or more miles farther than the distance in (b), complete the rest of this form. If the distance is less than 35 miles, you cannot take a deduction for moving expenses. This rule does not apply to members of the armed forces.

1 Transportation expenses in moving household goods and personal effects **1**

2 Travel, meals, and lodging expenses in moving from former to new residence **2**

3 Pre-move travel, meals, and lodging expenses in searching for a new residence after getting your job **3**

4 Temporary living expenses in new location or area during any 30 consecutive days after getting your job . . . **4**

5 Total. Add lines 3 and 4 . . . . **5**

6 Enter the smaller of line 5 or $1,500 ($750 if married filing a separate return and you lived with your spouse who also started work during the tax year) . . **6**

7 Expenses for: (Check only one box)
  (a) ☐ sale or exchange of your former residence; or,
  (b) ☐ if renting, settlement of unexpired lease on your former residence . . **7**

8 Expenses for: (Check only one box)
  (a) ☐ buying a new residence; or,
  (b) ☐ if renting, getting a lease on a new residence **8**

9 Total. Add lines 6, 7, and 8 . . . . **9**

Note: Amounts on lines 7(a) and 8(a) not deducted because of the $3,000 (or $1,500) limit on moving expenses may generally be used either to decrease the gain on the sale of your residence, or to increase the basis of your new residence. See "Double Benefits" in Instructions.

10 Enter the smaller of line 9 or $3,000 ($1,500 if married, filing a separate return, and you lived with your spouse who also started work during the tax year) **10**

11 Total moving expenses. Add lines 1, 2, and 10 . . . . **11**

12 Reimbursements and allowances received for this move. Do not report amounts included on your Form W-2 . . . . **12**

13 If line 12 is less than line 11, enter the difference here and on Form 1040, line 22 . . . . . . **13**

14 If line 12 is larger than line 11, enter the difference here and on Form 1040, line 20, as "Excess moving reimbursement" **14**

General Instructions

Paperwork Reduction Act Notice.—The Paperwork Reduction Act of 1980 says we must tell you why we are collecting this information, how we will use it, and whether you have to give it to us. We ask for the information to carry out the Internal Revenue laws of the United States. We need it to ensure that you are complying with these laws and to allow us to figure and collect the right amount of tax. You are required to give us this information.

A. Who May Deduct Moving Expenses.— If you moved your residence because of a change in the location of your job, you may be able to deduct your moving expenses. You may qualify for a deduction whether you are self-employed or an employee. But you must meet certain tests of distance and time, explained below. If you need more information, please get **Publication 521**, Moving Expenses.

Note: If you are a U.S. citizen or resident who moved to a new principal work place **outside** the United States or its possessions, get Form 3903F, Foreign Moving Expense Adjustment.

(1) *Distance Test.*—Your new job location must be at least 35 miles farther from your former residence than your old job location was. For example, if your former job was 3 miles from your former residence, your new job must be at least 38 miles from that residence. If you did not have an old job location, your new job must be at least 35 miles from your former residence. (The distance between the two points is the shortest of the commonly traveled routes between the points.)

(2) *Time Test.*—If you are an employee, you must work full time for at least 39 weeks during the 12 months right after you move. If you are self-employed, you

must work for at least 39 weeks during the first 12 months and a total of 78 weeks during the 24 months right after you move.

You may deduct your moving expenses for 1981 even if you have not met the "time" test before your 1981 return is due. You may do this if you expect to meet the 39-week test by the end of 1982 or the 78-week test by the end of 1983. If you have not met the test by then, you will have to do one of the following:

● Amend your 1981 tax return on which you deducted moving expenses. To do this, use Form 1040X, Amended U.S. Individual Income Tax Return.

● Report as income on your tax return for the year you cannot meet the test the amount you deducted on your 1981 return.

(Continued on back)

343-162-1   Form **3903** (1981)

If you do not deduct your moving expenses on your 1981 return, and you later meet the time test, you may file an amended return for 1981, taking the deduction. To do this, use Form 1040X.

B. Exceptions to the Distance and Time Tests.—You do not have to meet the time test if your job ends because of death, disability, transfer for the employer's benefit, or layoff or other discharge besides willful misconduct.

If you are in the armed forces, you do not have to meet the distance and time tests if the move is due to a permanent change of station. A permanent change of station includes a move in connection with and within 1 year of retirement or other termination of active duty. In figuring your moving expenses, do not deduct any moving expenses for moving services that were furnished by the military or that were reimbursed to you and that you did not include in income. However, you may deduct any unreimbursed moving expenses you have subject to the dollar limits. Also, treat each move for yourself or your spouse or your dependents to or from separate locations as a single move.

C. Moving Expenses in General.—You can deduct most but not all of your moving expenses.
Examples of expenses you CAN deduct are:
- Travel, meal, and lodging expenses during the move to the new residence.
- Temporary living expenses in the new location.
- Pre-move travel expenses.

Examples of expenses you CANNOT deduct are:
- Loss on the sale of your house.
- Mortgage penalties.
- Cost of refitting carpets and draperies.
- Losses on quitting club memberships.

The line-by-line instructions below explain how to figure the expenses you can deduct. The items listed must be the reasonable amounts you spent for the move. The expenses apply only to your family and dependent household members. They do not apply to employees such as a servant, governess, or nurse.

Line-by-Line Instructions

To see whether you meet the "distance" test, fill in the number of miles for questions (a) and (b) at the top of the form. If you meet the test in (c), continue with the items that follow.

Line 1, Household Goods and Personal Effects.—In figuring this amount, include the actual cost of packing, crating, moving, storing in transit, and insuring your household goods and personal effects.

Line 2, Travel Expenses.—Figure in this amount the costs of travel from your old residence to your new residence. These include transportation, meals, and lodging on the way, including costs for the day you arrive. You may take this travel deduction for only one trip. However, all the members of your household do not have to travel together and at the same time. If you use your own car, you may figure the expenses in either of two ways:
(a) Actual out-of-pocket expenses for gasoline, oil, and repairs. (Keep records to verify the amounts.)
(b) At the rate of 9 cents a mile. (Attach a sheet of paper showing your figures to verify mileage.)

Line 3, Pre-move Expenses.—Include in this amount the costs of travel before you move in order to look for a new residence. You may deduct the costs only if the following apply:
(a) If you began the house-hunting trip after you got the job;
(b) And if you returned to your old residence after looking for a new one;

(c) And if you traveled to the general location of the new work place primarily to look for a new residence.

Your deduction for pre-move travel is not limited to any number of trips by you or your household members. Your house-hunting does not have to be successful to qualify for this deduction. If you used your own car, figure transportation costs the same way as in the instructions for line 2. If you are self-employed, you can deduct these house-hunting costs only if you had already made substantial arrangements to begin work in the new location.

Line 4, Temporary Living Expenses.—Include in this amount the costs of meals and lodging while occupying temporary quarters in the area of your new place of work. You may include these costs for any period of 30 consecutive days after you get the job. If you are self-employed, you can count these temporary living expenses only if you had already made substantial arrangements to begin work in the new location.

Line 5, Total.—Add the amounts in lines 3 and 4.

Line 6.—Enter either the amount on line 5 or $1,500, whichever is smaller. (If you are married filing a separate return and you lived with your spouse who also started work during the tax year, enter either the amount on line 5 or $750, whichever is smaller.)

Lines 7 and 8, Expenses for the Sale, Purchase, or Lease of a Residence.—You may include in these amounts some costs when you sell or buy a residence and when you settle or get a lease. Examples are:
- Sales commissions.
- Advertising costs.
- Attorney's fees.
- Title and escrow fees.
- State transfer taxes.
- Costs to settle an unexpired lease or buy a new lease.

Examples of expenses you **CANNOT** include are:
- Costs to improve the residence to help it sell.
- Charges for payment or prepayment of interest.
- Payments or prepayments of rent.

Check the appropriate box (a) or (b) for line 7 and for line 8 when you enter the amounts for these two lines.

Line 9, Total.—Add lines 6, 7, and 8.

Line 10.—Enter either the amount on line 9 or $3,000, whichever is smaller. (If you are married filing a separate return and you lived with your spouse who also started working during the tax year, enter either the amount on line 9 or $1,500, whichever is smaller.)

Line 11, Total Moving Expenses.—Add lines 1, 2, and 10.

Line 12, Reimbursements and Allowances.—Include all reimbursements and allowances for moving expenses in income. In general, Form W–2 includes such reimbursements and allowances. However, check with your employer if you are in doubt. Your employer is required to give you a statement showing a detailed breakdown of reimbursements or payments of moving expenses. Form 4782, Employee Moving Expense Information, may be used for this purpose. Use line 12 for reporting reimbursements and allowances if they are not included elsewhere on Form 1040 or related schedules.

Line 13.—If line 12 is *less than* line 11, subtract line 12 from line 11. Enter the result here and on Form 1040, line 22.

Line 14.—If line 12 is *more than* line 11, subtract line 11 from line 12. Enter the result here and on Form 1040, line 20. Next to the amount, write "Excess moving reimbursement."

Double Benefits.—You cannot take double benefits. For example, you cannot use the moving expense on line 7 that became part of your moving expense deduction to lower the amount of gain on the sale of your old residence. You also cannot use the moving expense on line 8 that became part of your moving expense deduction to add to the cost of your new residence. (See Form 2119, Sale or Exchange of Principal Residence, to figure the gain to report on the old residence and the adjusted cost of the new one.)

Dollar Limitations.—Lines 1 and 2 (costs of moving household goods and costs of travel to your new residence) are not limited to any amount. All the other costs (lines 3, 4, 7, and 8) together cannot be more than $3,000. In addition, line 3 (house-hunting trip costs) and line 4 (temporary living costs) together cannot be more than $1,500. These are overall per-move limits.
There are some special cases:
(a) Both you and your spouse began work at new work places and shared the same new residence: You must consider this as one move rather than two if you shared the same new residence at the end of 1981. If you file separate returns, costs for lines 3, 4, 7, and 8 are limited to $1,500 per move for each of you. Costs of house-hunting and temporary living expenses (lines 3 and 4) are limited to $750 for each of you.
(b) Both you and your spouse began work at new work places but you moved to separate new residences: Report moving expenses separately. If you file separate returns, each of you is limited to $3,000 for lines 3, 4, 7, and 8; and to $1,500 for lines 3 and 4. If you file a joint return, the limits are $6,000 for lines 3, 4, 7, and 8; and $3,000 for lines 3 and 4.

Qualified Retired People or Survivors Living Outside the United States.—There are special rules for moving expenses to a U.S. residence for qualified retired people or survivors. If you meet the requirements below, treat your moving expenses as if you incurred them because of a move to a new principal work place located in the United States.

Use this form instead of Form 3903F, Foreign Moving Expense Adjustment. You do not have to meet the time test, discussed in instruction A, but you are subject to the dollar limitations and distance test that apply to moves within the United States (contained in this form).

Retired People.—You may be able to claim moving expenses if both your former principal work place and your former residence were outside the United States. This deduction is for moving expenses to a new U.S. residence in connection with your actual retirement.

Survivors.—If you are the spouse or dependent of a deceased person whose principal work place at the time of death was outside the United States, you may be able to claim some moving expenses. You must meet the following requirements:
- The moving expenses are for a move which begins within 6 months after the death of the decedent.
- The move is to a U.S. residence from a former residence outside the United States.
- At the time of death, the decedent and you shared your former residence.

Form **2106**

Department of the Treasury
Internal Revenue Service

Employee Business Expenses

(Please use Form 3903 to figure moving expense deduction.)
▶ Attach to Form 1040.

OMB No. 1545-0139

1981

Your name	Social security number	Occupation in which expenses were incurred
Employer's name	Employer's address	

Paperwork Reduction Act Notice.—The Paperwork Reduction Act of 1980 says we must tell you why we are collecting this information, how we will use it, and whether you have to give it to us. We ask for the information to carry out the Internal Revenue laws of the United States. We need it to ensure that you are complying with these laws and to allow us to figure and collect the right amount of tax. You are required to give us this information.

Instructions

Use this form to show your business expenses as an employee during 1981. Include amounts:
- You paid as an employee;
- You charged to your employer (such as by credit card);
- You received as an advance, allowance, or repayment.

Several publications available from IRS give more information about business expenses:

Publication 463, *Travel, Entertainment, and Gift Expenses.*

Publication 529, *Miscellaneous Deductions.*

Publication 587, *Business Use of Your Home.*

Publication 508, *Educational Expenses.*

Part I.—You can deduct some business expenses even if you do not itemize your deductions on Schedule A (Form 1040). Examples are expenses for travel (except commuting to and from work), meals, or lodging. List these expenses in Part I and use them in figuring your adjusted gross income on Form 1040, line 31.

Line 2.—You can deduct meals and lodging costs if you were on a business trip away from your main place of work. Do not deduct the cost of meals you ate on one-day trips when you did not need sleep or rest.

Line 3.—If you use a car you own in your work, you can deduct the cost of the business use. Enter the cost here after figuring it in Part IV. You can take either the cost of your actual expenses (such as gas, oil, repairs, depreciation, etc.) or you can use the standard mileage rate.

The mileage rate is 20 cents a mile up to 15,000 miles. After that, or for all business mileage on a fully depreciated car, the rate is 11 cents a mile. If you use the standard mileage rate to figure the cost of business use, the car is considered to have a useful life of 60,000 miles of business use at the maximum standard mileage rate. After 60,000 miles of business use at the maximum rate, the car is considered to be fully depreciated. (For details, see **Publication 463.**)

Caution: You cannot use the mileage rate for a leased vehicle.

Figure your mileage rate amount and add it to the business part of what you spent on the car for parking fees, tolls, interest, and State and local taxes (except gasoline tax).

Line 4.—If you were an outside salesperson with other business expenses, list them on line 4. Examples are selling expenses or expenses for stationery and stamps. An outside salesperson does all selling outside the employer's place of business. A driver-salesperson whose main duties are service and delivery, such as delivering bread or milk, is not an outside salesperson. (For details, see **Publication 463.**)

Line 5.—Show other business expenses on line 5 if your employer repaid you for them. If you were repaid for part of them, show here the amount you were repaid. Show the rest in Part II.

Part II.—You can deduct other business expenses only if (a) your employer did not repay you, and (b) you itemize your deductions on Schedule A (Form 1040). Report these expenses here and under Miscellaneous Deductions on Schedule A. (For details, see **Publication 529.**)

You can deduct expenses for business use of the part of your home that you exclusively and consistently use for your work. If you are not self-employed, your working at home must be for your employer's convenience. (For business use of home, see **Publication 587.**)

If you show education expenses in Part I or Part II, you must fill out Part III.

Part III.—You can deduct the cost of education that helps you keep or improve your skills for the job you have now. This includes education that your employer, the law, or regulations require you to get in order to keep your job or your salary. Do not deduct the cost of study that helps you meet the basic requirements for your job or helps you get a new job. (For education expenses, see **Publication 508.**)

Part IV, line 8—Depreciation

Cars placed in service **before 1/1/81:**

You must continue to use either the standard mileage rate or the method of depreciation you used in earlier years. You cannot change to either of the new methods available in 1981.

Cars placed in service **after 12/31/80:**

If you placed a car in service in 1981 and you do not use the standard mileage rate, you must use the new Accelerated Cost Recovery System (ACRS). One method lets you deduct the following percentages of your cost basis regardless of what month you placed the car in service:

1981—25%
1982—38%
1983—37%

Example: You bought a new car, without a trade-in, for $10,000 in September 1981, and used it 60% for business. Your basis for depreciation is $6,000 ($10,000 × 60%). For 1981 your depreciation deduction is $1,500 ($6,000 × 25%). If your percentage of business use changes in 1982, you must refigure your basis for depreciation.

There is also an alternate ACRS method under which you may use a straight-line method over a recovery period of 3, 5, or 12 years.

Note: *If you use the mileage rate, you are considered to have made an election to exclude this vehicle from ACRS.*

You do not have to consider salvage value in either of these methods. Please see **Publication 463** for details on how to figure the deduction under either method.

PART I.—Employee Business Expenses Deductible in Figuring Adjusted Gross Income on Form 1040, Line 31

1 Fares for airplane, boat, bus, taxicab, train, etc. . . . .

2 Meals and lodging . . . .

3 Car expenses (from Part IV, line 21) . . . .

4 Outside salesperson's expenses (see Part I instructions above) ▶

5 Other (see Part I instructions above) ▶

6 Add lines 1 through 5 . . . .

7 Employer's payments for these expenses if not included on Form W-2 . . . .

8 Deductible business expenses (subtract line 7 from line 6). Enter here and include on Form 1040, line 23 .

9 Income from excess business expense payments (subtract line 6 from line 7). Enter here and include on Form 1040, line 20 . . . .

PART II.—Employee Business Expenses that are Deductible Only if You Itemize Deductions on Schedule A (Form 1040)

1 Business expenses not included above (list expense and amount) ▶

2 Total. Deduct under Miscellaneous Deductions, Schedule A (Form 1040) . . . .

Form **2106** (1981)

Form 2106 (1981)   Page **2**

PART III.—Information About Education Expenses Shown in Part I or Part II

1 Name of educational institution or activity ▶ _____

2 Address ▶ _____

3 Did you need this education to meet the basic requirements for your job? . . . . ☐ Yes ☐ No

4 Will this study program qualify you for a new job? . . . . ☐ Yes ☐ No

5 If your answer to question 3 or 4 is Yes, you cannot deduct these expenses. If No, explain (1) why you are getting the education, and (2) what the relationship was between the courses you took and your job. (If you need more space, attach a statement.) ▶ _____

_____

6 List your main subjects, or describe your educational activity ▶ _____

_____

PART IV.—Car Expenses (Use either your actual expenses or the mileage rate.)

	Car 1	Car 2	Car 3
A. Number of months you used car for business during 1981 . .	_____ months	_____ months	_____ months
B. Total mileage for months in line A	_____ miles	_____ miles	_____ miles
C. Business part of line B mileage	_____ miles	_____ miles	_____ miles

Actual Expenses (Include expenses on lines 1–5 for only the months shown in line A, above.)

	Car 1	Car 2	Car 3
1 Gasoline, oil, lubrication, etc.			
2 Repairs			
3 Tires, supplies, etc.			
4 Other: **(a)** Insurance			
(b) Taxes			
(c) Tags and licenses			
(d) Interest			
(e) Miscellaneous			
5 Total (add lines 1 through 4(e))			
6 Business percentage of car use (divide line C by line B, above)	%	%	%
7 Business part of car expense (multiply line 5 by line 6) . . .			
8 Depreciation (see instructions on front) . . . . **Caution:** If you use ACRS, skip line 9 and enter the amount from line 8 on line 10.			
9 Divide line 8 by 12 months			
10 Multiply line 9 by line A, above			
11 Total (add line 7 and line 10; then skip to line 19)			

Mileage Rate

12 Enter the smaller of (a) 15,000 miles or (b) the combined mileages from line C, above . . . . _____ miles

13 Multiply line 12 by 20¢ (11¢ if car is fully depreciated) and enter here . . . . _____

14 Enter any combined mileage from line C that is over 15,000 miles . . . . . _____ miles

15 Multiply line 14 by 11¢ and enter here . . . . _____

16 Total mileage expense (add lines 13 and 15) . . . . _____

17 Business part of car interest and State and local taxes (except gasoline tax) . . . . _____

18 Total (add lines 16 and 17) . . . . _____

Summary

19 Enter amount from line 11 or line 18, whichever you used . . . . _____

20 Parking fees and tolls . . . . _____

21 Total (add lines 19 and 20). Enter here and in Part I, line 3 . . . . _____

Form **2119**	**Sale or Exchange of Principal Residence**	OMB No. 1545–0072
Department of the Treasury Internal Revenue Service	▶ See instructions on back. ▶ Attach to Form 1040 for year of sale (see instruction C).	**1981** 24

Note: *Do not include expenses you are deducting as moving expenses.*

Name(s) as shown on Form 1040 | Your social security number

		Yes	No
1 (a)	Date former residence sold ▶		
(b)	Enter the face amount of any mortgage, note (for example second trust), or other financial instrument on which you will receive periodic payments of principal or interest from this sale ▶		
(c)	Have you ever postponed any gain on the sale or exchange of a principal residence?		
(d)	If you were on active duty in the U.S. Armed Forces or outside of the U.S. after the date of sale of former residence, enter dates. From ____ to ____		
2 (a)	Date you bought new residence. (If none bought, so state). ▶		
(b)	If you constructed new residence, date construction began ▶ date occupied ▶		
(c)	Did you use both the old and new properties as your principal residence?		
(d)	Are any rooms in either residence rented out or used for business for which a deduction is allowed? . . . . . (If "Yes" do not include gain on the rented or business portion in line 7; instead include in income on Form 4797.)		

Part I Computation of Gain and Adjusted Sales Price

3	Selling price of residence. (Do not include selling price of personal property items.)	**3**	
4	Commissions and other expenses of sale not deducted as moving expenses	**4**	
5	Amount realized (subtract line 4 from line 3)	**5**	
6	Basis of residence sold **6**		
7	Gain on sale (subtract line 6 from line 5). (If line 6 is more than line 5, enter zero and do not complete the rest of form.) If you bought another principal residence during the allowed replacement period or you elect the one time exclusion in Part III, continue with this form. Otherwise, enter the gain on Schedule D (Form 1040), line 2a or 9a. **7**		
	If you haven't replaced your residence, do you plan to do so within the replacement period? ☐ Yes ☐ No		
	(If "Yes" see instruction C.)		
8	Fixing-up expenses (see instructions for time limitations.)	**8**	
9	Adjusted sales price (subtract line 8 from line 5)	**9**	

Part II Computation of Gain to be Postponed and Adjusted Basis of New Residence

10	Cost of new residence	**10**	
11	Gain taxable this year (Subtract line 10 from line 9. Do not enter more than line 7.) If line 10 is more than line 9, enter zero. Enter any taxable gain on Schedule D (Form 1040), line 2a or 9a. If you were 55 or over on the date of sale, see Part III	**11**	
12	Gain to be postponed (subtract line 11 from line 7)	**12**	
13	Adjusted basis of new residence (subtract line 12 from line 10)	**13**	

Part III Computation of Exclusion, Gain to be Reported, and Adjusted Basis of New Residence

		Yes	No
14 (a)	Were you 55 or over on date of sale?		
(b)	Was your spouse 55 or over on date of sale? . . . . (If you answered "No" to 14(a) and 14(b), do not complete the rest of form.)		
(c)	If you answered "Yes" to 14(a) or 14(b) did you own and use the property sold as your principal residence for a total of at least 3 years (except for short temporary absences) of the 5-year period before the sale? . . . (If you are 65 or over and 1(a) is before 7/26/81, see instruction D.)		
(d)	If you answered "Yes" to 14(c), do you elect to take the once in a lifetime exclusion of the gain on the sale? . . (If "Yes," check yes box and complete the rest of Part III. If "No," return to Part II, line 12 above.)		
(e)	At time of sale, was the residence owned by: ☐ you, ☐ your spouse, ☐ both of you?		
(f)	Social security number of spouse, at time of sale, if different from number on Form 1040 ▶ .... (Enter "none" if you were not married at time of sale.)		

15 (a)	If line 1(a) is before 7/21/81, enter the smaller of line 7 or $100,000 ($50,000, if married filing separate return) . .	**15(a)**	
(b)	If line 1(a) is after 7/20/81, enter the smaller of line 7 or $125,000 ($62,500, if married filing separate return) . . .	**15(b)**	
16	Part of gain included (subtract line 15a or 15b from line 7)	**16**	
17	Cost of new residence. If you did not buy a new principal residence, enter "None." Then enter the gain from line 16 on Schedule D (Form 1040), line 9a, and do not complete the rest of Form 2119	**17**	
18	Gain taxable this year. (Subtract the sum of lines 15 and 17 from line 9. The result cannot be more than line 16.) If line 17 plus line 15 is more than line 9, enter zero. Enter any taxable gain on Schedule D (Form 1040), line 9a	**18**	
19	Gain to be postponed (subtract line 18 from line 16)	**19**	
20	Adjusted basis of new residence (subtract line 19 from line 17)	**20**	

For Paperwork Reduction Act Notice, see back of form.   343-143-1   Form **2119** (1981)

Paperwork Reduction Act Notice.—We ask for the information to carry out the Internal Revenue laws of the United States. We need it to ensure that you are complying with these laws and to allow us to figure and collect the right amount of tax. You are required to give us this information.

General Instructions

A. Purpose of Form.—Use this form to report any gain on the sale of your principal residence whether or not you replace it with a new principal residence. A taxable gain must be reported on Schedule D (Form 1040). A loss is not deductible.

B. Postponement of Gain on Sale of Principal Residence.—Unless you elect to exclude it according to Instruction D, gain from the sale of your principal residence may have to be postponed if:

(1) within 18 months (2 years if line 1(a) is after 7/20/81) before or 2 years after the sale, you buy and occupy another principal residence; or

(2) before the sale or within 2 years after the sale, you begin construction of a new principal residence and occupy it within 18 months (2 years if line 1(a) is after 7/20/81) before and 2 years after the sale.

Use Parts I and II to figure the gain that must be postponed.

Note: If you are on active duty in the U.S. Armed Forces for more than 90 days or living and working outside the United States, after the date of sale of your old residence, that time is not counted in figuring your replacement period. However, this replacement period is never permitted to extend beyond 4 years after the date of sale.

Any gain postponed in the year you sell your old residence is subtracted from the cost of your new residence, giving you a lower cost basis in your new residence. If you sell the new residence in a later year and do not replace it, the postponed gain will be taxed in that year. However, see instruction D. If you do replace it, you may continue to postpone the gain.

Principal Residence.—Postponing gain applies only to the sale of your principal residence. Usually, the home in which you live is your principal residence. For example, this may be a house, houseboat, house trailer, cooperative apartment, or condominium.

If you have more than one residence, your principal residence is the one you physically occupy most of the time. If you change your principal residence more than once during the replacement period, only the last residence bought qualifies as your new residence for the purpose of postponing gain, unless you sold the residence because of a job relocation and are allowed a moving expense deduction.

C. When to File.—File this form for the year of sale whether or not you have already replaced your principal residence.

If you plan to replace your residence but have not done so by the time you file your return, and the replacement period has not expired, attach Form 2119 to Form 1040 for the year of sale, but complete lines 1(a), 2(a), and 3 through 7 only.

If you replace your residence after your return is filed but within the replacement period, and it costs you at least as much as the adjusted sales price of your old residence, you should notify in writing the Director of the Internal Revenue Service Center where you filed your return and attach another Form 2119 for the year of sale.

If your new residence costs less than the adjusted sales price of your old residence, or if you do not buy or start construction of your new residence within the replacement period, you must file Form 1040X with attached Schedule D and a new Form 2119 for the year of sale showing the amount of the gain you are required to report. Interest will be charged on the additional tax due on this gain.

If you paid tax on the gain from the sale of your old residence, and buy a new residence within the replacement period, file Form 1040X with attached Form 2119 if you are entitled to a refund.

D. Exclusion of Gain on Sale of Residence.—If you sold your principal residence, you may elect to exclude from your income part or all of the gain on the sale if:

(1) you were 55 or over on the date of the sale;

(2) you owned and occupied your residence for periods totaling at least 3 years within the 5 year period ending on the date of sale; and

(3) neither you nor your spouse has previously elected this exclusion after July 26, 1978.

Caution: However, you may choose not to make this election this year, since it is a once-in-a-lifetime election.

If you meet these requirements, you may elect to exclude up to the amounts specified on line 15 of Form 2119. Make the election in Part III of Form 2119. If you are 65 or over on the date of sale, you may substitute 5 of the last 8 years for 3 of the last 5 years if the sale took place before 7/26/81.

The amount of gain excluded from your income is never taxed. The balance of the gain, in excess of the amount excluded, is taxed in the year of sale, unless you buy a new residence during the replacement period.

Generally, you may make or revoke an election to exclude gain on the sale of your principal residence at any time within 3 years from the due date, including extensions, of the return for the year the residence was sold. Use Form 1040X to amend your return.

If you and your spouse jointly hold the property and you file a joint return, only one of you must meet the age, ownership, and use requirements.

If the property is not jointly owned, only the spouse who owns the property must meet the requirements regardless of filing status on Form 1040.

If you are married at the time of sale, both you and your spouse must make the election to exclude the gain. If you do not file a joint return with that spouse, he or she must indicate consent to the election by writing in the bottom margin of Form 2119 or on an attached statement, "I consent to Part III election," and signing.

The election does not apply separately to you and your spouse. If you and your spouse make an election during marriage and later divorce, no further elections are available to either of you or to your new spouse if you remarry.

E. Consent of You and Your Spouse to Apply Separate Gain on Sale of Old Residence to Basis of New Residence.—Sometimes one spouse may own the old residence separately, but both spouses may own the new residence jointly (or vice versa). In such cases, the gain from the sale of the old residence on which tax is postponed and the resulting adjustment to the basis of the new residence may be divided between them. You and your spouse may make such a division only if:

(1) both of you use the old and the new residences as your principal residence; and

(2) both of you indicate consent in the bottom margin of Form 2119 or on an attached statement by writing: "We consent to have the basis of the new residence reduced by the gain on sale of the old residence." Both of you must sign this consent.

If both of you do not consent, you must determine the recognition of gain from the sale of the old residence in the regular way with no division.

Line-By-Line Instructions

Line 3. Selling Price of Residence.—Enter the amount of money you received, the amount of all notes, mortgages, or other liabilities to which the property was subject, and the fair market value of any other property you received.

Note: *Report interest from a note as income when received.*

Line 4. Commissions and Other Expenses of Sale.—This includes sales commissions, advertising expenses, attorney and legal fees, etc., incurred in order to sell the old residence. Loan charges, such as "loan placement fees" or "points" charged the seller, generally are selling expenses. Do not include amounts deducted as moving expenses.

Line 6. Basis of Residence Sold.—This includes the original cost of the property, commissions, and other expenses incurred in its purchase, plus the cost of improvements. Subtract any depreciation allowed or allowable, any casualty loss taken on the residence, any energy credit taken, and the postponed gain on the sale or exchange of a previous principal residence. For more information, see **Publication 551,** Basis of Assets.

Line 8. Fixing-up Expenses.—These are decorating and repair expenses incurred only to assist the sale of the old property. They must have been incurred for work performed within 90 days before the contract to sell was signed, and must have been paid for not later than 30 days after the sale. Do not include capital expenditures for permanent improvements or replacements which are added to the basis of the property sold.

Note: *Fixing-up expenses are considered* **only** *in figuring adjusted sales price to determine the gain on which tax is postponed. They are* **not** *deductible in determining the actual profit on the sale of your old residence.*

Lines 10 and 17. Cost of New Residence.—The cost of your new residence includes one or more of the following:

(a) cash payments;

(b) the amount of any mortgage or other debt on the new residence;

(c) commissions and other purchase expenses you paid that were not deducted as moving expenses;

(d) construction costs (when you build your own residence) made during the replacement period;

(e) if you buy rather than build your new residence, all capital expenditures made within the replacement period.

For more information, please get **Publication 523,** Tax Information on Selling Your Home, from most IRS offices.

Form **4726**
Department of the Treasury
Internal Revenue Service

Maximum Tax on Personal Service Income

▶ See instructions on back.

▶ Attach to Form 1040 (or Form 1041).

OMB No. 1545–0180

1981

30

Name(s) as shown on Form 1040 (or Form 1041) | Identifying number

Do not complete this form if—(a) Taxable income or personal service taxable income is less than the amount reportable on line 10.

(b) You elected income averaging; or

(c) On Form 1040, you checked box 3.

Personal Service Income			Deductions Against Personal Service Income (Do not include expenses deductible on Schedule A (Form 1040))		
Wages, salaries, tips, etc.			Moving expenses		
Other compensation			Employee business expenses		
Other (see instructions and list):			Other (see instructions and list):		
1 Total personal service income			**2** Total deductions against personal service income		

3 Personal service net income—Subtract total of line 2 from total of line 1 . . . . | **3** |

4 Adjusted gross income from Form 1040, line 32a (estates and trusts—see instructions) . . . . | **4** |

5 Divide the amount on line 3 by the amount on line 4. Enter result as a percentage. If more than 100%, enter 100%. Round to nearest 4 numbers . . . . . | **5** |

6 Taxable income from Form 1040, line 34 or Form 1041, line 25 . . . . | **6** |

7 Multiply the amount on line 6 by the percentage on line 5 . . . . | **7** |

8 Enter the total of your 1981 tax preference items. (Do not include your capital gain deduction.) . . | **8** |

9 Personal service taxable income. Subtract line 8 from line 7 . . . . | **9** |

10 If: on Form 1040, you checked box 1, enter $41,500 . . . .
on Form 1040, you checked box 2 or box 5, enter $60,000 . . . . .
on Form 1040, you checked box 4, enter $44,700 . . . . . .
you are filing Form 1041, enter $28,300 . . . . . . | **10** |

11 Subtract line 10 from line 9. If line 10 is more than line 9, do not complete rest of form . . . . | **11** |

12 Enter 50% of line 11 . . . . | **12** |

13 Tax on amount on line 6* . . . . | **13** |

14 Tax on amount on line 9* . . . . | **14** |

15 Subtract line 14 from line 13 . . . . | **15** |

16 If the amount on line 10 is: $41,500, enter $13,392 . . . . . .
$60,000, enter $19,678 . . . . . .
$44,700, enter $13,961 . . . . . .
$28,300, enter $9,839 . . . . . | **16** |

17 Add lines 15 and 16. . . . . | **17** |

18 Multiply line 17 by .0125 . . . . | **18** |

19 Subtract line 18 from line 17 . . . . | **19** |

20 Add lines 12 and 19. This is your maximum tax. (see instructions) . . . . | **20** |

Computation of Alternative Maximum Tax (Complete only if you have an entry on Schedule D, line 29.) . .

21 Enter amount from line 32 of Schedule D (Form 1040 or Form 1041) . . . . | **21** |

22 Enter smaller of line 9 or line 21 . . . . | **22** |

23 Enter amount from line 10 . . . . | **23** |

24 Subtract line 23 from line 22. If line 23 is more than line 22, do not complete rest of form . . . | **24** |

25 Enter 50% of line 24 . . . . | **25** |

26 Tax on amount on line 21* . . . . | **26** |

27 Tax on amount on line 22* . . . . | **27** |

28 Subtract line 27 from line 26 . . . . | **28** |

29 Add lines 16 and 28 . . . . | **29** |

30 Multiply line 29 by .0125 . . . . | **30** |

31 Subtract line 30 from line 29 . . . . | **31** |

32 Enter amount from line 34 of Schedule D (Form 1040 or Form 1041) . . . . | **32** |

33 Add lines 25, 31, and 32 (see instructions) . . . . | **33** |

*Use Tax Rate Schedules from Form 1040 or Form 1041 instructions. Do not use Tax Computation Worksheet.

For Paperwork Reduction Act Notice, see back of form.   343–176–1   Form **4726** (1981)

Instructions

(Section references are to the Internal Revenue Code)

Paperwork Reduction Act Notice.—The Paperwork Reduction Act of 1980 says we must tell you why we are collecting this information, how we will use it, and whether you have to give it to us. We ask for the information to carry out the Internal Revenue laws of the United States. We need it to ensure that you are complying with these laws and to allow us to figure and collect the right amount of tax. You are required to give us this information.

Purpose of Form.—This form may be to your advantage if you have personal service income and your tax rate is above 50%. For more information, see **Publication 909, Minimum Tax and Maximum Tax.**

Line 1. Personal service income.—In the spaces on line 1 show the kinds and amounts of personal service income from your Form 1040 or Form 1041. For an estate or trust, personal service income includes only income in respect of a decedent as defined below. Personal service income for an individual includes:

- wages, salaries, tips, and other compensation for personal services actually rendered.
- professional fees.
- bonuses.
- commissions on sales or insurance premiums.
- prizes and awards that are not gambling winnings.
- taxable pensions and annuities which arise from employer-employee relationship or from tax deductible contributions to a retirement plan.
- taxable group term life insurance.
- property you received as payment for services even if you later transferred the property to someone else.
- gains (except capital gains) and net earnings from the sale or transfer of an interest in, or license for the use of property (other than goodwill) that you created by your personal efforts.
- the portion of income you received from a corporation (including an electing small business corporation) that represents a reasonable allowance as compensation for the services you performed for the corporation.
- the entire amount you receive for professional services if you are a doctor, dentist, lawyer, architect, accountant, etc., and you are personally responsible for the services performed. This is true even if your assistants perform all or part of the services.
- income you receive from a noncorporate trade or business where both personal services and capital are material income producing factors. In this case, your personal service income is a reasonable allowance as compensation for the personal services actually rendered, but not more than the net profits of the business.
- an item of gross income in respect of a decedent if the gross income would have been personal service income for the decedent had he or she lived and received the amount.
- personal service income of a nonresident alien if it is from sources in the U.S. and is effectively connected with the conduct of a trade or business in the U.S.

Personal service income does not include:

- interest and dividends (including undistributed taxable income from an electing small business corporation).
- other distributions of corporate earnings and profits.
- gambling gains.
- gains treated as capital gains.
- premature or excess distributions from a qualified employee pension plan under section 72(m)(5).
- lump-sum distributions from pension, etc., plans taxed under sections 402(a)(2), 402(e) and 403(a)(2).
- certain distributions from Individual Retirement Accounts or Annuities described in sections 408(e)(2), (3), (4), (5), and 408(f).
- redemption of retirement bonds includible in income under section 409 (b) or (c).

Line 2. Deductions against personal service income.—In the spaces on line 2 show the kind and amount of each deduction that is related to your personal service income and is required to be taken into account in determining adjusted gross income.

Examples of these are:

- allowable deduction for expenses from a trade or business from which you received personal service income.
- allowable deduction for expenses from performing services as an employee.
- allowable deduction for payments to a Keogh plan.
- allowable deduction for payments to an IRA.
- allowable deduction for moving expenses.
- deductions allowable to an individual who is a shareholder-employee of an electing small business corporation for the excess of amounts included in gross income due to overpayment on his or her behalf by a corporation to a qualified pension plan over amounts not received as benefits.
- a net operating loss deduction to the extent that the net operating losses carried to the taxable year are properly allocable to or chargeable against personal service income.
- allowable deduction for certain expenses of living abroad under section 913.

When the expenses of a business are more than the income from that business, and both personal services and capital are material income producing factors, deduct only part of the expenses against personal service income. To figure your deduction, multiply the total business expenses of that business by the ratio of a reasonable amount of pay for your services over the gross receipts of that business. You must make the computation separately for each business with a loss. You cannot apply the profits or losses of one business against the profits or losses of another.

Note: *Do not include in line 2, expenses which are properly deductible on Schedule A (Form 1040).*

Line 4. Adjusted gross income.—If you are an estate or trust, adjusted gross income is determined the same as for an individual.

Line 5.—Round percentage to nearest four numbers. For example, a percentage of 68.8456% should be rounded to 68.85%.

Line 8.—Enter on this line the following tax preference items:

- adjusted itemized deductions.
- accelerated depreciation on real and personal property.
- amortization of certified historic structures, certified pollution control facilities, railroad rolling stock, on-the-job training facilities and child care facilities.
- reserves for losses on bad debts of financial institutions.
- stock options.
- depletion.
- intangible drilling costs.

See Form 6251 for adjusted itemized deductions and Form 4625 for the other tax preference items. If you are an estate or trust, see Form 4626 instead of Form 4625.

If there are no tax preference items because of section 58(h), indicate this on line 8.

Lines 20 and 33.—This is your maximum tax. If line 20 is less than your tax by using the tax rate schedule, income averaging, or alternative tax, enter it on Form 1040, line 35 and check the box labeled "Form 4726". If you are an estate or trust, enter this amount on Form 1041, line 26a and write "Form 4726" in the margin. However, if you had an entry on line 29 of Schedule D (Form 1040 or Form 1041), complete lines 21 through 33. If line 33 is less than line 20, use the line 33 amount instead of line 20.

Short Period Returns.—If you are required to prepare a return of less than twelve months, your tax is determined by placing your taxable income, personal service net income, adjusted gross income, and items of tax preference on an annual basis.

1982 Tax Planning Section

If you keep your records on 1982 income and expenses on the following pages, it will make the preparation of your 1982 return next year much easier. You will simply copy the information from these pages onto your return.

Note that there is only one column for dividend income. If you receive dividends that are a return of capital or are capital-gains dividends, identify them so that you won't include them with any regular dividends that are taxable as ordinary income.

Note also that there is no column for your regular salary income. The Form W-2 you receive from your employer will give you that necessary information.

CAPITAL GAINS AND LOSSES—1982
Short-Term Capital Gains and Losses—held for not more than one year

Securities or Property Sold	Date Sold	Date Purchased	Sales Price	Cost and Expense of Sale	Gain (or Loss)

CAPITAL GAINS AND LOSSES—1982
Long-Term Capital Gains and Losses—held for more than one year

Securities or Property Sold	Date Sold	Date Purchased	Sales Price	Cost and Expense of Sale	Gain (or Loss)

DEDUCTIBLE EXPENSES—1982

Date Paid	To Whom	Taxes	Interest	Alimony	Child Care*	Contributions	Medical	Other Disbursements** Explanation	Amount

*Qualifies for credit. See page 106.
**Energy expenditure qualifies for credit. See page 111.

TAXABLE INCOME—1982

Date Rec'd.	From Whom	Dividends	Interest	Rents and Royalties	Explanation	Other Income Amount

SUMMARY OF DEDUCTIBLE EXPENSES—1982

	Taxes	Interest	Alimony	Child Care*	Contributions	Medical	Other**
January, 1982							
February, 1982							
March, 1982							
April, 1982							
May, 1982							
June, 1982							
July, 1982							
August, 1982							
September, 1982							
October, 1982							
November, 1982							
December, 1982							
Totals							

*Qualifies for credit. See page 106.
**Energy expenditure qualifies for credit. See page 111.

INDEX

A

Abandoned spouses, head of household status........100
Abortion, legal..80, 81
Accident and health insurance premiums...........59, 79
   benefits received..59
Accidents. See Automobile accidents; Casualties
Accounting-certificate fees..69
Accounting method, choice of.....................................124
Accrual basis..124, 130
   and salaries paid in January..................................132
Adjusted gross income..19
   average deductions on..89
   chances of audit based on..................................119
   computation of..77
Adjusted net earnings...137
Adjustments to income. See also Employee business
   expenses; Moving expenses
   method of computing..161
   totaling..177
Adopted children
   alien..27
   deductions for..32
   legal expenses..12
Advance payments..123
   on earned-income credits....................................114
Advance rent..54
Advertising costs..132
Age, and filing requirements of resident aliens...........9
Age 55 or over
   home destroyed by casualty..................................46
   and sale of home................................43-44, 45-46
Age 65 or over. See also Elderly
   credit for elderly..103-105
   date of reaching..26
   and deceased spouse..26
   exemption for..26
   filing requirements..9
   and home sale........................11, 43-44, 45-46
   and Schedule, R and RP................................104-105
Aid to Dependent Children payments........................60
Air conditioner, as medical expense..........................81
Air terminal, trip to and from hotel............................72
Alcohol, used as fuel, credit for................................20
Alcoholics Anonymous..82
Alcoholism treatments..82
Aliens
   dual-status, required to itemize deductions...........78
   nonresident
      adopted..27
      spouse..9, 19
      spouse as head of household........................100
   resident, filing requirements....................................9
Alimony..75-76
   earmarked toward mortgage on jointly
      owned residence..76
   filing requirements and..20
   legal expenses for collection of............................76
   not covered by legal obligation..............................76
   paying for real-estate taxes, property insurance, and
      utility expenses..76
   in payment of property rights................................75
   periodic payments..75
   from securities in trust..76
All-Savers interest..36
Allocation method, for office-at-home expenses.......68
Allowances..60
   expense-account..134
   fixed, employee business expenses........................64
   and gross receipts..124
   to servicemen for quarters, subsistence, and
      uniforms..61
Alternative minimum tax..113
Amended return..99
Amortization..128
   forestration/reforestration......................................77
   royalties..54
Annuities..52
   See also Pensions
   fully taxable..49

Apartments, condominium and cooperative. See
   Cooperative apartments
Appraisal fees, for determining loss
   from casualties..94
Arithmetic errors on returns....................................119
Armed forces
   allowances and family allowances........................61
   dependents in..28
   living quarters..60
   payments in..61
   uniforms..69
Artificial teeth and limbs..79
Artistic works..60
"At risk" provisions..133
Athletic club membership, paid by employer............34
Audit of return
   and average deductions..89
   and correction on original return............................99
   and expense-account information not given........134
   reasons increasing chances of............................119
   statistical chances of..119
Automatic extension to file return,
   payment with..116
Automobile accidents..93-94
   damages to other person's car..............................95
Automobile expenses. See Automobiles; Car
   expenses; Travel and transportation
Automobiles
   disabled veterans..61
   investment credit for purchase of..........................74
   license and inspection fees..................................85
   modification for handicapped person......................80
   rebates..60
   repairs..93-94
   useful life of..74
Awards. See also Prizes and awards; Scholarships from
   court suits..59
   Public Health Service..59

B

Babysitter, payments to, during voluntary work for
   charitable organization..91
Bad debts..96
   business..128
   collected..128
   interest on..96
   proof of worthlessness of......................................96
   when to deduct..95-96
Baggage charges..70
Balance due..118
Bank credit-plan interest..87
Bankruptcy, and bad debts..96
Bar-exam fees..69
Barter transactions..60
Benefit performances..90
Bequests. See Gifts; Inheritances
Birth control expenditures....................................80, 81
Blindness
   exemption for..26
   legal..26
   seeing-eye dog and..83
Blood transfusions..81
"Blue Book" value of car..94
Bonds
   coupon..36
   holding..73
   interest on..34
   issued by church..90
   long- and short-term capital gains on sale of.........49
   Series E..36
   worthless..128
Bonuses..33,132
Braces..80
Broker, travel expenses to..96
Brokerage account..37
Bus drivers; meals away from home............................71
Business, principal place of..68
Business bad debt..96
Business deductions

See also Employee business expenses
   amortization..128
   amount allowed..132
   bad debts..128
   depletion allowances on natural resources...........128
   depreciation and obsolescence..............52-53, 129
   examples of..132-133
   form..127
   gifts..66
   insurance..130
   interest on business indebtedness........................130
   leased property improvements..............................133
   losses..133
   miscellaneous..132-133
   rent on business property....................................131
   repairs..131
   retirement plans and other employee benefit plans
      other than your share................................130
   taxes on business and business property..............131
   wages to employees..132
Business expenses. See Business deductions;
   Employee business expenses
Business income. See Profit or Loss from Business or
   Profession
Business insurance..130
Business-pleasure trips..65-66
Business and professional organizations dues..........66
Business or professional persons. See Self-employed
   persons
Business property
   casualty losses..132-133
   condemnation of..47
   leased, improvements on....................................133
   rent on..131
   repairs..131
   repairs vs. improvements....................................131
Business use of home..68

C

Campaign contributions. See Political contributions
Campaign expenses..69
Capital asset, description of..40
Capital expenses
   counting as support of dependent..........................27
   medical..77
   reconditioning of building....................................131
Capital-gain distributions........................36-37, 38, 49
Capital gains and losses. See also Gains and losses
   capital asset described..40
   carryover loss from 1964-79..................................40
   casualties, condemnations, and
      involuntary exchanges............................46-48
   deferred-payment sales....................................48-49
   deferred-payments sales without
      adequate interest..48
   filing requirements..39
   home, sale of..43-46
   long- and short-term on sales of
      stocks and bonds..49
   long-term......................................11, 39, 40, 113
   net, deduction from ordinary income........40, 43
   real estate, sale of..46
   sample Schedule D..41-42
   short-term..40
      bad debts as..96
   stock dividend sale..43
   stock rights..43
   stocks and other securities....................................43
Capital-gains property contribution............................88
Capital improvement, flood prevention structures....95
Capital items, purchase of for another person..........28
Car expenses..64
   See also Travel and transportation
   boosting deductions for..73
   for business and pleasure use........64, 72, 124, 130
   for business use..72, 110
   for charitable work..91
   credit for gasoline and oil taxes............................10
   for deductible moving expenses........................62-63

deduction for driving to work with tools..............73
itemized vs. optional deduction..............73
items included in..............72
mileage and per diem allowances..............64
optional allowances vs. actual costs..............63
repairs, boosting deduction for..............73
as support of dependent..............27
traffic violation fines..............73
for transportation to jury duty..............57
Car-pool expenses..............73, 96
Cartage..............126
Cash-basis taxpayer..............124
and salaries paid in January..............132
Cash gifts..............58
Casualties..............92-95
appraisal fees for loss determination..............95
as business deductions..............132-133
computation of loss..............93-95
deductible and nondeductible..............92
domestic mishaps..............94-95
gifts for repairs after..............94
how to deduct..............46-48, 92
insurance proceeds..............46, 94
loss of car in wreck..............94
nonaccident damage to car..............95
$100 limitation..............92, 93, 95
prevention of future, costs for..............95
proof of loss..............93
repair costs..............93-94, 95
replacement..............46
shrubs, damage to..............95
storm damage to business property..............94
trees, damage to..............95
uninsured damage from disaster..............94
when to deduct..............46-48, 94
Cemetery company, nonprofit, contribution to..........90
Certified mail, returns sent by..............134
Chair, reclining..............81
Charge accounts, finance charges
      for late payments..............87-88
Charity. See Contributions
Checks
      as proof of business expenses..............69
      undeposited..............124
Child-care credits..............14, 106-110
      during absence from work..............110
      and birthdate of child..............109
      calculation of amount..............106, 109-110
      and dependency exemptions..............29
      during education and training courses..............109
      form for..............107-108
      while job-hunting..............109
      meals and lodging for live-in housekeeper..........110
      medical expenses..............110
      for part-time workers..............110
      for payments to relatives for care of children..106
      qualifying for..............106
      school fees..............109
Child-placing agency, non-profit, payments for foster
      parenting from..............58
Child support payments..............75
Childbirth expenses. See Pregnancy and childbirth
      expenses
Children
      adopted alien..............27
      born during year..............31
      as employees..............132
      and estate taxes..............13
      exemptions for..............27-31
      married without income..............30-31
      support for..............28-29
      under 19, gross-income test and..............31
Christian Science Practitioners..............136
Christmas bonuses..............132
Church membership fee..............91
Cigarette taxes..............86
Cleaning and laundry expenses..............70
Clothing
      contributions of..............90
Club dues..............66
Cohabitors, as dependents..............32
"Collectibles," IRA
      investment in..............12
Commissions..............33
      advanced on drawing account as loan..............60

on policies bought by life-insurance agent for
      relatives..............34
Community-property laws, and credit for elderly.....104
Commuting expenses..............72, 96
      to school..............98
Compensation..............33-34
      See also Income; wages
      commissions on life insurance policies bought for
            relatives..............34
      and employer contributions to group life-insurance
            and/or group hospitalization plans..............33
      employer contributions to pension plan..............34
      employer contributions to profit-sharing or thrift
            plan..............34
      garnishments and attachments..............33
      health-reconditioning program..............34
      meals furnished by employer..............34
      payment for cancelled employment contract..........33
      payments withheld from wages..............33
      prizes and awards..............34
      property at reduced price as..............34
      services as..............33
      severance pay..............33
      supper money during overtime work..............34
      vacation fund payments..............33
Condemnations and threats of..............46-48
      of rental property..............47
Condominiums. See Cooperative apartments
      and condominiums
Contact lenses, medical-insurance against loss or
      damage to..............79
Containers and packages..............126
Contributions
      benefit performances..............90
      bonds..............90
      capital-gains property..............88
      car expenses..............91
      churches, in lieu of parochial school tuition..........90
      with credit card..............91
      date of..............89
      deductible amount..............14, 88
      meals and lodging during charitable work away from
            home..............91
      membership fee to church..............90
      merchandise..............89
      nondeductible..............89, 90
      "overpayment" to charitable organization as..........90
      political..............25, 102
      property..............88, 90
      qualifying organizations..............89
      raffles..............90
      records of..............91
      reporting method..............88
      services..............90
      stock..............88
      value of..............90
Cooperative apartments and condominiums..............45
      interest deductions..............85, 87
      residential energy credits..............111-112
      tax deductions..............85
Corporations
      nonqualifying for dividend exclusion..............38
      small-business..............55
Correspondence courses..............31, 98
Cost of goods sold
      inventory and..............125, 126
      labor costs..............125
      material and supplies costs..............125
      other costs..............126
      purchases and..............125
Cost pricing..............126
Cost sharing, for residential energy credits..............111
Court suits, awards from..............59
Credit card use
      for contribution..............91
      employer payment of employee business expenses
            with..............64
      expense account items paid by..............134
      finance charges..............87
Credit purchases. See Instalment purchases
Credits. See also Investment credit
      See also Earned-income credit
      for amount paid with application for automatic two-
            month extension..............116
      for car purchase..............74

child care..............106-110
earned-income, see Earned-income credit
      for the elderly..............10
      and community-property shares..............103
      and public retirement system income..............103
      Schedule R and RP for..............104-105
      for federal tax on special fuels and oils..............11, 117
      form for..............20, 102
      for overpayments..............114
      for political contributions..............20, 102
      for public retirement system income..............103
      refundable..............115-117
      regulated investment company..............117
Crutches..............80

D

Daily allowance rule..............69-70
Damages for personal injuries..............60
Date
      of birth
            of dependent..............31
            of taxpayers age 65..............26
      of contribution..............89
      of death of spouse..............26
      of divorce..............26
Day care costs. See Child-care credits
Deaf person
      special equipment for..............80
      special instruction for, as medical expense..........80
Death
      of dependent during year..............31
      of spouse..............26
Death benefits from employer..............58
Debts. See Bad debts; Interest
Declaration of estimated tax
      filing requirements..............118
      understimated..............118
Declining-balance method..............129
      200-percent..............129
Deductions. See also Adjustments to income; Business
      deductions
      acceleration of..............11
      alimony..............39, 75-76
      car expenses..............72-74
      for child adopted during year..............32
      choosing between Form 1040A
            and Form 1040..............20
      club dues..............11, 66
      energy tax credits..............111-112
      for friends and cohabitors..............32
      and housekeepers..............31
      itemized, see Itemized deductions
      of long- and short-term capital losses..............40, 43
      married-couple..............14
      for office at home..............68
      for repairs to rental property..............54
      standard, and rent income..............54
      state tax on stocks..............43
      vacation home expenses..............56
Deferred medical bills..............83
Deferred-payment sales..............48
      computation of value of notes..............49
      election of reporting method..............48
      on instalment method..............48-49
Degree candidates, fellowship for required part-time
      employment..............59
Department of Housing and Urban Development,
      assistance payments on behalf of mortgagors to
      mortgagees..............61
Department store employees, discounts on
      purchases..............34
Dependent-care credit..............14
      for disabled spouse..............109
      nurse for invalid mother..............109
Dependents..............26-31
      born during year..............31
      capital expenditures..............27
      child-care credit..............106-110
      criteria for..............27
      deceased during year..............31
      filing requirements..............9
      foster child..............32

friends and cohabitors............................32
gross-income test for.............................31
and head of household status..................100
married.................................30-31
medical expenses..............................80
out-of-home care for............................14
receiving Social Security payments...........28, 30
relatives of spouse............................32
required to itemize deductions..................78
in state institutions............................30
students, and free room and board..............30
summer camp payments for......................31
wedding costs for..............................30
wife not considered............................27
Depletion.................................54, 128
Depreciation...................................129
calculation of.................................129
first year..................................129
Form 4562.................................52-53
and investment credit..........................110
office at home..............................68
of property put in service in 1981.............129
salvage value and...........................129, 132
vacation homes..............................56, 57
Diaper service................................81
Diets, special, as medical expense...............80
Direct moving expenses...........................62
Disability allowances and pensions to veterans.....61
Disability-income exclusion.......................76
Disability pay to servicemen......................61
Disabled veterans................................61
Disasters
classified by President..........................94
gifts during................................94
proof of loss.................................93
Discounted loans.............................87, 130
Discounts
employee.................................34
business loans..............................130
Display material, transporting costs.............70
Dividends.................................36-38
choice of tax form..........................19-20
exclusions.................................15, 38, 43
filing requirements..........................10, 19, 36
on foreign stock, tax withheld on..............86
form for.................................35
left in account..............................37
life-insurance...............................37
liquidating................................37
mutual funds...............................38
mutual life-insurance or veterans'
life insurance.............................37
record-keeping on............................146
after sale of stock...........................37-38
on savings-and-loan-association accounts........37
stock.................................14-15, 37
veterans' insurance...........................37
Divorce. See also Alimony; Child support; Divorced
persons
attorney's fees for...........................76, 96
Divorced persons
claiming children as dependents.................28-29
and spousal IRA.............................12
Drought, damage from.........................92-93
Dues
club.................................66
gym.................................82
union.................................69

E

Earned income, defined.........................30
Earned-income credit
advance payments of...........................9, 114
eligibility.................................9, 21, 115
method of figuring............................21
refund.................................21
sample form for.............................22
worksheet.................................22, 115
Earned Income Credit Table......................147
Educational expenses..........................97-98
correspondence schools........................98
deductible and nondeductible..................97-98
for handicapped child..........................82

how to claim.................................98
to qualify for a better job......................97
to qualify for specialty.........................99
travel expenses and............................98
travel by teacher..............................98
voluntary.................................98
Elastic stockings................................80
Elderly. See also Age 65 or older; Credits, for elderly
Medicare benefits and premiums.................61
Employee benefit plans, as business deductions....130
Employee business expenses......................63-74
accounting to employer........................63
business gifts................................66
car purchase, investment credit for..............74
club dues.................................66
combined business-pleasure trip................65-66
deductible for office at home...................68
employment agency fees........................67
entertainment expenses........................65
excess allowance from employer.................63
Form 2106.................................157-158
mileage and per diem allowances................64
nondeductible...............................67
office-at-home...............................68
paid by employer through credit cards...........64
per diem allowance or reimbursement arrangement
with employer.............................69-70
physical examinations..........................67
record-keeping..............................69-70
with relative as employer.......................64
reporting method.............................63
reporting requirements.........................64
service uniform..............................67
subscriptions to professional journals............67
supporting proof.............................69
tools and supplies............................67
travel and transportation......................70-74
union dues.................................67
Employee discounts..............................34
Employers
allowance or reimbursement
arrangement with..........................69-70
guaranteed-annual-wage plan...................58
and IRAs.................................12
job credit.................................111
of participants in Federal Work Incentive (WIN)
program, and Work-Incentive Credit...........111
payment for moving expenses..................62-63
payments for group hospitalization plan..........33
payments for group life insurance..............33, 59
payments under employee's health-and-accident
insurance plan............................59
pensions paid for by..........................74
physical examinations required by...............67
reimbursement for business expenses.............63-64
reimbursement for employment agency fees.......67
reimbursement for medical expenses.............59
relatives
business expenses and........................64
and daily allowance rule.....................69-70
return of state workmen's compensation payments
to.................................59
supplemental unemployment benefits from........60
Employment. See also New employment
lump-sum distribution from pension or profit-
sharing plan at termination of................49
Employment agency fees.........................67, 97
Employment contract, payment for
cancellation of.............................33
Employment-related expenses,
and child-care credit.........................106
Endowment policies.............................58
Entertainment expenses.........................63, 65-67, 132
record-keeping..............................69-70
spouses.................................66-67
traveling expenses and........................70-74
Equipment, deductible as medical expense.........80
Errors, filing.................................119
Estates or trusts, filing requirements............10, 13, 55
Estimated-tax payments.........................114
refund credited on...........................117
underpayment..............................11, 118
Excess investment interest.......................87
Exclusions
disability-income............................76

dividend income.................................37-38, 43
and home sale..............................43-46
interest from dividends........................15, 38, 43
Exemptions. See also Support
for blindness................................26
for child born during year.....................31
and child support............................27-31
for dead spouse..............................26
for dependent dying during year................31
for divorced spouse...........................26
for foster child..............................32
for home sale by person 55 or older.............43-44
and joint returns with supported person..........27
and legal separation...........................27
number of, choice of form and..................19
sample form.................................26
for shared support............................29
for unemployment benefits.....................60
for vacation-home rental.......................57
"waiving".................................29
Expense-account deductions. See Employee business
expenses
Extensions.................................116
Eyeglasses.................................80

F

Fair rental value, computation of.................30
Family allowance
to servicemen's families........................61
to veterans.................................61
Farm property, condemnation of..................47
Farmers
credit for federal tax on special fuels and oils.....117
filing requirements...........................10
self-employment tax..........................136
Federal income tax withheld. See Withholding tax
Federal Unemployment Trust Fund payments.......60
Federal Work Incentive (WIN) program...........111
Fellowships. See also Scholarships
with part-time employment.....................58
research.................................58
FICA. See Social Security tax
Filing date.................................20, 134
Filing errors.................................119
Filing requirements............................9-10
Filing status.................................25, 100-101
Finance charges..............................87-88
See also Interest
Fines
for illegal strike.............................34
traffic.................................73
Fire insurance................................54
Fixing-up expenses.............................45
rental property..............................54
Floods, prevention costs.........................95
Foreign
bank, securities and other financial accounts......19
corporations, and dividend exclusion............38
tax credit.................................111
trust, grantors or transferors to................19
Foreign living expenses, excess..................77
Forestation/reforestation amortization.............77
Forfeited-interest penalty........................74
Forms. See also Schedules
physician's certification........................76
requiring use of form 1040.....................19-20
W-2.................................33, 114, 119
W-2G.................................114
W-2P.................................114
1040
use of guide for filling in.....................9
requirements for use of......................19-20
sample.................................23-24
1040A.................................10, 17-22, 139
1040-ES.................................20
1040X.................................99
2106.................................63, 157-158
2119.................................44, 159-160
2120.................................29
2210.................................19, 118
2439.................................117
2440.................................76
2441.................................107-108

2555 19
3468 110, 151-152
3903 61, 155-156
4136 10, 117
4562 52-53
4563 19
4726 161-162
4782 63
4797 49, 153-154
4868 19, 116
5329 74
5500-K 75
5695 111
6251 113
Foster children 27, 32
full-time students 31
Foster parents, payments to 58
Fraternal society, contributions to 89-90
Freight costs 126, 132
Friends, as dependents 32
Frost damage 95
Full-time students 31
Funeral and burial costs 83
Furniture, special, as medical expense 81

G

Gains and losses. *See also* Capital gains and losses
deduction method 40, 43
hobbies 123
supplemental 49, 153-154
Gambling income and losses 57, 96
Garage rent 72
Garnishments and attachments 33
credit for nonhighway use 117
Geothermal energy equipment 112
Gifts 58
See also Contributions
business 66
after casualties 94
loans to children 96
strike benefits to nonunion striker 58
Grants. *See* Fellowships; Scholarships
Graves, payment to nonprofit cemetery
company for care of 90
Gross income
of dependent children 27
and filing requirements 9
Gross-income test 31
Gross profit 127
Gross receipts, calculation of 124
Ground rents, redeemable 86
Group hospitalization plans 33, 79
Group life insurance
paid by employer 33
withheld from wages 33
Guaranteed-annual-wage-plan payments 58
Gym dues 82

H

Halfway house, child in 82
Handicapped persons
advance payment for lifetime care 83
special equipment for 80
Head of household 100-101
qualifying as 95-97, 100-101
Health insurance. *See also* Medical insurance
deductible and nondeductible 78-80
employer payments to 34, 59
excess payments 59, 83
withheld from wages 33
Hearing aids 80
Heat, light, and power costs 132
Hobby income or losses 123
Home
business use of 68
faulty construction 95
improvements for medical reasons 82
inherited 45
purchase of, and transfer taxes 85
rental and personal use 54
rental value, in figuring support of children 29
specially designed for paraplegic veterans 61
tax rebate on 86
taxpayer's, for traveling expenses deductions 70
vacation 45, 56
Home, sale of 10, 11, 39, 43-46
age, ownership, and use 43-44
costs 44, 62
and 18-month deadline on moving
into new home 45
exchanged for part payment on new home 45
filing requirements 10
fixing-up expenses 44
fixing-up expenses on new residence 45
inheritance of new residence 45
instalment basis 45, 48
as long-term capital gain 44
losses 44
by persons age 55 or older 43-44
and points 86
purchase of 11
purchase of new home in wife's name 45
real-estate tax deductions 85-86
replacement 43-45
summer home 45
table for computation of taxable gain
after new home purchase 45
Hospital volunteers 90
Hospitals, payments to interns and residents 59
Hotel, trip to and from air terminal 72
Household allowance 60
Household help 31, 82, 106
and child-care credit 109
during absence from job 110
meals and lodging for 110
for semi-invalid 80
Household maintenance, expenses
included in cost of 101
Housing, fair rental value of 30
Husband. *See* Spouse

I

Important Tax Developments, use of summary of 9
Improvements on business property,
compared with repairs 131
Income. *See also* Compensation;
Miscellaneous income
adjustments to, and choice between
Form 1040 and Form 1040A 19-20
alimony received 39
barter 60
from business or profession, *see* Profit or Loss from
Business or Profession, Schedule C
commissions and bonuses 33
record form for 165
and use of Form 1040A 19-20
jury fees 57
nontaxable 60-61
postponing 11
schedules for reporting 38
from sources other than wages, dividends, and
interest, forms for reporting 38
from sources in U.S. possessions, itemized
deductions and 78
tips 33
Income averaging 102
form for 149-150
Income-producing property, deductible taxes on 85
Income splitting, and joint return 25
Indirect moving expenses 62
Individual proprietor, education expenses 97
Individual retirement arrangement (IRA) 12, 74, 75
extensions 116
and filing requirements 19-20
and Medicare 61
premature distributions or undistributed 74
tax on excess 114
Inflation, and "indexing" tax brackets 11
Inheritances 58, 60
Injury
damages paid for 60
insurance payments 59
Insect damage 92, 95
Instalment sales
and gross receipts calculations 124
home 45
interest 86
of property 48-49
Institutionalized dependents 30
Insulation 111
energy tax credits for 111
Insurance. *See also* Health insurance; Life insurance
automobile 72
business 130
casualty losses 46
dividends 37
fire and liability 54, 59
paid by employer 59
for pay lost while ill 80, 83
payments for loss of body member, function, or
disfigurement 59
on rented business property 131
Interest
added to loans 87
All-Savers 36
exclusion 38
points as 86
Interest deductions 86-88
additional tax 87
bad debts 96
business indebtedness 130
cooperative apartment 85, 87
deductible and nondeductible 86-87
excess investment 86
filing requirements 10, 19
finance charges 87-88
forfeited, for premature withdrawal
of term account 74
inadequate, on deferred payment sales 48
on instalment purchases 87
on IRS tax refund 11
and mortgage assistance payments 86
mortgages 87
on one-year tax-exempt savings certificate 11
paid in advance 88
on partially rented home 87
reporting with standard deduction 87
Interest income
and choice of tax form 18-19
coupon bonds 36
credited to account 36
life insurance 36
and savings-and-loan-association accounts 37
Schedule B 35
from Series E bonds 36
from stocks, exclusion of 15
Interns, payments to 59
Inventories
and computation of purchases and sales 124
and cost of goods sold 125
at end of year, value of 126
loan to carry 130
pricing methods 126
Investment credit 110
form for 151-152
prior year, tax from recomputing 113
Invoice price 125
Involuntary conversions 46, 47-48
IRA. *See* Individual Retirement Arrangement
IRS, tax figured by 20
Itemized deductions
average claimed 87
contributions 86-87
correction of oversights on 1980 return 99
education expenses 97-99
foreign-tax credit 111
form for 19-20, 148
interest 86-88
losses from accidents, fires, storm,
or other casualty 92-95
medical expenses 78-83
miscellaneous 95
required 77-78
Schedule A for 10, 148
Schedule B for 148
vs. standard 77-78
summary of, calculation of 99
taxes 83-86
unusually large 119

J

Joint returns
  benefits of filing 25
  and child care credit 106
  excess Social Security tax on 20
  exclusions on interest from dividends on 15
  and exemptions for spouse 26
  and IRS figuring tax 20
  and nonworking spouse 25, 26
  signing 119
  with supported person 30
Jury fees 57

K

Keogh (H.R. 10) Retirement Plan 12-13, 74, 75
  extensions 116

L

Laboratory tests 80
Labor costs 125
Laetrile 80
Land. *See also* Real estate
  depreciation 129
Lawyer fees 96
  for alimony or separate-maintenance payments collection 95
  for divorce 76
Liability insurance 54
License fees 69, 72, 132
Life insurance 36, 96
  on business owner 130
  dividends and proceeds 38, 58, 60
  paid for another person 28
  transferred 58
Liquor bills 86
Living expenses. *See also* Room and board
  armed forces officers and personnel 60
  paid by fire insurance policy 59
  from pension or profit-sharing plan 42
Loan(s). *See also* Bad debts, Interest
  to children 96
  commissions advanced on drawing account as 60
  discounted 87
  for medical expenses 83
  repaid, principal of 60
Local income-tax refunds 39
Local taxes, deductible 84
Long-term capital gains and losses 39, 40
Losses. *See also* Casualties; Gains and losses
  appraisal fees for determination of 94
  business, "at risk" provisions 133
  business bad debts 128
  from business or profession 133
  business property, computation of 132
  car replacement 94
  computation of 93-95
  gambling 96
  nondeductible 96
  when to claim 94
Lottery tickets 57
Lump-sum payments
  for employment contracts 60
  to ex-spouse 76

M

Mailing date of contribution 89
Maintenance expenses, for vacation homes 57
Manufacturing enterprises
  labor costs 125
  material and supplies costs 125
  miscellaneous costs 126
Market pricing 126
Marriage, of dependent without income 30-31
Marriage penalty 14
Married person(s)
  filing requirements 9
  married-couple deduction 14
  medical-insurance premiums deductions 79
Married taxpayers living apart. *See also* Separated taxpayers; Single taxpayers
  and child-care credit 106
  filing as head of household 100
  nonresident alien spouse 19
Material and supplies costs 125
Maternity clothing 81
Meals. *See also* Meals and lodging
  furnished by employer 34
  "quiet business" 65
Meals and lodging expenses 70
  on business trips away from home overnight 71
  in city away from general place of employment 71
  during charitable work away from home 91
  free, for students 30
  furnished by employer 60
  in halfway house 82
  for live-in housekeeper 110
  as medical expense 80
  and new employment location 62
  in old-age home 82
  taxability of 34
Medicaid and Medicare payments 61, 80
Medical and dental license fees 69
Medical expenses. *See also* Medicaid, Medicare
  abortion, legal 80, 81
  air conditioner 81
  air conditioner for allergy 82
  alcoholism, treatment for 82
  anti-smoking treatments 82
  birth-control expenditures 80, 81
  capital expenses 81
  car expenses for travel to doctor's office 80
  and child-care credit 109
  computation of 78-79
  deductible, examples of 80
  deduction rules 79-83
  deferred 83
  and dependency exemptions 29
  excess health insurance payments 83
  excess reimbursement 59
  general drug purchases 79
  handicapped child in special school 82
  health club dues 82
  household help 82
  illegal operations and treatments 81
  maintenance in halfway house 82
  nurse accompanying patient for special treatment, traveling expenses 81
  nursing home 82
  other than doctor and hospital bills 80
  paid to nonprofessional 82
  of partially supported nondependents 80
  physical examinations required by employer 69
  pregnancy and childbirth 81
  prepaid 83
  psychiatric care 82
  reimbursed 59, 83
  remedial reading courses for brain-damaged child 82
  seeing-eye dog 83
  transportation 81
  trip as 81
  vacuum cleaner for dust allergy 82
  vasectomy, legal 80, 81
Medical insurance 70-72
  See also Health insurance
  for loss or damage to contact lenses 79
  Medicare 61
  for prescription drug costs 79
Medical and surgical appliances 79
Medicare. *See also* Medicaid
  deductions for premiums 61, 80
  and support figuring 30
Medicines and drugs 79
  See also Prescription drugs
Membership fee, church 90
Mental illness or defect, psychiatric care for 82
Merchandise
  casualty loss 93-94
  on consignment 126
  evaluation of 126
  inventory at end of year 126
  sold, cost of 124-126
Mileage allowances 70
  for car used for charitable work
  for travel to jury duty
  vs. itemized deductions 7
Military. *See* Armed forces
Minimum tax 113
Miscellaneous deductions 95
  bad debts 96
  expenses for seeking new employment 96, 97
  travel expenses to broker's office 96
Miscellaneous income 57-61
  accident-and-health policy payments 59
  award from court suit 59
  company-financed supplemental-unemployment benefits 58
  death benefits from spouse's employer 58
  employer reimbursement of medical expenses 59
  from endowment policy 58
  excess health insurance payments 59
  fellowship with part-time employment 58
  fire insurance policy payments for living expenses 59
  foster parent payments 58
  gifts 58
  hospital interns and residents, payments to 59
  inheritances 58
  insurance payments for bodily injury 59
  jury fees 57
  lottery winnings and other gambling gains and losses 57
  notary fees 57
  prizes 57
  public-assistance payments 58
  Public Health Service awards 59
  research fellowships 58-59
  scholarships 58
  Social Security benefits 58
  state workmen's-compensation payments 59
  unemployment benefits 58
  union-financed unemployment, strike and lockout benefits 58
  Veterans Administration benefits 59
Mortgage assistance payments 60-61
  interest and real estate taxes 86
Mortgage payments. *See also* Instalment sales
  assumed by buyer 48
  from alimony, on jointly owned property 76
  interest paid in advance 88
  interest portion of 87
Mortgage points 86
Mortgage prepayment penalty 86
Moving, to new principal job site, and home sale 43
Moving expenses 62-63
  filing requirements 62-63
  form for 155-156
  reimbursement for 62
Multiple-support agreement 29
  and head of household status 101
Mustering-out pay 61
Mutual funds 38
  tax credit 117

N

Natural resource investments, depletion 128
Net earnings
  adjusted 137
  non-farm self-employment, computation of 136
Net profit or loss 136
New employment. *See also* Moving expenses
  expenses incurred in seeking 33, 96, 97
  interview expenses 33
  and more than one home sale in 18 months 43
New plant or location, trip to find 72
Nonfarm optional method 136, 137
Nonqualifying corporations, for dividend exclusion 38
Nonresident aliens
  adopted children 27
  spouse of 9, 100
Nontaxable income 60-61
Nonunion striker, strike benefits to 58
Notary fees 57
Note discount interest 86
Notes, valuation of 49

...g patient for special treatment,
   ...payments for...81
...d mother, and dependent-care credit....109
...born baby...81
...y school costs..109
...ng home...82

O

Office at home..68
   allocation of expenses of.................................68
   for nonemployees...68
   in undivided room..68
Old-age home. See Retirement home
Options income..28
Outside salesperson...68
Overhead expenses, manufacturing.............126
"Overnight" trips...71
Overpayment of taxes...19
   FICA and RRTA taxes......................................116
   Social Security...20
Overtime, supper money from employer during....34

P

Painting, as repair..131
Paraplegic veterans, specially designed homes for....61
Parents
   child-care payments to, see Child care credit
   dependent..28
   and head of household status.................100-101
   and Medicare payments....................................30
   on Social Security....................................28, 29-30
   in state institutions...30
Parking fees...70
Parochial school, contribution to church
   in lieu of tuition...90
Part-time employment, and child-care credit.....110
Partnerships, filing requirements.......................10
Patents, royalty producing, amortization...........54
Payments and credits.....................................116-118
   amount paid with Form 4868............................116
   credit for federal tax on special fuels.............117
   credit from 1980 return...................................114
   earned-income credit...........................115, 116
   estimated-tax payments in 1981......................114
   excess FICA and RRTA tax withheld...............116
   regulated investment company credit.............117
   total..117
   withholding tax..114
Penalties
   for inflated valuations on property.............11-12
   on IRA or Keogh plan excesses........................13
   for late real-estate tax payment.......................87
   for underpayment of estimated tax.........11, 15, 118
Pensions. See also Annuities
   cost of..50
   employee...34
   employer contributions.....................................50
   form for..50
   fully taxable...49
   lump-sum distribution.......................................49
   reporting method..50
   to soldiers' widows...61
   veterans..61
Per diem allowance..69-70
Personal exemption...26
   age 65 or older...26
Personal service income, maximum tax on,
   form for...161-162
Physical therapy..82
Physicians, deductions for costs of
   qualifying for specialty...............................97, 99
Physician's certification form..............................76
"Points"...86
Political contributions, credit for................19, 102
Pollution-control expenses.................................128
Postage...132
Pregnancy and childbirth expenses.....................81
Prescription drugs, medical-insurance for cost of.....79
Presidential election campaign contribution........25
Pricing methods...126

Principal place of business
   more than one..68
   travel to minor place of business
      or employment from......................................71
Principal residence. See Main home
Principal of repaid loans.....................................60
Prizes and awards.......................................34, 57
Profit or Loss from Business or Profession Schedule
   "at risk" provisions...133
   cost of goods sold and/or operations.......124-126
   deductions, see Business deductions
   expense-account information for employees.......134
   filing requirements..123
   gross profit..127
   net profit or loss, computation of..................133
   other income..127
   sample form..121-122
   total income..127
Profit-sharing plan
   employer contributions to.................................34
   lump-sum distribution................................49, 51
Proof
   of business expenses..69
   of filing date of tax return.............................134
   of spending per diem allowance........................70
Property. See also Business property
   as compensation..34
   contribution..88
   deferred payment sales
      on instalment method................................48-49
      without adequate interest.............................48
   depreciation, see Depreciation
   estate taxes and..13
   lost or misplaced..96
   personal, sale of...39
   rented, expenses paid on.................................131
   rights, alimony in payment of..........................75
   sale or exchange of, see Capital gains and losses
   valuations, penalty for inflation of..............11-12
Psychiatric care...82
Public assistance payments.........................58, 60
Public Health Service awards..............................59
Public library, contribution to.............................89
Public retirement system income credit.............103
Public-utility companies, stock dividends......14-15

Q

"Quiet meal rule"...65

R

Raffles, income from..90
Railroad Retirement tax, excess withheld..........116
Railroad Unemployment Insurance
   Act payments..58, 60
Real estate, sale of..46
   See also Home, sale of
Real-estate taxes
   interest for late payments.................................87
   paid by another person......................................85
   paid with mortgage payments...........................85
   rebate...86
   after sale of home..85-86
Real property, instalment sale of.................48-49
Rebates
   automobile..60
   and gross receipts..124
Receivables outstanding....................................124
"Reciprocal meals"..65
Records
   of contributions...91
   entertainment expenses....................................69
   1982 Tax Planning Section for.................163-166
   for Repair Allowance method.........................131
   traveling expenses..69
Redeemable ground rents...................................86
Refunds...117
   See also Earned-income credit
   amount refunded and amount credited
      on 1982 estimated tax................................117
   excess FICA and RRTA tax withheld...............116

federal income tax..39
   filing..9, 116
   for residential energy credits...............111-112
   state and local income tax..............................39
Regulated investment company credit...............117
Reimbursements
   business expenses......................................63-74
   car expenses...73
   employment agency fees...................................67
   medical expenses.......................................79, 83
   moving expenses..62-63
   per diem..69-70
Relatives
   child-care payments to....................................110
   close...27
   delayed wages to...132
   qualifying as dependents for head of
      household status..100
   renting property below normal rental value.....54
   of spouse..32
   wages paid to..131
Religious orders, members of...........................136
Remedial reading courses....................................82
Renovations...131
Rent income. See also Rent and royalty income;
      Rental property
   advance rent..54
   below normal rental value.................................54
   for breaking lease...54
   business property...131
   from family members...54
   filing requirements...10
   security payments...54
   vacation homes...56
Rent and royalty income or loss..................50-54
   See also Rent income
   deductible expenses..54
   form for..50
   how to report..51
   and joint ownership...54
   and personal use of rental property..................54
Rental property. See also Rent income
   condemnation of..47
   improvements, depreciation on.......................130
   payment for breaking lease...............................54
   personal use..54
   in service after 1980...51
Rented home
   residential energy credits.......................111-112
   tax rebate on..86
Repairs...93
   automobile..72
   business property...131
Research fellowships......................................58-59
Reserve for bad debts.......................................128
Reservists' service uniform expenses..................69
Resident aliens, filing requirements.....................9
Residential energy credits.........................111-112
   carryover for unused......................................112
   cost sharing...112
   figuring...112
   items included and not included in................112
   for all principal residences............................112
   for solar, wind, or geothermal
      energy equipment.............................111-112
   when to take..111
Residents, hospital, payments to.........................59
Resumes, for new employment............................96
Retirement, under age 65 with total disability.....76
Retirement home..82
   parent in, and head of household status.........101
   prepaid lump-sum care fee................................83
Retirement pay, veterans......................................61
Retirement plans, as business deductions.........130
Returns. See also Audits; Joint returns
   common errors...119
   and gross receipts..124
   proof of filing date...134
   signing..119
Revenue-sharing, Census Bureau questions for.......25
Room and board. See Meals and lodging
Royalties. See also Rent or royalty income or loss
   filing requirements...10
   how to report..54
   from natural resources, depletion.....................54

S

Sabbatical leave, teacher's travel during....98
Safe-deposit boxes....96
Salaries. *See* Compensation; Wages
Sales and exchanges. *See also* Capital gains and losses; Gains and losses
  home....10, 43-46
  instalment basis....48-49
  personal property....39
  stock....10
Salespersons
  business expenses....63, 64
  prizes and awards....34
Sales tax, computing deductions....85
Sample cases, transporting costs for....70
Savings-bond purchase plan payments, withheld from wages....33
Savings certificates, one-year tax exempt....11
Savings plans, employer contributions to....34
Schedules
  A....10, 78, 86, 88, 148
  B....35
  C....10, 121-122
  D....41-42
  E....50-51
  G....19, 149-150
  R....104
  RP....105
  SE....135
  filing requirements....10
  for reporting income from sources other than wages, dividends, and interest....38
Scholarships....58
  Public Health Service awards....59
  and support for child....28, 30
  teaching expenses income....58
School fees, and child-care credit....110
"Seconds"....126
Securities income, as alimony payments....76
Security deposit....54
Seeing-eye dogs....80, 83
Self-employed persons. *See also* Profit or Loss from Business or Profession
  education expenses....98
  filing requirements....9, 10
  Social Security Self-Employment tax....10
  Keogh and Individual Retirement Plans....74, 75
  qualifying for specialty....99
  travel and transportation expenses....70
Self-employment income, taxable....138
Self-employment tax....113
  computation of....135-138
  and computation of net earnings from non-farm self-employment....136
  form....135
  higher than required....136
  maximum amount subject to....137
  for members of religious orders and Christian Science practitioners....136
  nonfarm optional method....136-137
  reporting....19, 138
SEP....74
Separate maintenance payments....75-76
Separated persons
  exemption....27
  filing requirements....9, 21-22
Separation agreement, out-of-court....76
Servicemen. *See* Armed forces
Services
  barter transactions....60
  as compensation....33
  contributions....90
Severance pay....33, 60
"Short" tax form. *See* Forms, 1040A
Short-term gains and losses....40, 43
Shrubs, frost damage....95
Simplified employee pension....74
Single persons
  filing requirements....9
  living with person of opposite sex, deductions for....33
Signing return....119
Small-business corporations, reporting income or loss from....55
Smoking, treatment to break habit....82
Social Security. *See also* Social Security benefits
  account number
    on check or money order in payment of taxes 118
    for nonworking spouse....25
    on Schedule E....49
  Medicare B insurance....80
  to child....30
  and credit for the elderly....103-105
  dependents with....28, 29-31
  exemption....57
Social Security tax. *See also* Self-employment tax
  excess withheld....116
  hospital-insurance tax included in....79, 80
  overpayment on....20
  on tips....9, 19
Solar-energy equipment....111-112
Specialty, qualifying for....99
Spouse. *See also* Married taxpayers
  accompanying on business trip....71
  deceased and death benefits from employer...26, 58
  dependent relatives of....32
  disabled....106, 108
  divorced....26
  as employee....132
  entertainment expenses....67
  exemptions for....26
  full-time student....106
    and child-care credit....110
  itemizing deductions on separate return....78
  joint return with....25
  personal exemption for....26-27
  purchase of home in name of....45
  name on return....25
  nonresident alien....19
    and head-of-household status....100
  surviving, estate taxes and....13
Standard deductions
  and interest deductions....87-88
  vs. itemized deductions....78
  and tax deductions....84-86
  income-tax refunds....39
State
  taxes....83-84
    on stock....43
  welfare-agency work relief program payments....60
  workmen's compensation payments....59
Stationery....132
Stocks. *See also* Dividend income
  contribution....88
  as dividend....37-38
  and estate taxes....13
  exclusion....15
  figuring capital gains and losses....40, 43
  foreign, tax on dividends....86
  holding....73
  holding period....40
  long- and short-term capital gains on sales of....49
  of public-utility companies....14-15
  purchased with proceeds of condemned rental property....49
  sale of....10, 47
  state tax....43
Stock ownership in employer corporation, and business deductions....66
Storm damage....94
Storm windows....112
Straddles....11
Straight-line method....129
Strike, illegal, penalty paid for....34
Strike benefits, paid by union to nonunion striker...58
Students
  and child-care credits....109
  earning over $1000....31
  with free room and board....30
  full-time....31
  with scholarships, exemption for....28, 30
Sub-pay, repayment....77
Subscriptions to professional journals....67, 96
Summer camp payments....31
Summer home. *See* Vacation home
Supplemental gains or losses....49, 153-154
Supplemental Income Schedule. *See* Annuities; Estates or trusts; Pensions; Rents; Royalties; Schedules, E
Supplies and materials....132
Support. *See also* Children; Dependents
  affirmative step to provide....30
  capital expenditures counting as....27
  for divorced spouse....26
  of elderly, and Medicare benefits and premiums....61
  figuring....28-31
  postponed....30
  for relative of spouse living in separate house....32
  shared....28
Supported persons, joint returns with....27
Swimming pool, as medical expense....81

T

Tables....139-146
  depreciation....129
  Earned Income Credit....147
  tax rate schedules....146
Tangible personal property
  contributions....90
  depreciable, and investment credit....110
  depreciation rule for....129
  records of contributions....91
Tax
  balance due....118
  calculation of....100-102
  estimated-, payments....114
  figured by IRS on Form 1040A....20
  income averaging....102
  overpayments....114
  unpaid....19-20
  withholding....114
Tax-Computation Schedule TC....77
Tax counsel fees....96
Tax Court decisions
  on drought loss....92-93
  on fees....15
  on mileage allowance for travel to jury duty....57
  on office at home....68
  on "overnight" trips....71
  on summer camp payments....31
  on trees destroyed by insects....95
Tax home....70-73
Tax laws. *See also* Tax Court decisions
  changes in....11-15
Tax Planning Section....163-166
Tax Rate Schedules....146
Tax rebate for tenant....86
Tax refunds, interest on....11, 34
Tax tables....139-145
  and exemptions....26
  and filing status....25
  use of....20, 100, 139
Taxable income, compared with gross income....31
Taxes. *See also particular type of*
  automobile....72, 85
  on business and business property....131
  on Canadian stock dividends....86
  cigarettes....86
  cooperative apartment....85
  deducted, and use of standard deduction....85
  deductible and nondeductible....83-86
  deductible from rental property....54
  FICA....113, 116
  FICA and RRTA on tips, uncollected....113
  on gasoline and oil....10
  and homes qualifying for mortgage assistance payments....86
  on individual Retirement Arrangement excess...114
  for local improvements....54
  minimum....113
  paid for another person....28, 85
  on pension plan....34
  real-estate, paid to bank....85
  rebate on real-estate taxes on home....86
  from recomputing prior-year investment credit..113
  on rented property....131
  RRTA....116
  sales-tax tables....85

...t, *see* Self-employment tax
...ls and oils, credit for.............117
.........................43
.........................85
.........................72

...s
...alty paid for illegal strike.............34
...aveling expenses.............98
...elephone and telegraph.............132
Television show prizes.............57
Temporary job assignments, visits home from.............72
Theft
  of business property.............132
  proof of.............92, 93
  value of property.............95
  when to claim.............95, 133
Tips
  cost of.............70
  form for reporting.............161-162
  reporting as income.............33
  Social Security taxes on.............9, 19
  unreported and uncollected tax on.............113
Tires and tubes, for business vehicle.............131
Tolls.............70
Tools, driving to work with.............73
Tools and supplies.............67
Total adjustments.............77
Total income
  and choice of tax form.............19
  and loss from business.............133
Trade name expenses.............128
Trademark expenses.............128
Traffic fines.............73
Transfer taxes.............85
Transient workers.............71
Travel and transportation expenses.............70-74
  See also Car expenses; Moving expenses
  from air terminal to hotel.............72
  to attend college.............97
  to broker's office.............96
  business or income producing.............65-66
  charitable.............91
  cleaning and laundering.............70
  combined business-pleasure trip.............65-66
  commutation costs.............72
  deductible.............70
  and definition of "home".............70

entertainment expenses and.............70
to jury duty.............57
medical.............80, 81
and more than one place of employment.............71
of nurse accompanying patient for
  special treatment.............81
paid by prospective employer.............33
and per diem allowance.............69-70
record-keeping.............69
and seeking new employment.............96
spouse accompanying on trip.............71
tax home and family home.............70-71
taxi fares.............72
teachers.............98
transient workers.............71
trip to find new location or new plant.............72
visits home from temporary job.............72
to warmer climate as medical expense.............81
within city.............72
Trees, destroyed by insects.............92, 95
Truckdriver, meals away from home.............71
Trucks, tires and tubes for.............131
Trusts
  filing requirements.............10
  foreign.............20

U

Underpayment of estimated tax.............11, 118
Unemployment compensation.............19, 57
  employer financed.............58, 60
  exempt and not exempt.............60
  union financed.............58
  worksheet for figuring taxability.............56
Uniforms.............67
Union
  dues.............67
  strike benefits to nonunion striker.............58
  unemployment, strike, and lockout benefits.............58

V

Vacation
  as prize.............34

with business trip.............66
Vacation fund payments.............33
Vacation home
  expenses.............56
  sale and replacement of.............45
Vasectomy, legal.............80, 81
Veterans
  paraplegic, specially designed homes for.............61
  payments to.............59-61
Veterans Administration benefits.............59, 60, 61
Visits home from temporary job.............72
Vitamins and minerals.............80
Vouchers, for business expenses.............63

W

Wages, salaries, etc. *See also* Compensation
  Christmas bonuses.............132
  delayed payment.............132
  paid in January for last week of year.............132
  paid to spouse.............132
  paid to yourself.............132
Wedding expenses.............30
Weight-reduction programs.............82
Wheelchairs.............80
Widows and widowers
  filing requirements.............9
  of soldiers, pensions.............60
  tax rates.............101
Wife. *See* Spouse
Will, fees for preparation of.............96
Wind energy equipment.............112
Withholding tax
  increased, estimated-tax payments and.............118
  penalties for false information.............15
  refund.............9
  total.............114
Work Incentive (WIN) Program credit.............111
Work relief program payments.............60
Workmen's compensation.............59

X

X-rays.............80